Kamisama Kiss

Hana to Yume Comics
KAMISAMA KISS
Julietta Suzuki 5
PRICE 400 + TAX
Hana to Yume Comics

5

Story & Art by

Julietta Suzuki

CHARACTERS

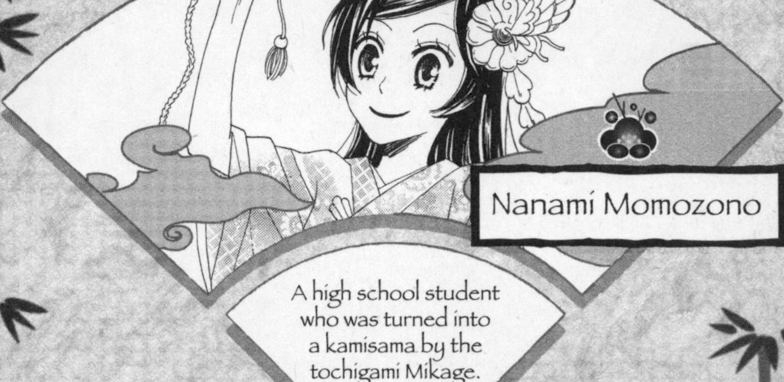

Nanami Momozono

A high school student who was turned into a kamisama by the tochigami Mikage.

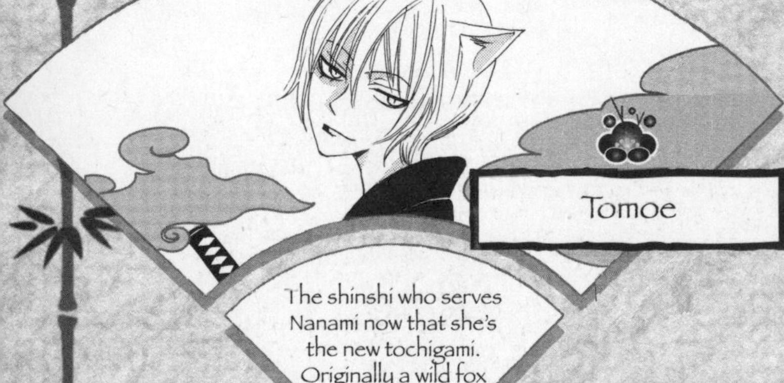

Tomoe

The shinshi who serves Nanami now that she's the new tochigami. Originally a wild fox ayakashi.

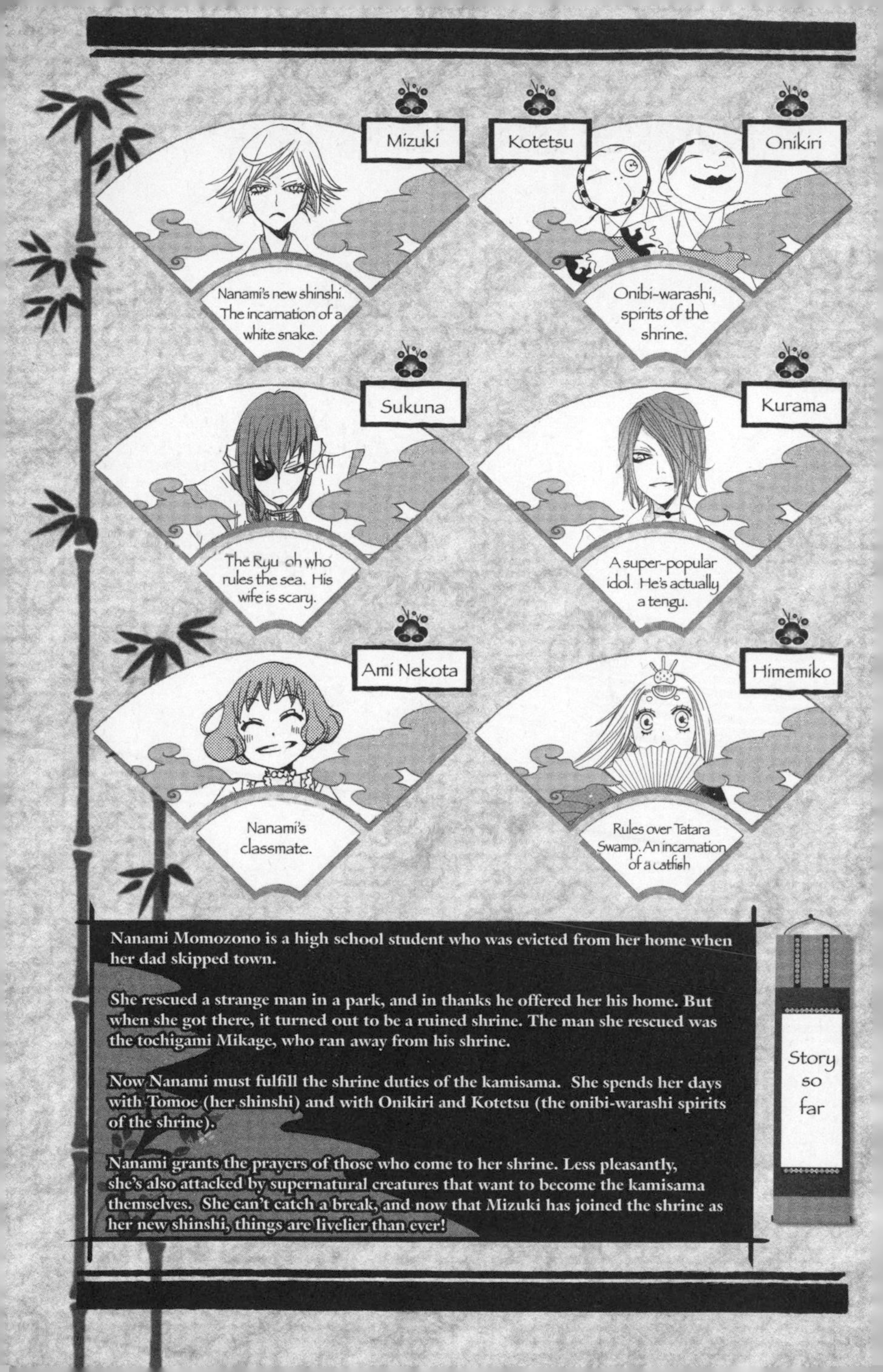
Kotetsu
Onikiri
Onibi-warashi, spirits of the shrine.
Mizuki
Nanami's new shinshi. The incarnation of a white snake.
Kurama
A super-popular idol. He's actually a tengu.
Sukuna
The Ryu oh who rules the sea. His wife is scary.
Himemiko
Rules over Tatara Swamp. An incarnation of a catfish
Ami Nekota
Nanami's classmate.

Story so far

Nanami Momozono is a high school student who was evicted from her home when her dad skipped town.

She rescued a strange man in a park, and in thanks he offered her his home. But when she got there, it turned out to be a ruined shrine. The man she rescued was the tochigami Mikage, who ran away from his shrine.

Now Nanami must fulfill the shrine duties of the kamisama. She spends her days with Tomoe (her shinshi) and with Onikiri and Kotetsu (the onibi-warashi spirits of the shrine).

Nanami grants the prayers of those who come to her shrine. Less pleasantly, she's also attacked by supernatural creatures that want to become the kamisama themselves. She can't catch a break, and now that Mizuki has joined the shrine as her new shinshi, things are livelier than ever!

Kamisama Kiss

Volume 5
CONTENTS

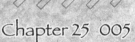

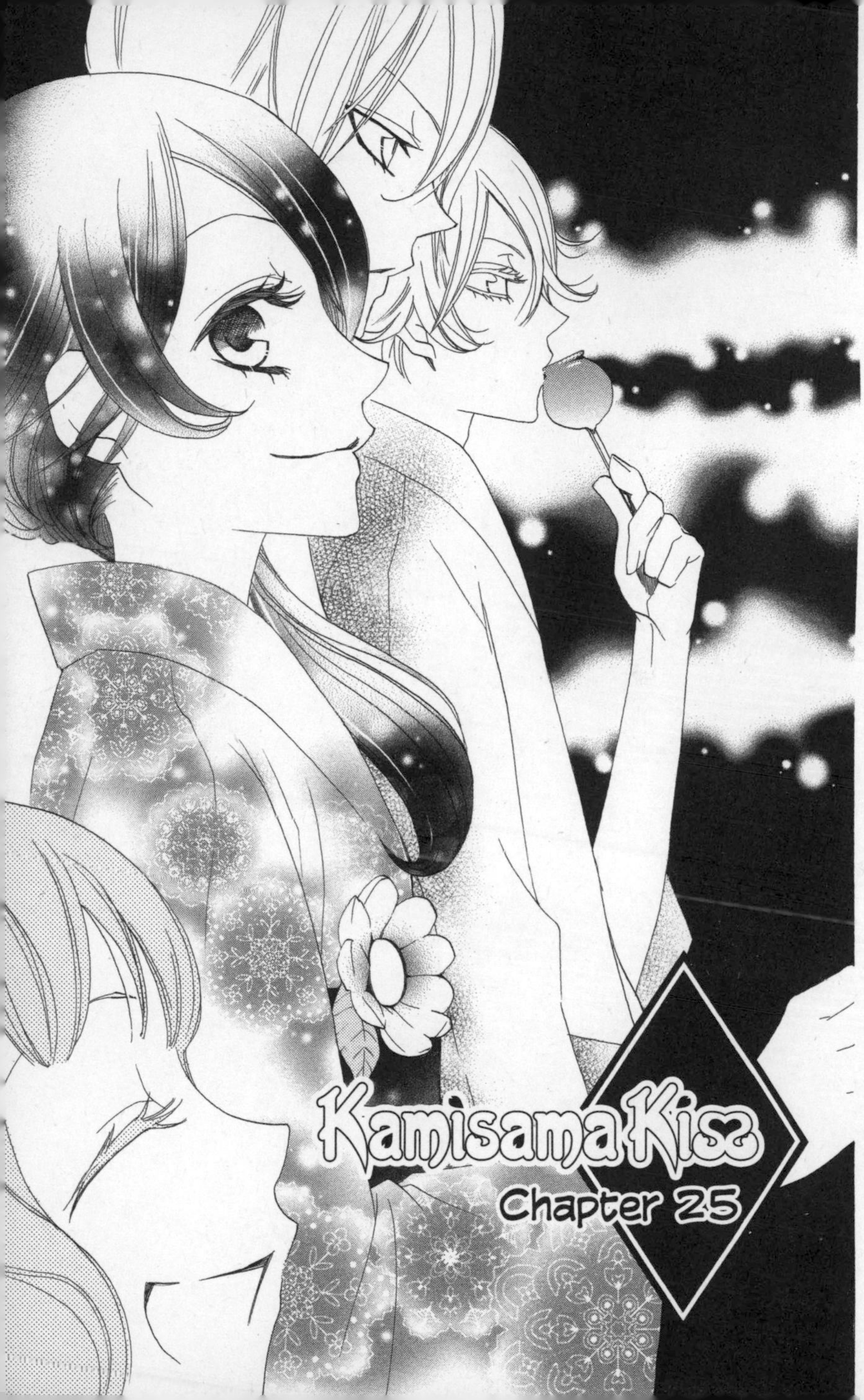
Kamisama Kiss
Chapter 25

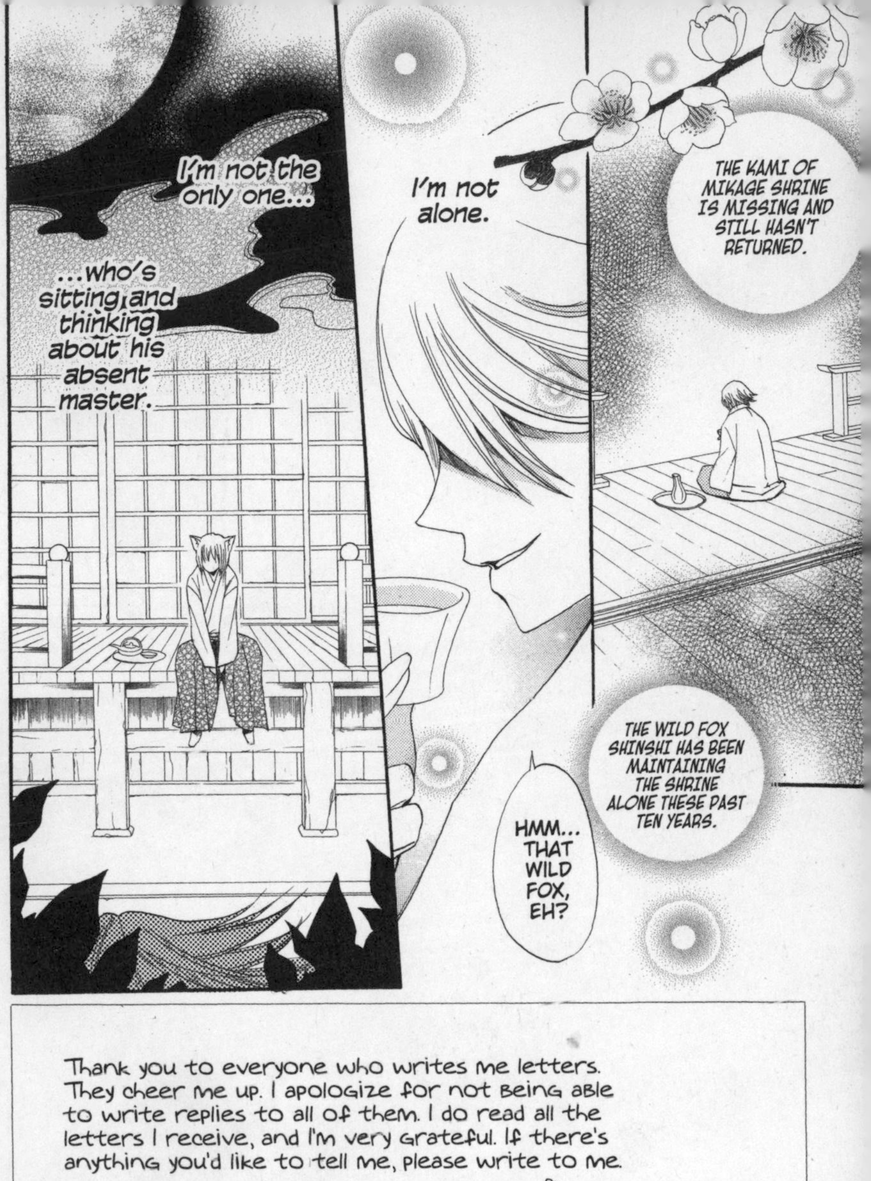
THE KAMI OF MIKAGE SHRINE IS MISSING AND STILL HASN'T RETURNED.
THE WILD FOX SHINSHI HAS BEEN MAINTAINING THE SHRINE ALONE THESE PAST TEN YEARS.
HMM... THAT WILD FOX, EH?
I'm not alone.
I'm not the only one...
...who's sitting and thinking about his absent master.

Thank you to everyone who writes me letters. They cheer me up. I apologize for not being able to write replies to all of them. I do read all the letters I receive, and I'm very grateful. If there's anything you'd like to tell me, please write to me.

Nowadays I'm very sleepy all the time. It's a mystery. Is it because it's winter? Is this the season for hibernating? I wish I could wake up properly.

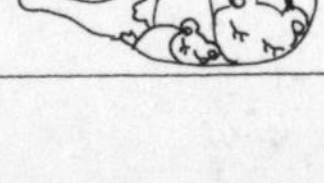

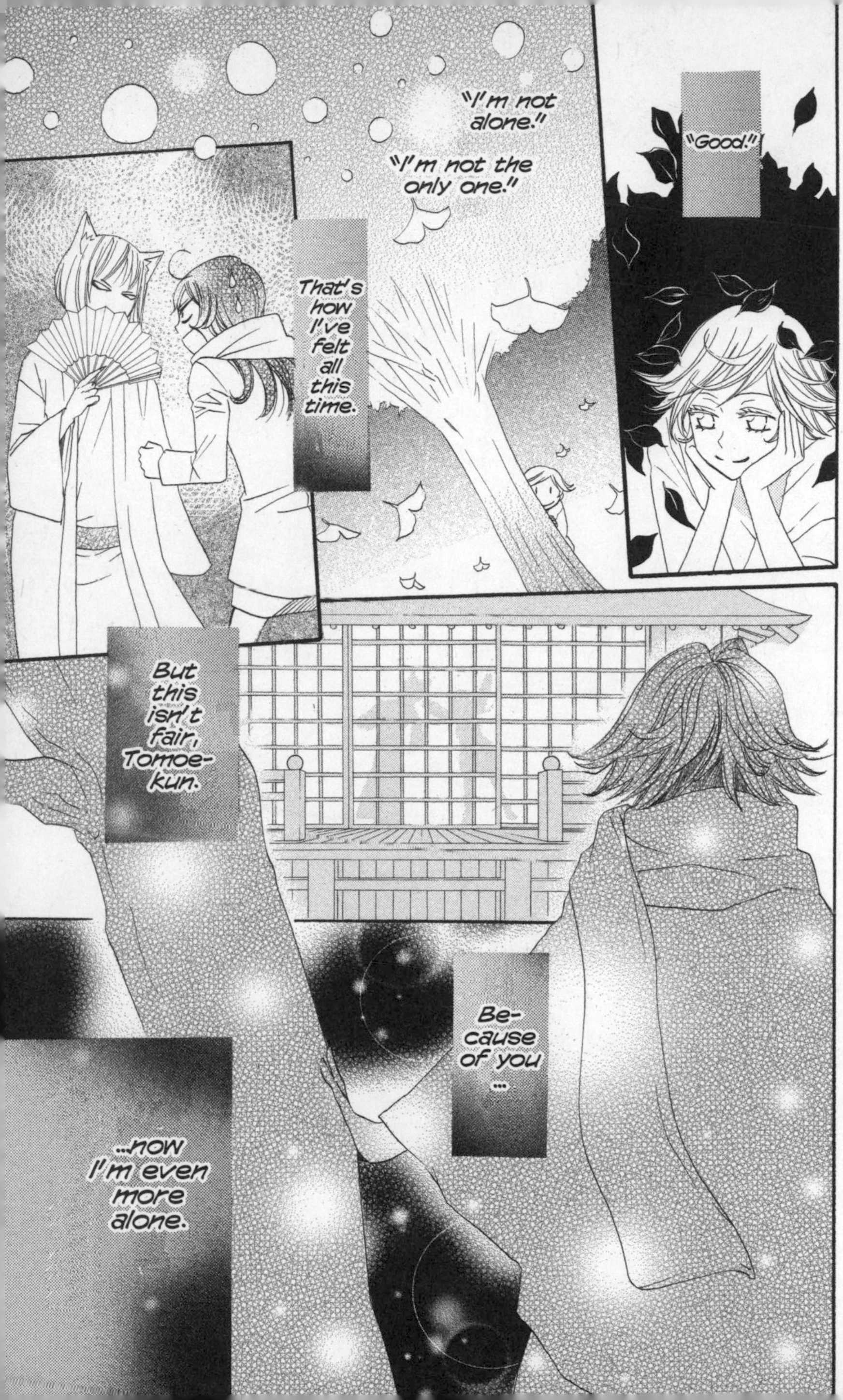
"Good!"
"I'm not alone."
"I'm not the only one."
That's how I've felt all this time.
But this isn't fair, Tomoe-kun.
Be-cause of you...
...now I'm even more alone.

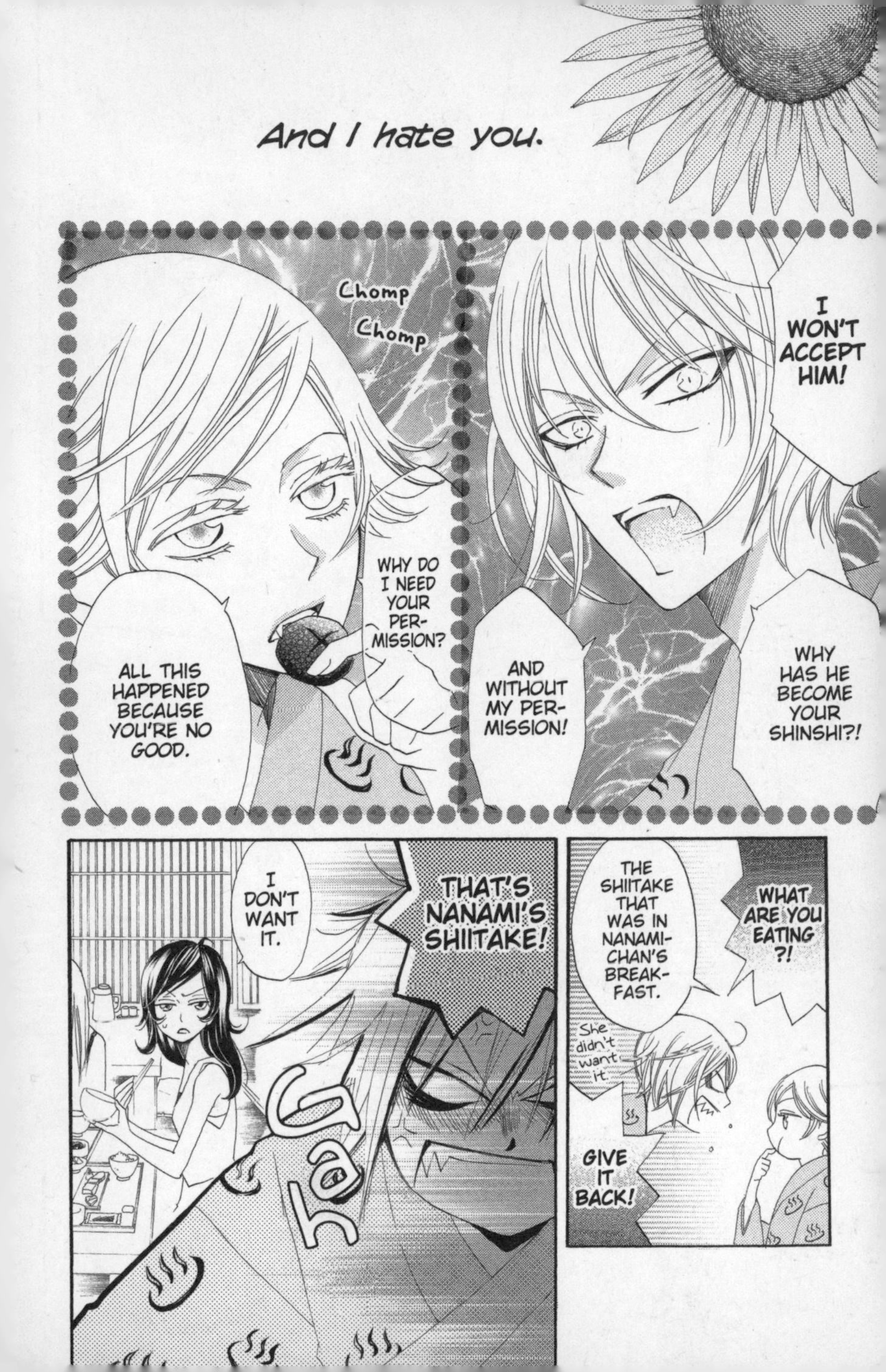
And I hate you.
Chomp
Chomp
I WON'T ACCEPT HIM!
WHY HAS HE BECOME YOUR SHINSHI?!
AND WITHOUT MY PER-MISSION!
WHY DO I NEED YOUR PER-MISSION?
ALL THIS HAPPENED BECAUSE YOU'RE NO GOOD.
WHAT ARE YOU EATING?!
THE SHIITAKE THAT WAS IN NANAMI-CHAN'S BREAK-FAST.
She didn't want it
GIVE IT BACK!
THAT'S NANAMI'S SHIITAKE!
I DON'T WANT IT.
Gah

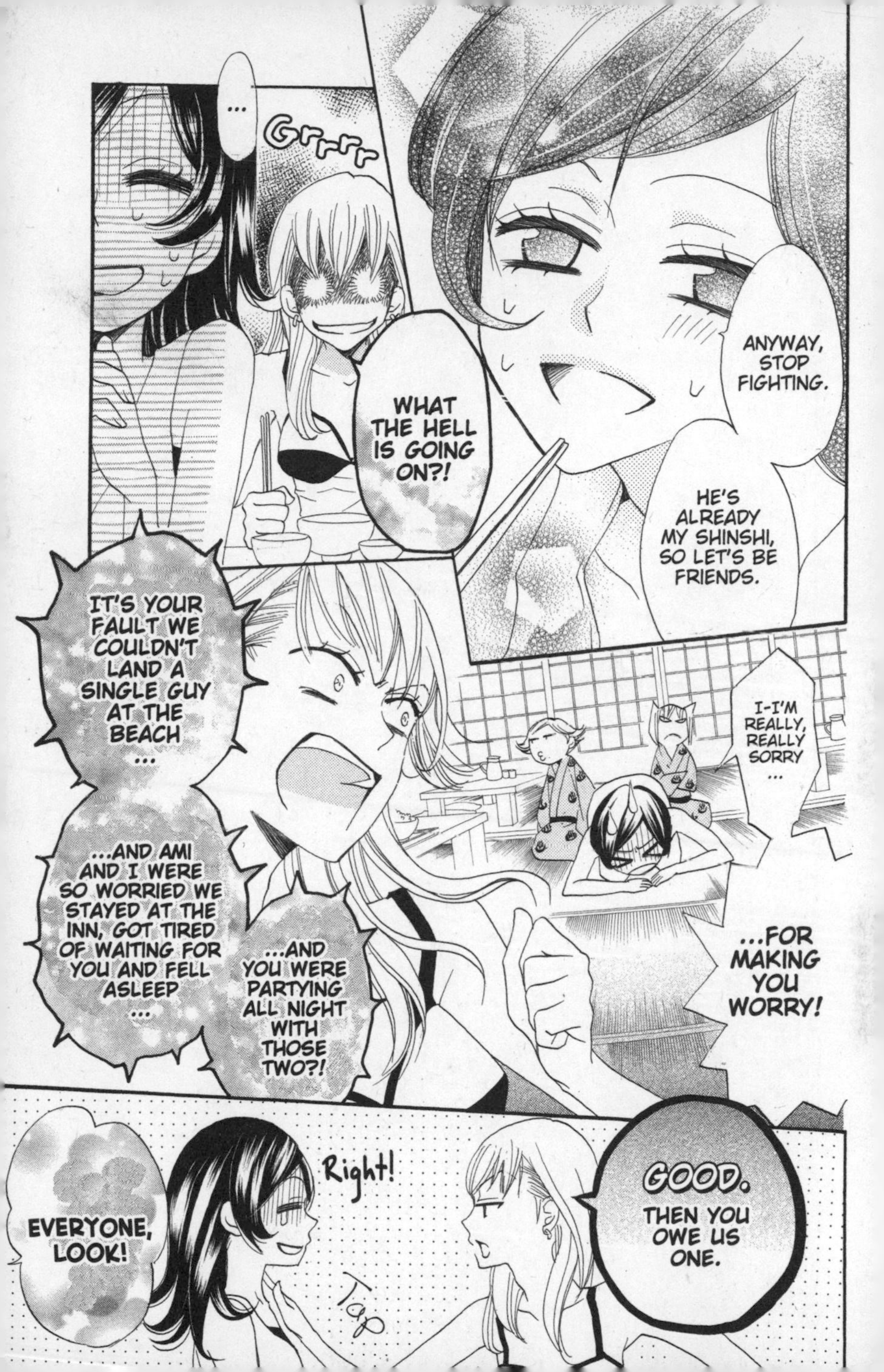
ANYWAY, STOP FIGHTING.
HE'S ALREADY MY SHINSHI, SO LET'S BE FRIENDS.
...
Grrrr
WHAT THE HELL IS GOING ON?!
IT'S YOUR FAULT WE COULDN'T LAND A SINGLE GUY AT THE BEACH...
...AND AMI AND I WERE SO WORRIED WE STAYED AT THE INN, GOT TIRED OF WAITING FOR YOU AND FELL ASLEEP...
...AND YOU WERE PARTYING ALL NIGHT WITH THOSE TWO?!
I-I'M REALLY, REALLY SORRY...
...FOR MAKING YOU WORRY!
GOOD. THEN YOU OWE US ONE.
Right!
EVERYONE, LOOK!
Tap

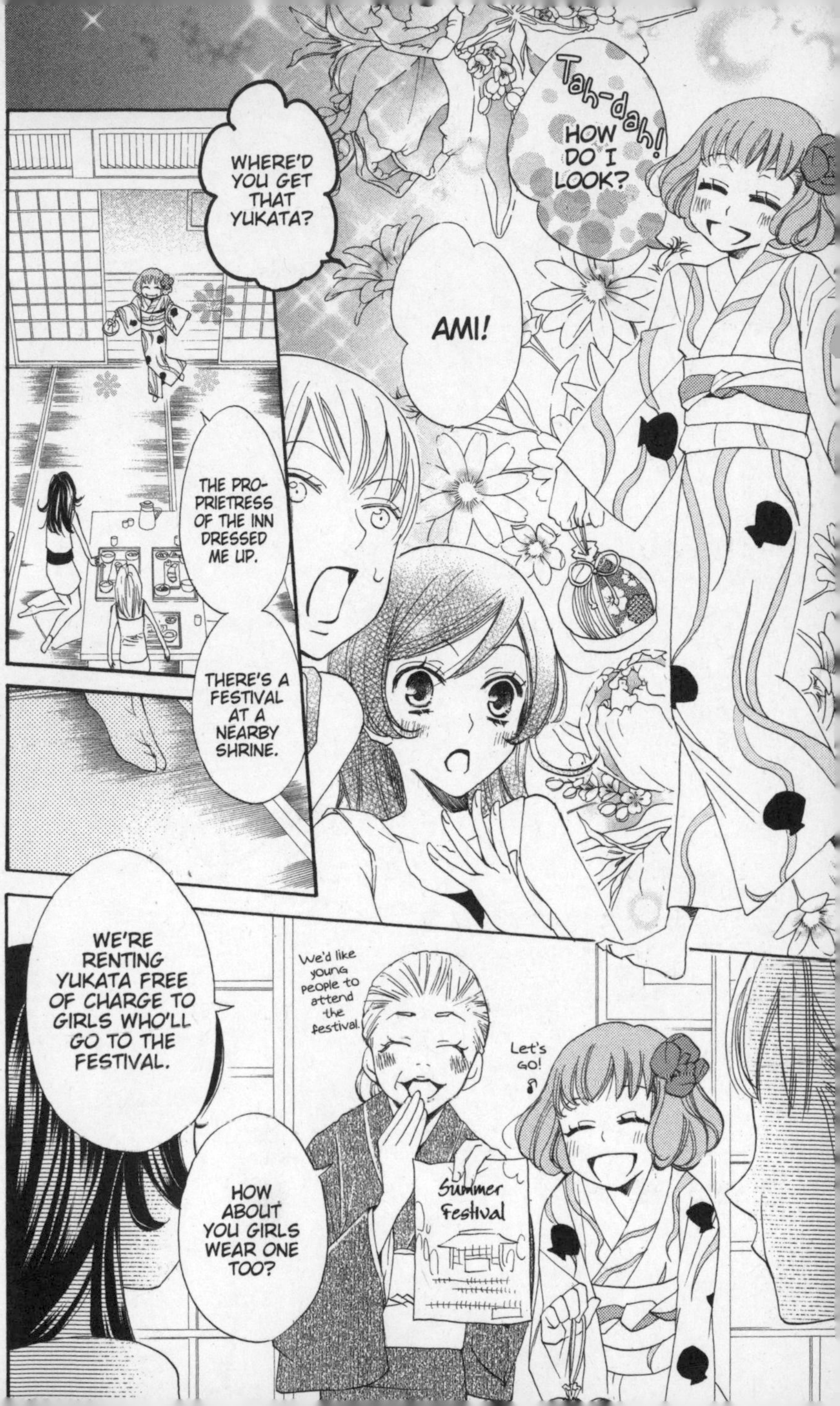
Tah-dah! HOW DO I LOOK?
AMI!
WHERE'D YOU GET THAT YUKATA?
THE PROPRIETRESS OF THE INN DRESSED ME UP.
THERE'S A FESTIVAL AT A NEARBY SHRINE.
Let's GO!
We'd like young people to attend the festival.
WE'RE RENTING YUKATA FREE OF CHARGE TO GIRLS WHO'LL GO TO THE FESTIVAL.
Summer Festival
HOW ABOUT YOU GIRLS WEAR ONE TOO?

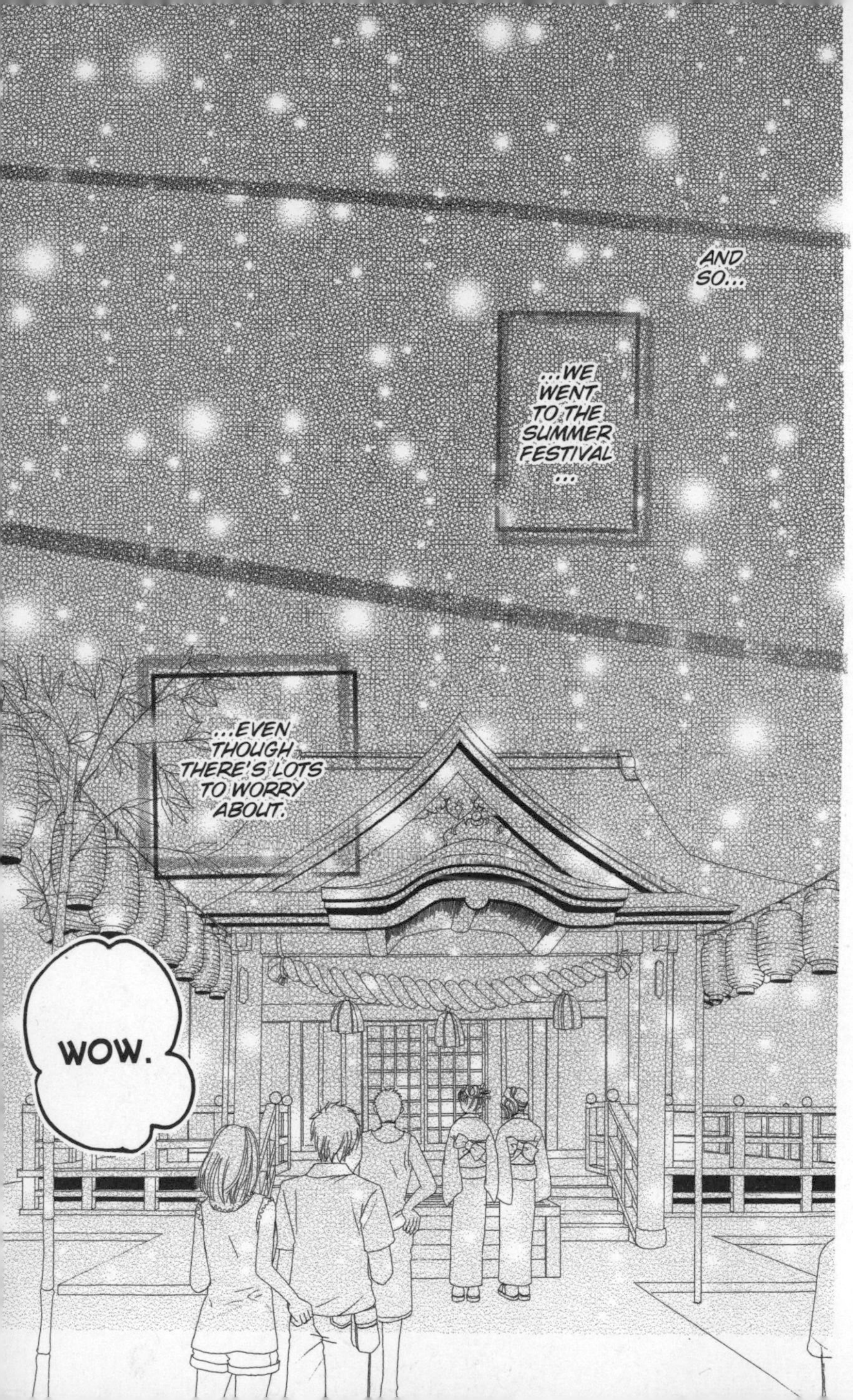
AND SO...
...WE WENT TO THE SUMMER FESTIVAL...
...EVEN THOUGH THERE'S LOTS TO WORRY ABOUT.
WOW.

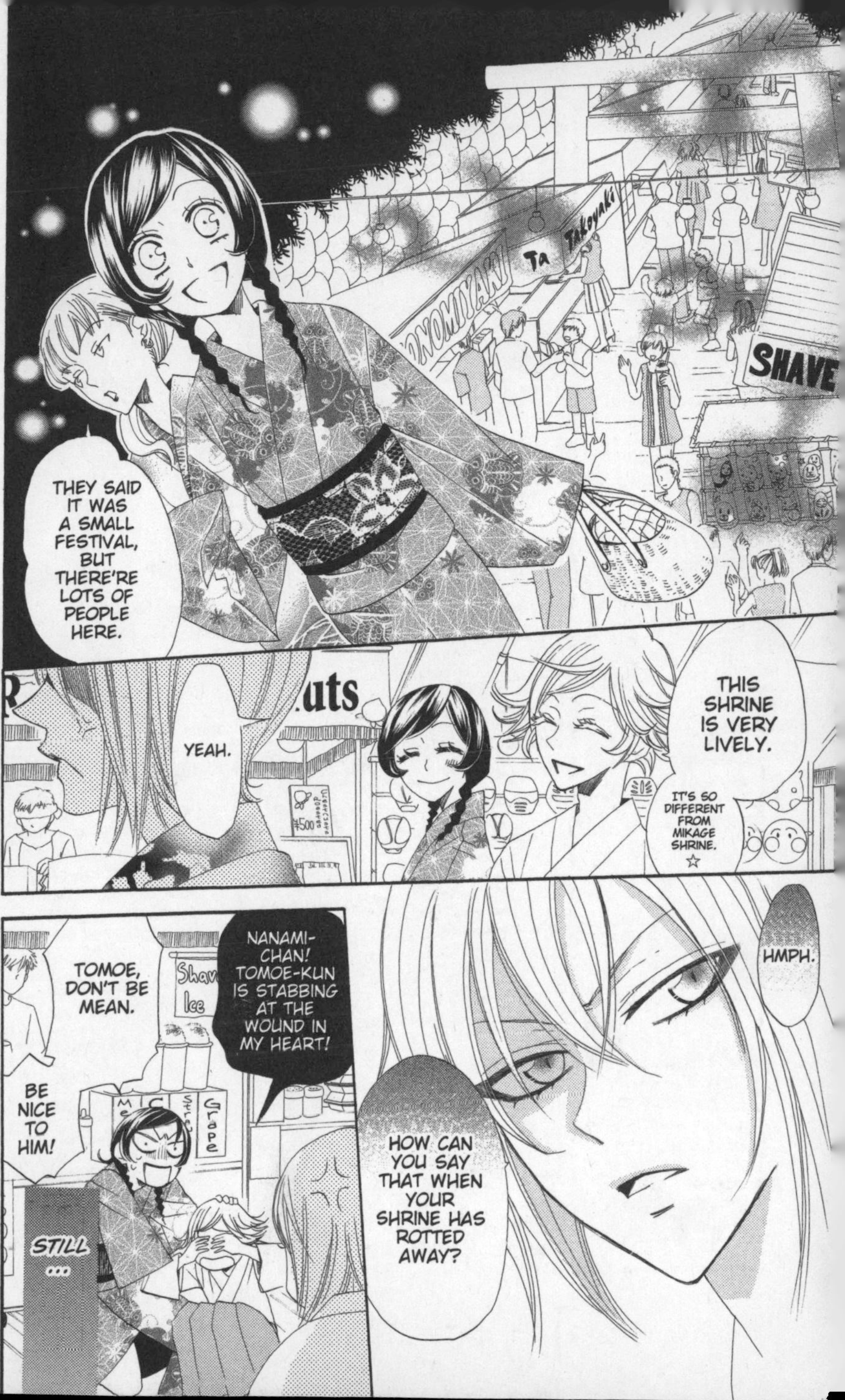
THEY SAID IT WAS A SMALL FESTIVAL, BUT THERE'RE LOTS OF PEOPLE HERE.
SHAVE
THIS SHRINE IS VERY LIVELY.
IT'S SO DIFFERENT FROM MIKAGE SHRINE. ☆
YEAH.
HMPH.
HOW CAN YOU SAY THAT WHEN YOUR SHRINE HAS ROTTED AWAY?
NANAMI-CHAN! TOMOE-KUN IS STABBING AT THE WOUND IN MY HEART!
TOMOE, DON'T BE MEAN.
BE NICE TO HIM!
STILL...

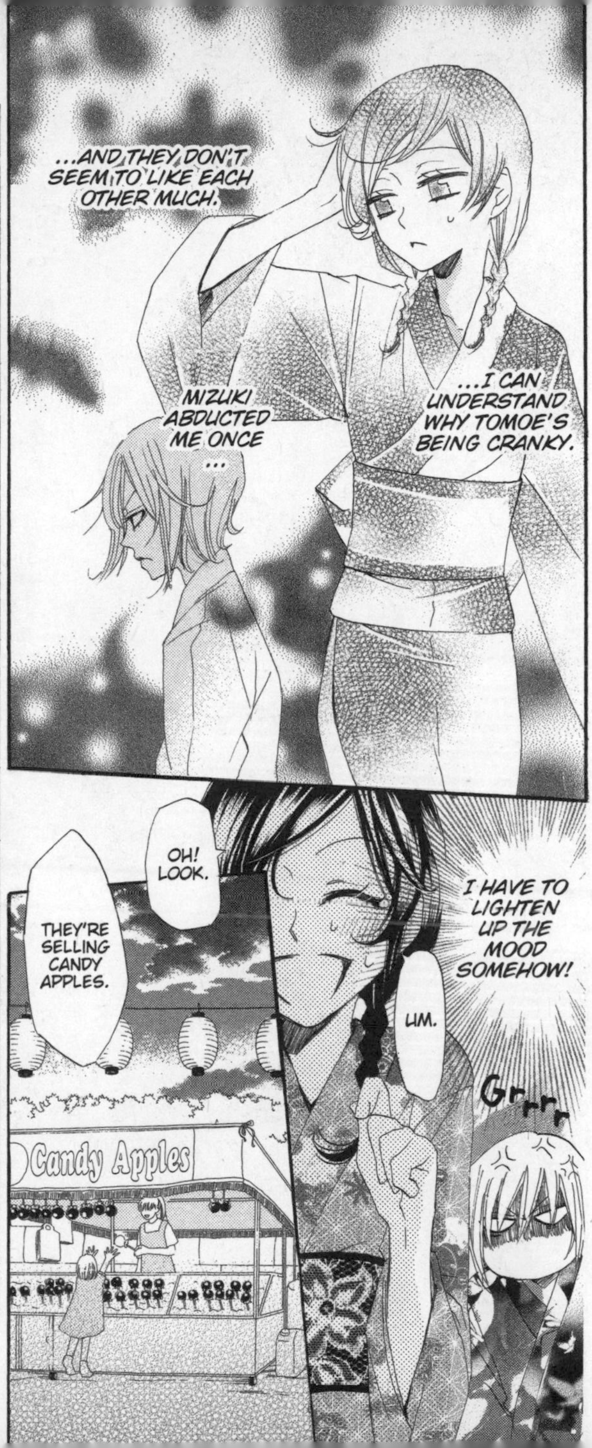
...AND THEY DON'T SEEM TO LIKE EACH OTHER MUCH.
MIZUKI ABDUCTED ME ONCE...
...I CAN UNDERSTAND WHY TOMOE'S BEING CRANKY.
I HAVE TO LIGHTEN UP THE MOOD SOMEHOW!
UM.
Grrrr
OH! LOOK.
THEY'RE SELLING CANDY APPLES.
Candy Apples

Hello! Thank you for reading this volume!

The other day I went to Ikaho Onsen for the first time. Onsen are good. I love them. I put flowers of sulfur in my bath at home. I feel my heart and body both become clean, and I also warm up in the bath. Next time I'd like to go to an onsen in Yamanashi prefecture. Ooh.

I really love the incense I bought at Ikaho, "The Fragrance of Ikaho".

The Fragrance of Ikaho

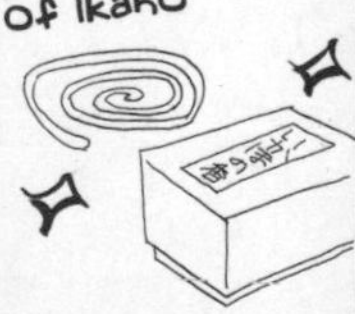

This incense is only sold in Ikaho, and it smells wonderful. I wish I'd bought more of it. I recommend it. ☆

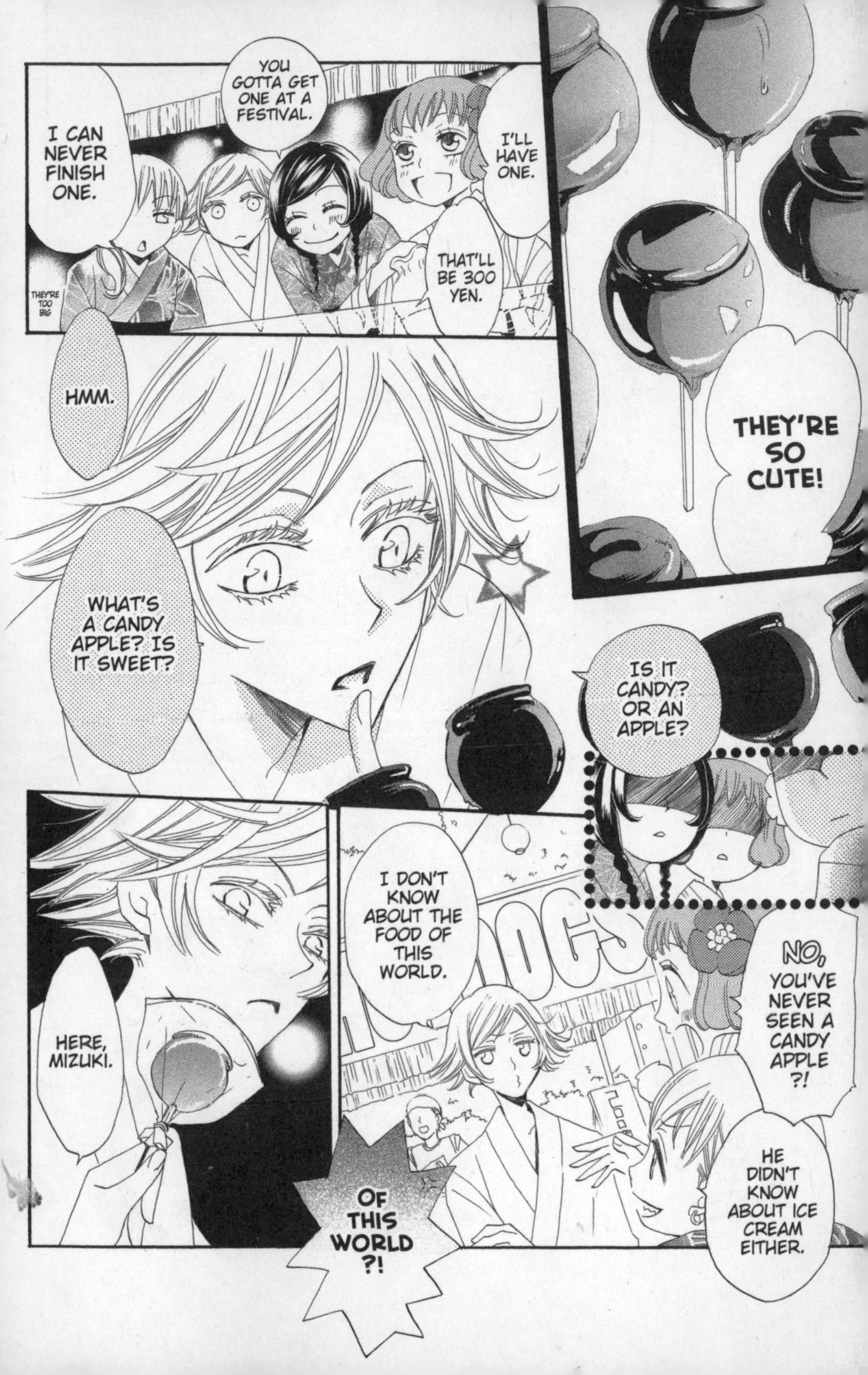
THEY'RE SO CUTE!
I'LL HAVE ONE.
YOU GOTTA GET ONE AT A FESTIVAL.
THAT'LL BE 300 YEN.
I CAN NEVER FINISH ONE.
THEY'RE TOO BIG
HMM.
WHAT'S A CANDY APPLE? IS IT SWEET?
IS IT CANDY? OR AN APPLE?
NO, YOU'VE NEVER SEEN A CANDY APPLE?!
I DON'T KNOW ABOUT THE FOOD OF THIS WORLD.
HE DIDN'T KNOW ABOUT ICE CREAM EITHER.
OF THIS WORLD?!
HERE, MIZUKI.

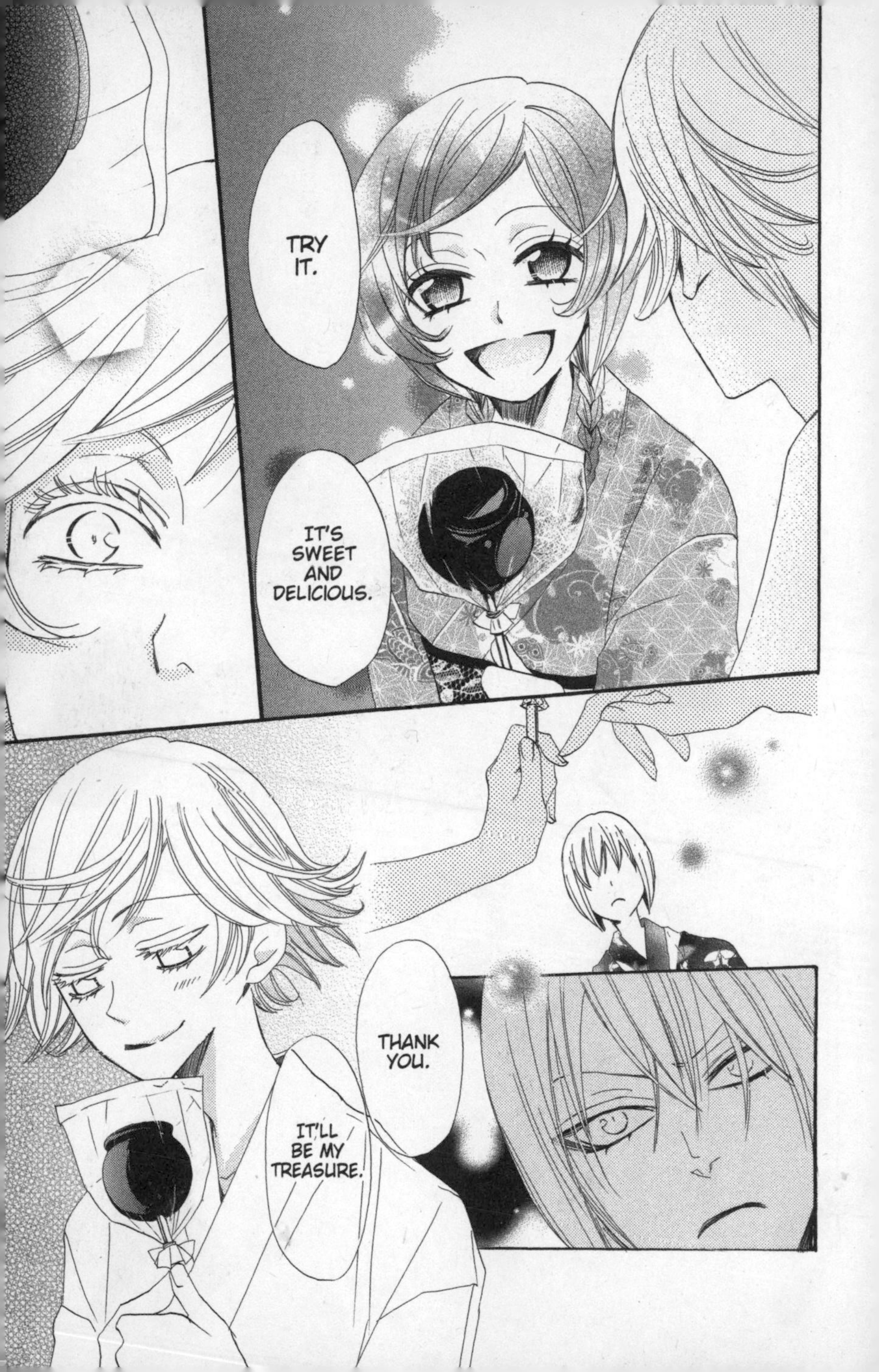
TRY IT.
IT'S SWEET AND DELICIOUS.
THANK YOU.
IT'LL BE MY TREASURE.

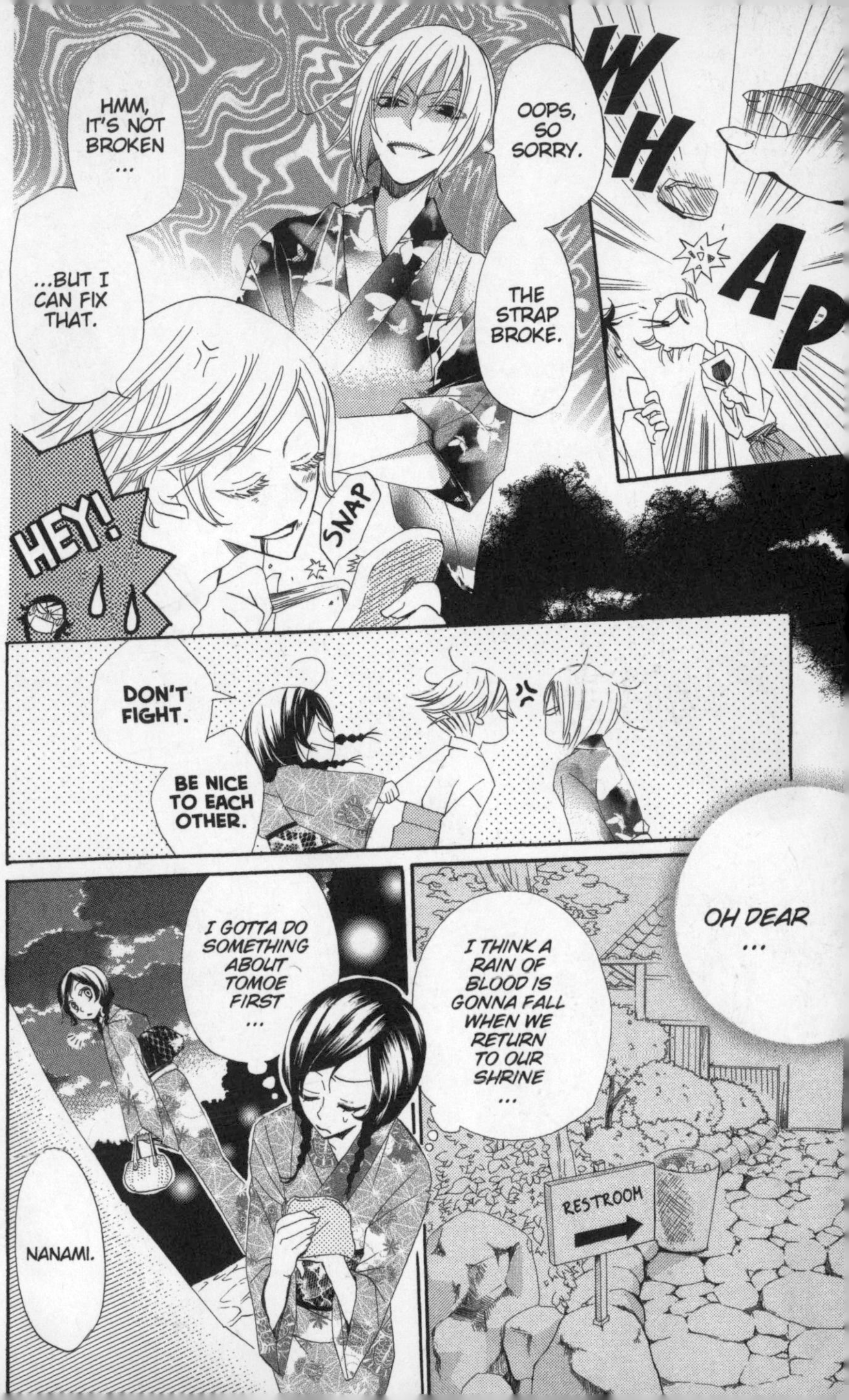
WHAP
OOPS, SO SORRY.
THE STRAP BROKE.
HMM, IT'S NOT BROKEN ...
...BUT I CAN FIX THAT.
SNAP
HEY!
DON'T FIGHT.
BE NICE TO EACH OTHER.
OH DEAR ...
I THINK A RAIN OF BLOOD IS GONNA FALL WHEN WE RETURN TO OUR SHRINE ...
RESTROOM
I GOTTA DO SOMETHING ABOUT TOMOE FIRST ...
NANAMI.

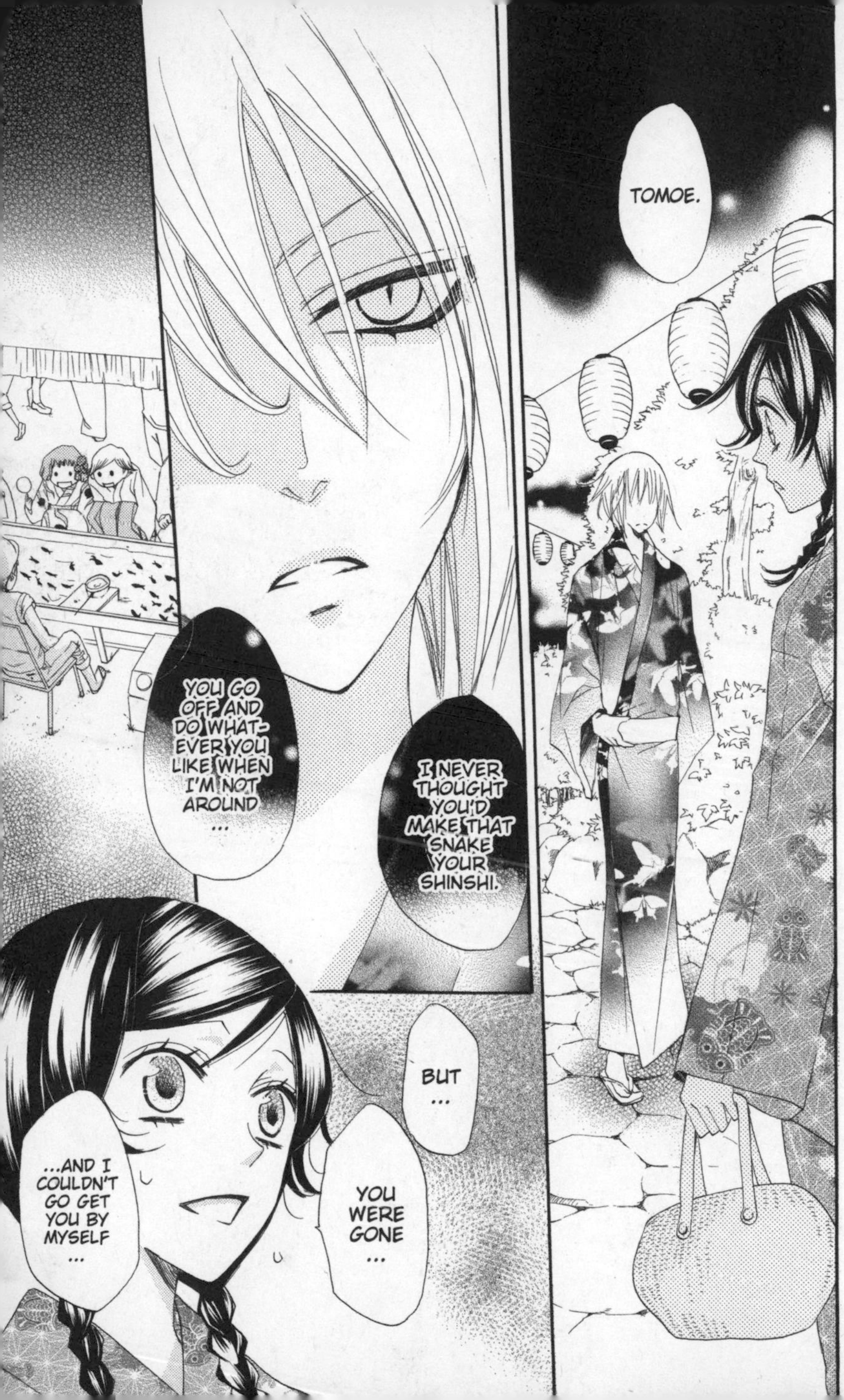
TOMOE.
I NEVER THOUGHT YOU'D MAKE THAT SNAKE YOUR SHINSHI.
YOU GO OFF AND DO WHATEVER YOU LIKE WHEN I'M NOT AROUND ...
BUT ...
YOU WERE GONE ...
...AND I COULDN'T GO GET YOU BY MYSELF ...

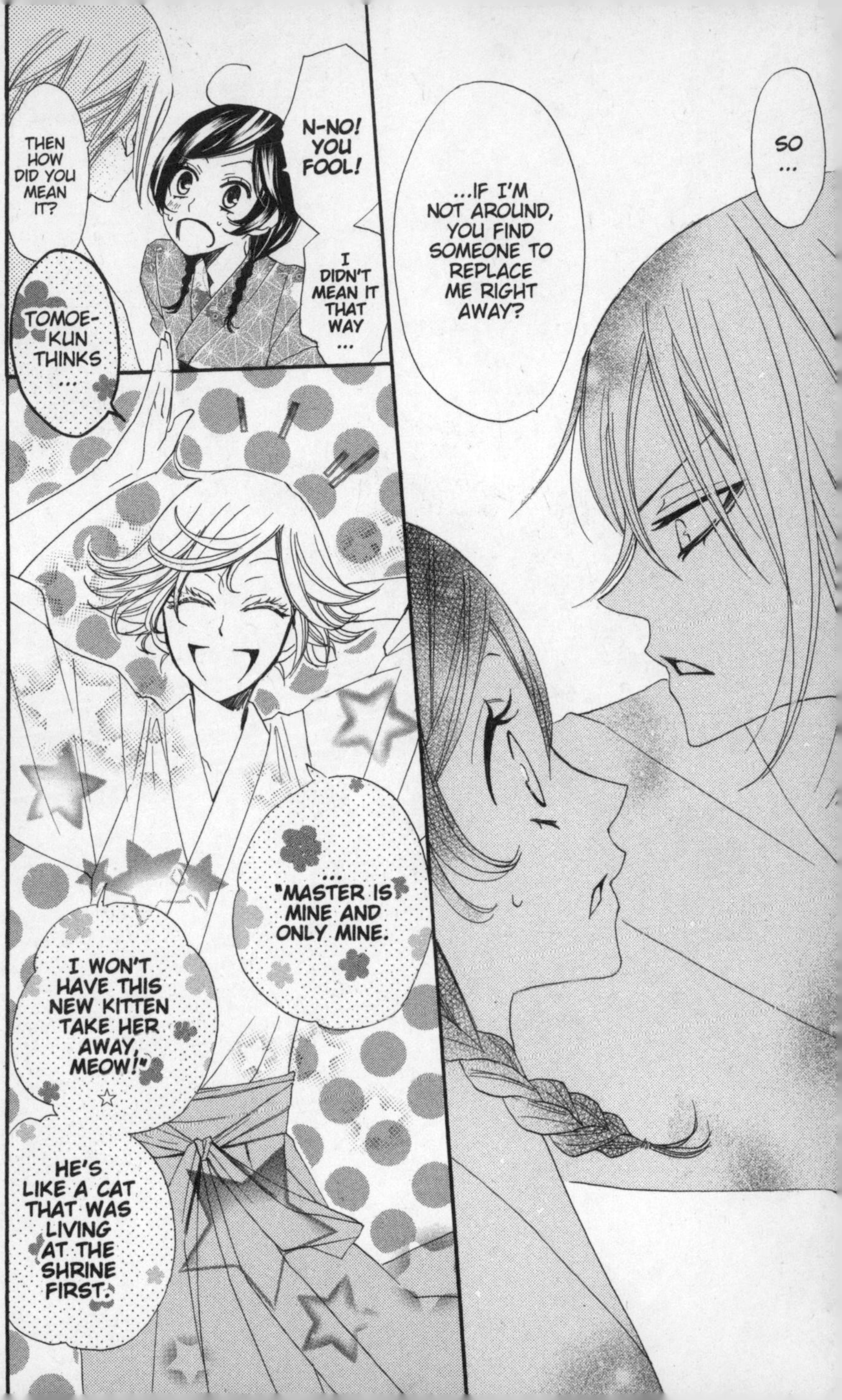
SO ...
...IF I'M NOT AROUND, YOU FIND SOMEONE TO REPLACE ME RIGHT AWAY?
N-NO! YOU FOOL!
I DIDN'T MEAN IT THAT WAY ...
THEN HOW DID YOU MEAN IT?
TOMOE-KUN THINKS ...
... "MASTER IS MINE AND ONLY MINE.
I WON'T HAVE THIS NEW KITTEN TAKE HER AWAY, MEOW!" ☆
HE'S LIKE A CAT THAT WAS LIVING AT THE SHRINE FIRST.

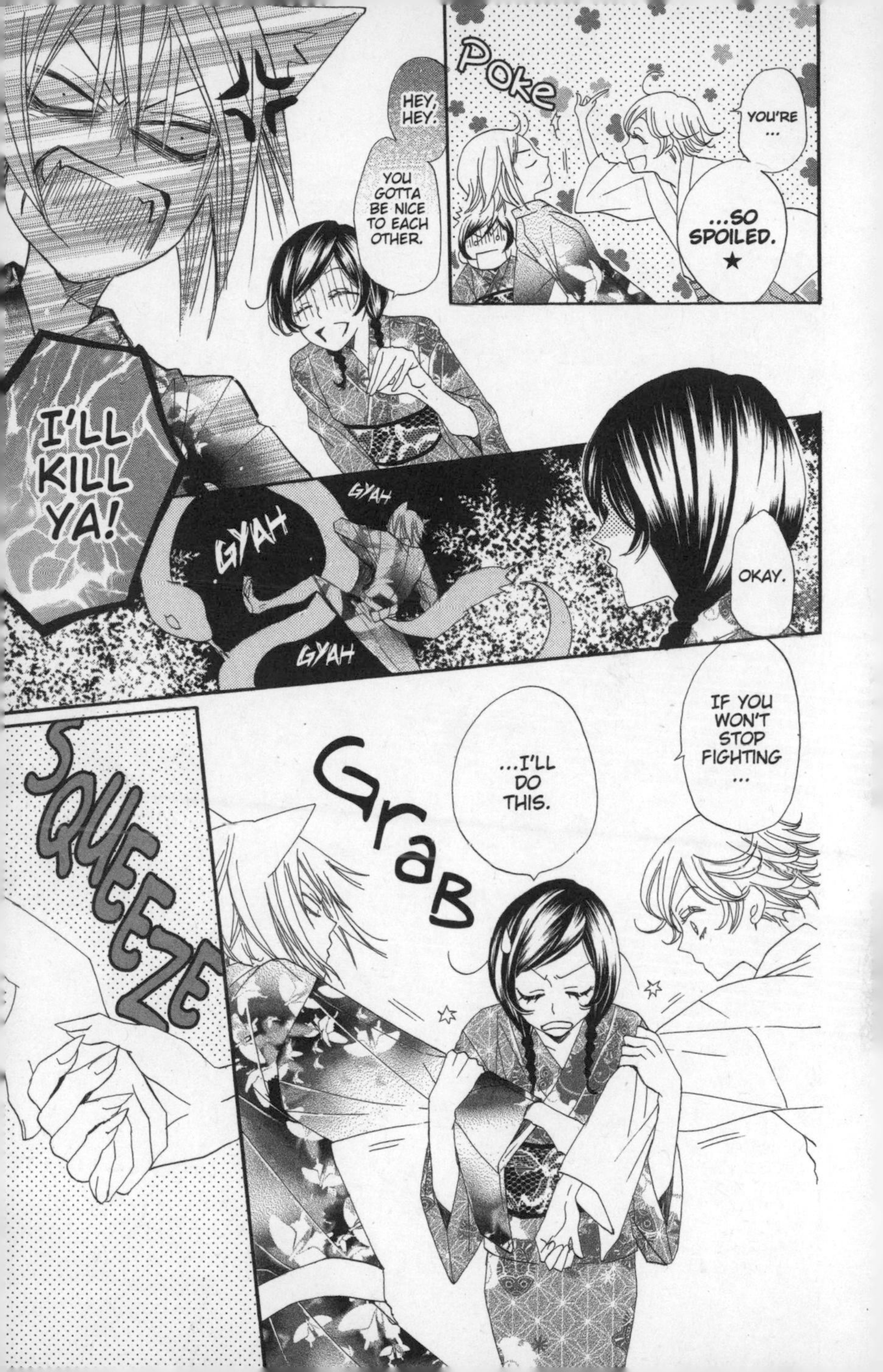
Poke
YOU'RE ...
...SO SPOILED. ★
HEY, HEY.
YOU GOTTA BE NICE TO EACH OTHER.
I'LL KILL YA!
OKAY.
GYAH
GYAH
GYAH
IF YOU WON'T STOP FIGHTING ...
...I'LL DO THIS.
GraB
SQUEEZE

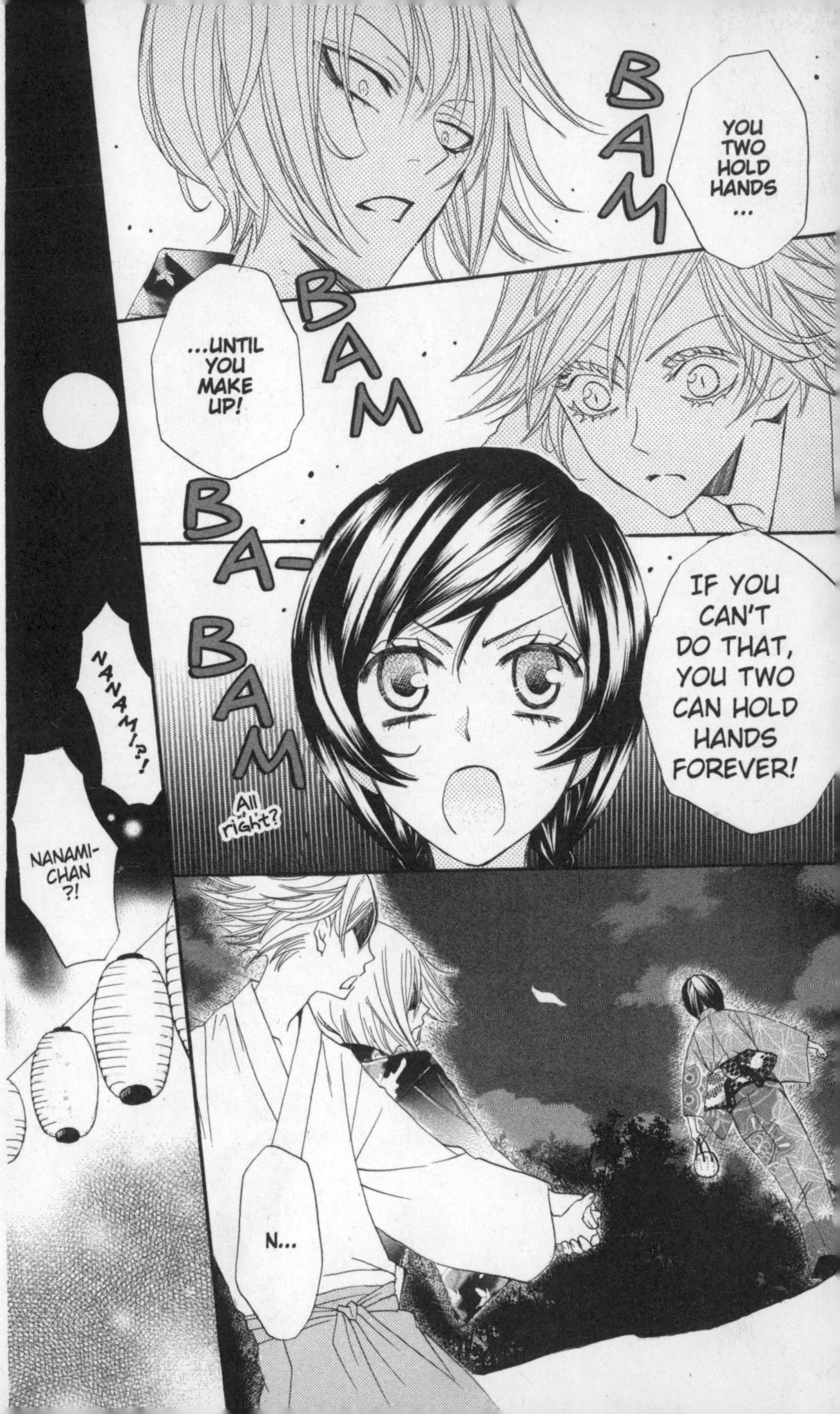
BAM
YOU TWO HOLD HANDS ...
BAM
...UNTIL YOU MAKE UP!
BA-BAM
IF YOU CAN'T DO THAT, YOU TWO CAN HOLD HANDS FOREVER!
All right?
NANAMI?!
NANAMI-CHAN ?!
N...

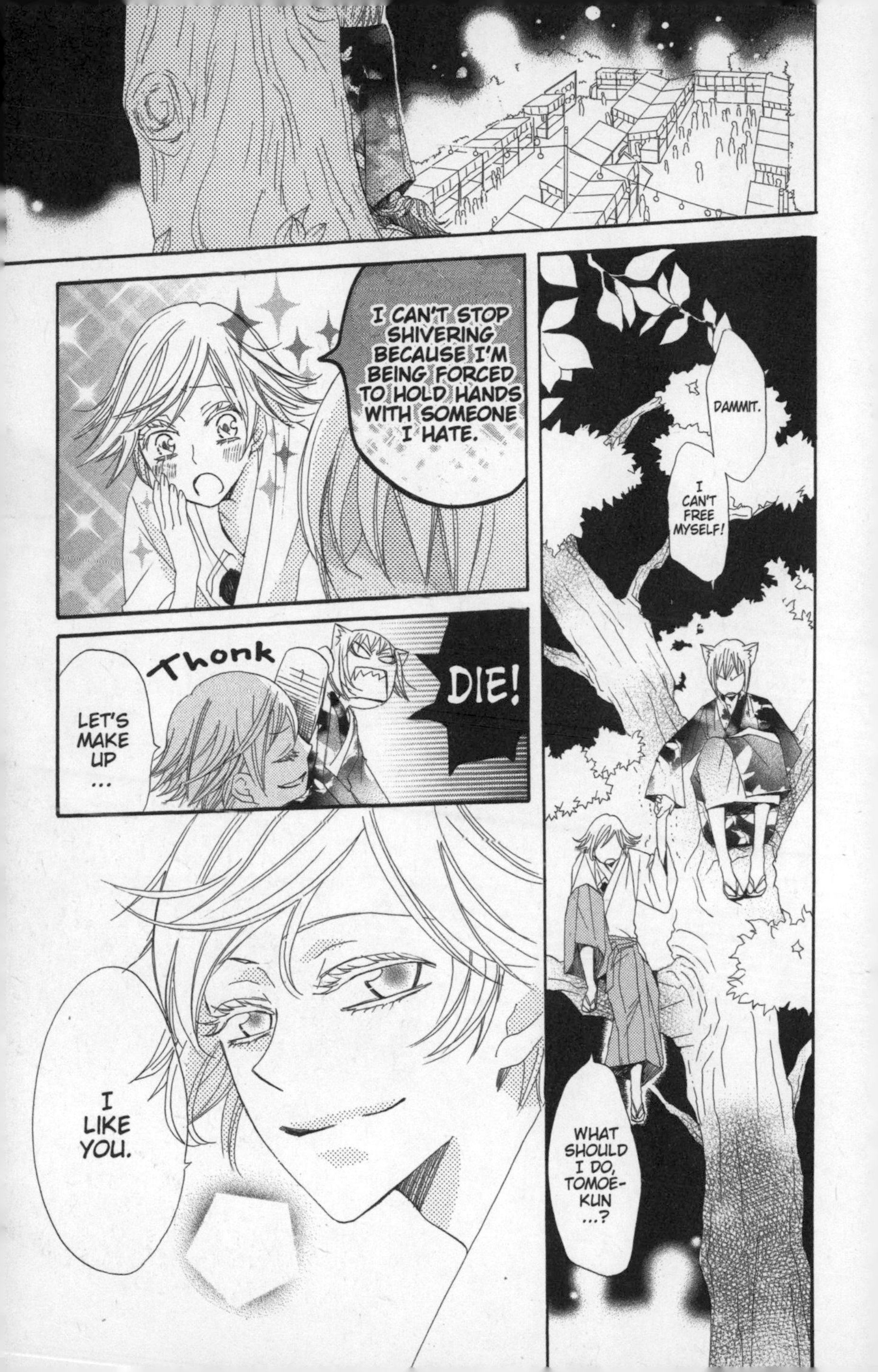
DAMMIT.
I CAN'T FREE MYSELF!
WHAT SHOULD I DO, TOMOE-KUN ...?
I CAN'T STOP SHIVERING BECAUSE I'M BEING FORCED TO HOLD HANDS WITH SOMEONE I HATE.
DIE!
Thonk
LET'S MAKE UP ...
I LIKE YOU.

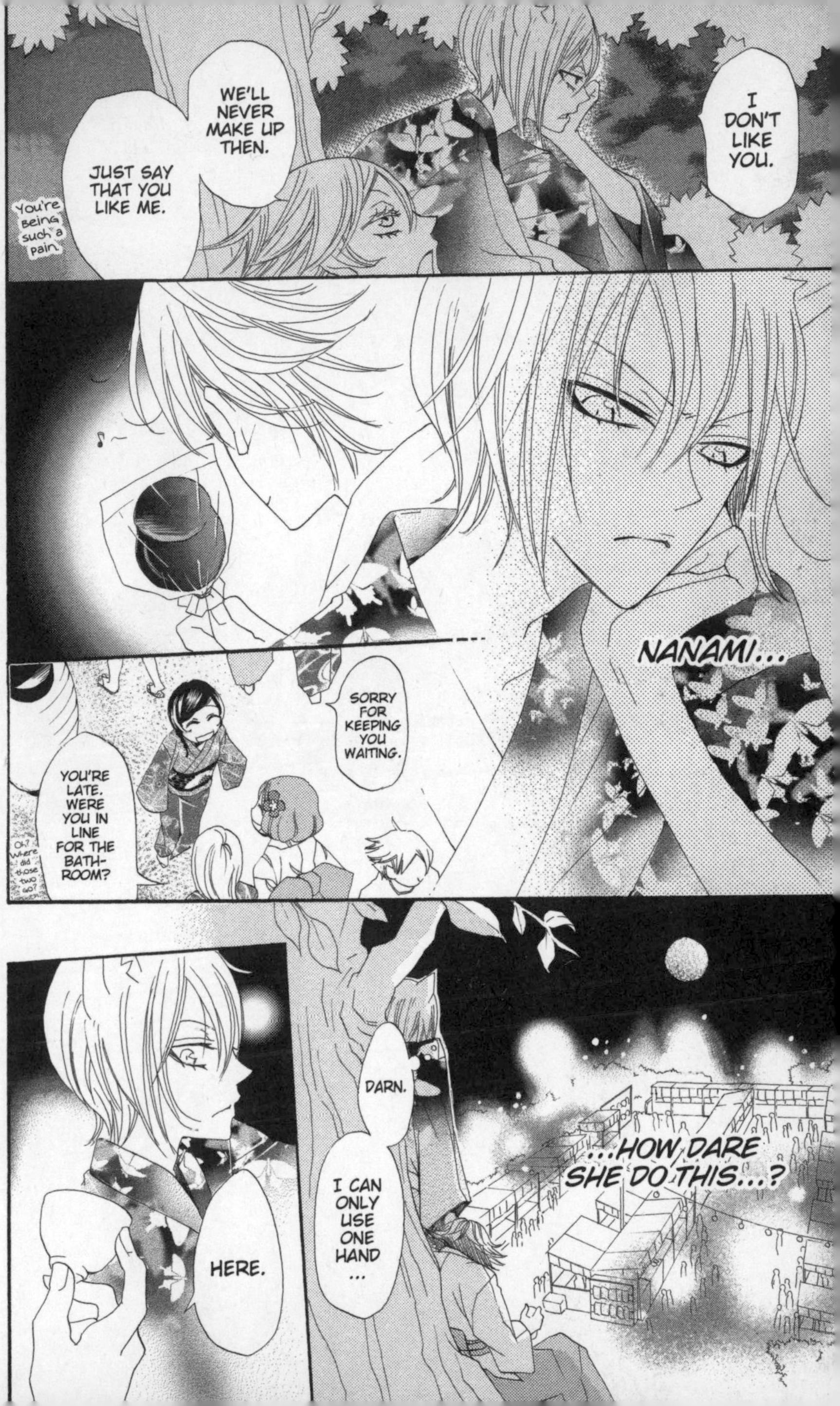
I DON'T LIKE YOU.
WE'LL NEVER MAKE UP THEN.
JUST SAY THAT YOU LIKE ME.
You're being such a pain.
NANAMI...
♪~
SORRY FOR KEEPING YOU WAITING.
YOU'RE LATE. WERE YOU IN LINE FOR THE BATHROOM?
Oh? Where did those two go?
...HOW DARE SHE DO THIS...?
DARN.
I CAN ONLY USE ONE HAND ...
HERE.

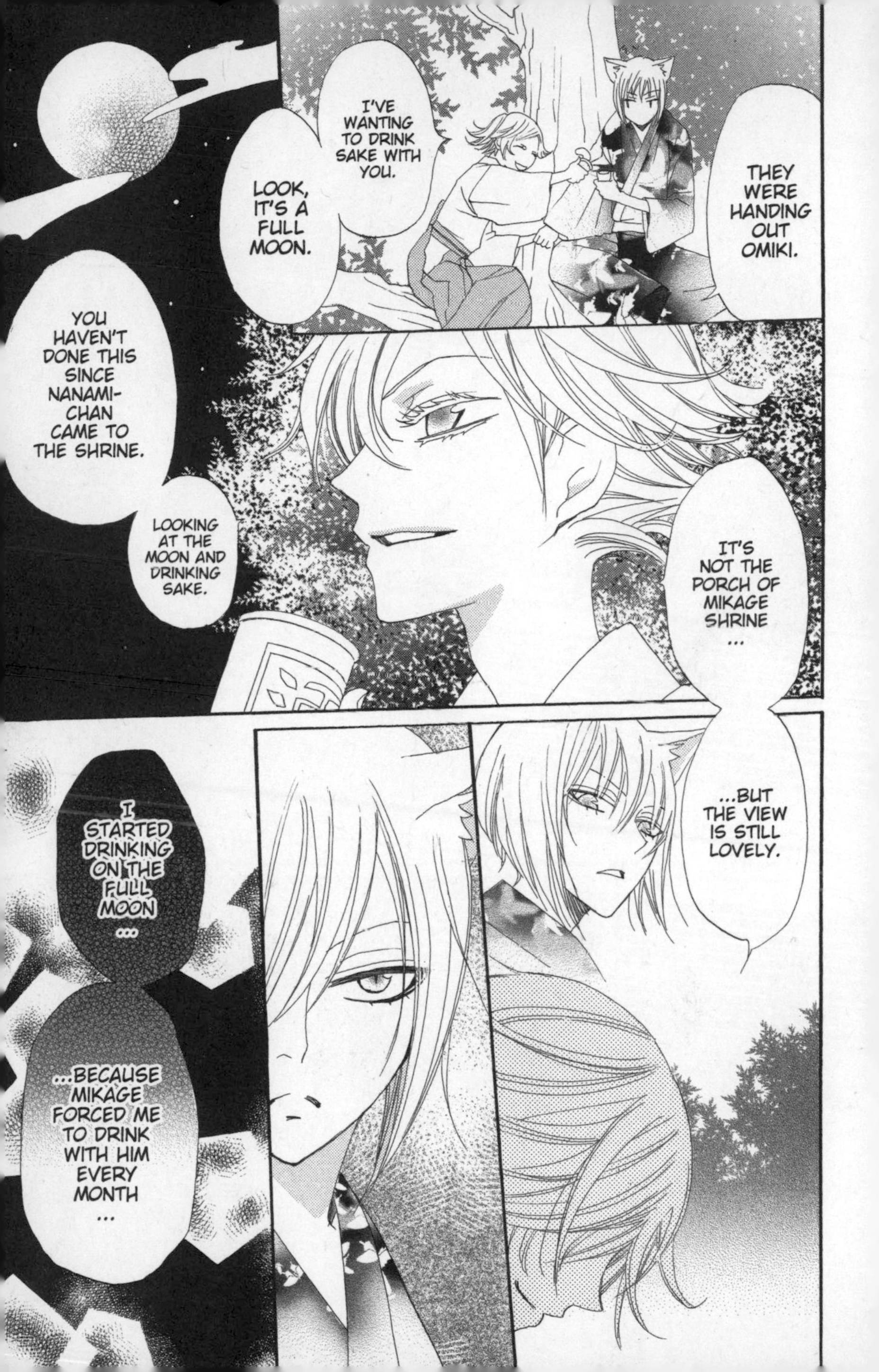
THEY WERE HANDING OUT OMIKI.
I'VE WANTING TO DRINK SAKE WITH YOU.
LOOK, IT'S A FULL MOON.
YOU HAVEN'T DONE THIS SINCE NANAMI-CHAN CAME TO THE SHRINE.
LOOKING AT THE MOON AND DRINKING SAKE.
IT'S NOT THE PORCH OF MIKAGE SHRINE ...
...BUT THE VIEW IS STILL LOVELY.
I STARTED DRINKING ON THE FULL MOON ...
...BECAUSE MIKAGE FORCED ME TO DRINK WITH HIM EVERY MONTH ...

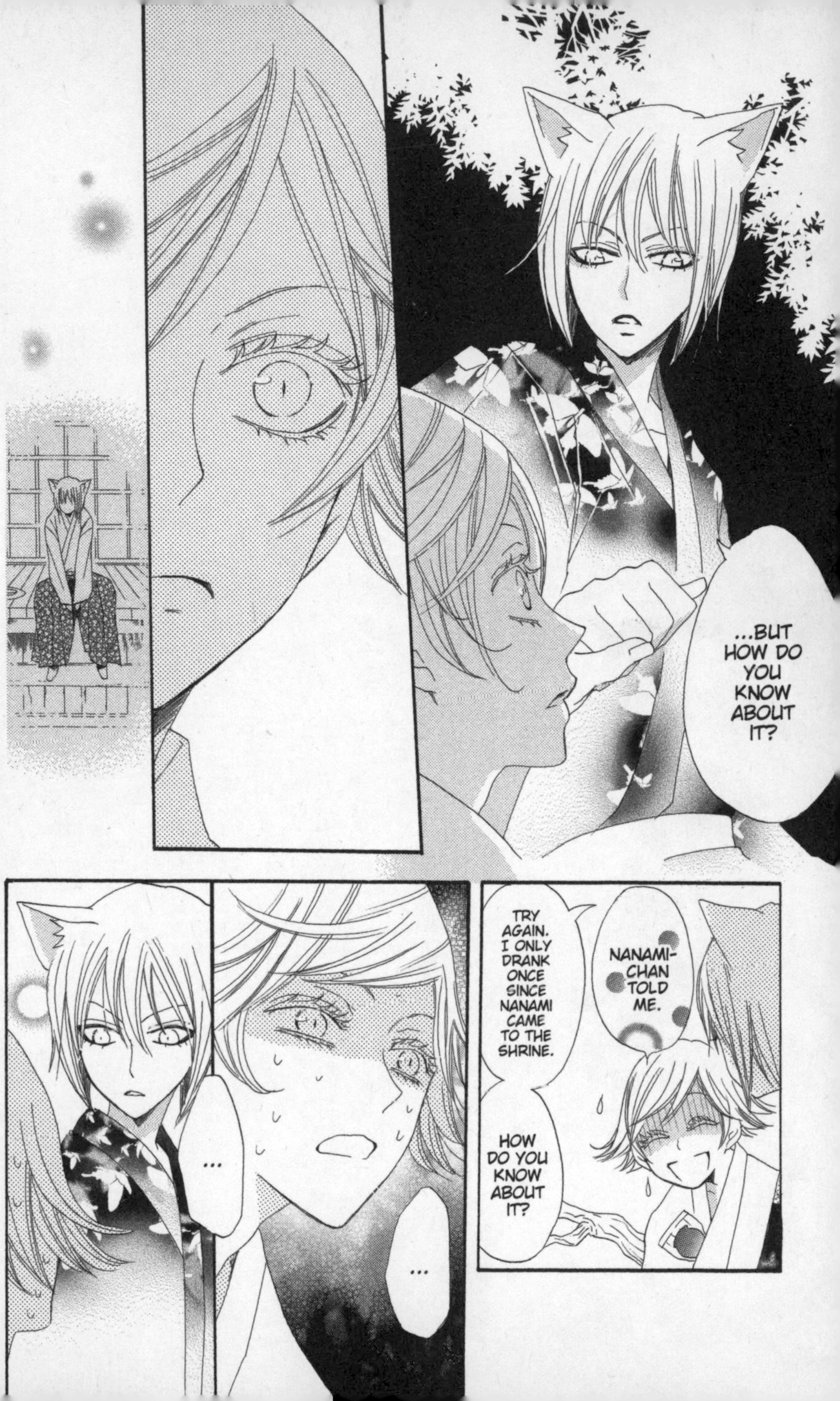
...BUT HOW DO YOU KNOW ABOUT IT?
NANAMI-CHAN TOLD ME.
TRY AGAIN. I ONLY DRANK ONCE SINCE NANAMI CAME TO THE SHRINE.
HOW DO YOU KNOW ABOUT IT?
...
...

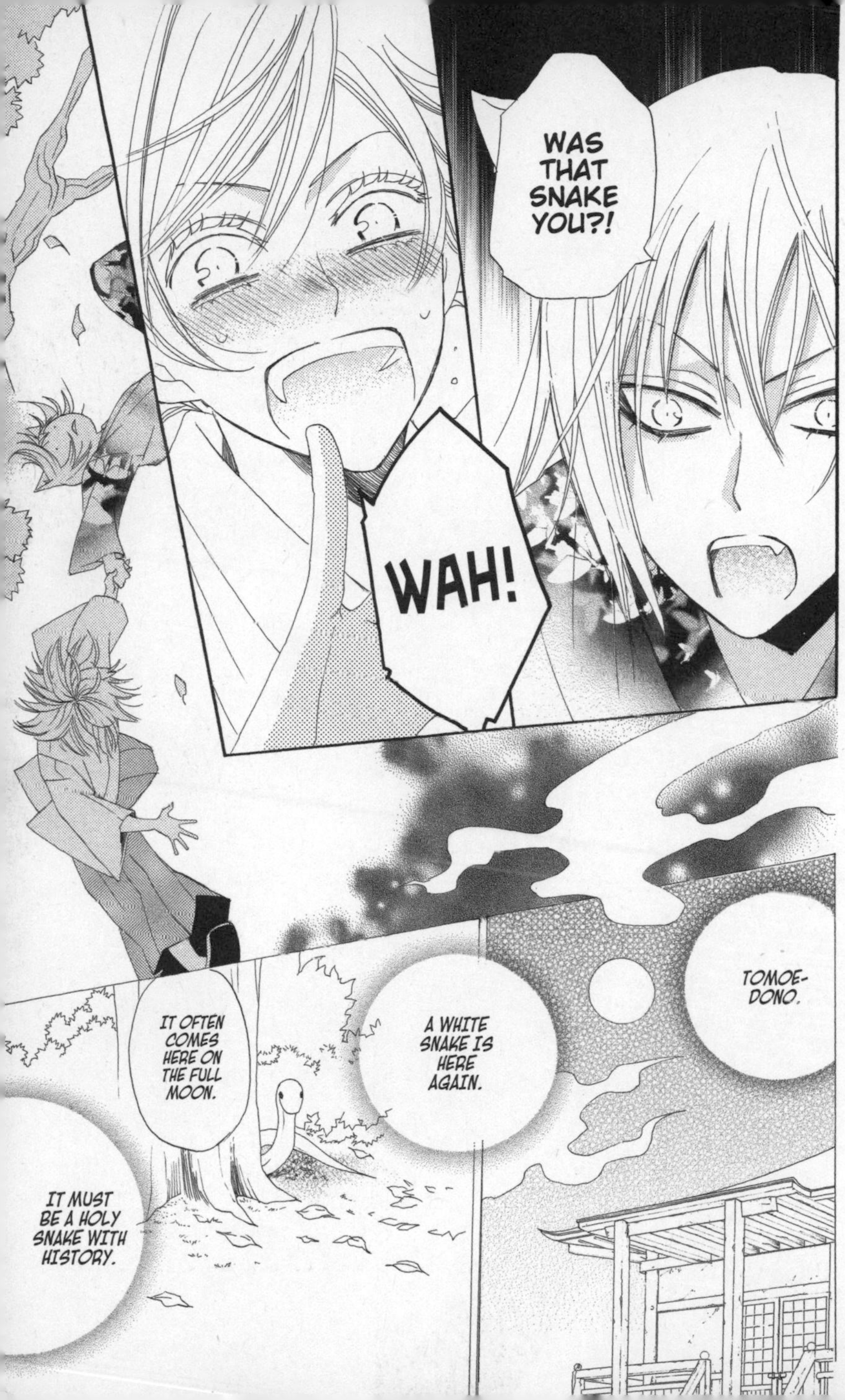
WAS THAT SNAKE YOU?!
WAH!
TOMOE-DONO.
A WHITE SNAKE IS HERE AGAIN.
IT OFTEN COMES HERE ON THE FULL MOON.
IT MUST BE A HOLY SNAKE WITH HISTORY.

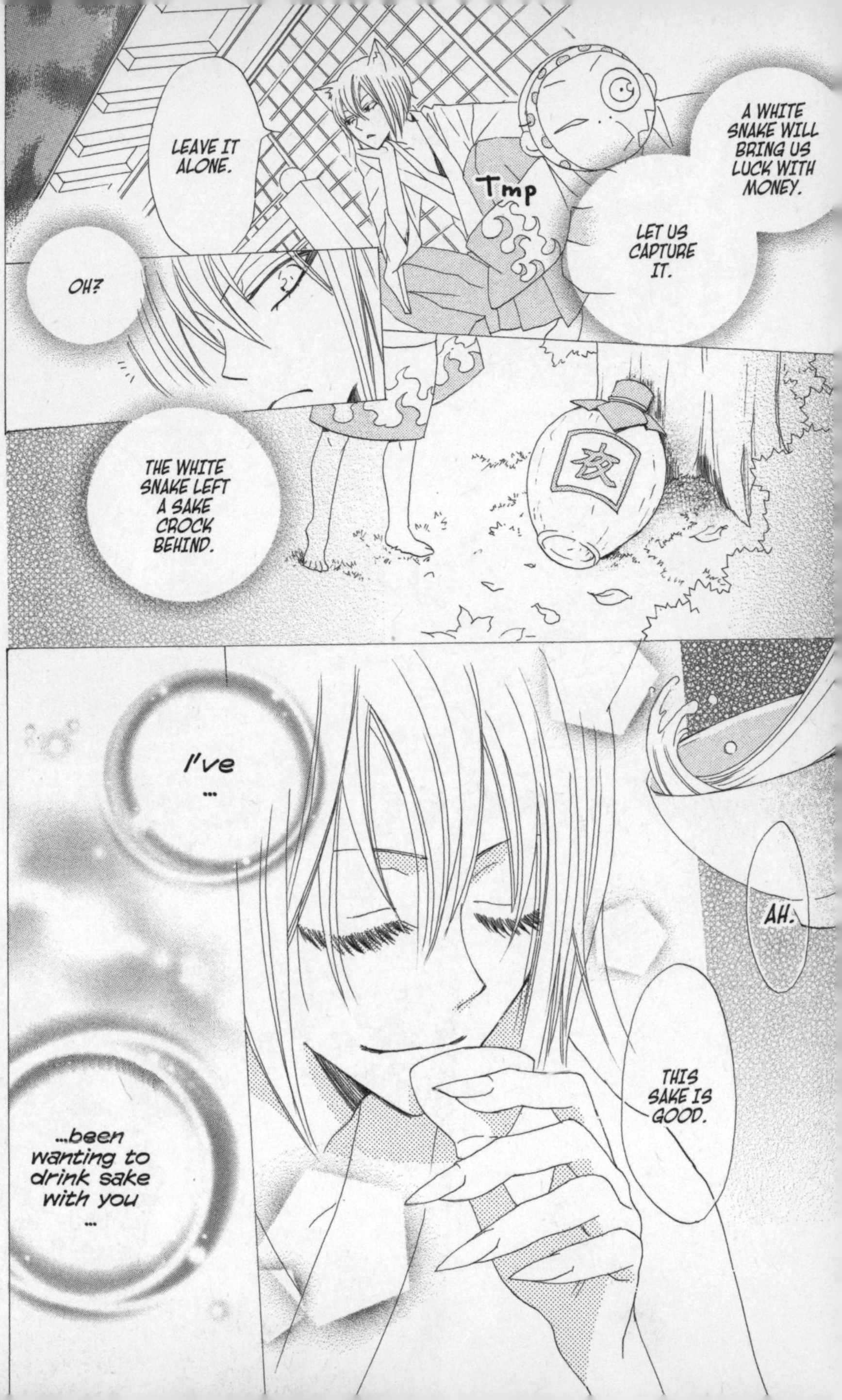
A WHITE SNAKE WILL BRING US LUCK WITH MONEY.
LET US CAPTURE IT.
Tmp
LEAVE IT ALONE.
OH?
夜
THE WHITE SNAKE LEFT A SAKE CROCK BEHIND.
AH.
THIS SAKE IS GOOD.
I've ...
...been wanting to drink sake with you ...

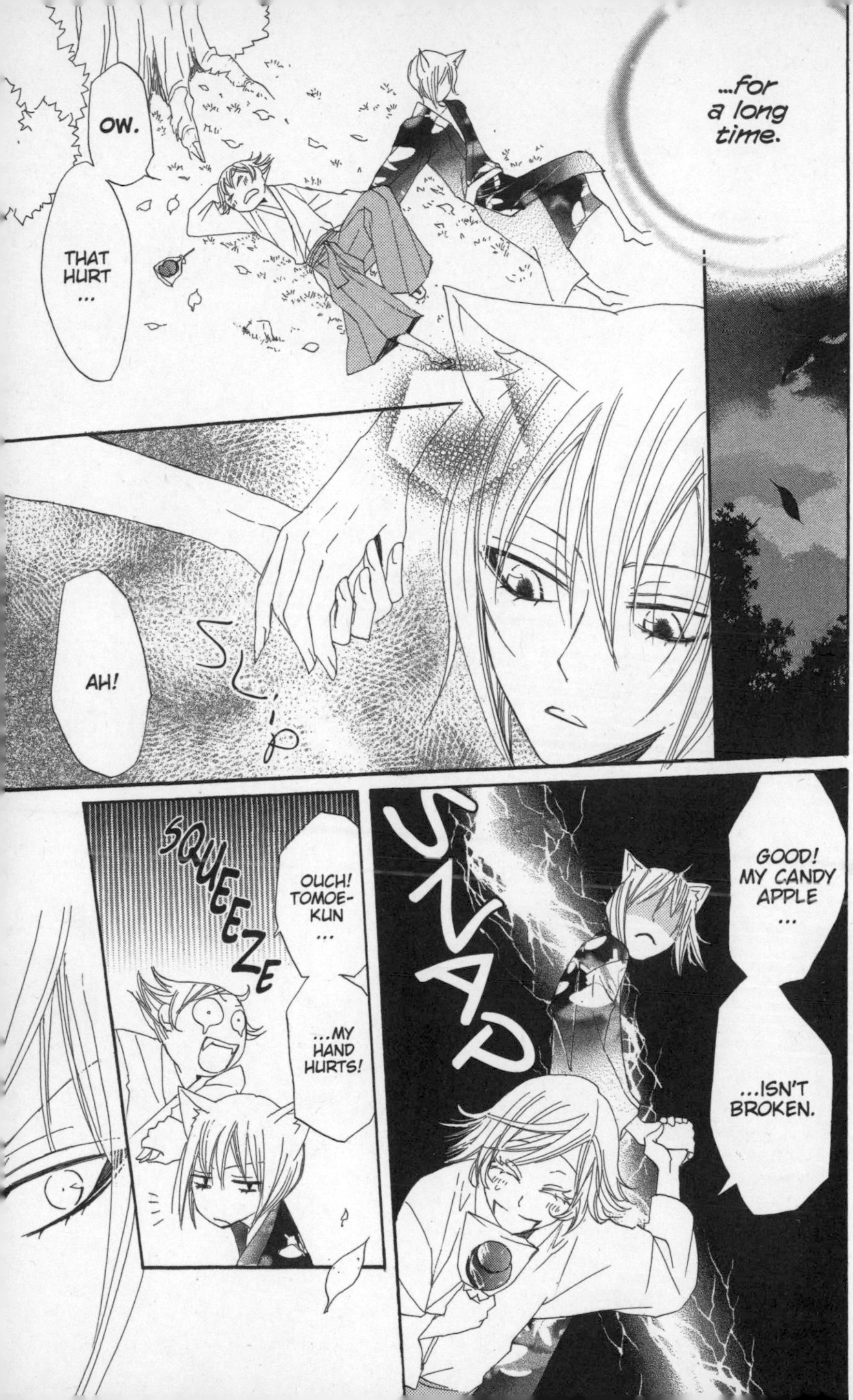
...for a long time.
OW.
THAT HURT ...
AH!
SLIP
SNAP
GOOD! MY CANDY APPLE ...
...ISN'T BROKEN.
SQUEEZE
OUCH! TOMOE-KUN ...
...MY HAND HURTS!

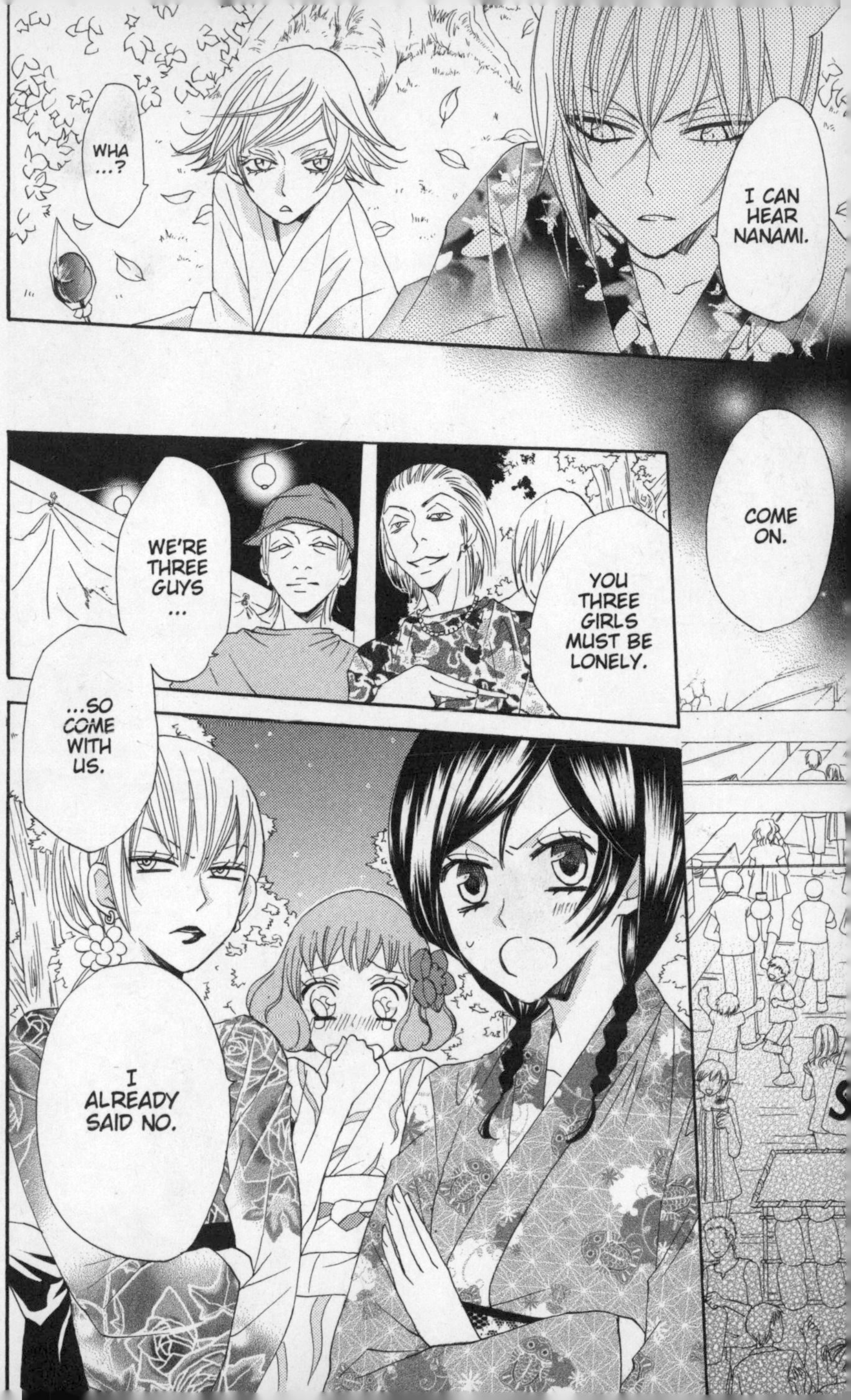
I CAN HEAR NANAMI.
WHA...?
COME ON.
YOU THREE GIRLS MUST BE LONELY.
WE'RE THREE GUYS...
...SO COME WITH US.
I ALREADY SAID NO.

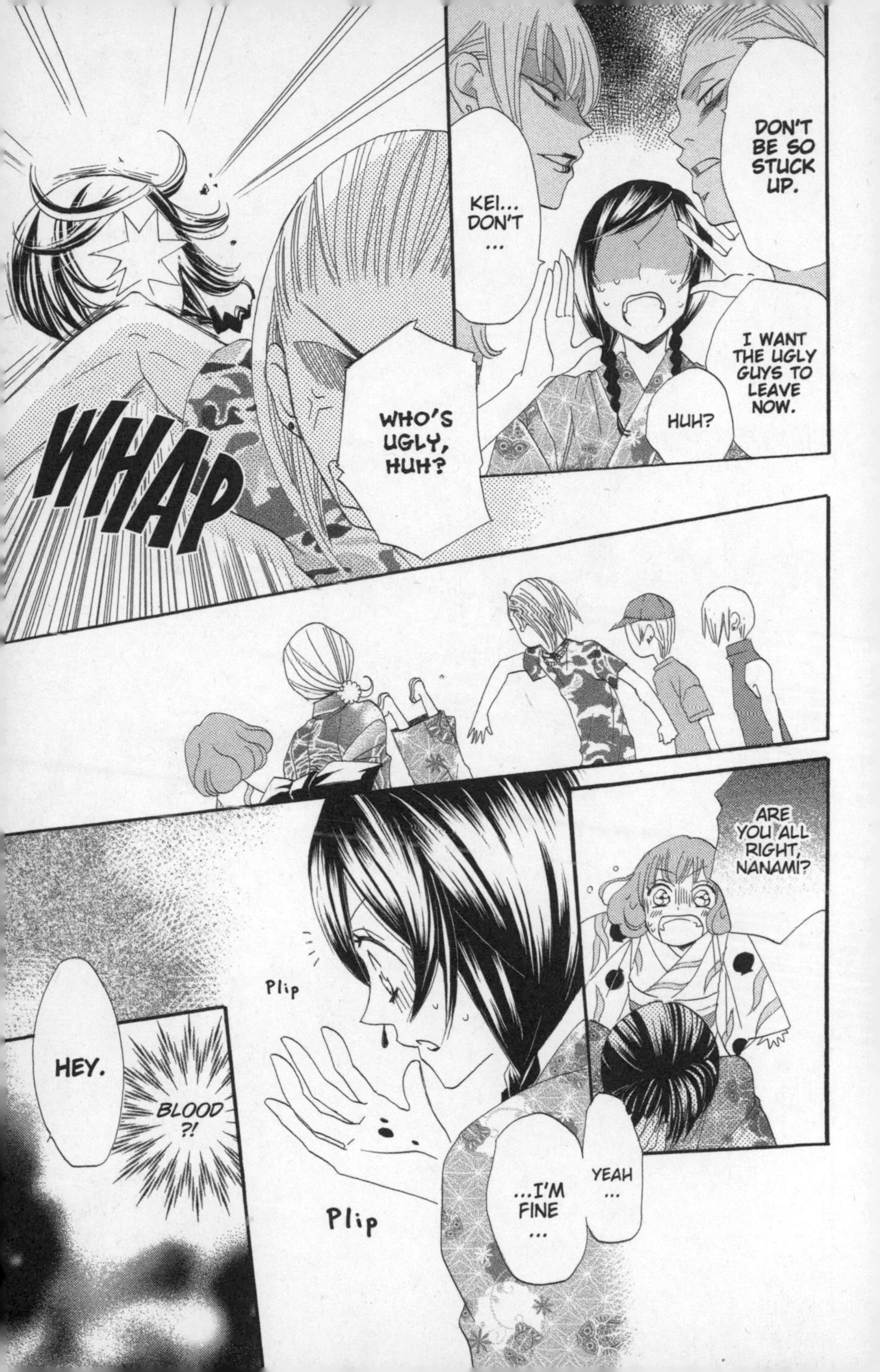
DON'T BE SO STUCK UP.
KEI... DON'T ...
I WANT THE UGLY GUYS TO LEAVE NOW.
HUH?
WHO'S UGLY, HUH?
WHAP
ARE YOU ALL RIGHT, NANAMI?
YEAH ...
...I'M FINE ...
Plip
Plip
HEY.
BLOOD ?!

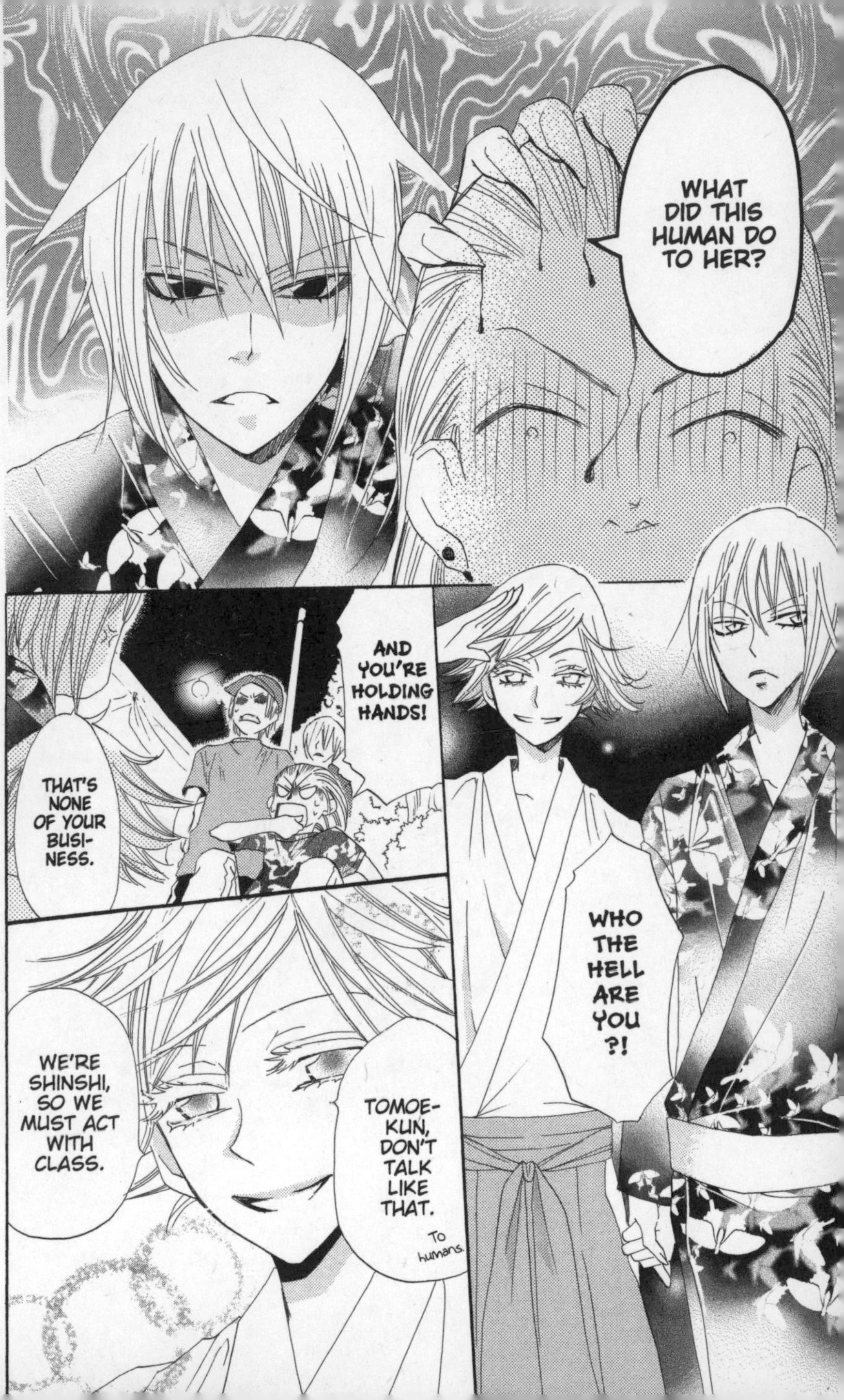
WHAT DID THIS HUMAN DO TO HER?
WHO THE HELL ARE YOU?!
TOMOE-KUN, DON'T TALK LIKE THAT.
To humans.
AND YOU'RE HOLDING HANDS!
THAT'S NONE OF YOUR BUSINESS.
WE'RE SHINSHI, SO WE MUST ACT WITH CLASS.

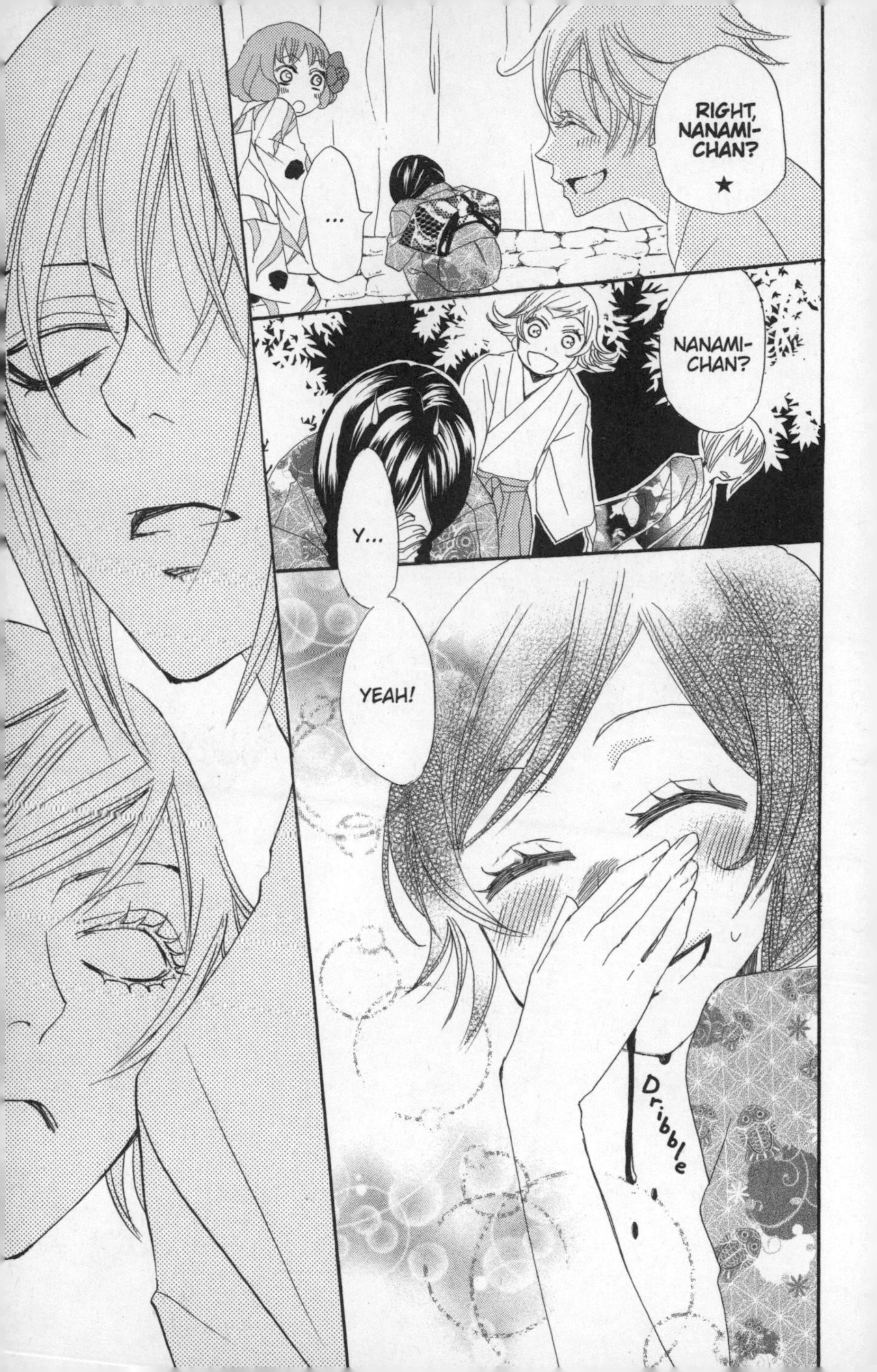
RIGHT, NANAMI-CHAN? ★
...
NANAMI-CHAN?
Y...
YEAH!
Dribble

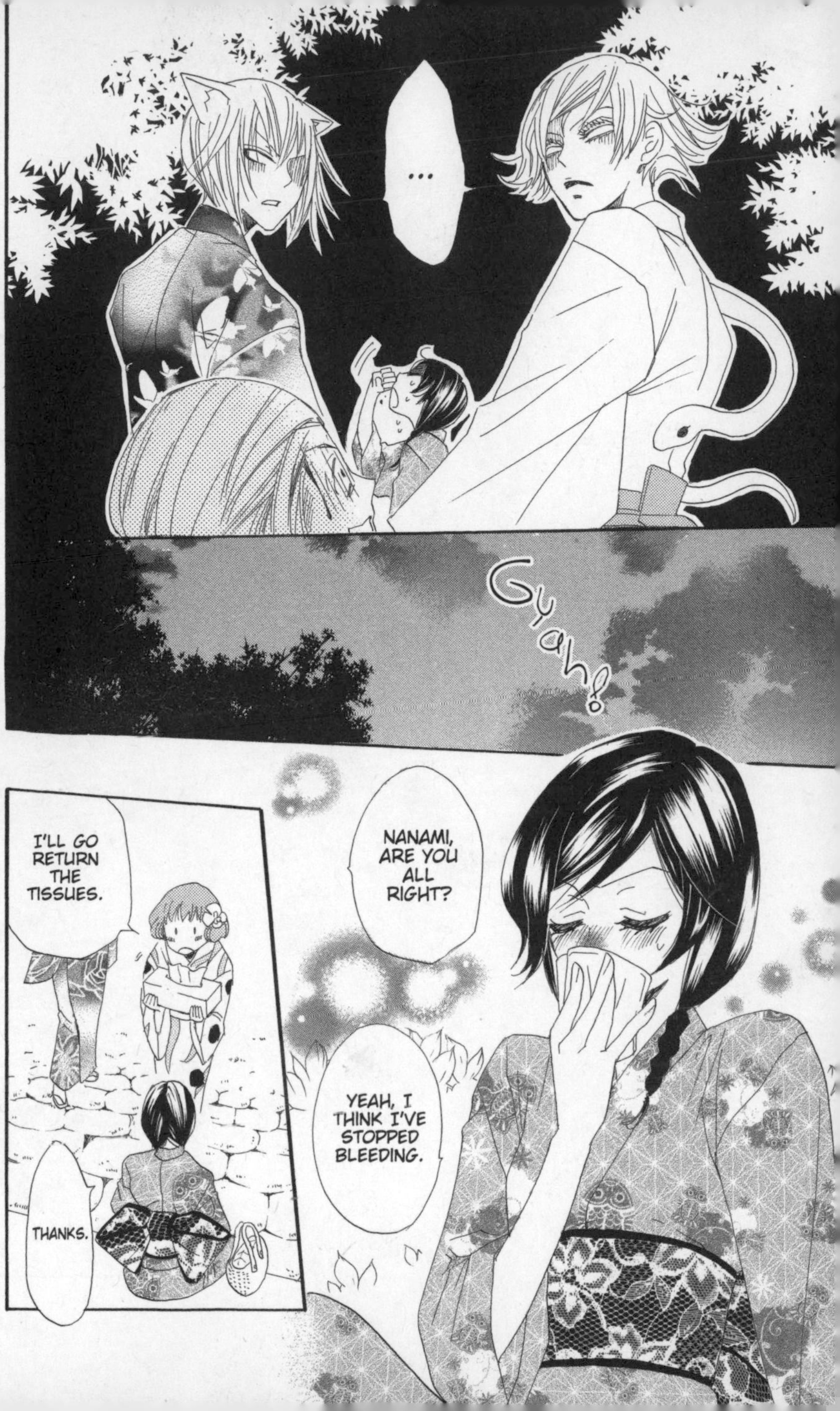
...
Gyah!
NANAMI, ARE YOU ALL RIGHT?
YEAH, I THINK I'VE STOPPED BLEEDING.
I'LL GO RETURN THE TISSUES.
THANKS.

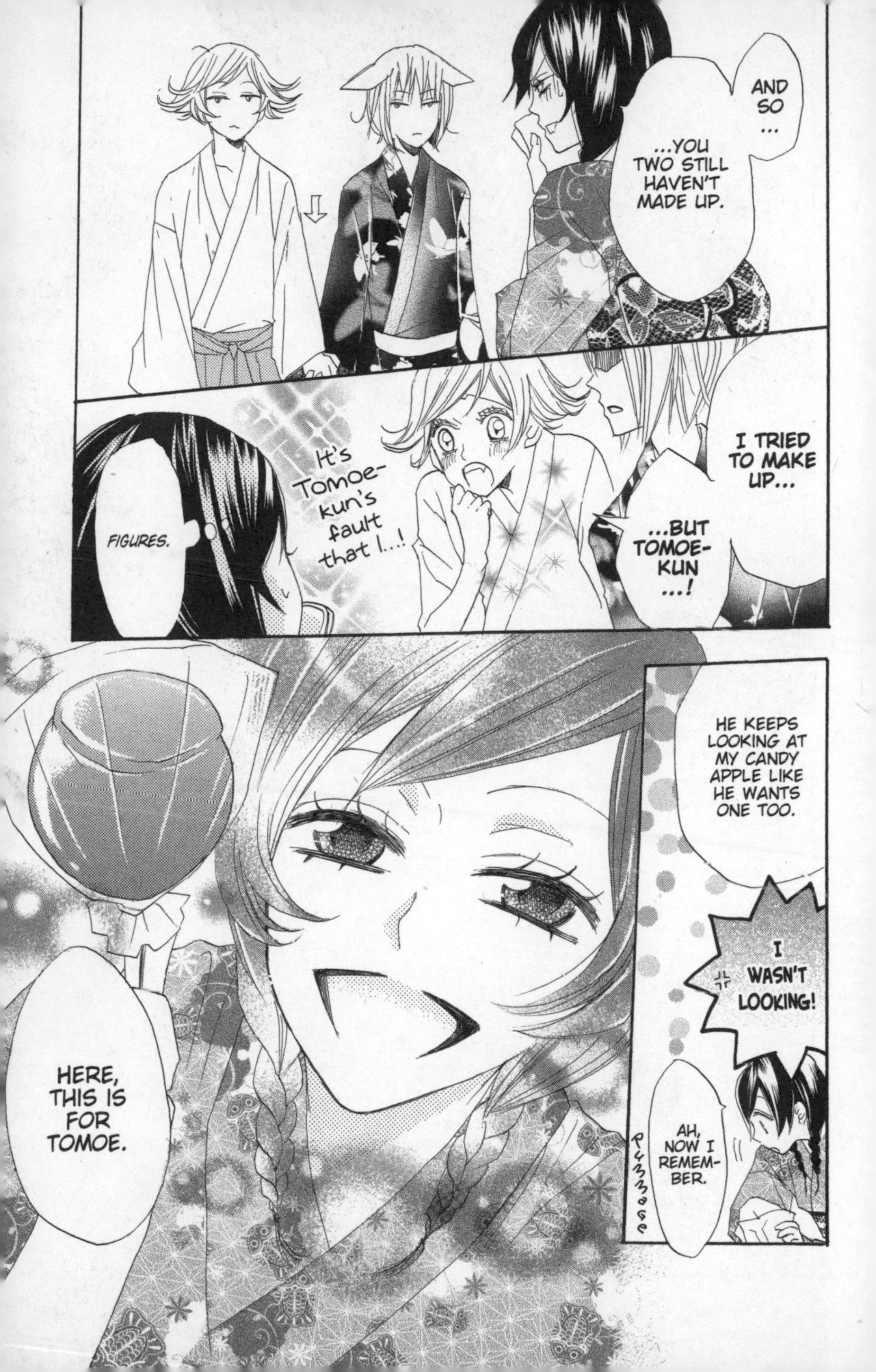
AND SO ...
...YOU TWO STILL HAVEN'T MADE UP.
I TRIED TO MAKE UP...
...BUT TOMOE-KUN ...!
It's Tomoe-kun's fault that I...!
FIGURES.
HE KEEPS LOOKING AT MY CANDY APPLE LIKE HE WANTS ONE TOO.
I WASN'T LOOKING!
AH, NOW I REMEMBER.
HERE, THIS IS FOR TOMOE.

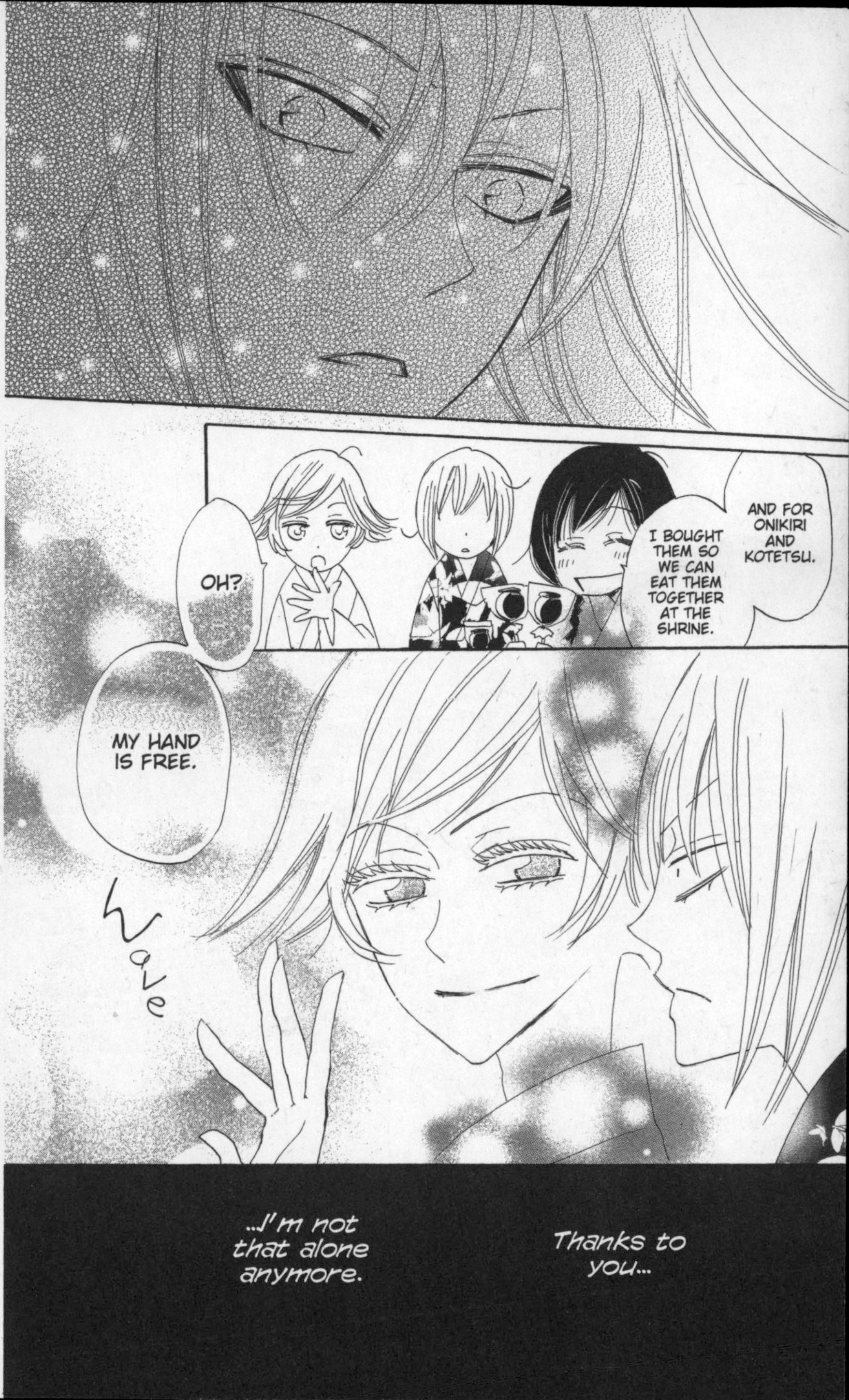
AND FOR ONIKIRI AND KOTETSU.
I BOUGHT THEM SO WE CAN EAT THEM TOGETHER AT THE SHRINE.
OH?
MY HAND IS FREE.
Wave
Thanks to you...
...I'm not that alone anymore.

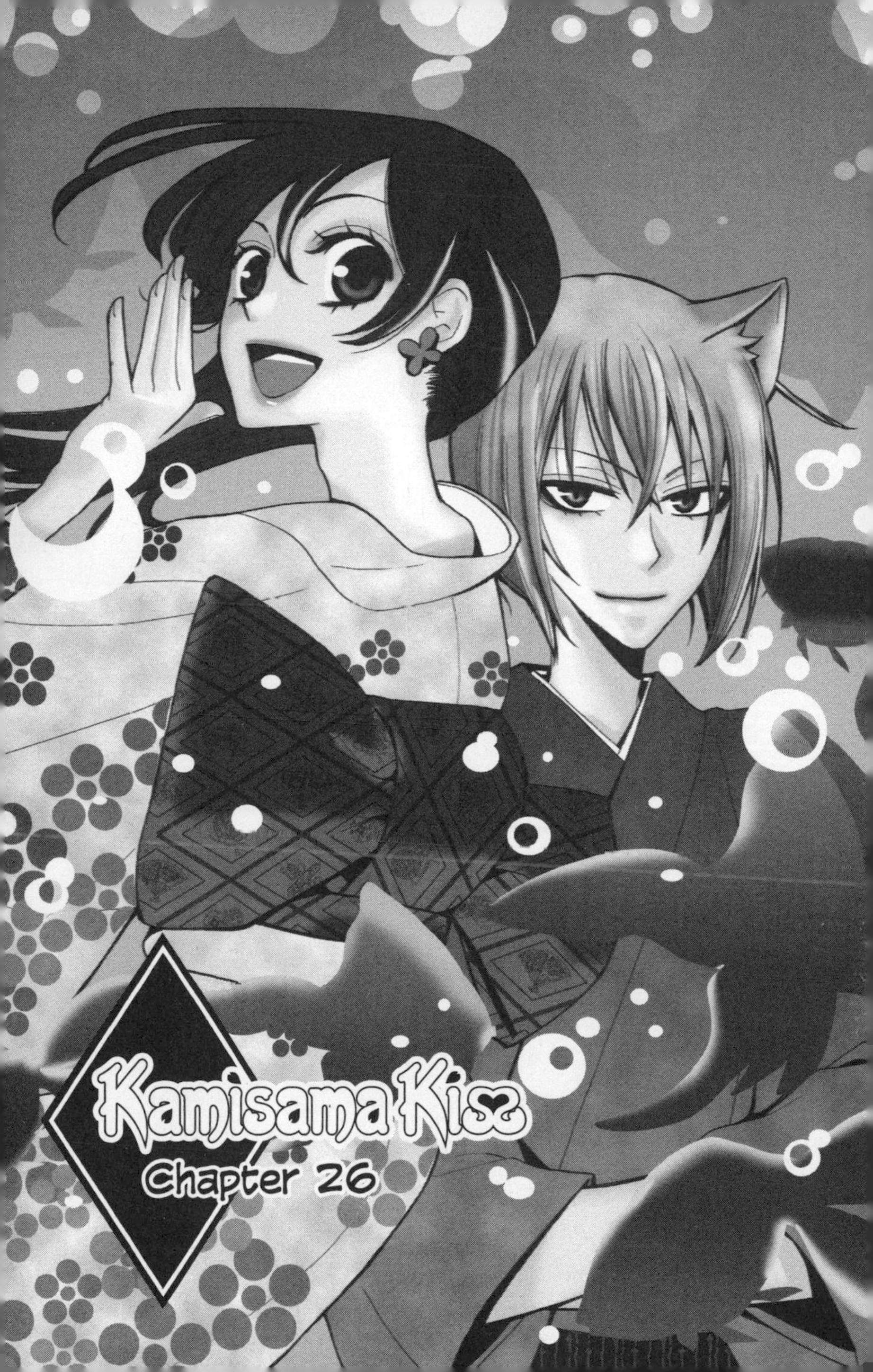
Kamisama Kiss
Chapter 26

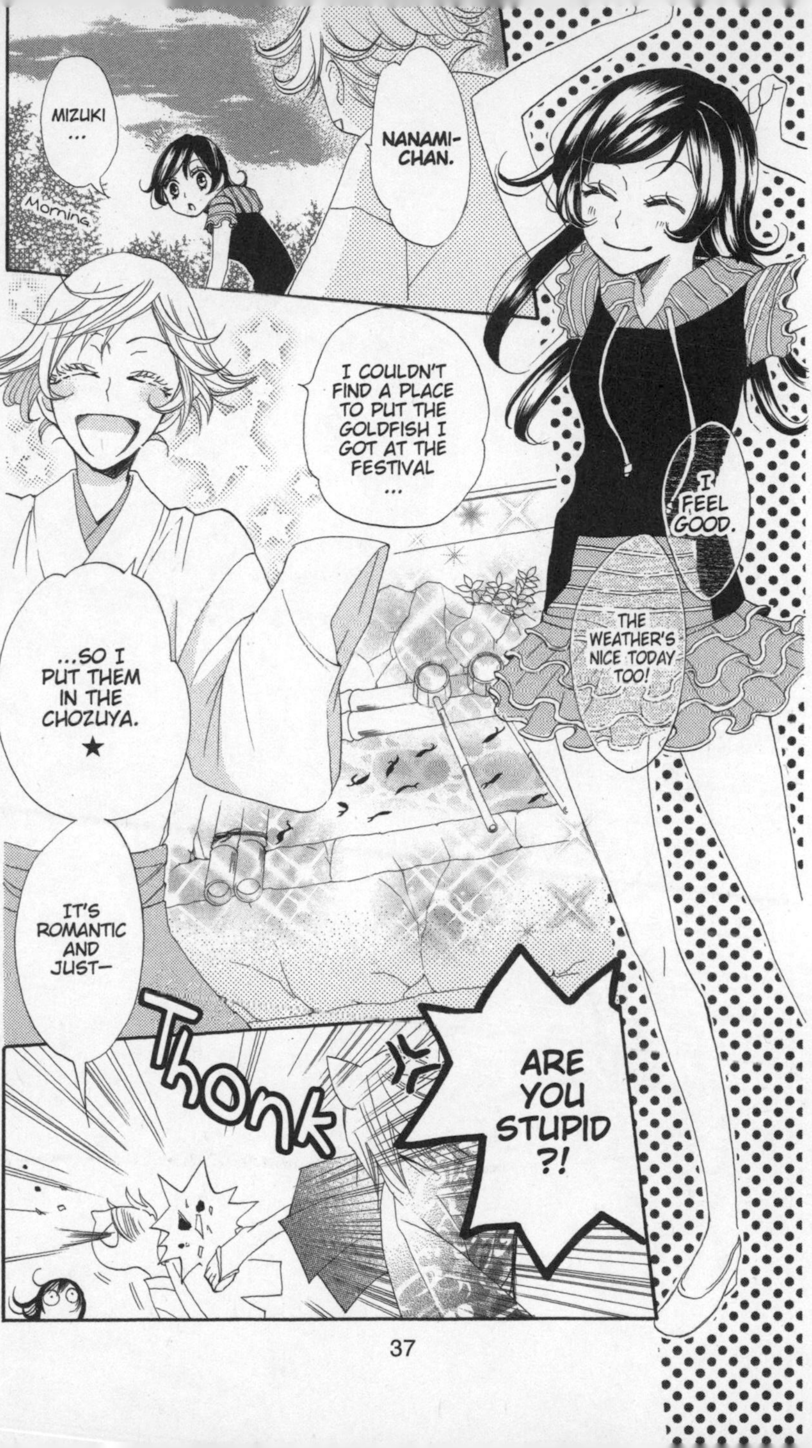
I FEEL GOOD.
THE WEATHER'S NICE TODAY TOO!
NANAMI-CHAN.
MIZUKI ...
Morning
I COULDN'T FIND A PLACE TO PUT THE GOLDFISH I GOT AT THE FESTIVAL ...
...SO I PUT THEM IN THE CHOZUYA. ★
IT'S ROMANTIC AND JUST—
ARE YOU STUPID ?!
Thonk

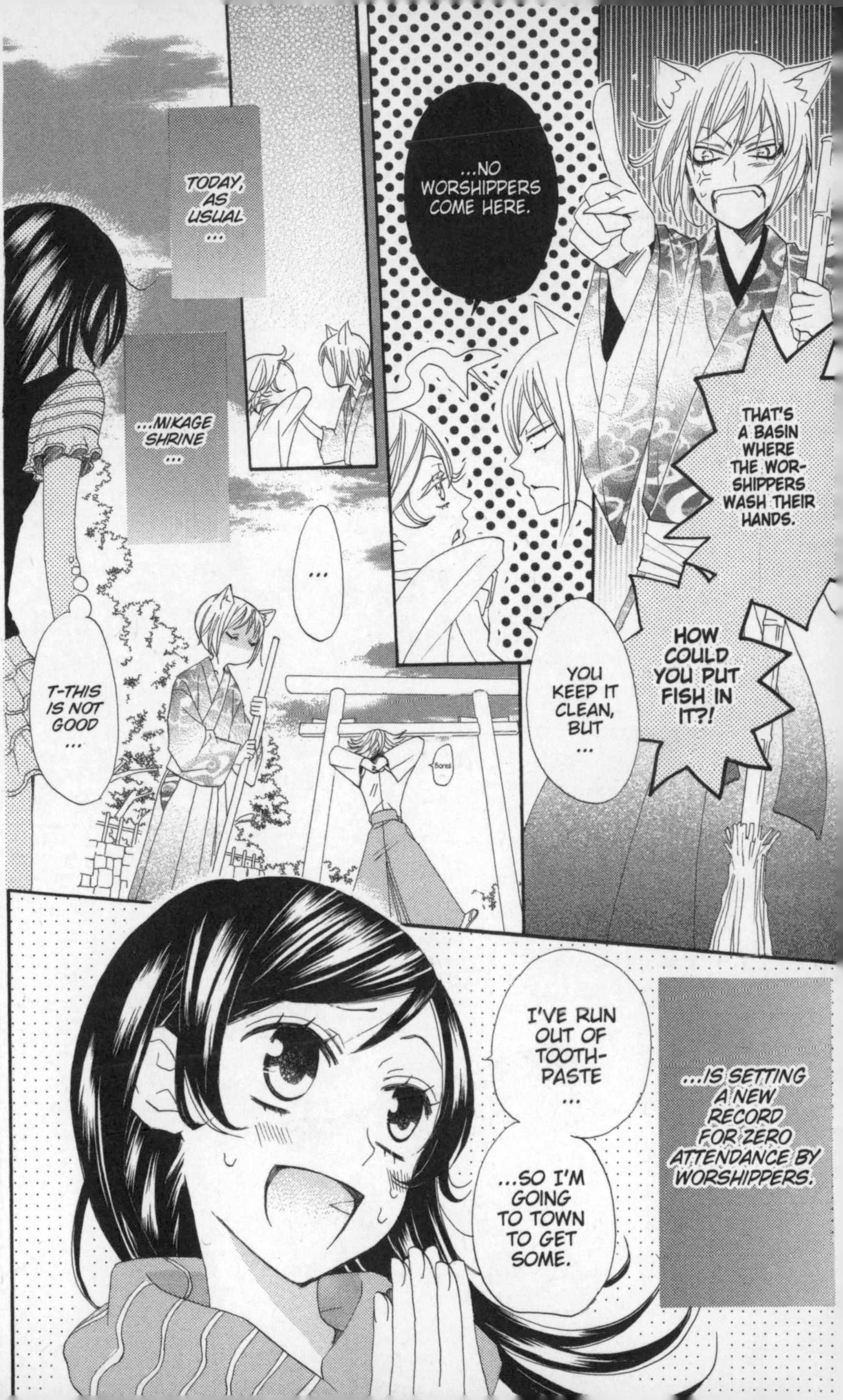
THAT'S A BASIN WHERE THE WOR-SHIPPERS WASH THEIR HANDS.
HOW COULD YOU PUT FISH IN IT?!
...NO WORSHIPPERS COME HERE.
YOU KEEP IT CLEAN, BUT ...
...
Bored
TODAY, AS USUAL ...
...MIKAGE SHRINE ...
T-THIS IS NOT GOOD ...
...IS SETTING A NEW RECORD FOR ZERO ATTENDANCE BY WORSHIPPERS.
I'VE RUN OUT OF TOOTH-PASTE ...
...SO I'M GOING TO TOWN TO GET SOME.

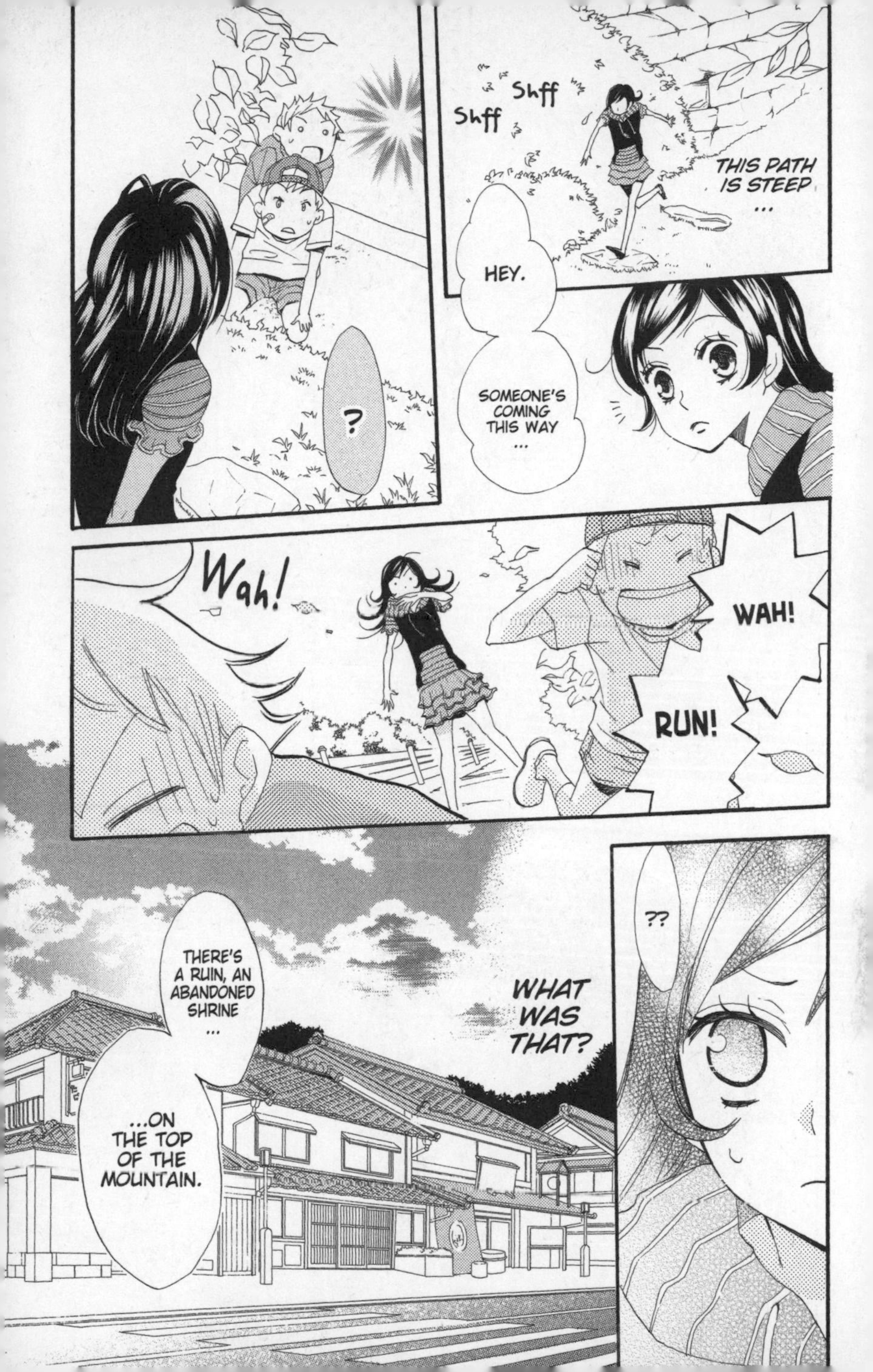
Shff
Shff
THIS PATH IS STEEP ...
HEY.
SOMEONE'S COMING THIS WAY ...
?
WAH!
RUN!
Wah!
??
WHAT WAS THAT?
THERE'S A RUIN, AN ABANDONED SHRINE ...
...ON THE TOP OF THE MOUNTAIN.

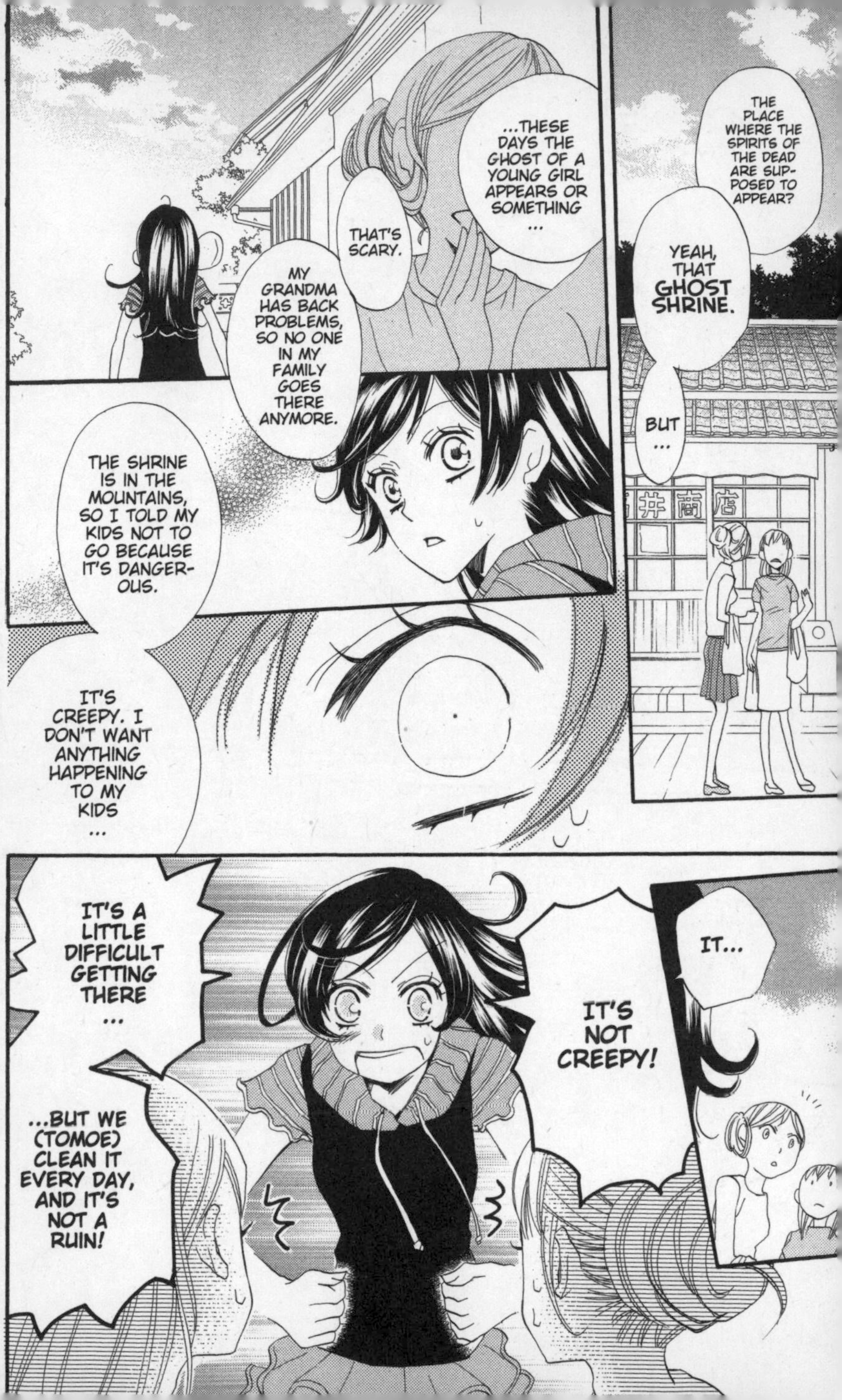
THE PLACE WHERE THE SPIRITS OF THE DEAD ARE SUPPOSED TO APPEAR?
YEAH, THAT GHOST SHRINE.
BUT ...
井商店
...THESE DAYS THE GHOST OF A YOUNG GIRL APPEARS OR SOMETHING ...
THAT'S SCARY.
MY GRANDMA HAS BACK PROBLEMS, SO NO ONE IN MY FAMILY GOES THERE ANYMORE.
THE SHRINE IS IN THE MOUNTAINS, SO I TOLD MY KIDS NOT TO GO BECAUSE IT'S DANGER-OUS.
IT'S CREEPY. I DON'T WANT ANYTHING HAPPENING TO MY KIDS ...
IT...
IT'S NOT CREEPY!
IT'S A LITTLE DIFFICULT GETTING THERE ...
...BUT WE (TOMOE) CLEAN IT EVERY DAY, AND IT'S NOT A RUIN!

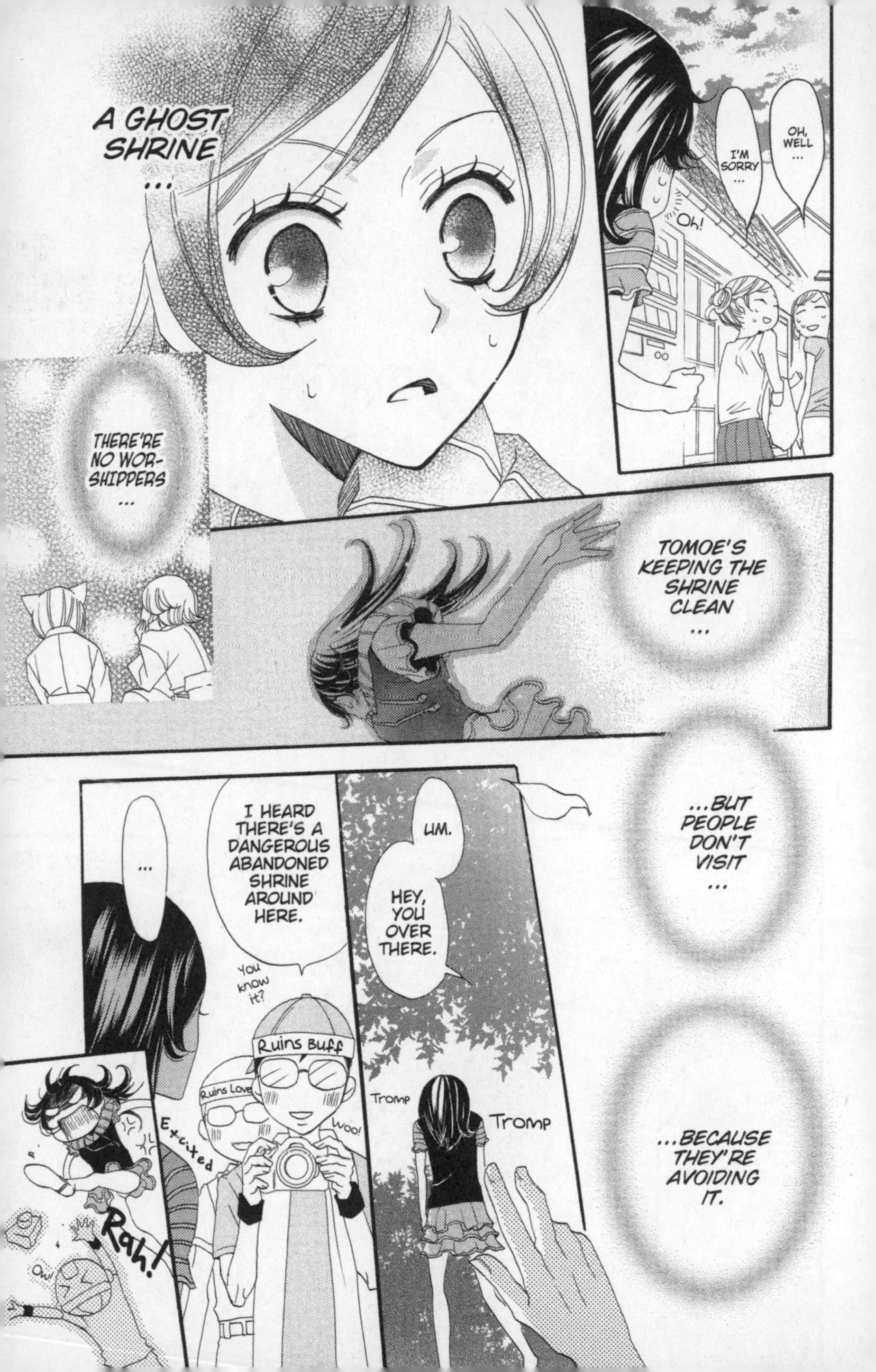
OH, WELL ...
I'M SORRY ...
Oh!
A GHOST SHRINE ...
THERE'RE NO WOR-SHIPPERS ...
TOMOE'S KEEPING THE SHRINE CLEAN ...
...BUT PEOPLE DON'T VISIT ...
UM.
HEY, YOU OVER THERE.
Tromp
Tromp
...BECAUSE THEY'RE AVOIDING IT.
I HEARD THERE'S A DANGEROUS ABANDONED SHRINE AROUND HERE.
...
You know it?
Ruins Buff
Ruins Love
Woo!
Excited
Rah!
Ow!

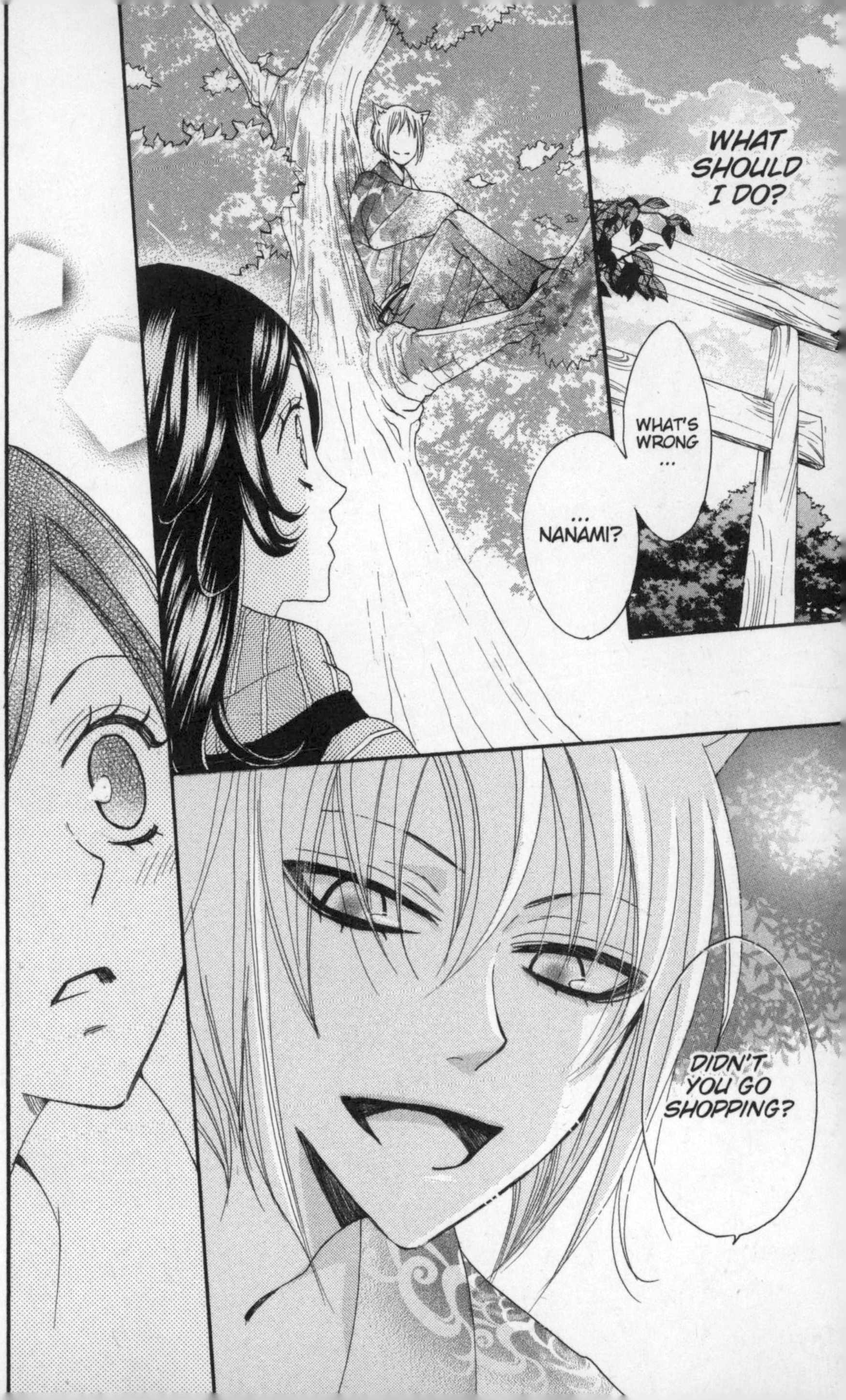
WHAT SHOULD I DO?
WHAT'S WRONG ... ... NANAMI?
DIDN'T YOU GO SHOPPING?

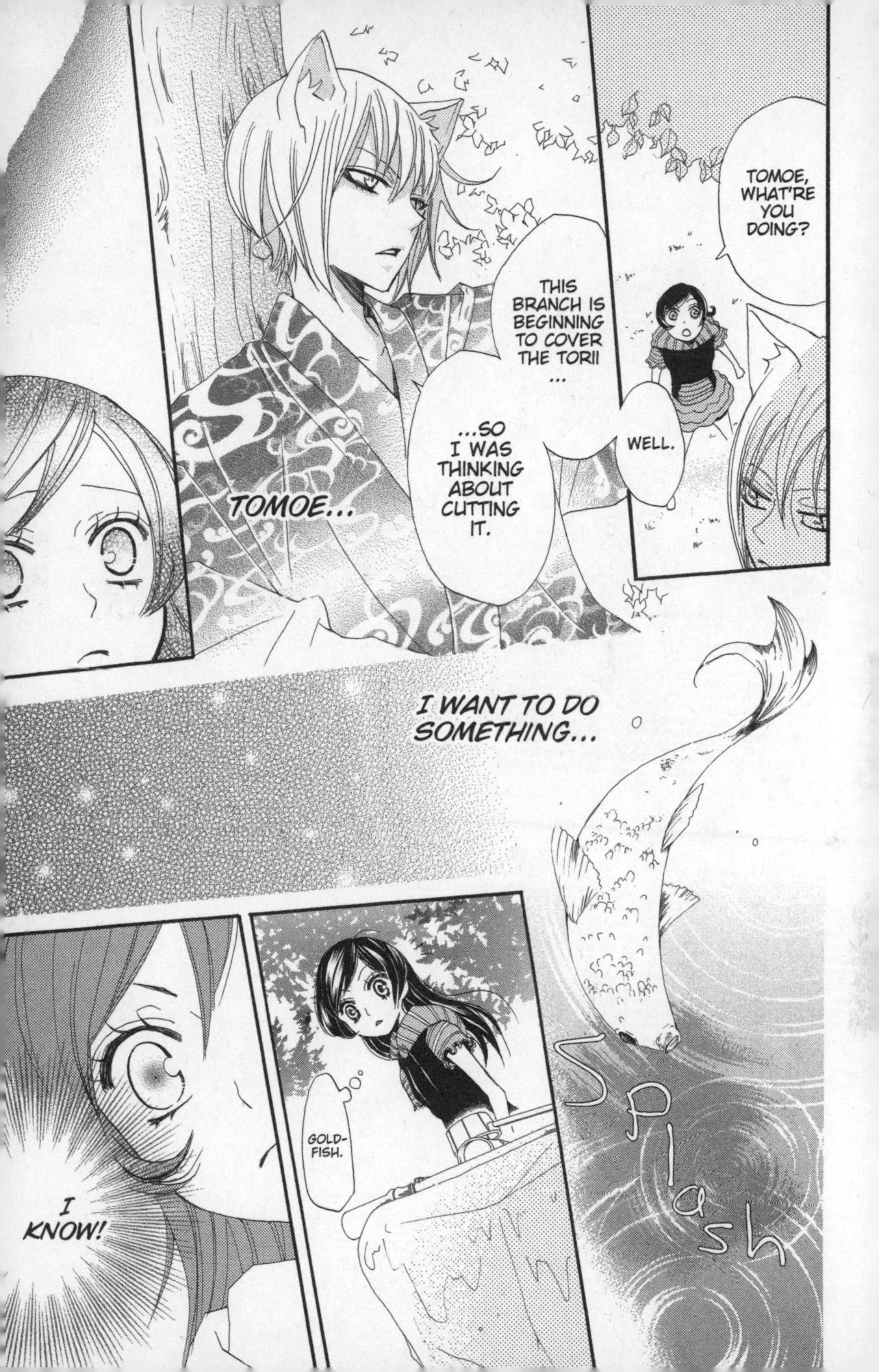
TOMOE, WHAT'RE YOU DOING?
WELL.
THIS BRANCH IS BEGINNING TO COVER THE TORII ...
...SO I WAS THINKING ABOUT CUTTING IT.
TOMOE...
I WANT TO DO SOMETHING...
Splash
GOLD-FISH.
I KNOW!

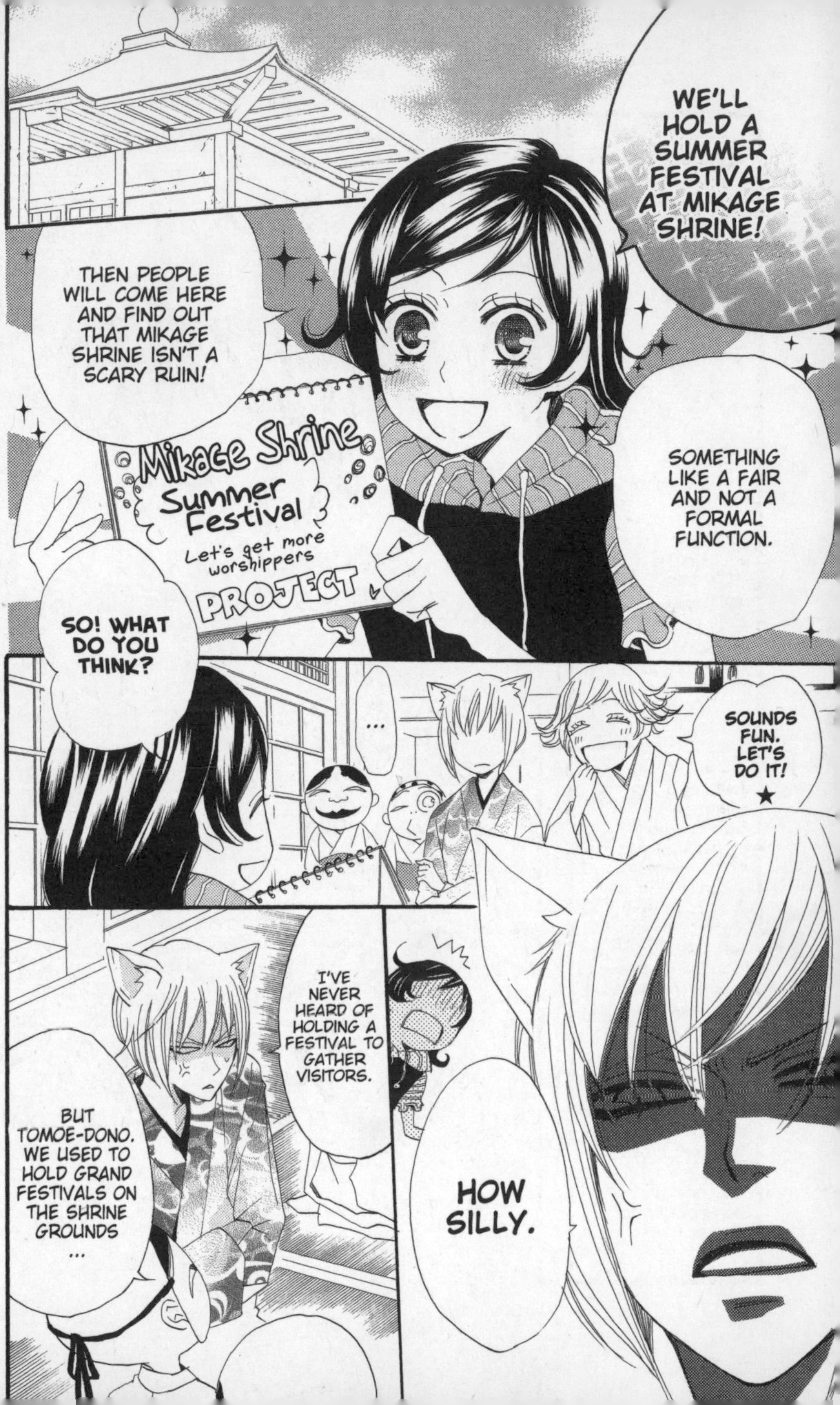
WE'LL HOLD A SUMMER FESTIVAL AT MIKAGE SHRINE!
SOMETHING LIKE A FAIR AND NOT A FORMAL FUNCTION.
THEN PEOPLE WILL COME HERE AND FIND OUT THAT MIKAGE SHRINE ISN'T A SCARY RUIN!
Mikage Shrine
Summer Festival
Let's get more worshippers
PROJECT
SO! WHAT DO YOU THINK?
SOUNDS FUN. LET'S DO IT! ★
...
HOW SILLY.
I'VE NEVER HEARD OF HOLDING A FESTIVAL TO GATHER VISITORS.
BUT TOMOE-DONO. WE USED TO HOLD GRAND FESTIVALS ON THE SHRINE GROUNDS ...

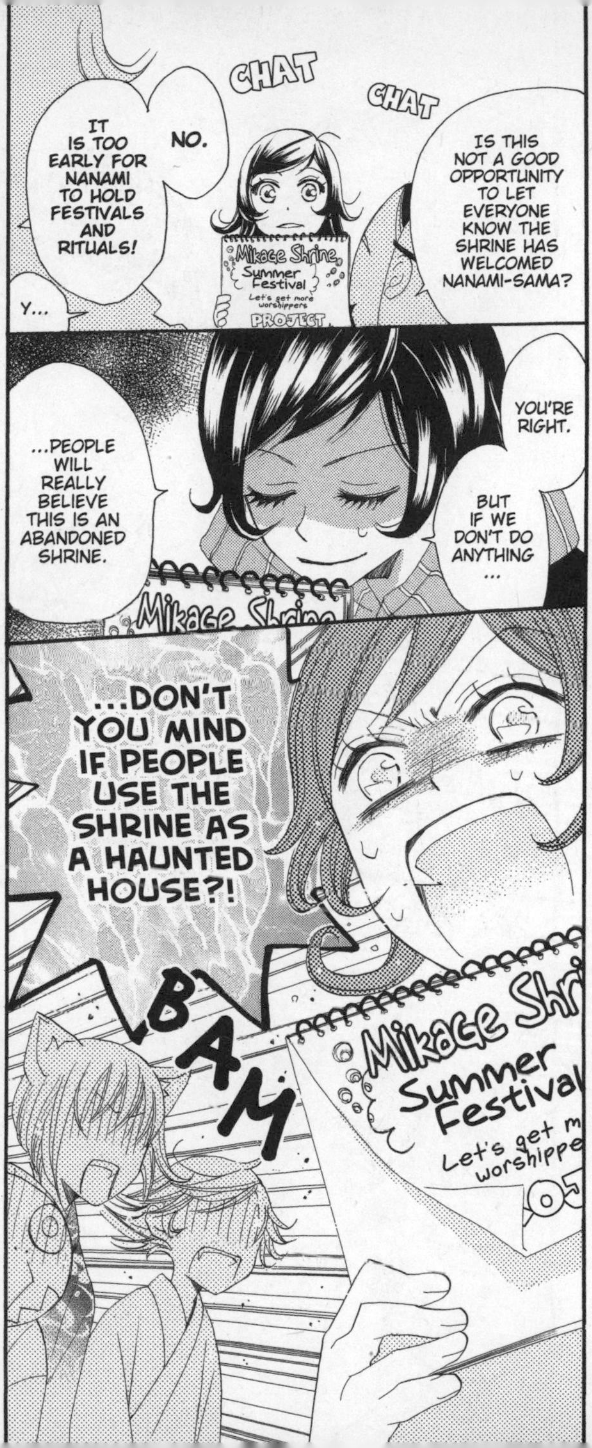
IS THIS NOT A GOOD OPPORTUNITY TO LET EVERYONE KNOW THE SHRINE HAS WELCOMED NANAMI-SAMA?
CHAT
CHAT
NO.
IT IS TOO EARLY FOR NANAMI TO HOLD FESTIVALS AND RITUALS!
Y...
Mikage Shrine Summer Festival Let's get more worshippers PROJECT
YOU'RE RIGHT.
BUT IF WE DON'T DO ANYTHING ...
...PEOPLE WILL REALLY BELIEVE THIS IS AN ABANDONED SHRINE.
...DON'T YOU MIND IF PEOPLE USE THE SHRINE AS A HAUNTED HOUSE?!
BAM

A friend bought me a kumade at a Tori no Ichi fair.

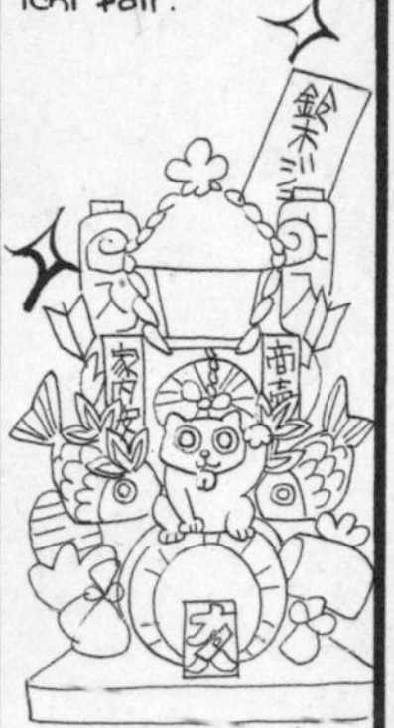

All sorts of lucky things are included in this! I was so happy. Thank you! Thank you!

I've never been to a Tori no Ichi fair, and I've wanted to go at least once. It's nice to participate in Japanese festivals and events! I feel the #1 event is the end of the year and the start of the New Year. I feel very excited at the atmosphere where everyone in town is preparing for the New Year, combined with the cold winter temperature.

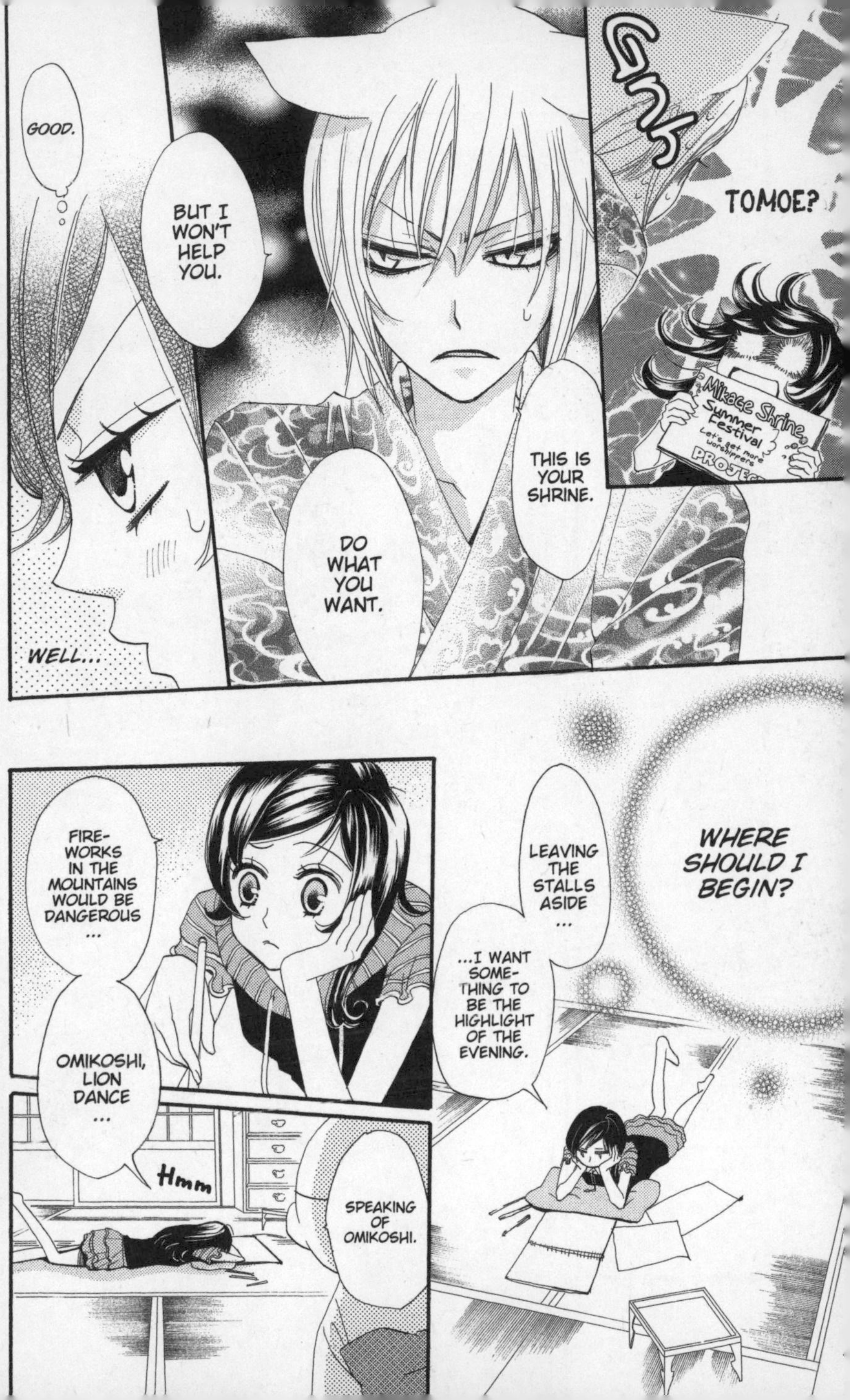
Gnh
TOMOE?
Mikage Shrine Summer Festival
Let's get more worshippers
PROJEC
THIS IS YOUR SHRINE.
DO WHAT YOU WANT.
BUT I WON'T HELP YOU.
WELL...
GOOD.
WHERE SHOULD I BEGIN?
LEAVING THE STALLS ASIDE...
...I WANT SOMETHING TO BE THE HIGHLIGHT OF THE EVENING.
FIRE-WORKS IN THE MOUNTAINS WOULD BE DANGEROUS...
OMIKOSHI, LION DANCE...
Hmm
SPEAKING OF OMIKOSHI.

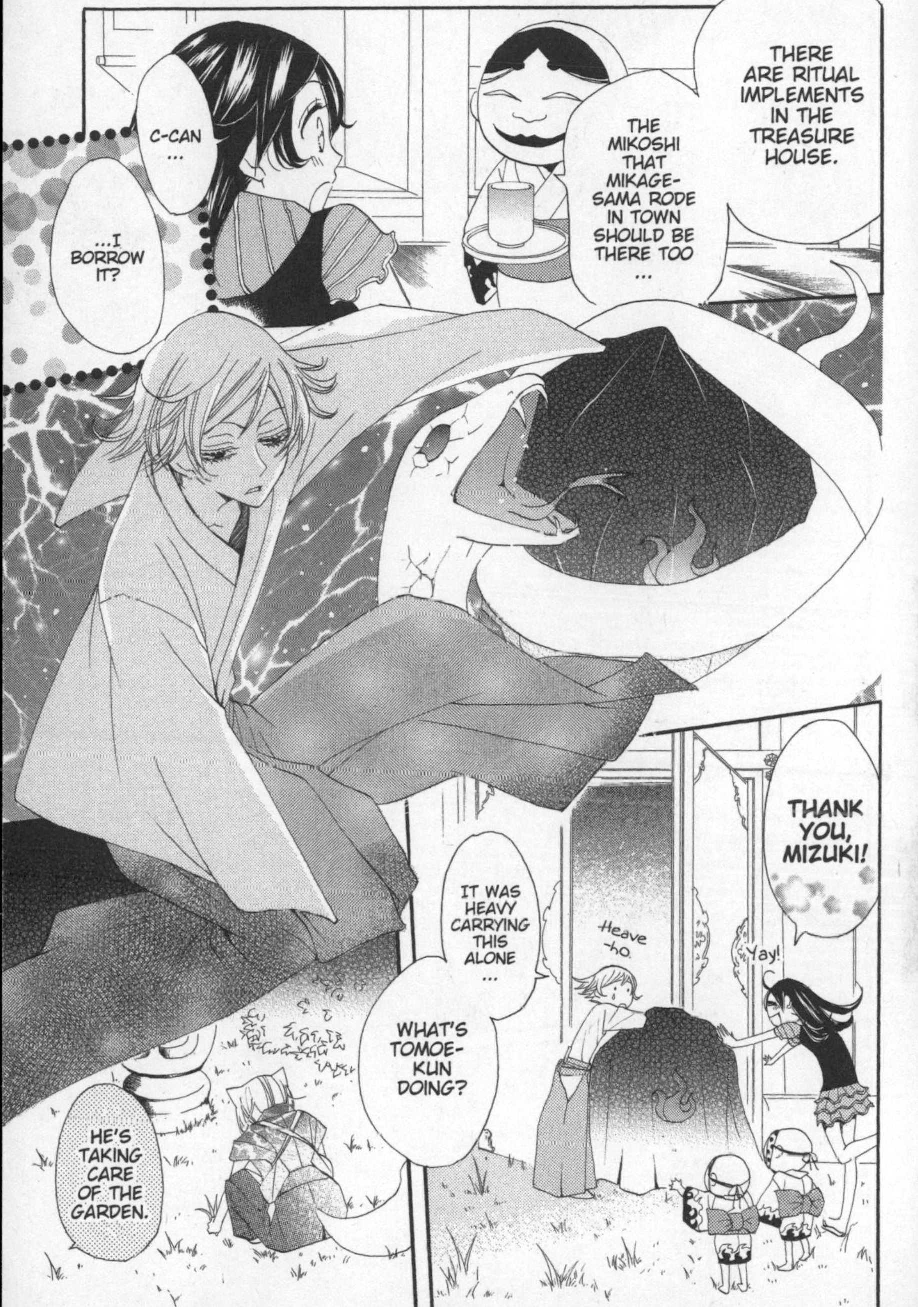
THERE ARE RITUAL IMPLEMENTS IN THE TREASURE HOUSE.
THE MIKOSHI THAT MIKAGE-SAMA RODE IN TOWN SHOULD BE THERE TOO...
C-CAN...
...I BORROW IT?
THANK YOU, MIZUKI!
Yay!
Heave-ho.
IT WAS HEAVY CARRYING THIS ALONE...
WHAT'S TOMOE-KUN DOING?
HE'S TAKING CARE OF THE GARDEN.

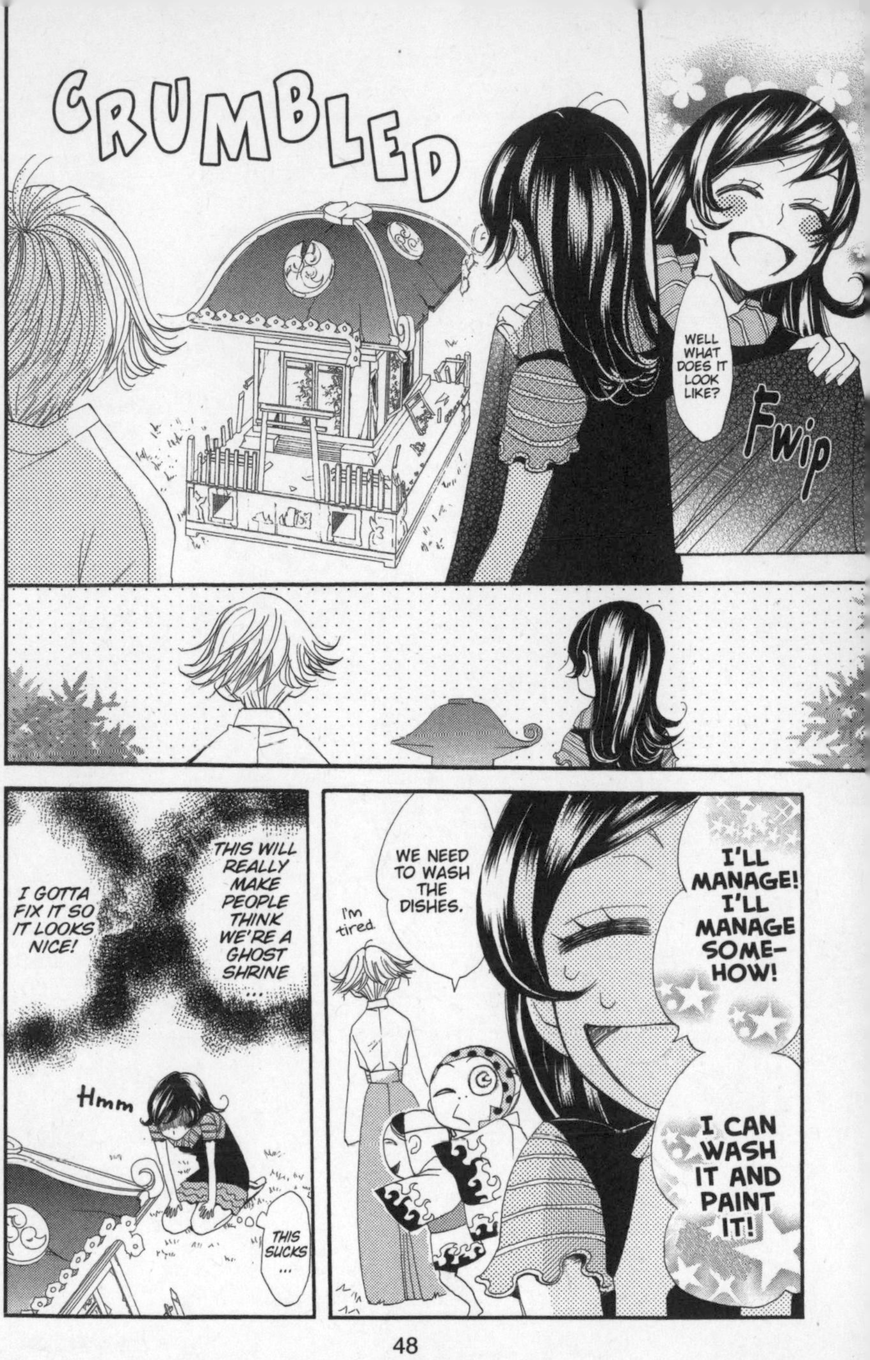
WELL WHAT DOES IT LOOK LIKE?
Fwip
CRUMBLED
I'LL MANAGE! I'LL MANAGE SOME-HOW!
WE NEED TO WASH THE DISHES.
I'm tired.
I CAN WASH IT AND PAINT IT!
THIS WILL REALLY MAKE PEOPLE THINK WE'RE A GHOST SHRINE...
I GOTTA FIX IT SO IT LOOKS NICE!
Hmm
THIS SUCKS...

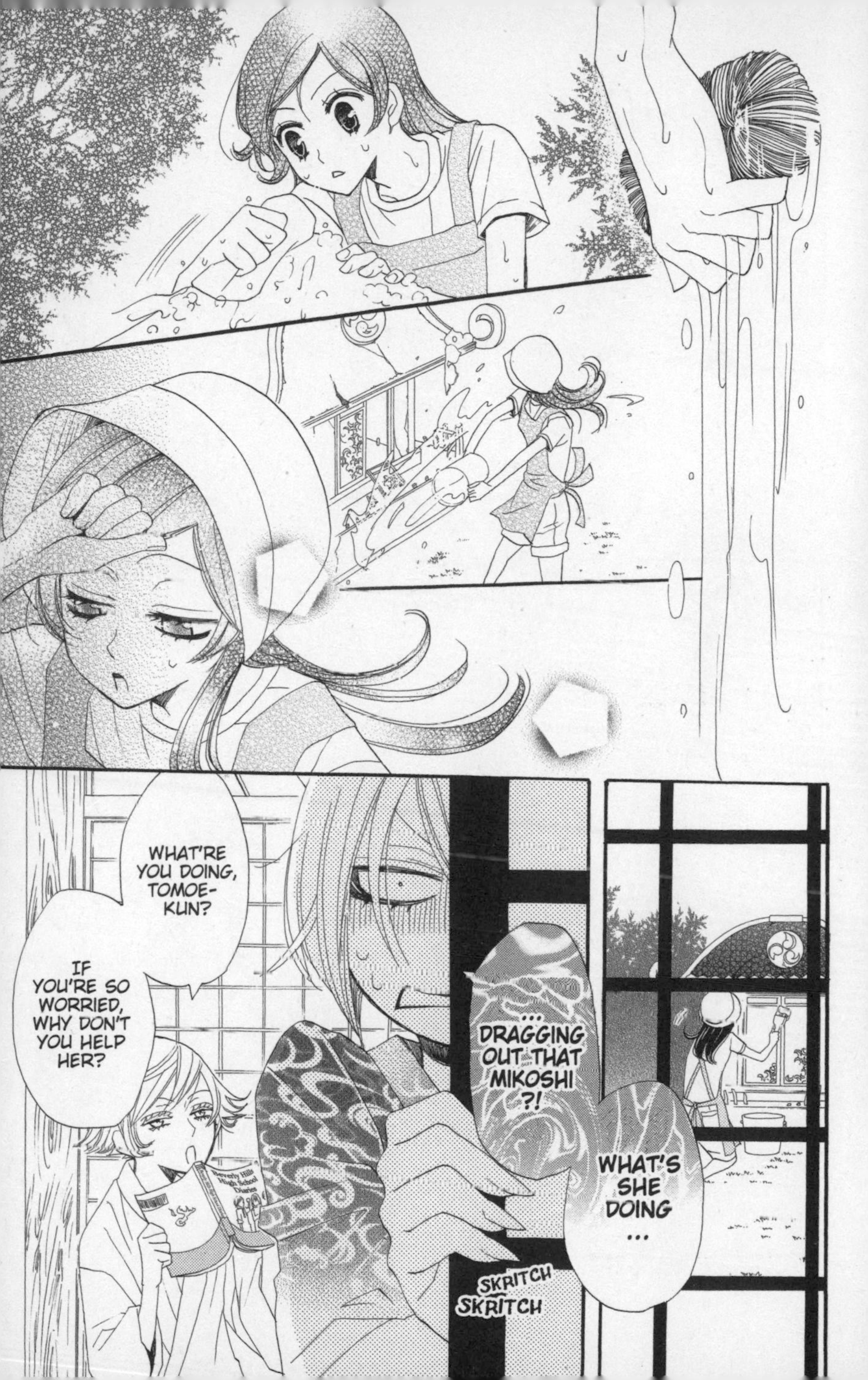
WHAT'S SHE DOING ...
... DRAGGING OUT THAT MIKOSHI ?!
SKRITCH SKRITCH
WHAT'RE YOU DOING, TOMOE-KUN?
IF YOU'RE SO WORRIED, WHY DON'T YOU HELP HER?
Beverly Hills High School Diaries

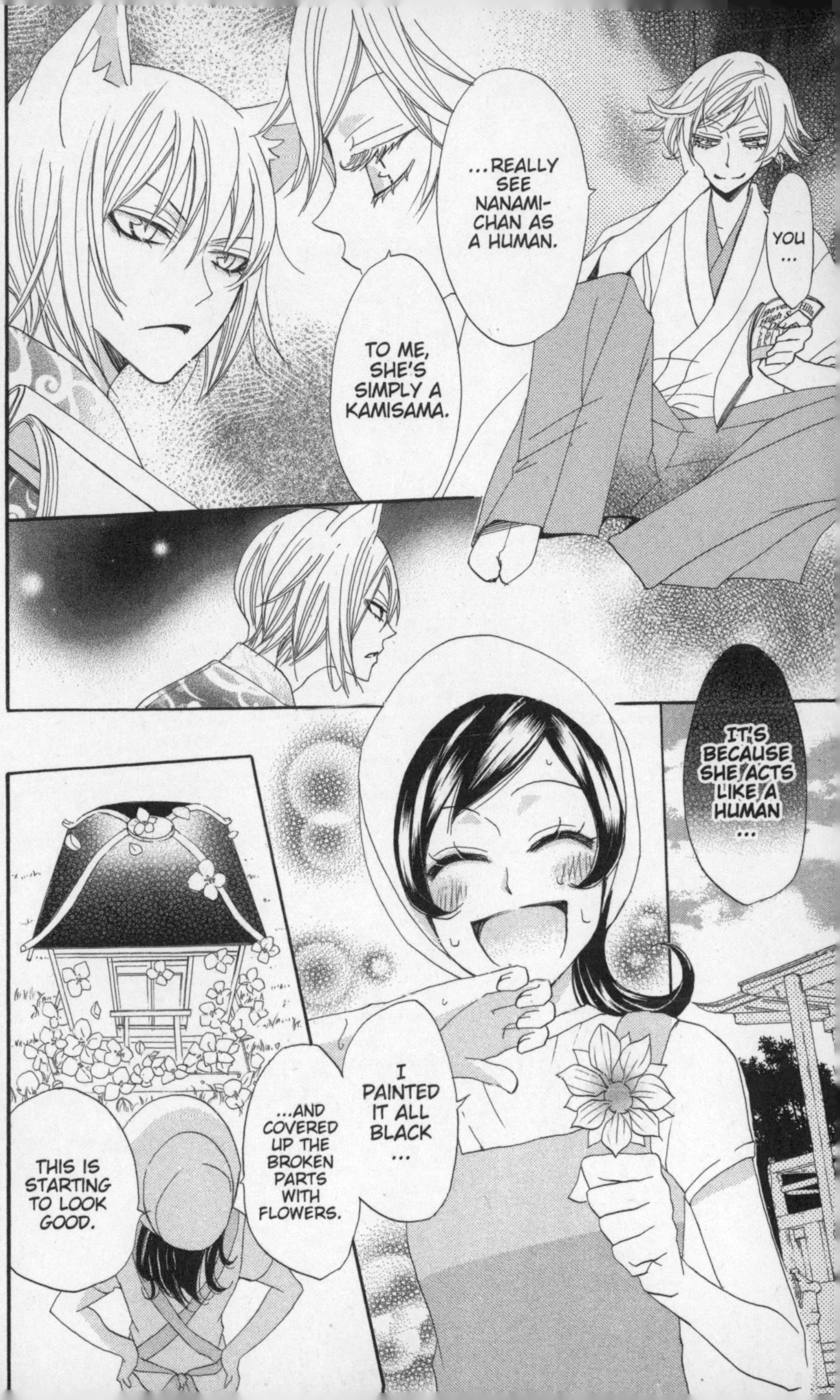
YOU ...
...REALLY SEE NANAMI-CHAN AS A HUMAN.
TO ME, SHE'S SIMPLY A KAMISAMA.
IT'S BECAUSE SHE ACTS LIKE A HUMAN ...
I PAINTED IT ALL BLACK ...
...AND COVERED UP THE BROKEN PARTS WITH FLOWERS.
THIS IS STARTING TO LOOK GOOD.

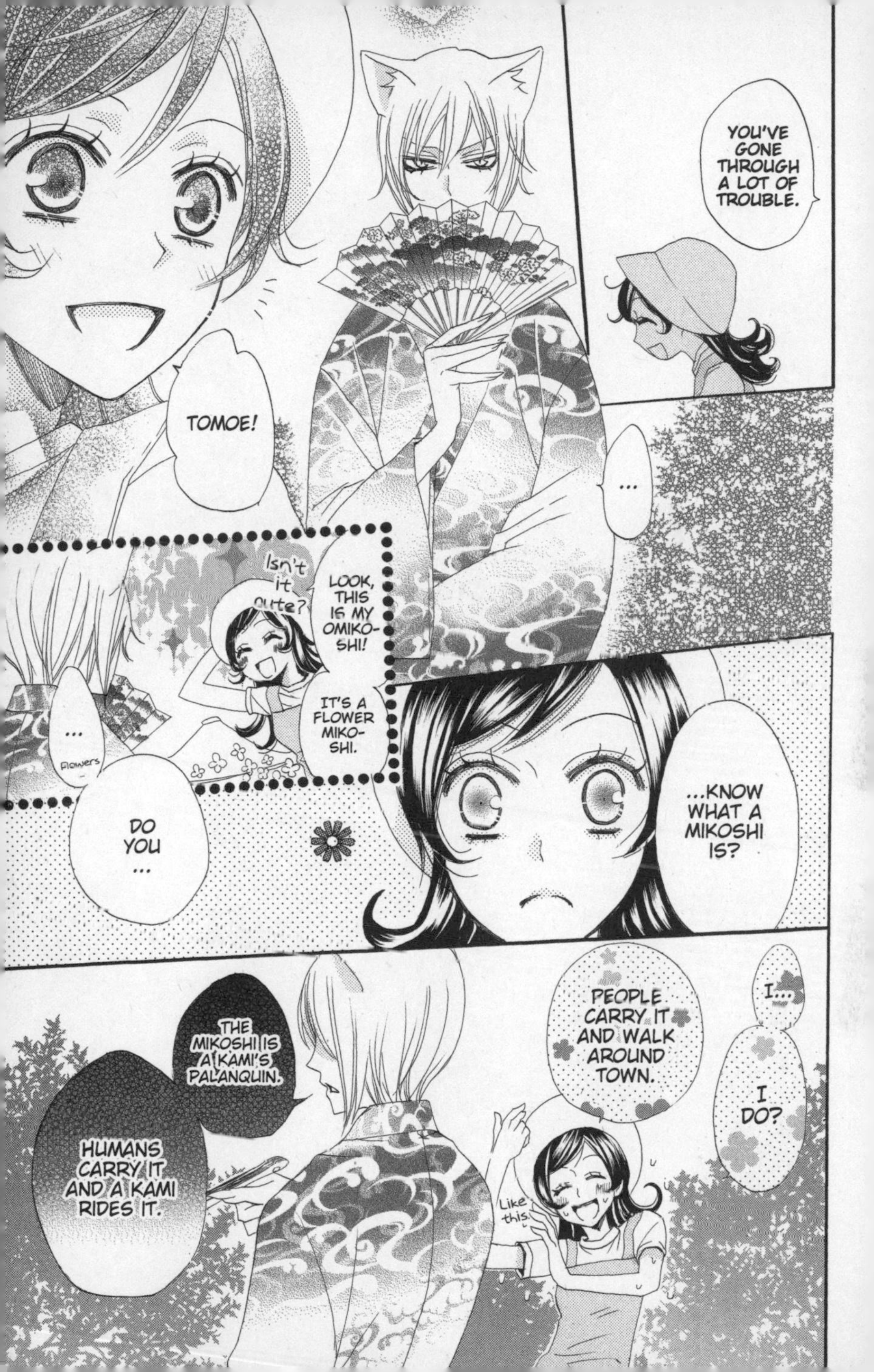
YOU'VE GONE THROUGH A LOT OF TROUBLE.
TOMOE!
...
LOOK, THIS IS MY OMIKOSHI!
Isn't it cute?
IT'S A FLOWER MIKOSHI.
...
Flowers
DO YOU ...
...KNOW WHAT A MIKOSHI IS?
I...
I DO?
PEOPLE CARRY IT AND WALK AROUND TOWN.
Like this.
THE MIKOSHI IS A KAMI'S PALANQUIN.
HUMANS CARRY IT AND A KAMI RIDES IT.

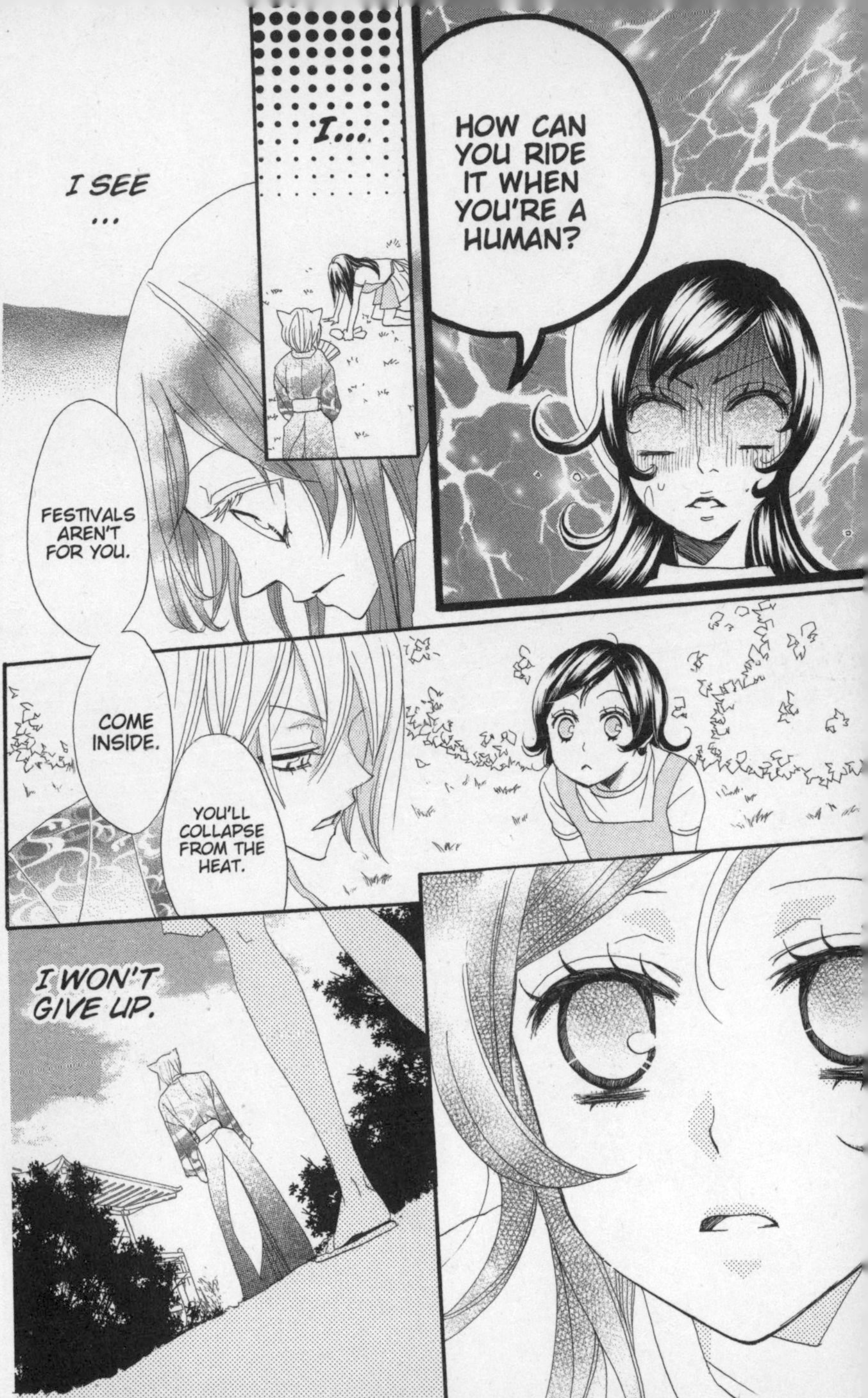
HOW CAN YOU RIDE IT WHEN YOU'RE A HUMAN?
I...
I SEE ...
FESTIVALS AREN'T FOR YOU.
COME INSIDE.
YOU'LL COLLAPSE FROM THE HEAT.
I WON'T GIVE UP.

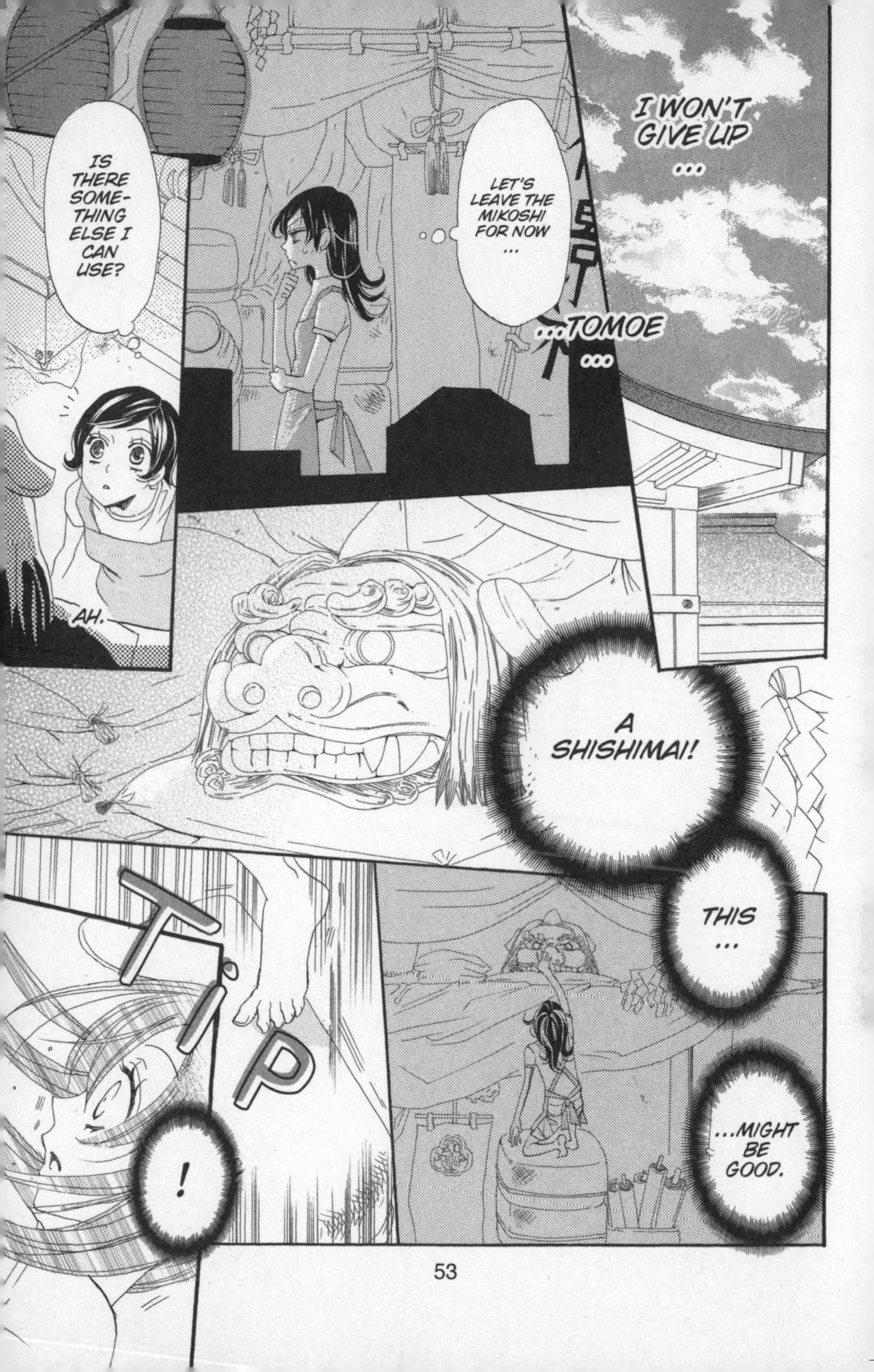
I WON'T GIVE UP ...
...TOMOE ...
LET'S LEAVE THE MIKOSHI FOR NOW ...
IS THERE SOME-THING ELSE I CAN USE?
AH.
A SHISHIMAI!
THIS ...
...MIGHT BE GOOD.
TIP
!

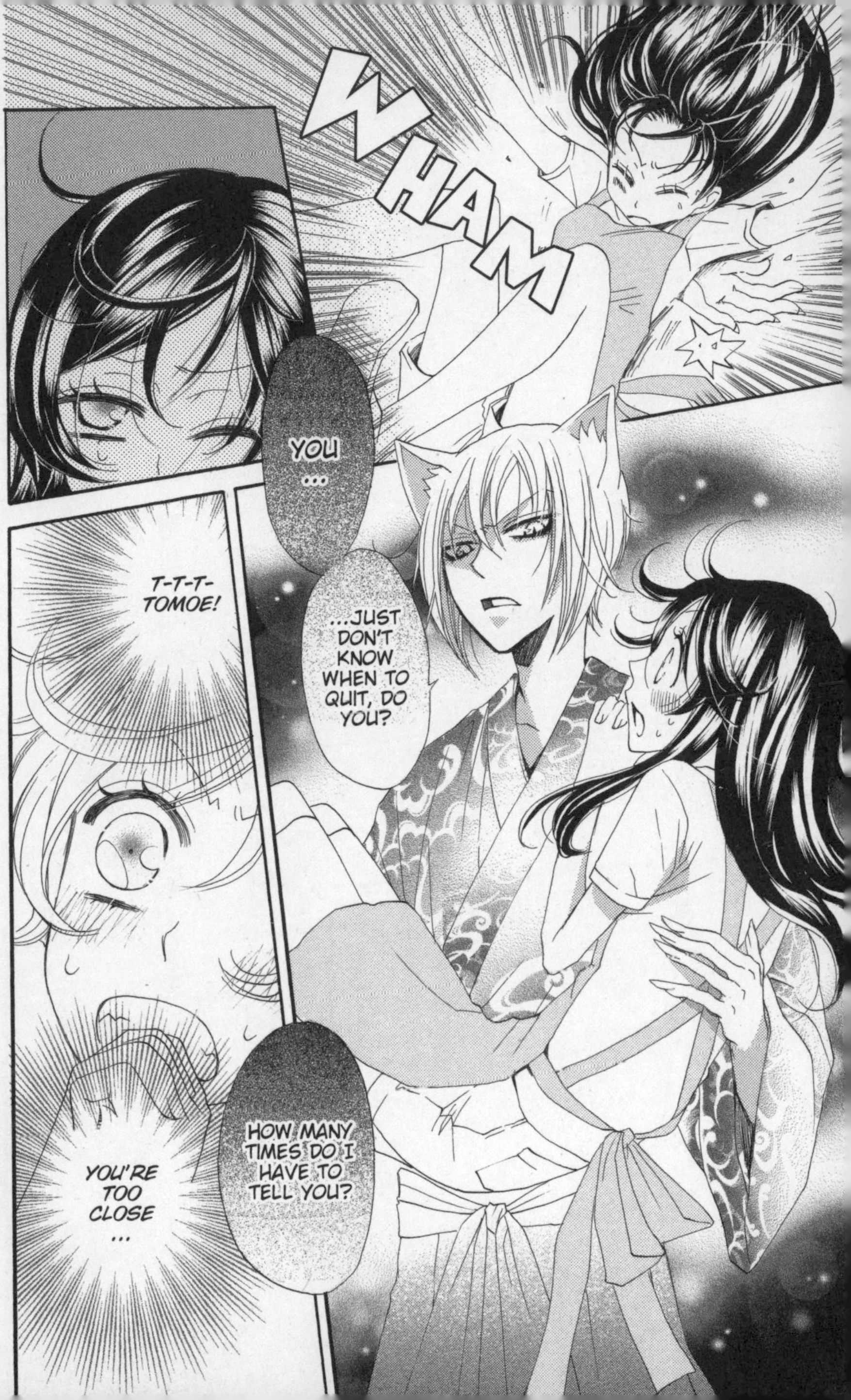
WHAM
YOU ...
...JUST DON'T KNOW WHEN TO QUIT, DO YOU?
HOW MANY TIMES DO I HAVE TO TELL YOU?
T-T-T-TOMOE!
YOU'RE TOO CLOSE ...

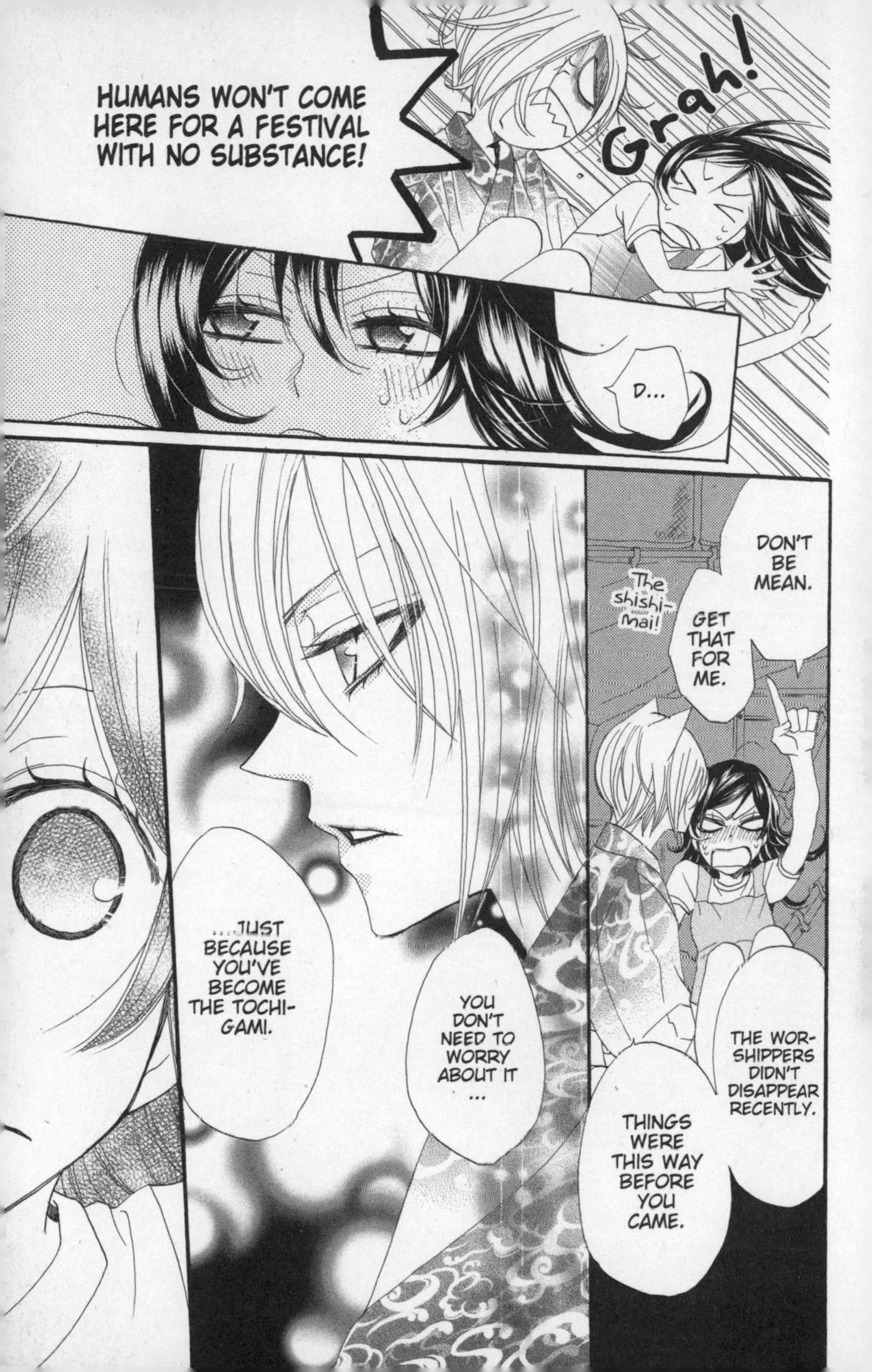
Grah!
HUMANS WON'T COME HERE FOR A FESTIVAL WITH NO SUBSTANCE!
D...
DON'T BE MEAN.
GET THAT FOR ME.
The shishi-mai!
THE WORSHIPPERS DIDN'T DISAPPEAR RECENTLY.
THINGS WERE THIS WAY BEFORE YOU CAME.
YOU DON'T NEED TO WORRY ABOUT IT ...
...JUST BECAUSE YOU'VE BECOME THE TOCHIGAMI.

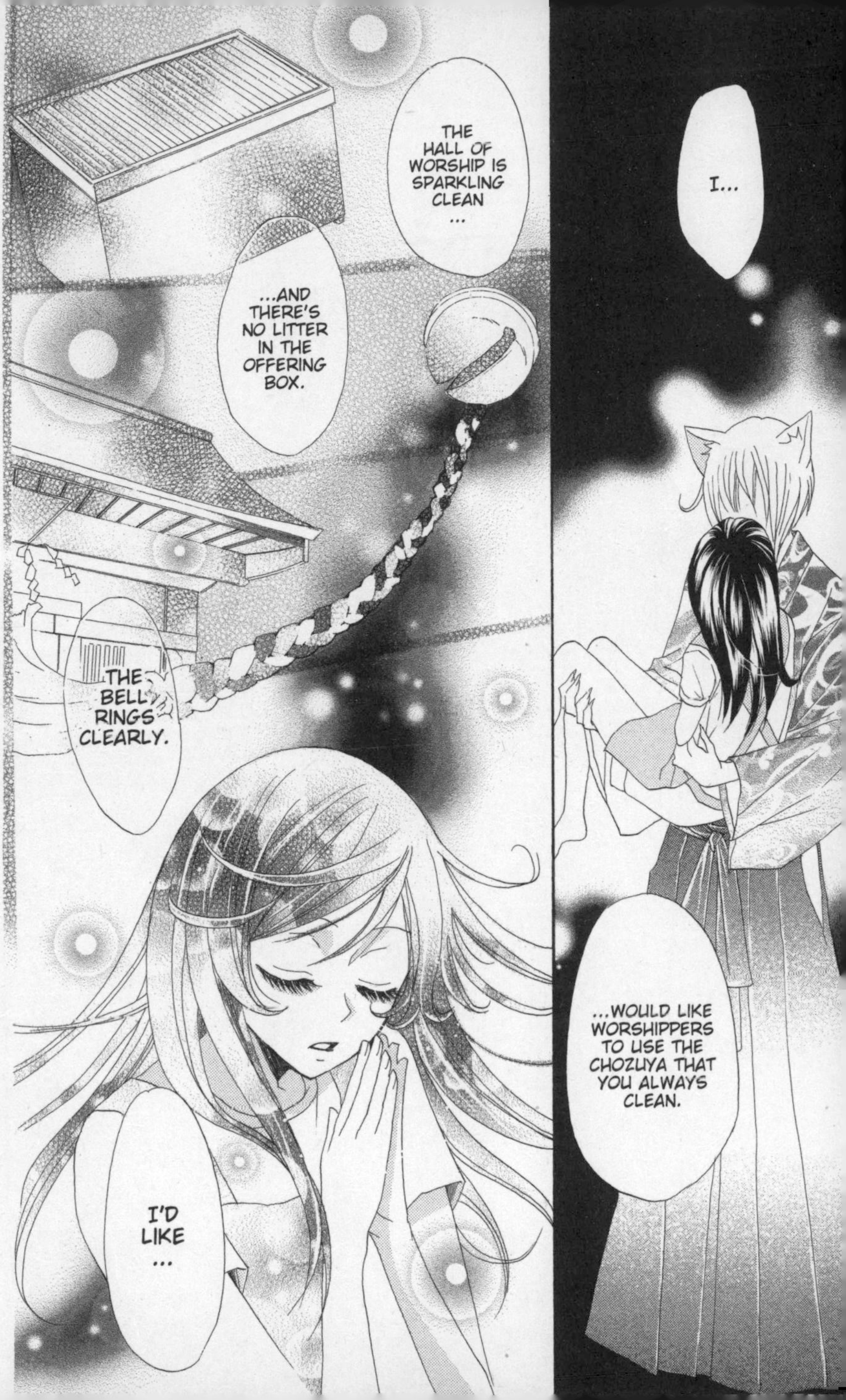
I...
...WOULD LIKE WORSHIPPERS TO USE THE CHOZUYA THAT YOU ALWAYS CLEAN.
THE HALL OF WORSHIP IS SPARKLING CLEAN ...
...AND THERE'S NO LITTER IN THE OFFERING BOX.
THE BELL RINGS CLEARLY.
I'D LIKE ...

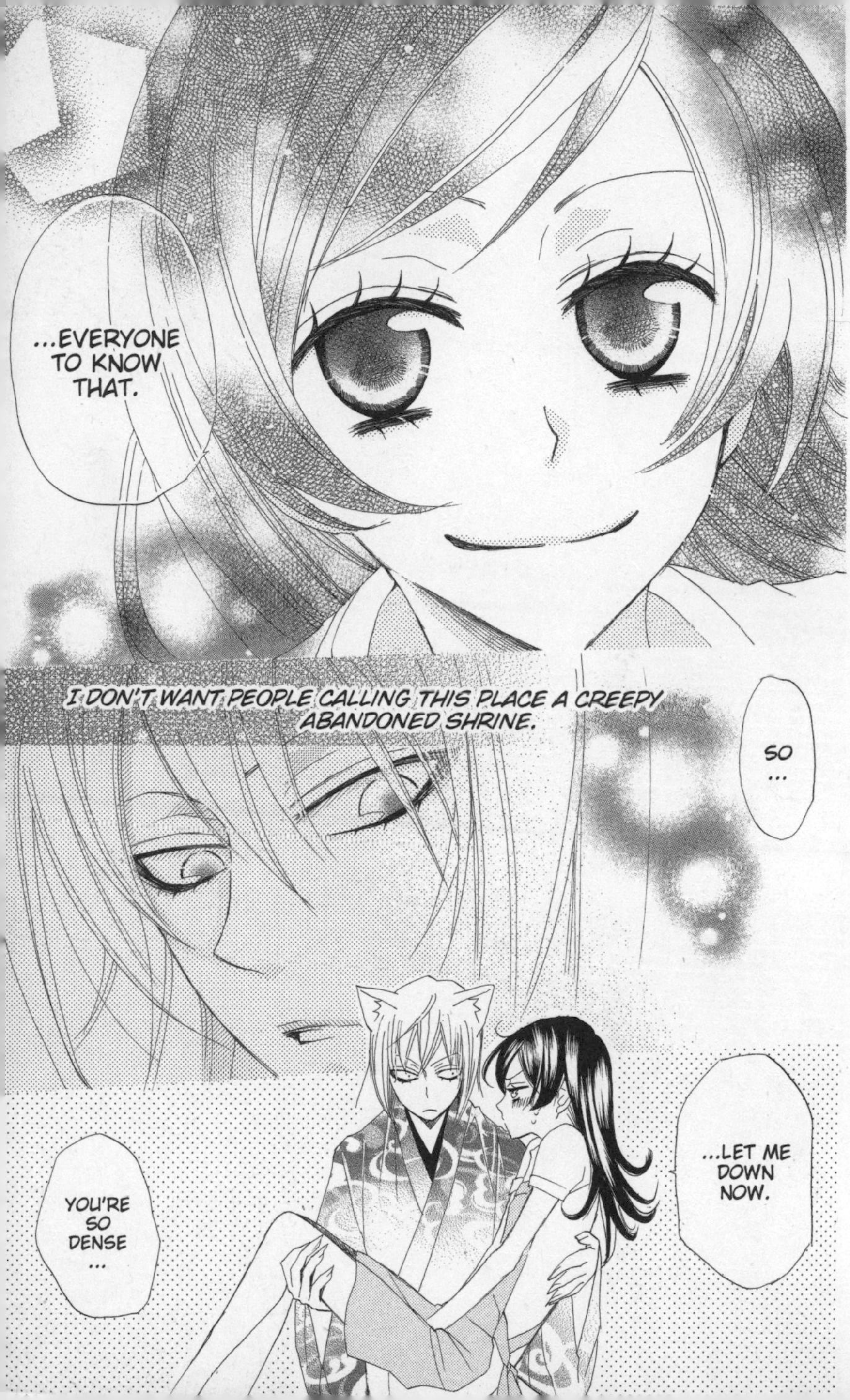
...EVERYONE TO KNOW THAT.
I DON'T WANT PEOPLE CALLING THIS PLACE A CREEPY ABANDONED SHRINE.
SO ...
...LET ME DOWN NOW.
YOU'RE SO DENSE ...

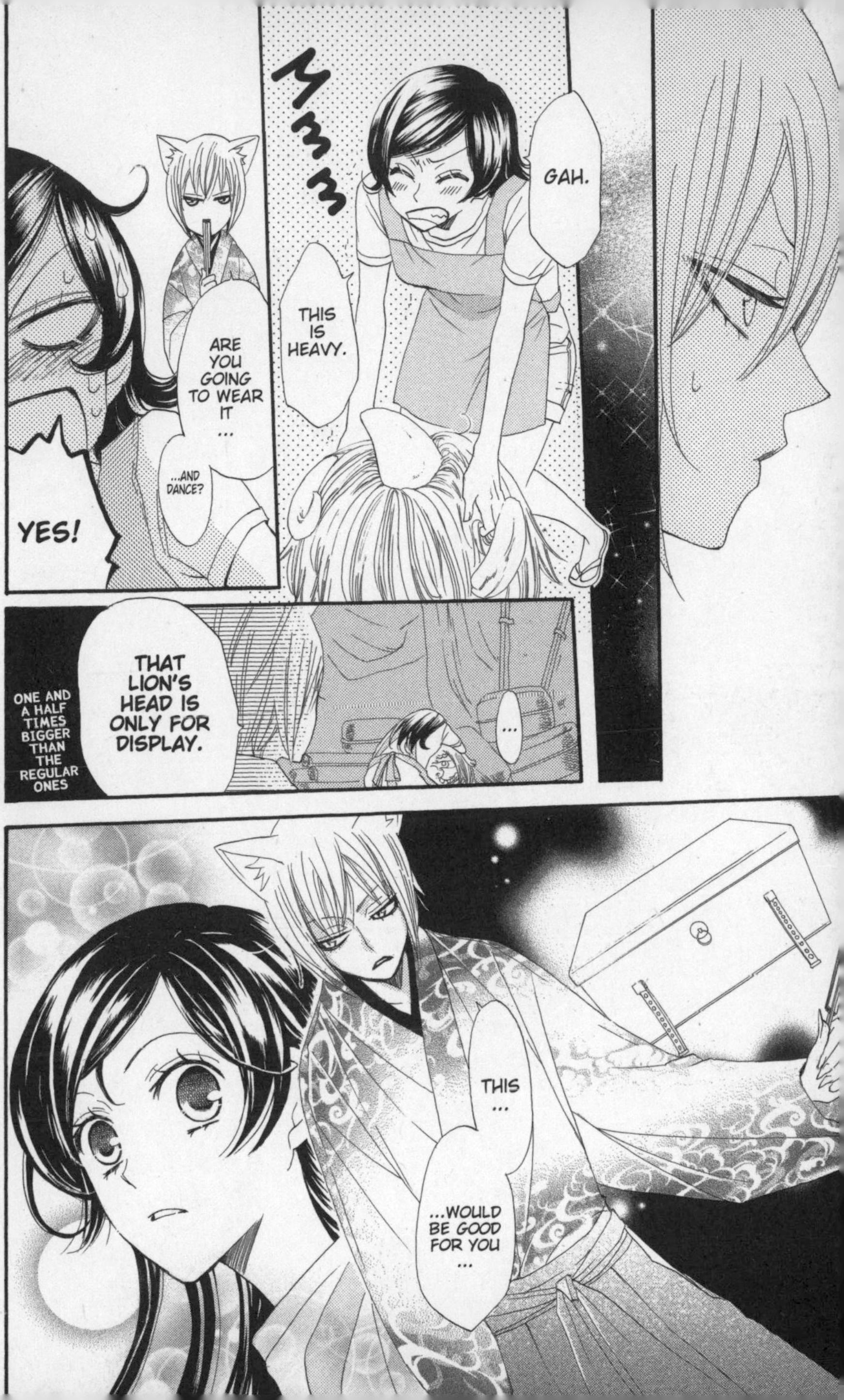
GAH.
MMM
THIS IS HEAVY.
ARE YOU GOING TO WEAR IT ...
...AND DANCE?
YES!
...
THAT LION'S HEAD IS ONLY FOR DISPLAY.
ONE AND A HALF TIMES BIGGER THAN THE REGULAR ONES
THIS ...
...WOULD BE GOOD FOR YOU ...

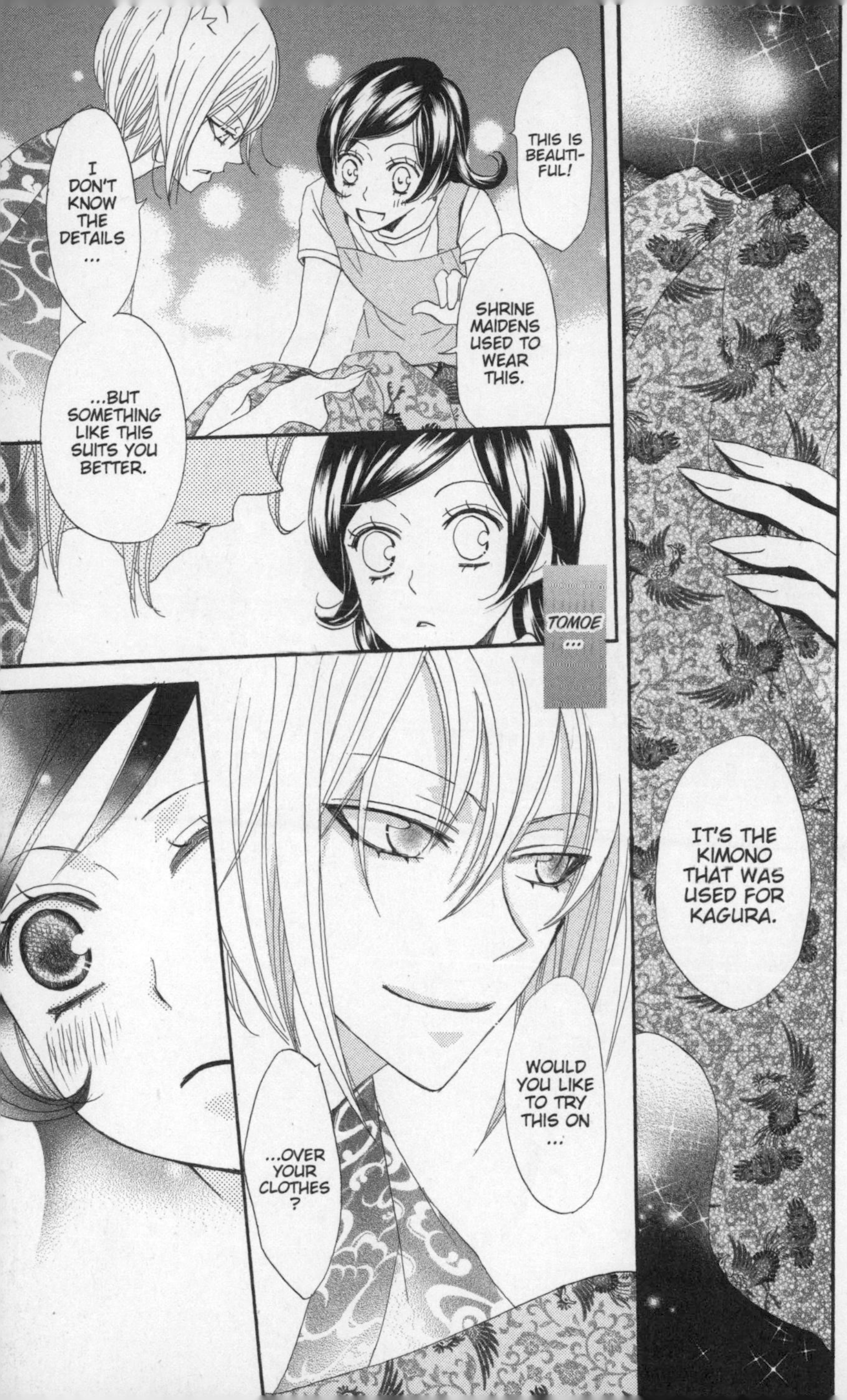
IT'S THE KIMONO THAT WAS USED FOR KAGURA.
THIS IS BEAUTIFUL!
SHRINE MAIDENS USED TO WEAR THIS.
I DON'T KNOW THE DETAILS ...
...BUT SOMETHING LIKE THIS SUITS YOU BETTER.
TOMOE ...
WOULD YOU LIKE TO TRY THIS ON ...
...OVER YOUR CLOTHES ?

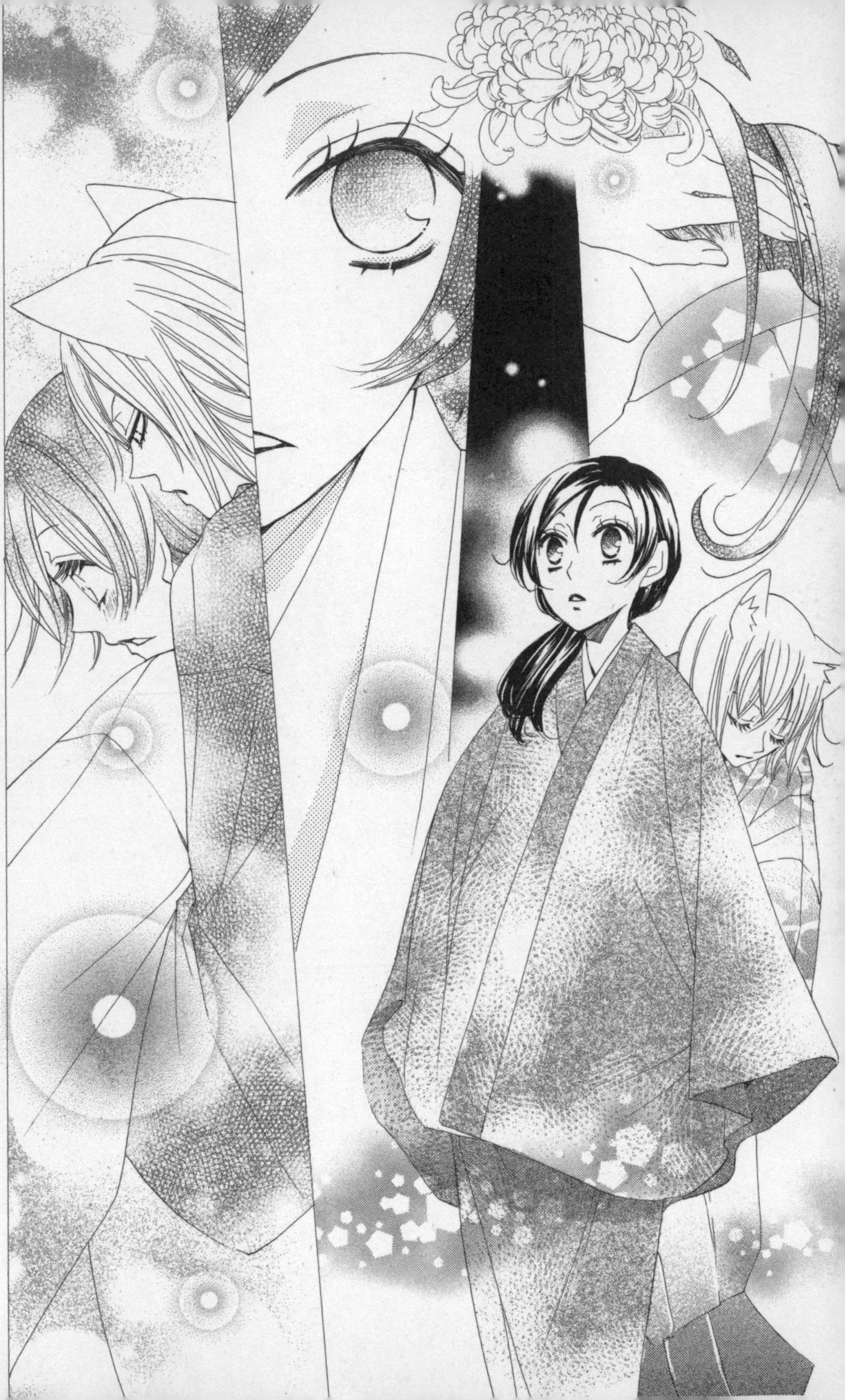

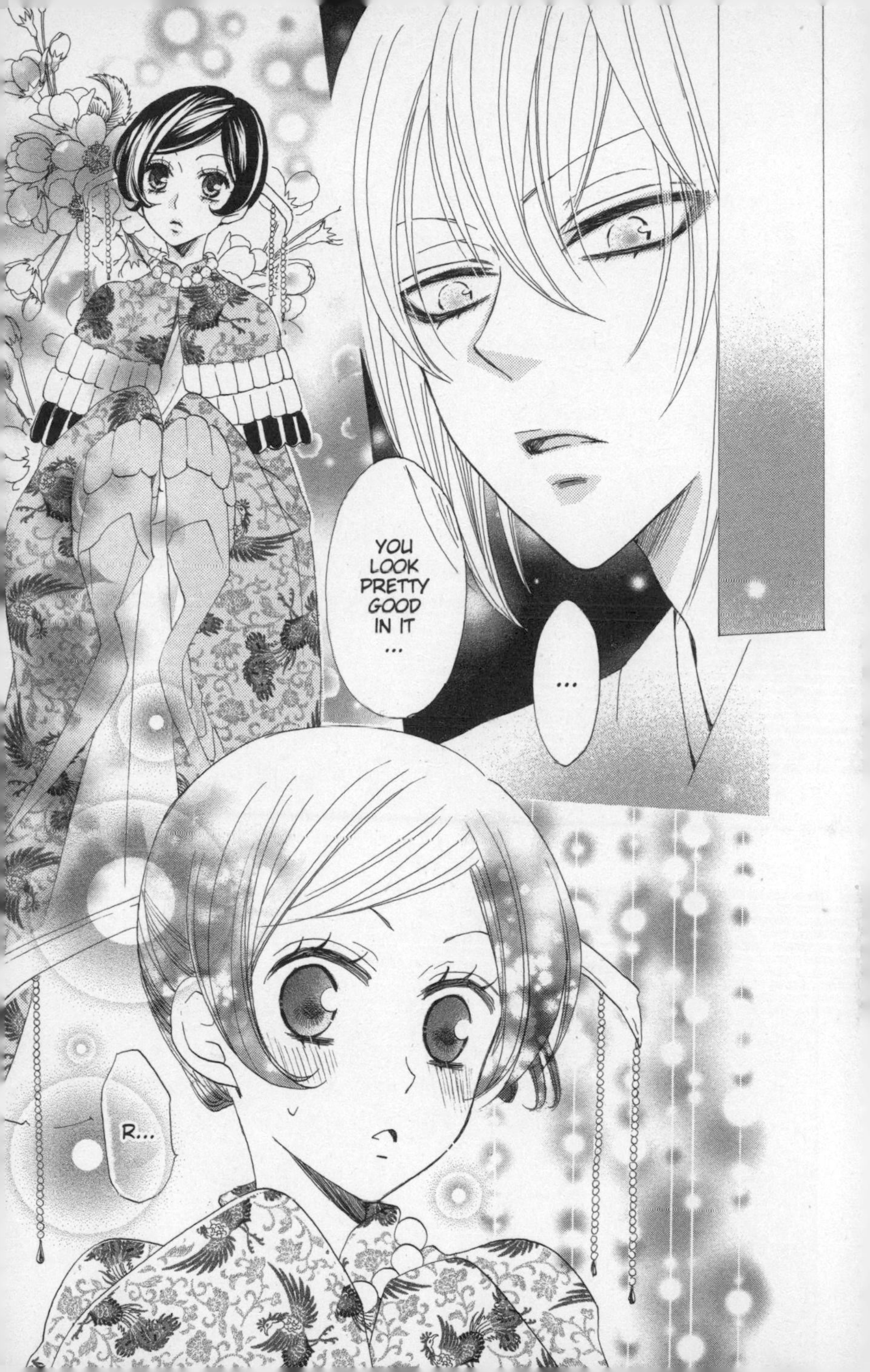
...
YOU LOOK PRETTY GOOD IN IT ...
R...

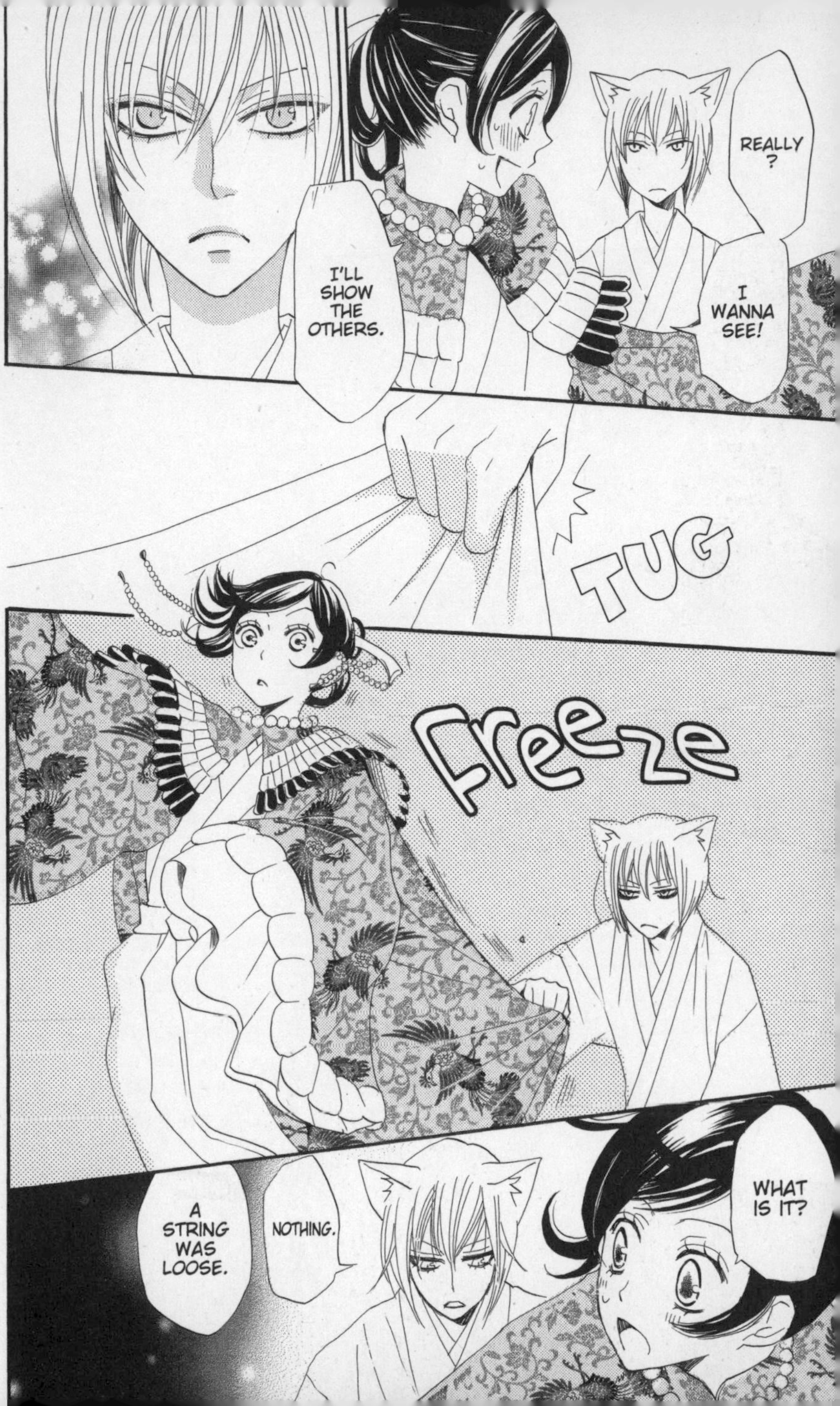
REALLY?
I WANNA SEE!
I'LL SHOW THE OTHERS.
TUG
Freeze
WHAT IS IT?
NOTHING.
A STRING WAS LOOSE.

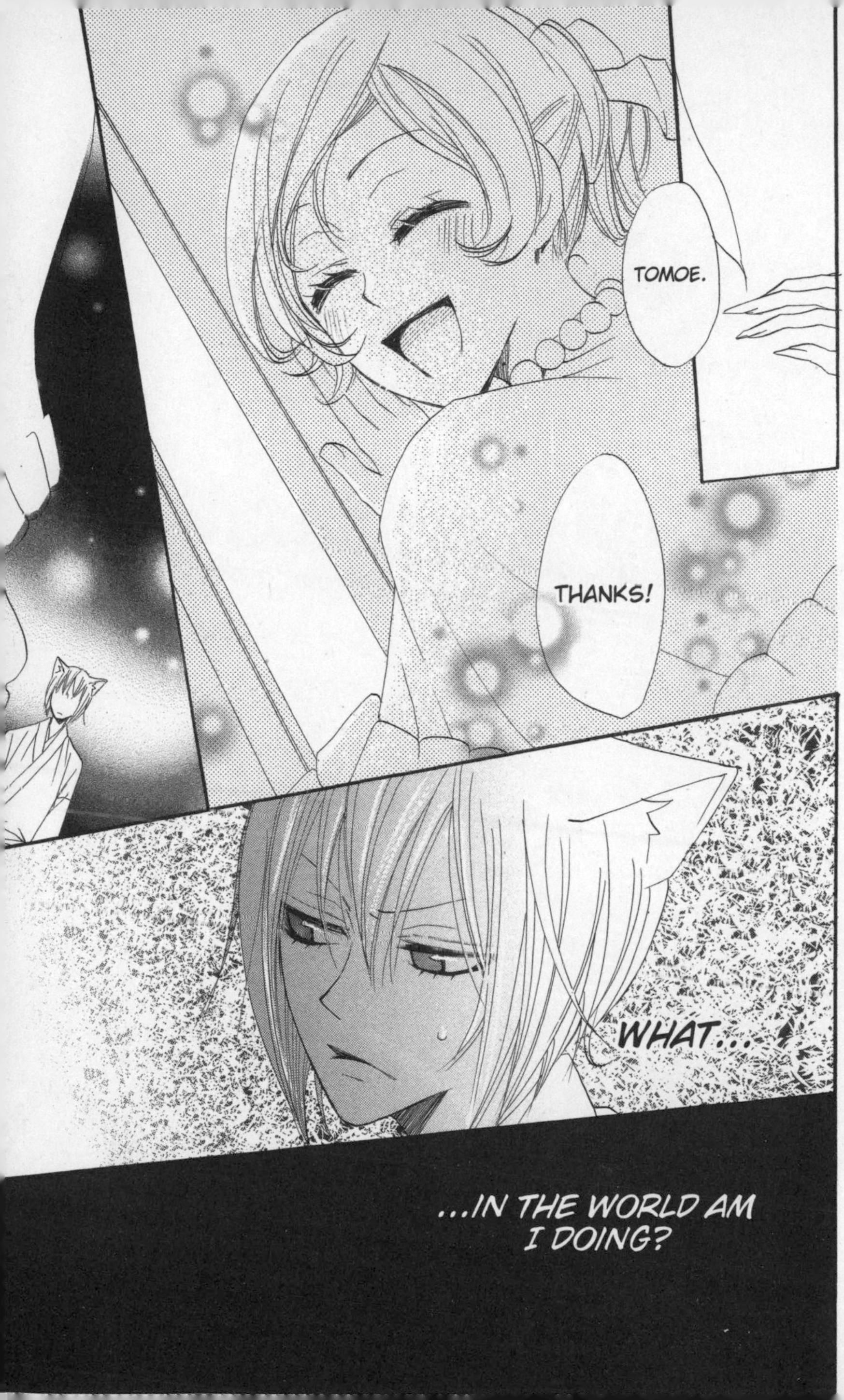
TOMOE.
THANKS!
WHAT...
...IN THE WORLD AM I DOING?

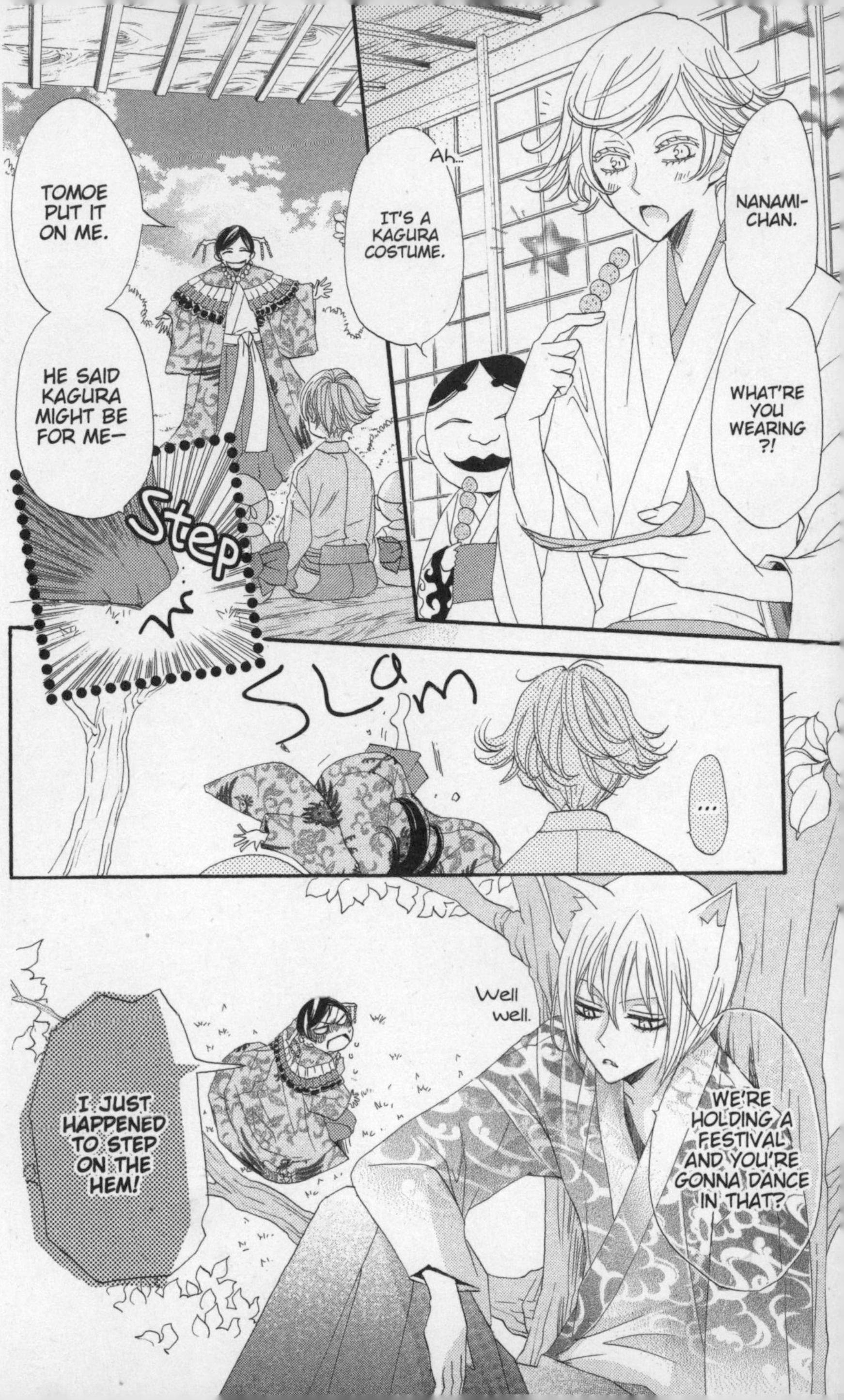
NANAMI-CHAN.
WHAT'RE YOU WEARING ?!
Ah...
IT'S A KAGURA COSTUME.
TOMOE PUT IT ON ME.
HE SAID KAGURA MIGHT BE FOR ME—
Step
SLAM
...
Well well.
WE'RE HOLDING A FESTIVAL AND YOU'RE GONNA DANCE IN THAT?
I JUST HAPPENED TO STEP ON THE HEM!

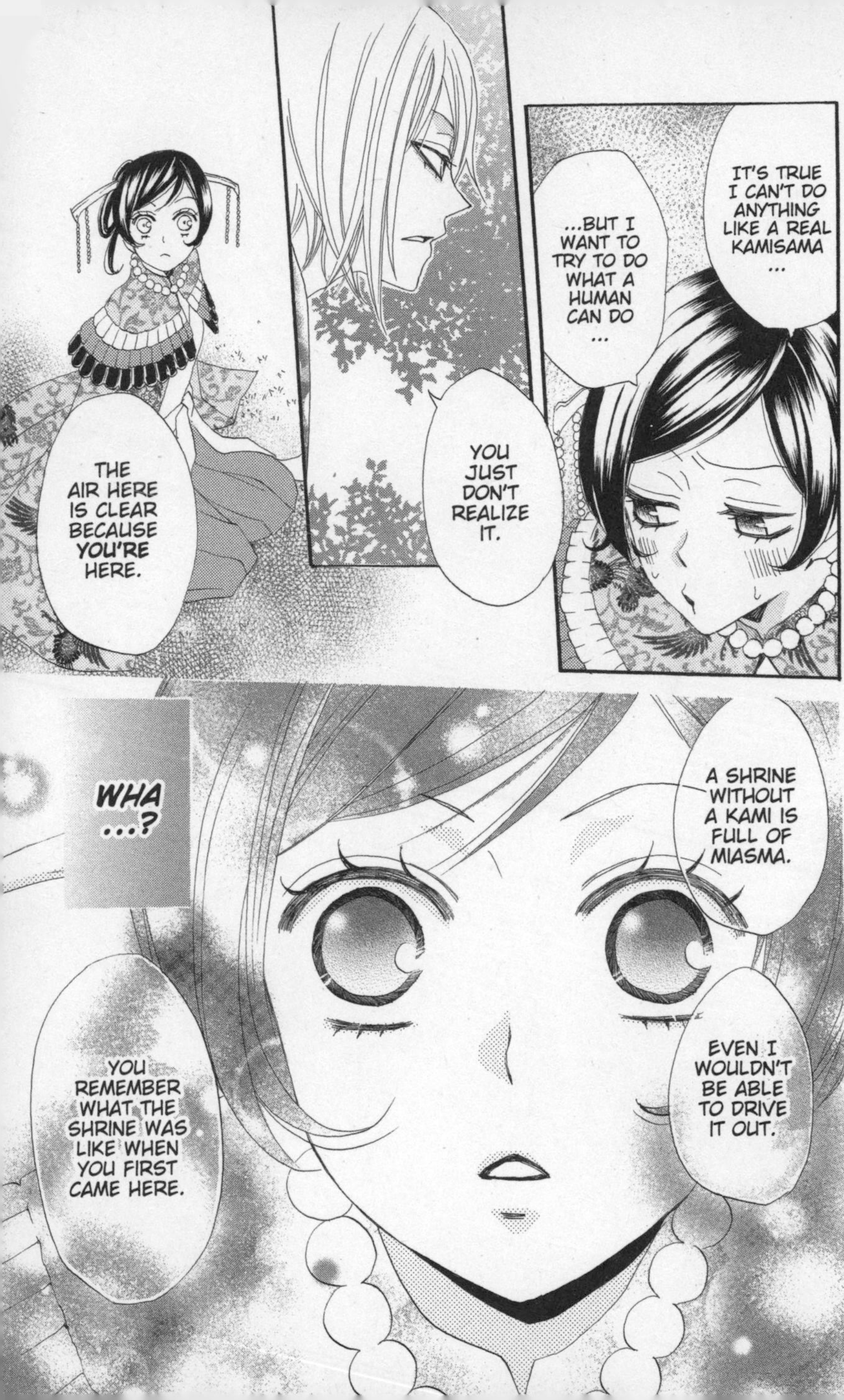
IT'S TRUE I CAN'T DO ANYTHING LIKE A REAL KAMISAMA ...
...BUT I WANT TO TRY TO DO WHAT A HUMAN CAN DO ...
YOU JUST DON'T REALIZE IT.
THE AIR HERE IS CLEAR BECAUSE YOU'RE HERE.
A SHRINE WITHOUT A KAMI IS FULL OF MIASMA.
WHA ...?
EVEN I WOULDN'T BE ABLE TO DRIVE IT OUT.
YOU REMEMBER WHAT THE SHRINE WAS LIKE WHEN YOU FIRST CAME HERE.

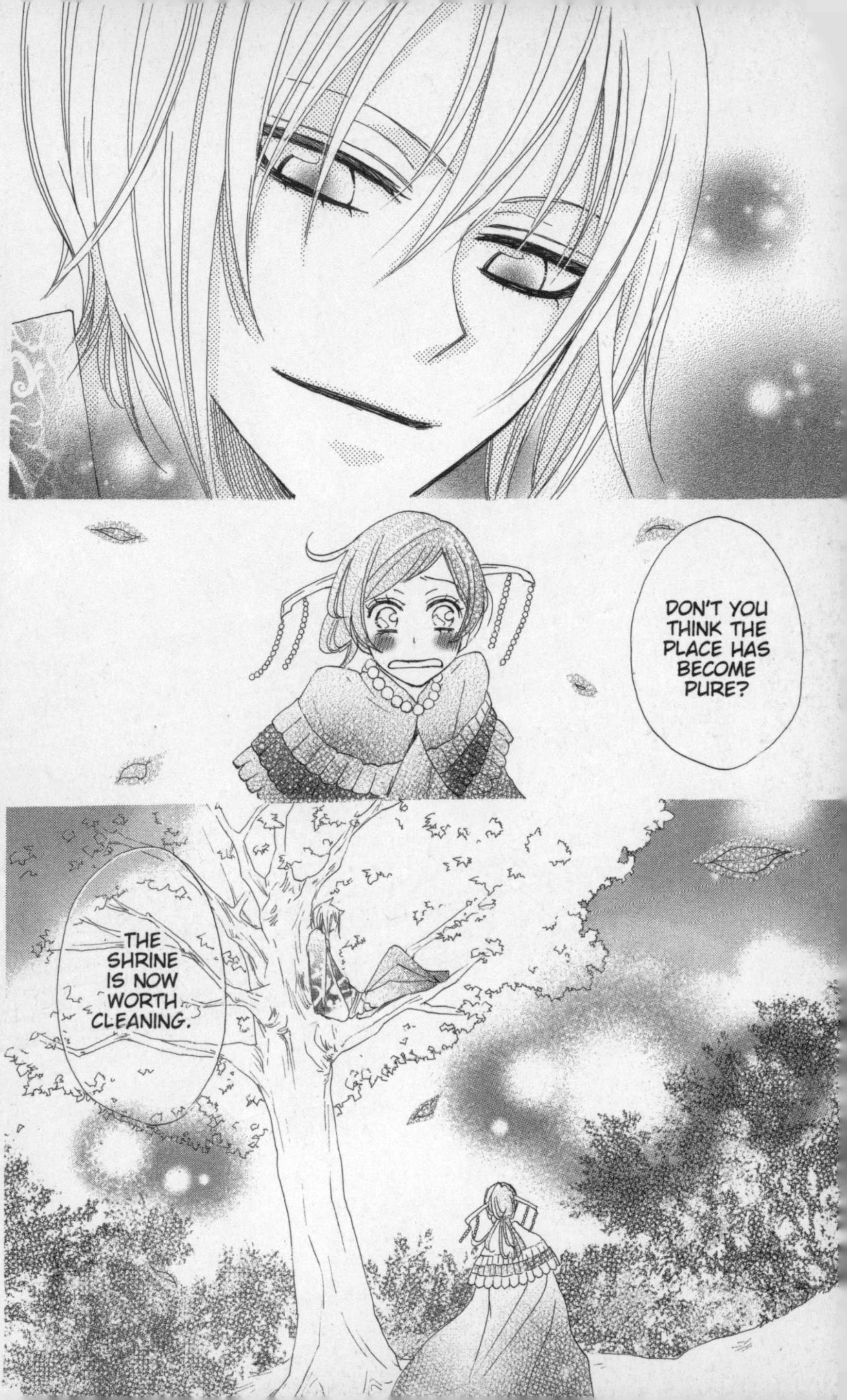
DON'T YOU THINK THE PLACE HAS BECOME PURE?
THE SHRINE IS NOW WORTH CLEANING.

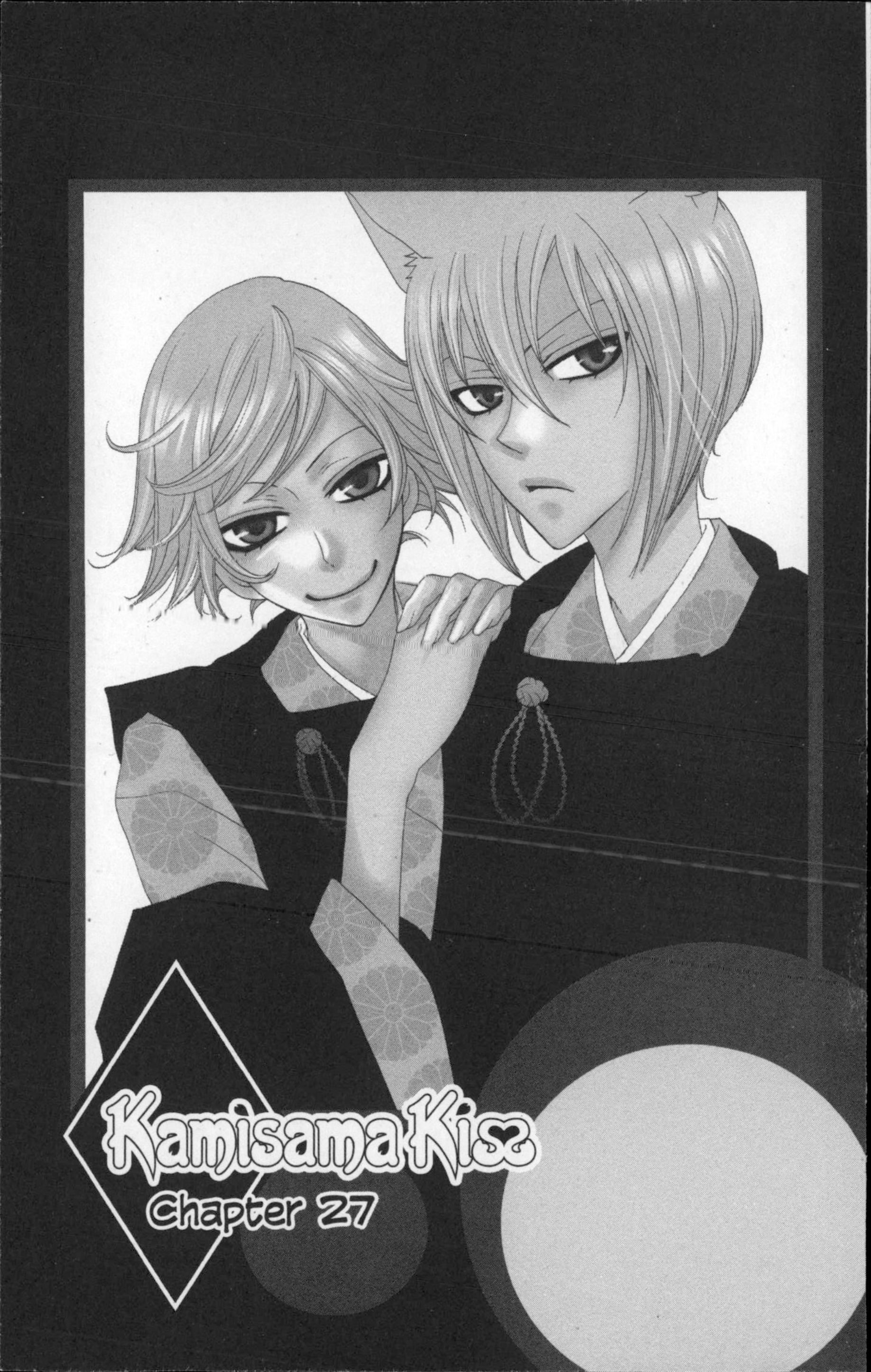
Kamisama Kiss
Chapter 27

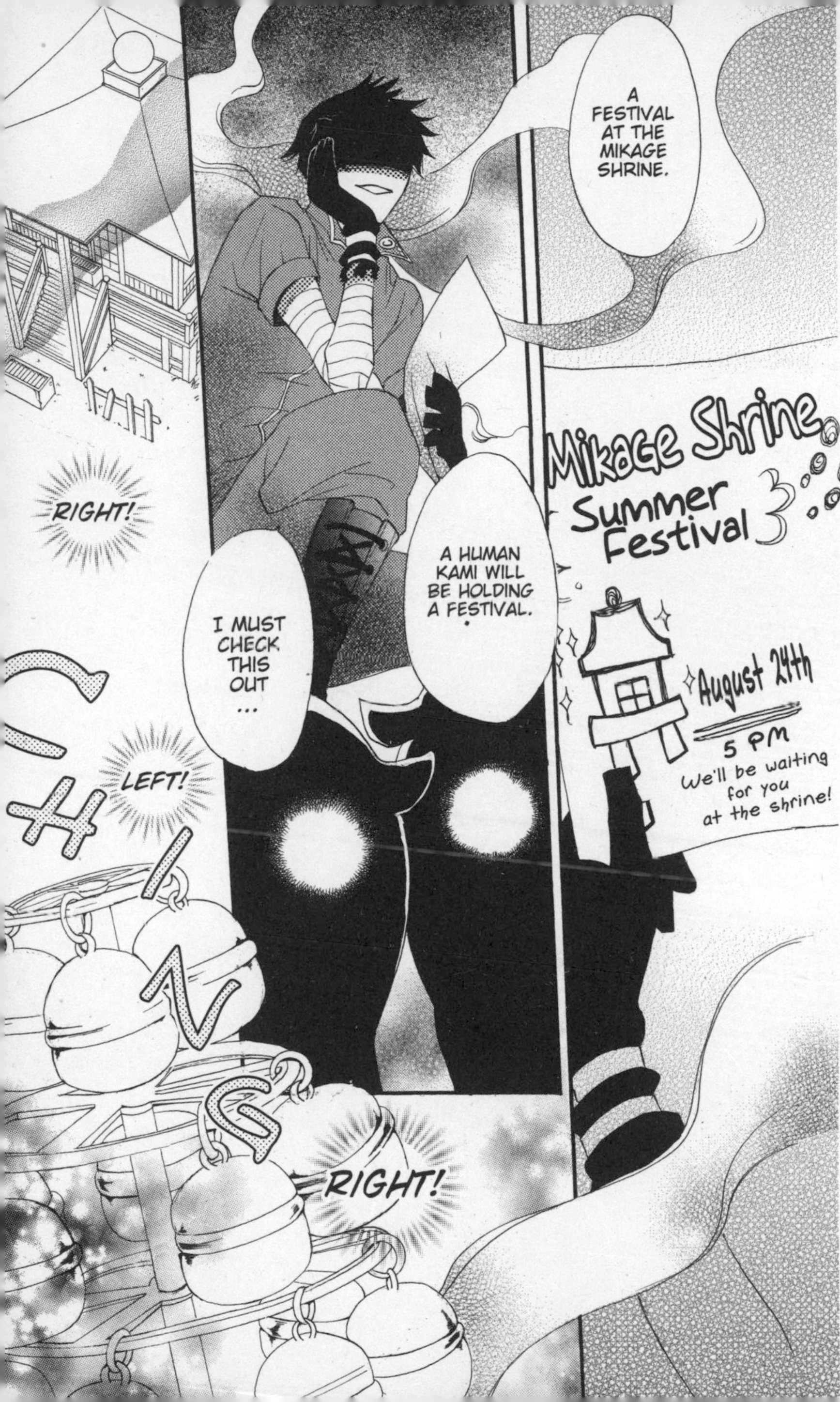
A FESTIVAL AT THE MIKAGE SHRINE.
Mikage Shrine
Summer Festival
August 24th
5 PM
We'll be waiting for you at the shrine!
A HUMAN KAMI WILL BE HOLDING A FESTIVAL.
I MUST CHECK THIS OUT...
RIGHT!
LEFT!
RIGHT!
CHING

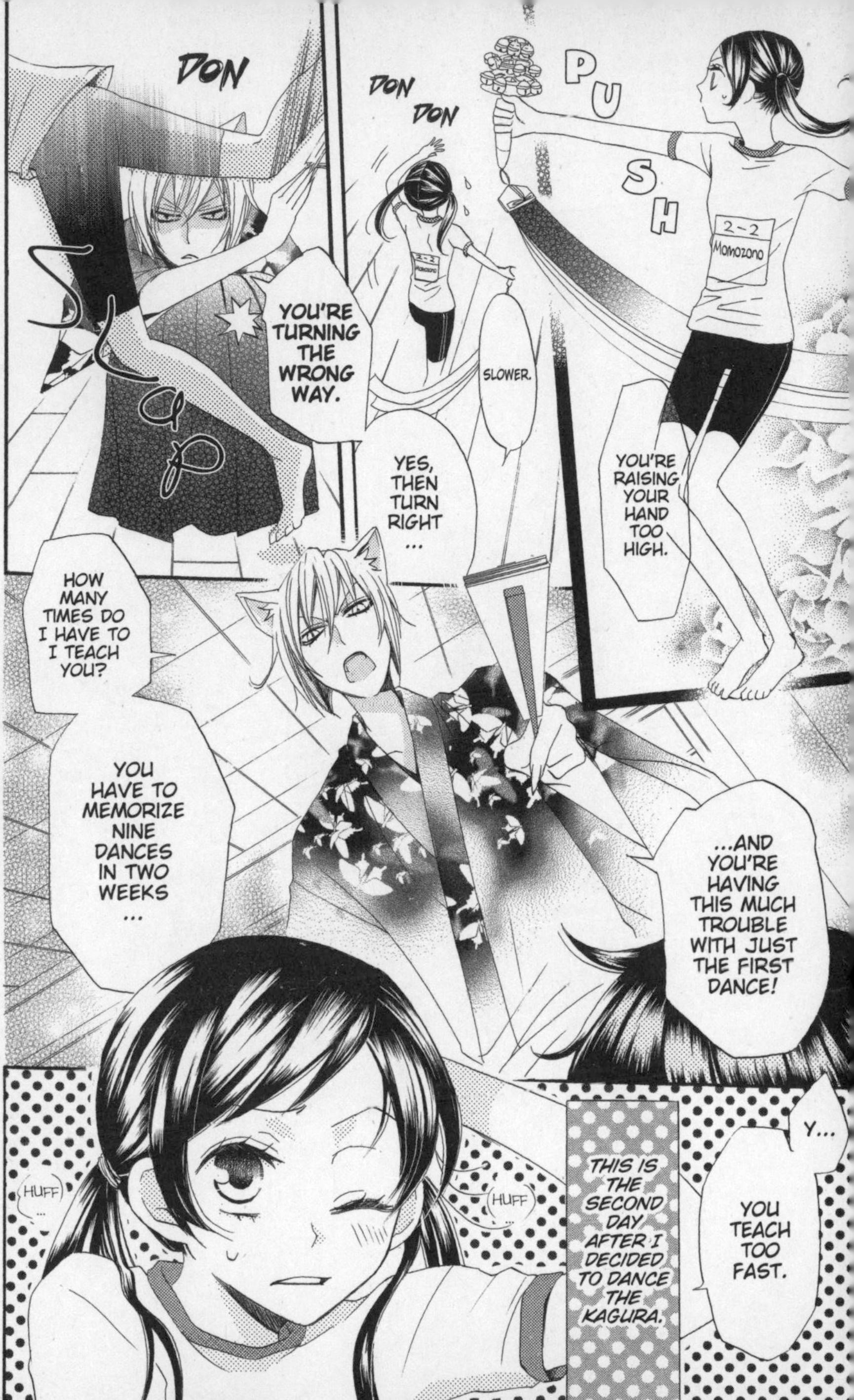
PUSH
2-2 Momozono
YOU'RE RAISING YOUR HAND TOO HIGH.
DON DON
SLOWER.
YES, THEN TURN RIGHT...
DON
SLAP
YOU'RE TURNING THE WRONG WAY.
HOW MANY TIMES DO I HAVE TO I TEACH YOU?
YOU HAVE TO MEMORIZE NINE DANCES IN TWO WEEKS...
...AND YOU'RE HAVING THIS MUCH TROUBLE WITH JUST THE FIRST DANCE!
Y...
YOU TEACH TOO FAST.
THIS IS THE SECOND DAY AFTER I DECIDED TO DANCE THE KAGURA.
(HUFF HUFF)...

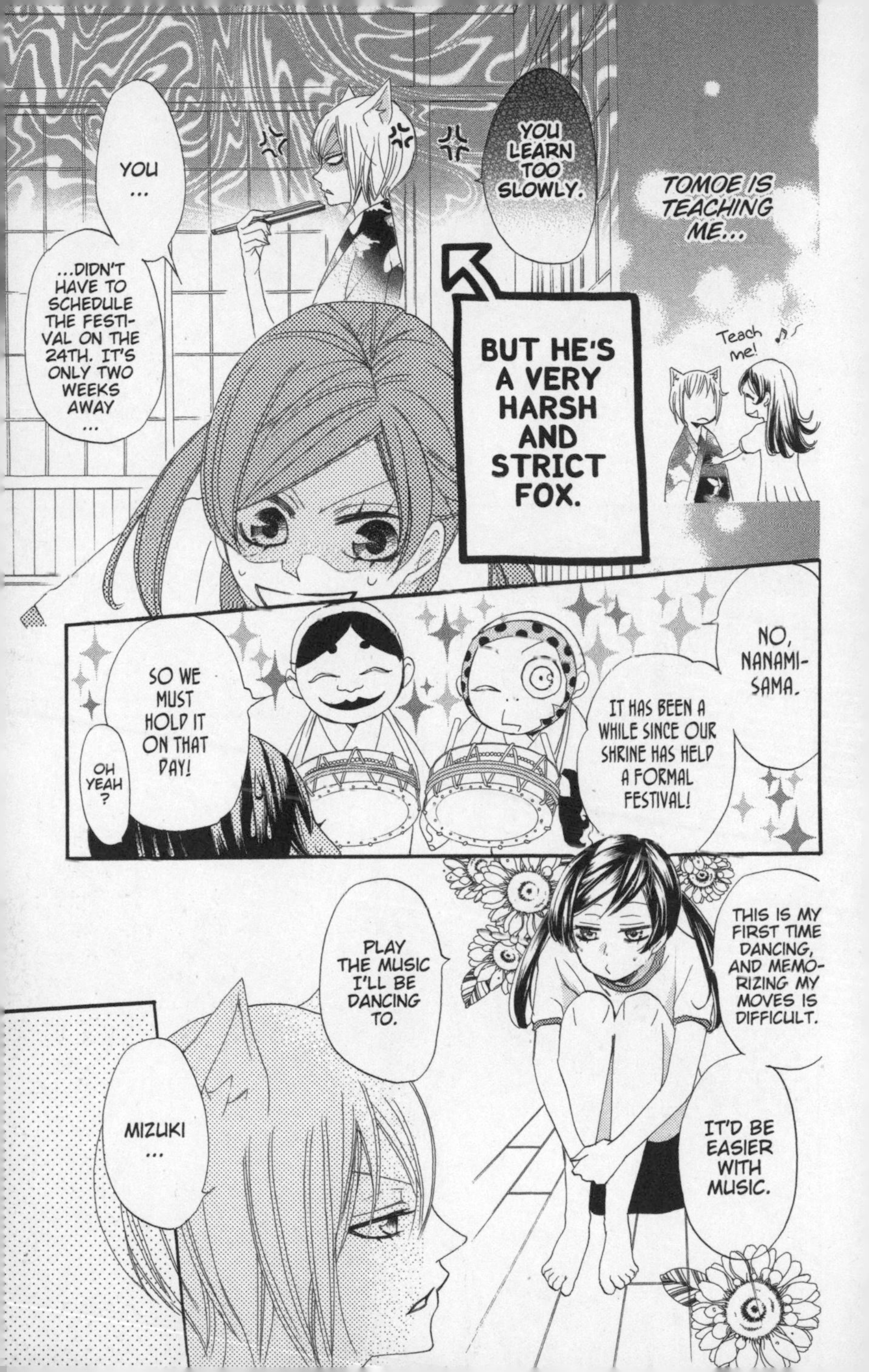
TOMOE IS TEACHING ME...
Teach me!
BUT HE'S A VERY HARSH AND STRICT FOX.
YOU LEARN TOO SLOWLY.
YOU ...
...DIDN'T HAVE TO SCHEDULE THE FESTIVAL ON THE 24TH. IT'S ONLY TWO WEEKS AWAY ...
NO, NANAMI-SAMA.
IT HAS BEEN A WHILE SINCE OUR SHRINE HAS HELD A FORMAL FESTIVAL!
SO WE MUST HOLD IT ON THAT DAY!
OH YEAH?
THIS IS MY FIRST TIME DANCING, AND MEMORIZING MY MOVES IS DIFFICULT.
IT'D BE EASIER WITH MUSIC.
PLAY THE MUSIC I'LL BE DANCING TO.
MIZUKI ...

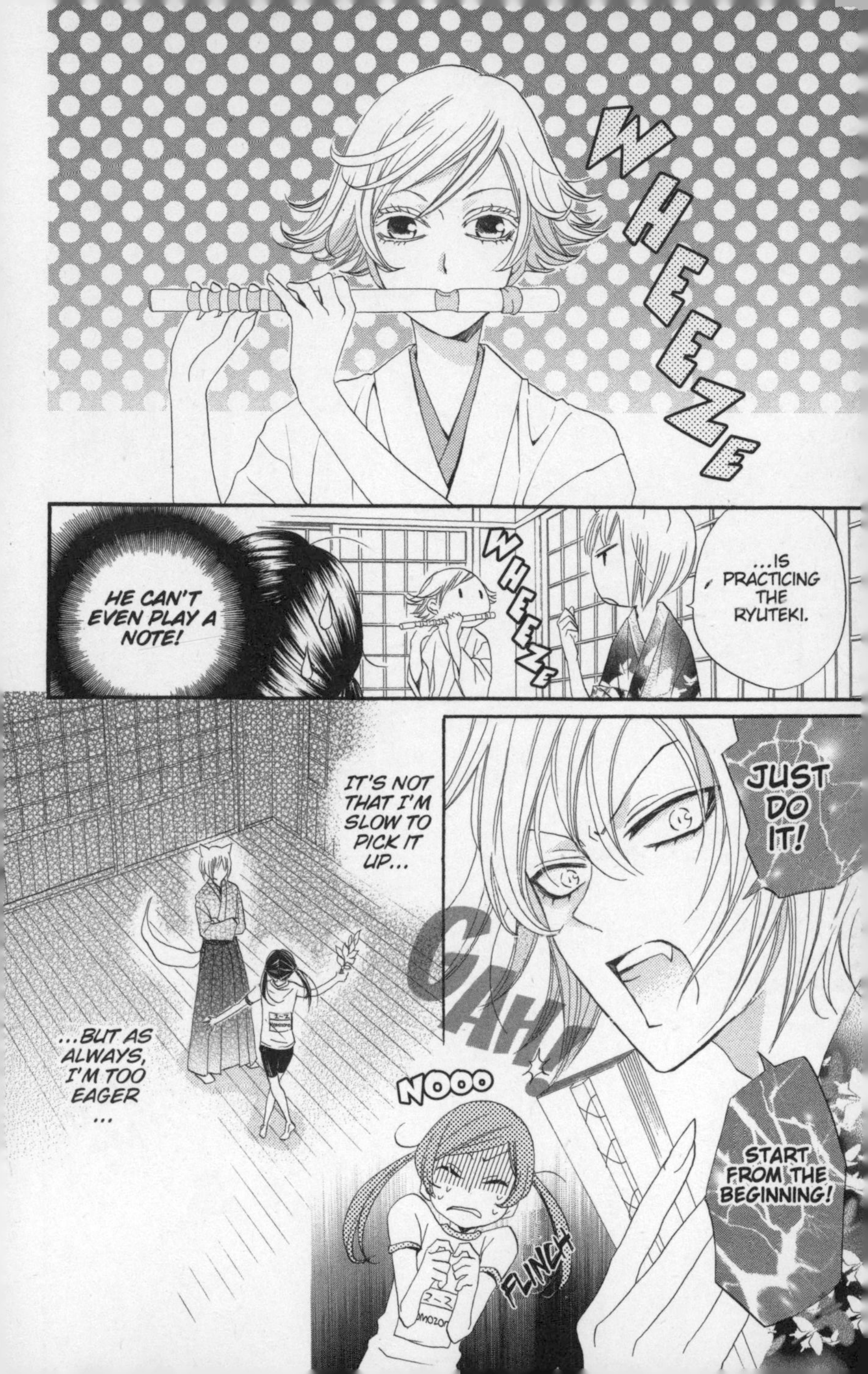
WHEEZE
...IS PRACTICING THE RYUTEKI.
WHEEZE
HE CAN'T EVEN PLAY A NOTE!
JUST DO IT!
GAH!
START FROM THE BEGINNING!
NOOO
FLINCH
IT'S NOT THAT I'M SLOW TO PICK IT UP...
...BUT AS ALWAYS, I'M TOO EAGER...

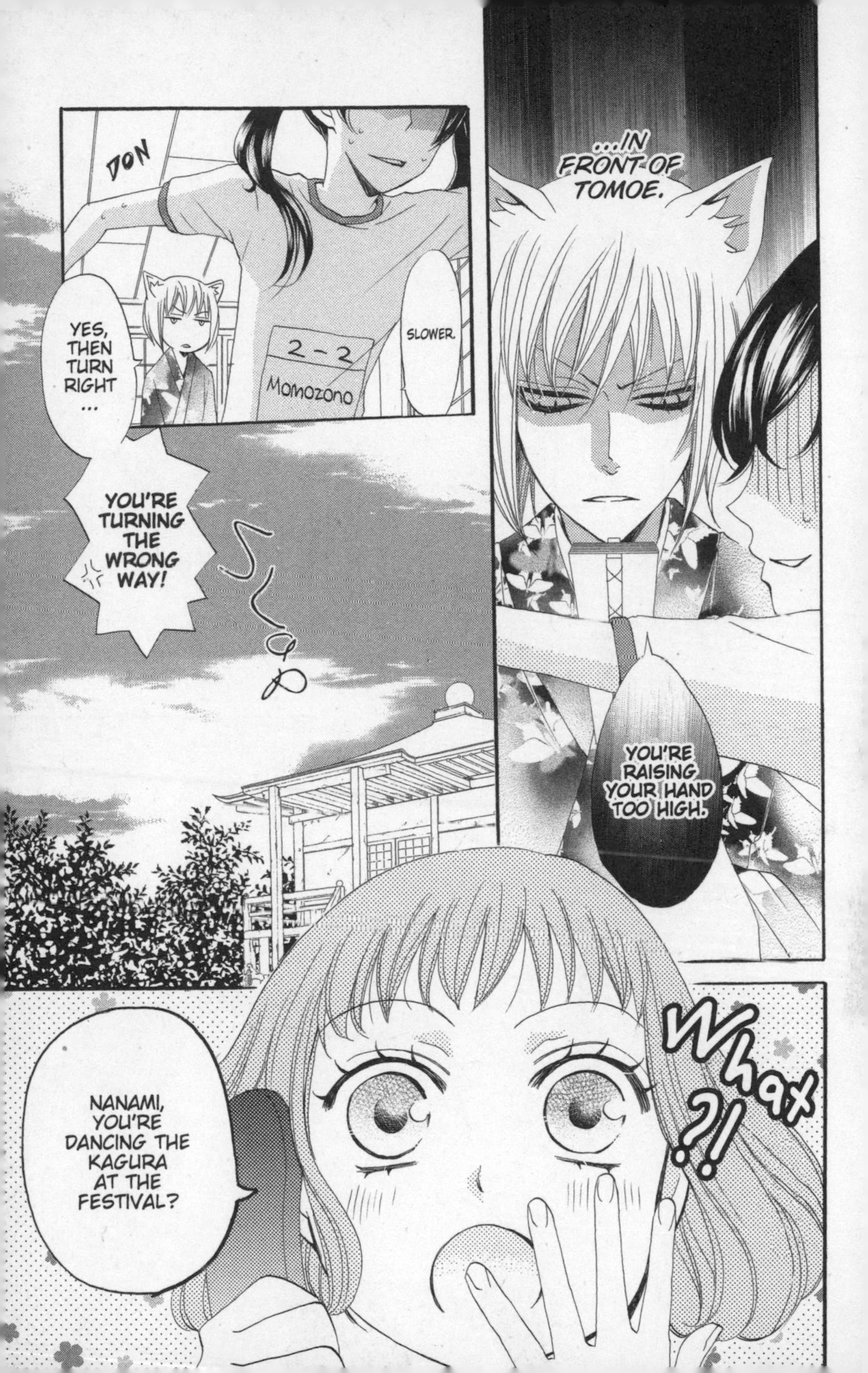
...IN FRONT OF TOMOE.
YOU'RE RAISING YOUR HAND TOO HIGH.
DON
SLOWER.
2-2
Momozono
YES, THEN TURN RIGHT...
YOU'RE TURNING THE WRONG WAY!
What?!
NANAMI, YOU'RE DANCING THE KAGURA AT THE FESTIVAL?

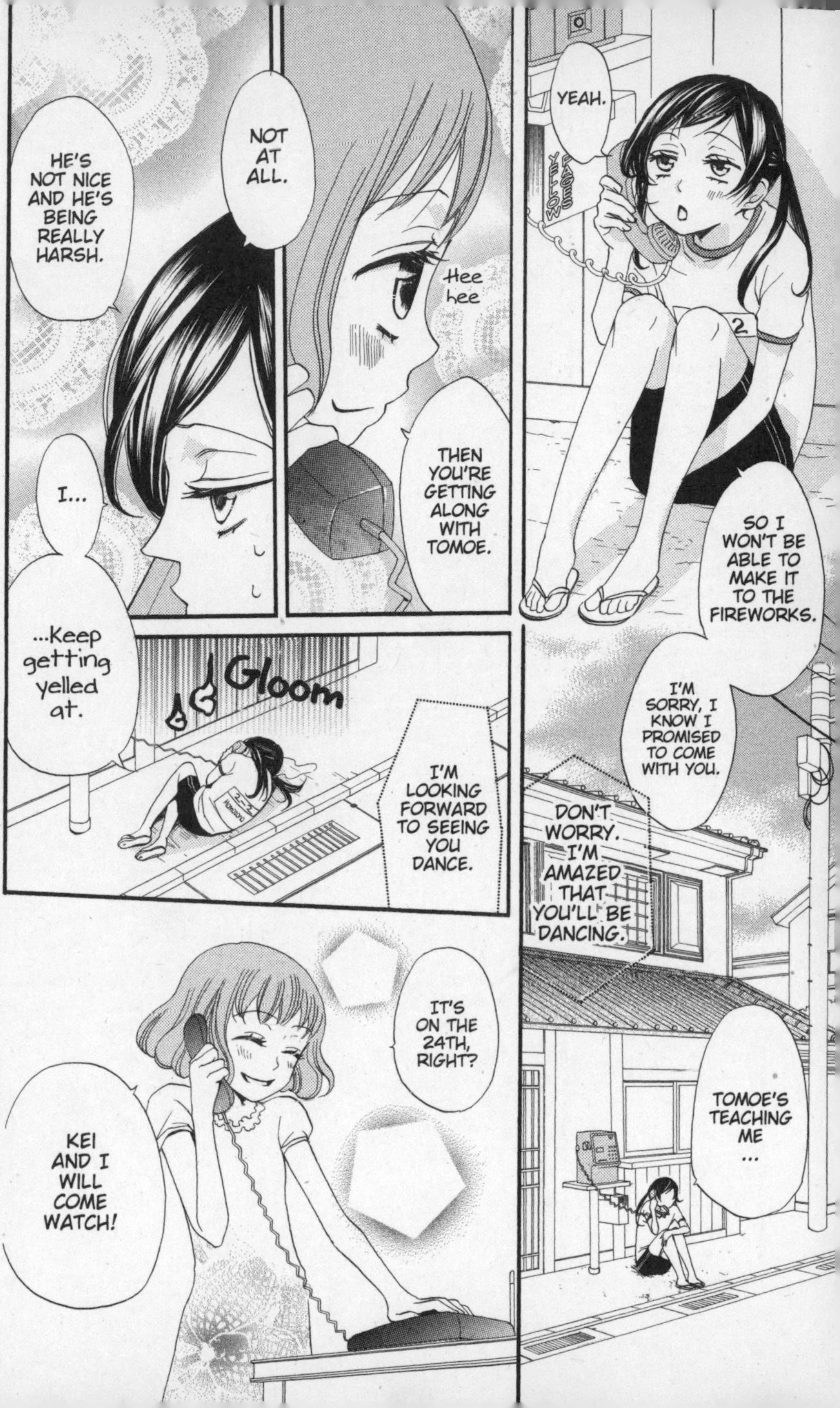
YEAH.
SO I WON'T BE ABLE TO MAKE IT TO THE FIREWORKS.
I'M SORRY, I KNOW I PROMISED TO COME WITH YOU.
DON'T WORRY. I'M AMAZED THAT YOU'LL BE DANCING.
TOMOE'S TEACHING ME...
YELLOW PAGES
Hee hee
THEN YOU'RE GETTING ALONG WITH TOMOE.
NOT AT ALL.
HE'S NOT NICE AND HE'S BEING REALLY HARSH.
I...
...Keep getting yelled at.
Gloom
I'M LOOKING FORWARD TO SEEING YOU DANCE.
IT'S ON THE 24TH, RIGHT?
KEI AND I WILL COME WATCH!

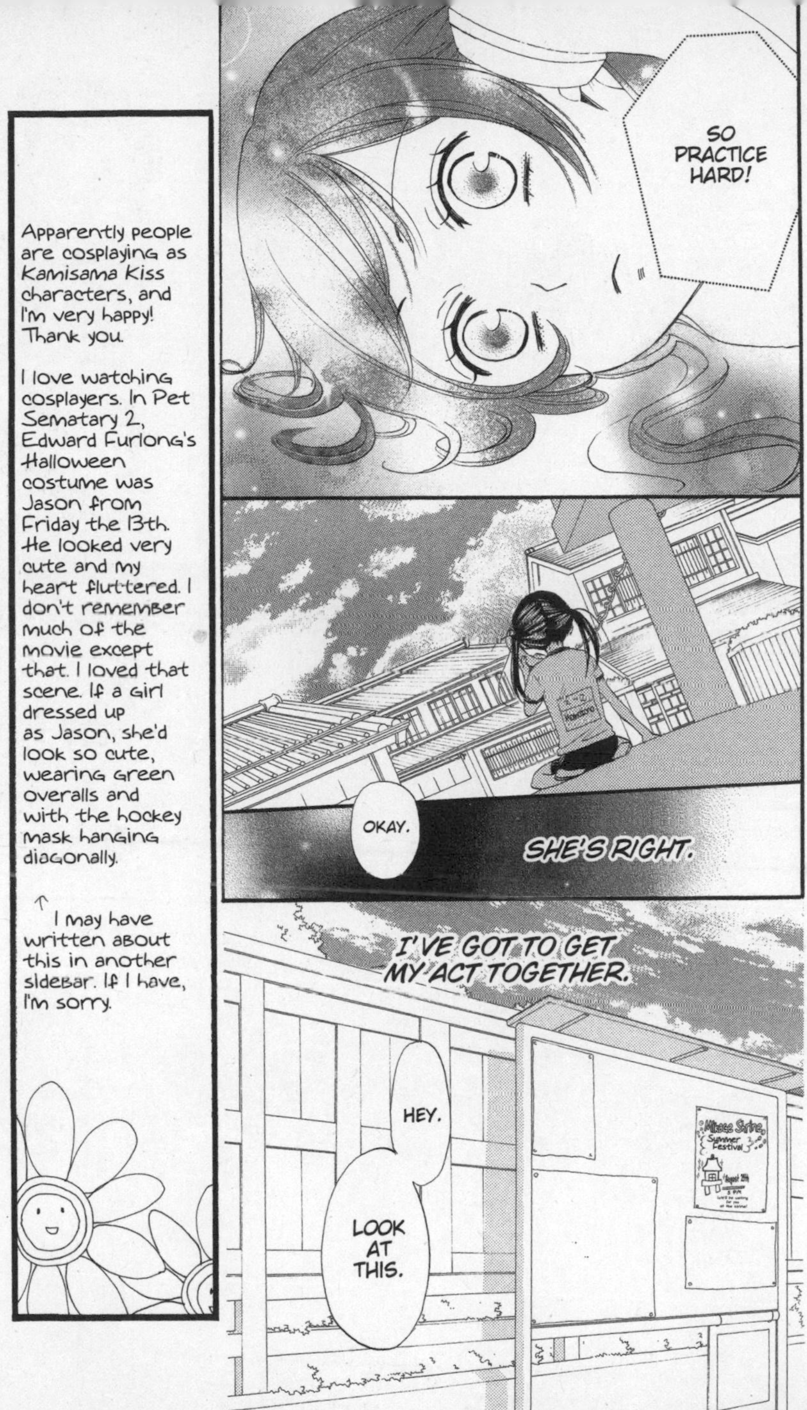
SO PRACTICE HARD!
OKAY.
SHE'S RIGHT.
I'VE GOT TO GET MY ACT TOGETHER.
HEY.
LOOK AT THIS.
Mikage Shrine
Summer Festival

Apparently people are cosplaying as Kamisama Kiss characters, and I'm very happy! Thank you.

I love watching cosplayers. In Pet Sematary 2, Edward Furlong's Halloween costume was Jason from Friday the 13th. He looked very cute and my heart fluttered. I don't remember much of the movie except that. I loved that scene. If a girl dressed up as Jason, she'd look so cute, wearing green overalls and with the hockey mask hanging diagonally.

↑ I may have written about this in another sidebar. If I have, I'm sorry.

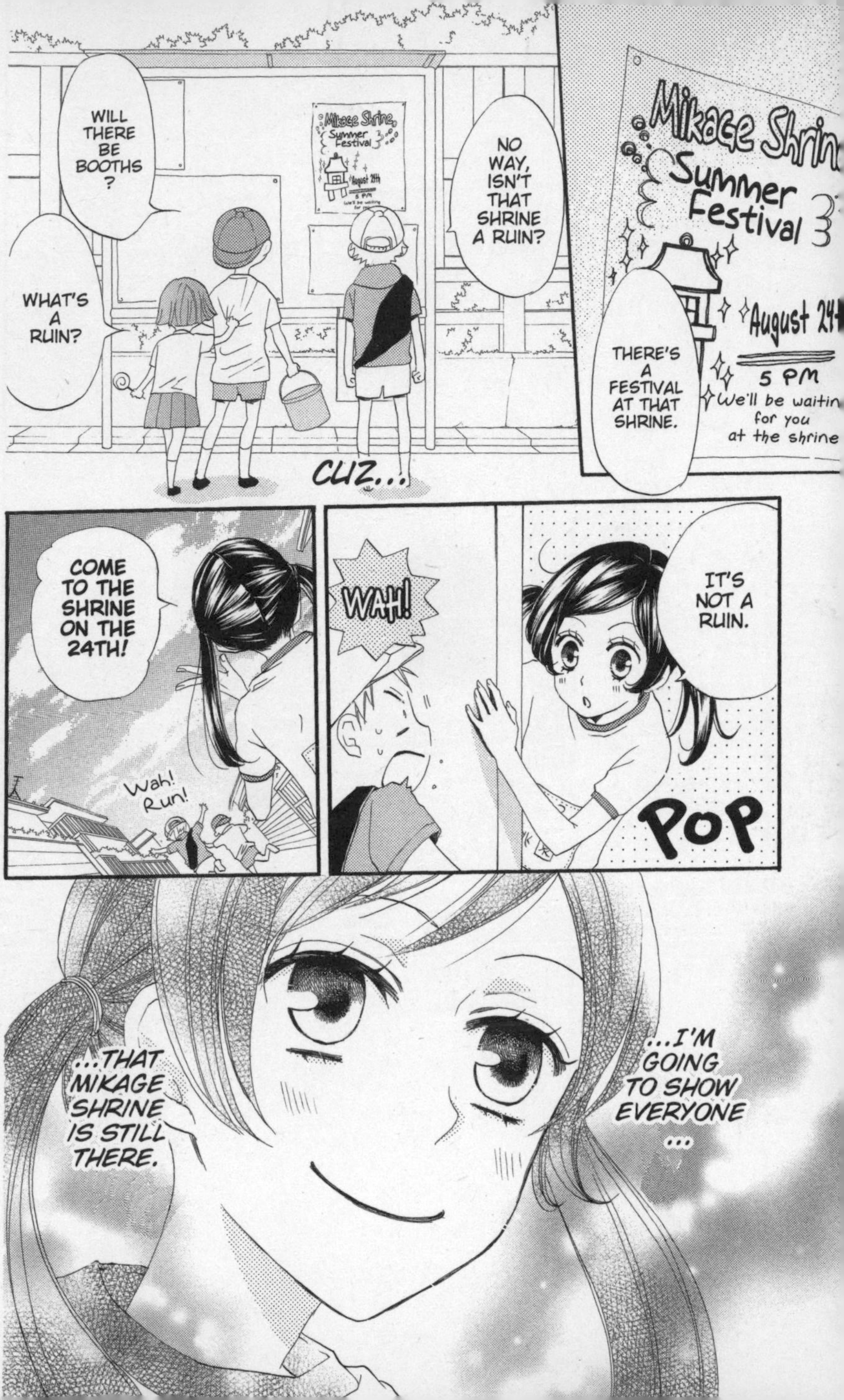
Mikage Shrin
Summer Festival
August 24
5 PM
We'll be waitin
for you
at the shrine
THERE'S A FESTIVAL AT THAT SHRINE.
NO WAY, ISN'T THAT SHRINE A RUIN?
Mikage Shrine
Summer Festival
August 24th
5 PM
WILL THERE BE BOOTHS?
WHAT'S A RUIN?
CUZ...
IT'S NOT A RUIN.
POP
WAH!
COME TO THE SHRINE ON THE 24TH!
Wah! Run!
...I'M GOING TO SHOW EVERYONE ...
...THAT MIKAGE SHRINE IS STILL THERE.

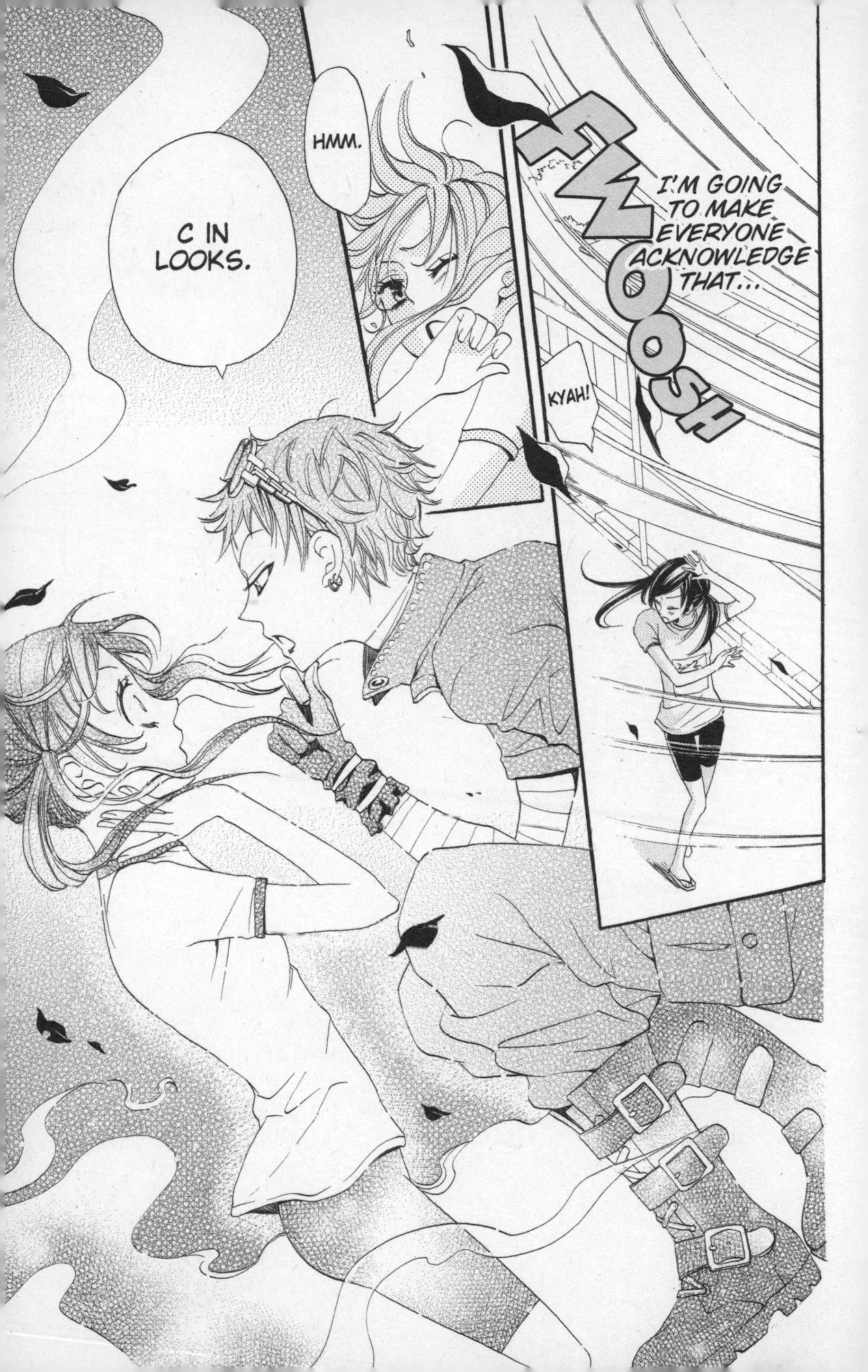
FWOOSH
I'M GOING TO MAKE EVERYONE ACKNOWLEDGE THAT...
KYAH!
HMM.
C IN LOOKS.

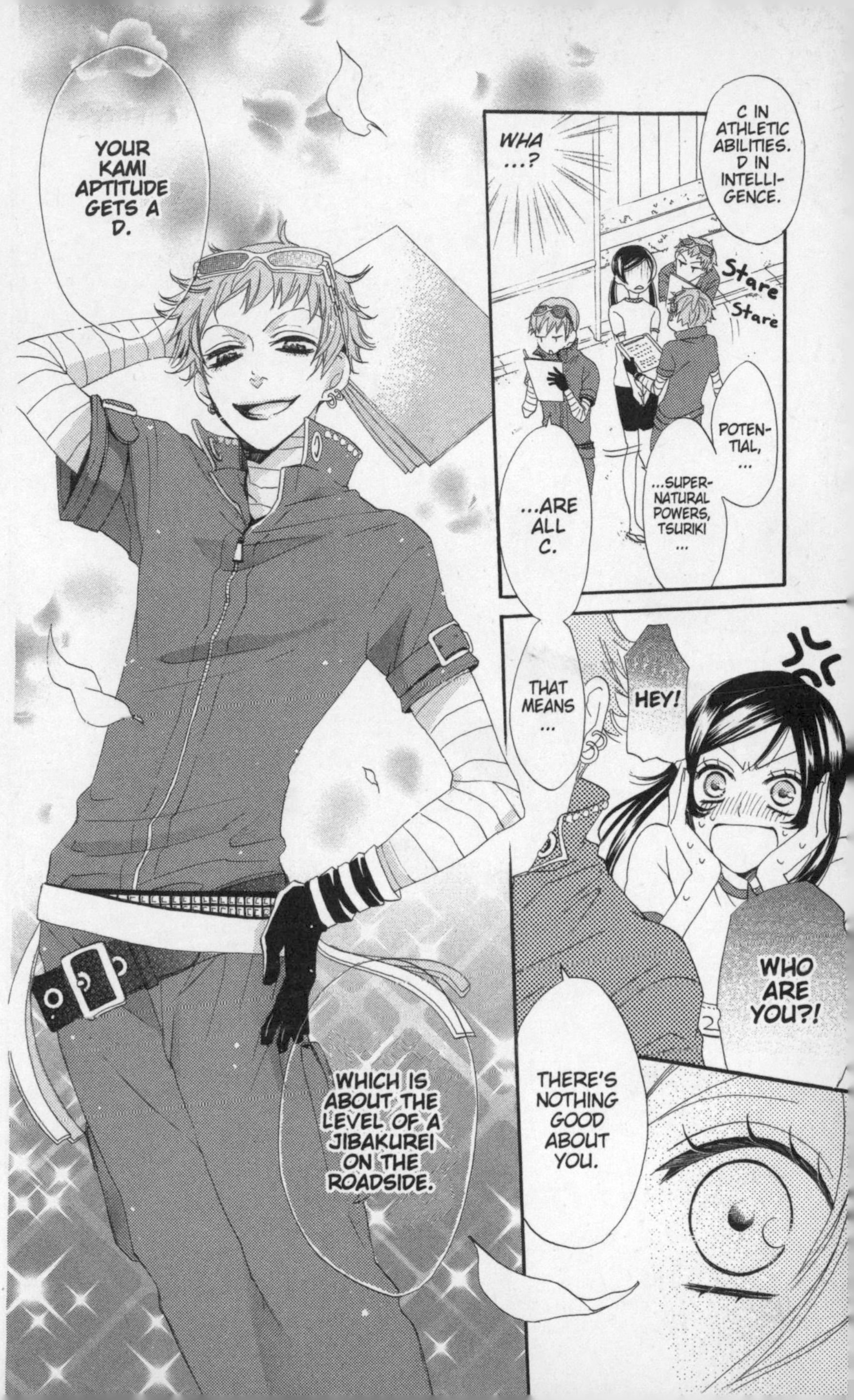
C IN ATHLETIC ABILITIES. D IN INTELLI-GENCE.
WHA ...?
Stare
Stare
POTEN-TIAL, ...
...SUPER-NATURAL POWERS, TSURIKI ...
...ARE ALL C.
THAT MEANS ...
HEY!
WHO ARE YOU?!
THERE'S NOTHING GOOD ABOUT YOU.
YOUR KAMI APTITUDE GETS A D.
WHICH IS ABOUT THE LEVEL OF A JIBAKUREI ON THE ROADSIDE.

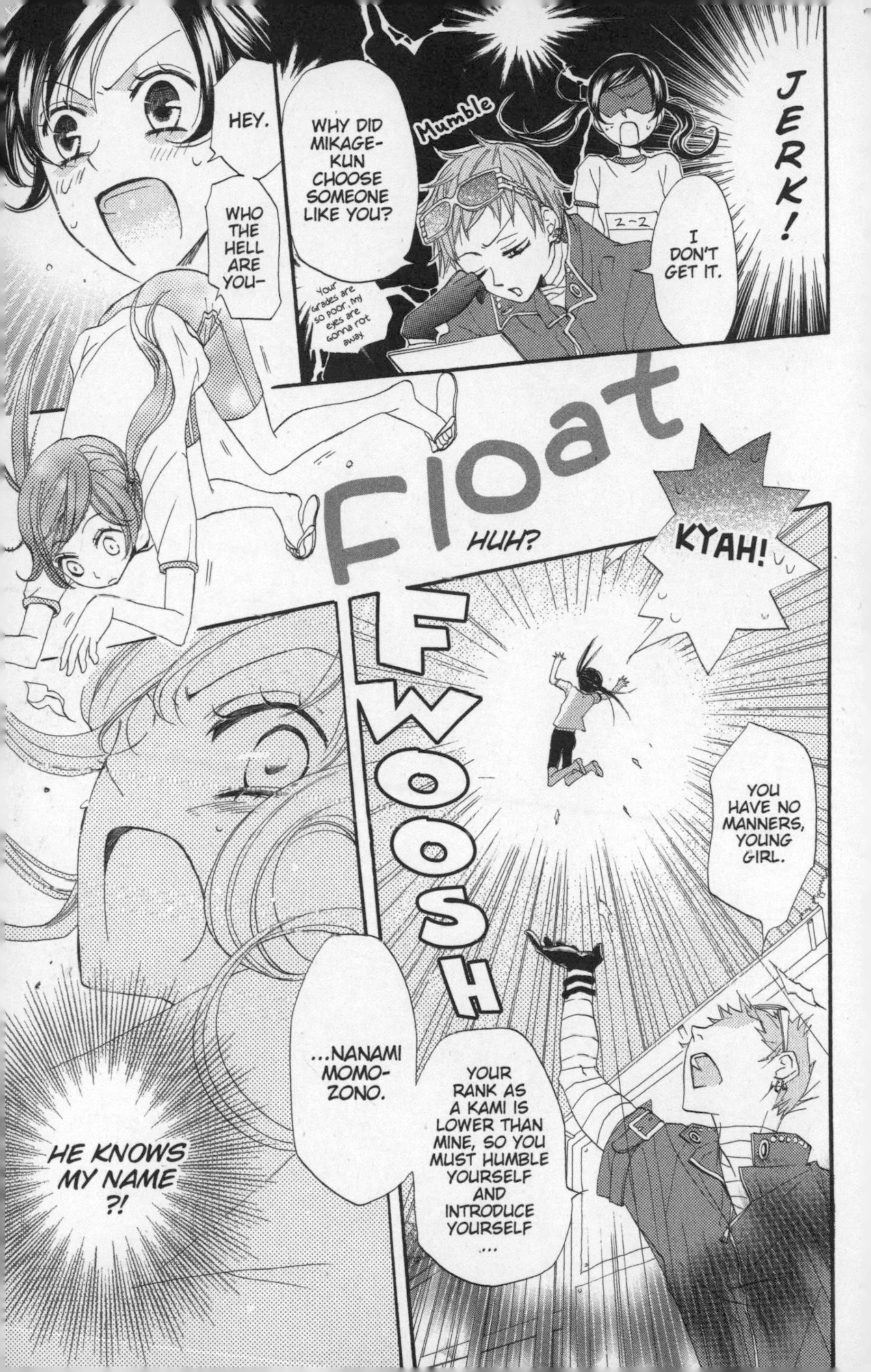
JERK!
I DON'T GET IT.
WHY DID MIKAGE-KUN CHOOSE SOMEONE LIKE YOU?
Mumble
Your Grades are so poor, my eyes are gonna rot away.
HEY.
WHO THE HELL ARE YOU-
Float
HUH?
KYAH!
FWOOSH
YOU HAVE NO MANNERS, YOUNG GIRL.
YOUR RANK AS A KAMI IS LOWER THAN MINE, SO YOU MUST HUMBLE YOURSELF AND INTRODUCE YOURSELF ...
...NANAMI MOMOZONO.
HE KNOWS MY NAME ?!

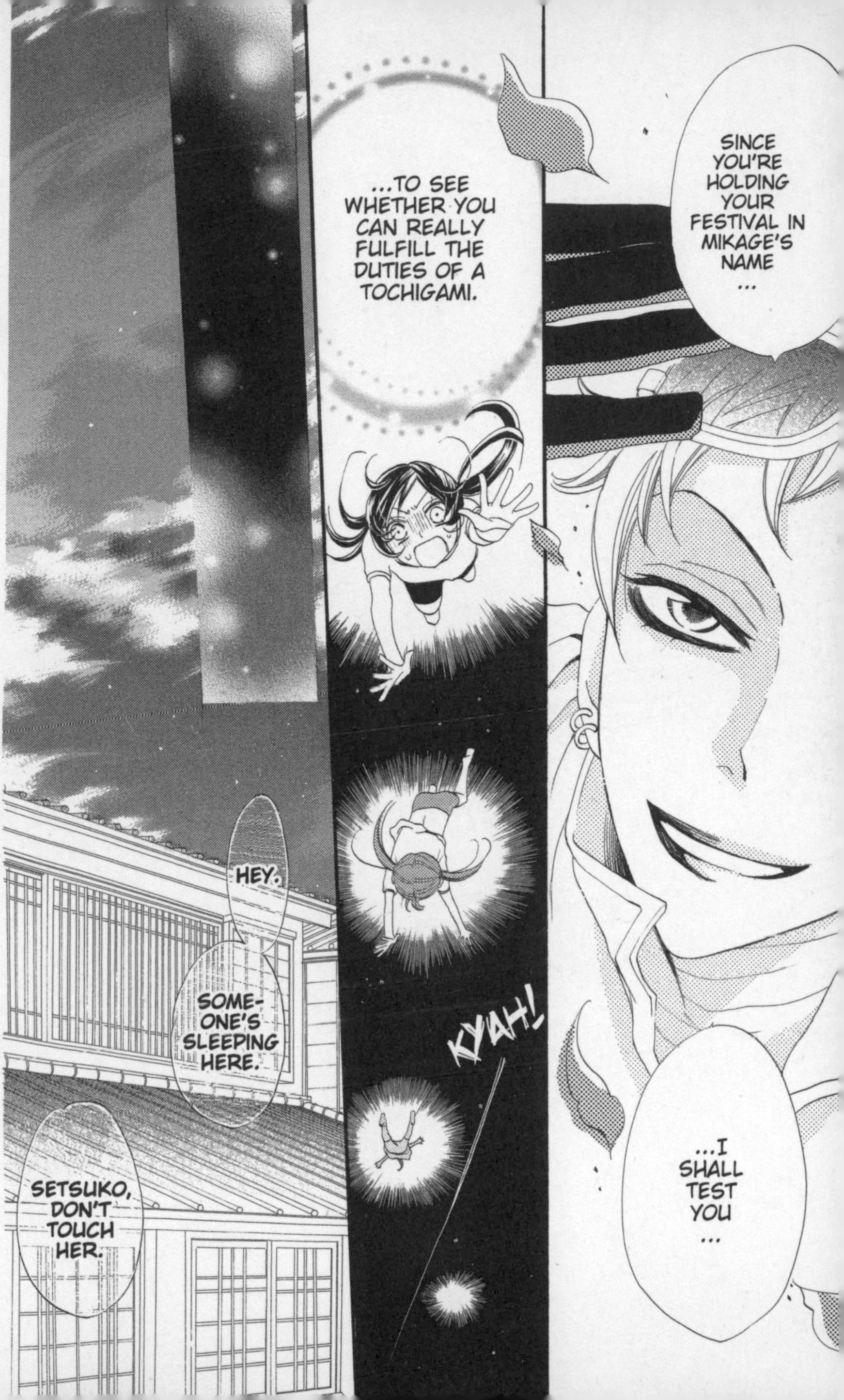
SINCE YOU'RE HOLDING YOUR FESTIVAL IN MIKAGE'S NAME ...
...I SHALL TEST YOU ...
...TO SEE WHETHER YOU CAN REALLY FULFILL THE DUTIES OF A TOCHIGAMI.
KYAH!
HEY.
SOME-ONE'S SLEEPING HERE.
SETSUKO, DON'T TOUCH HER.

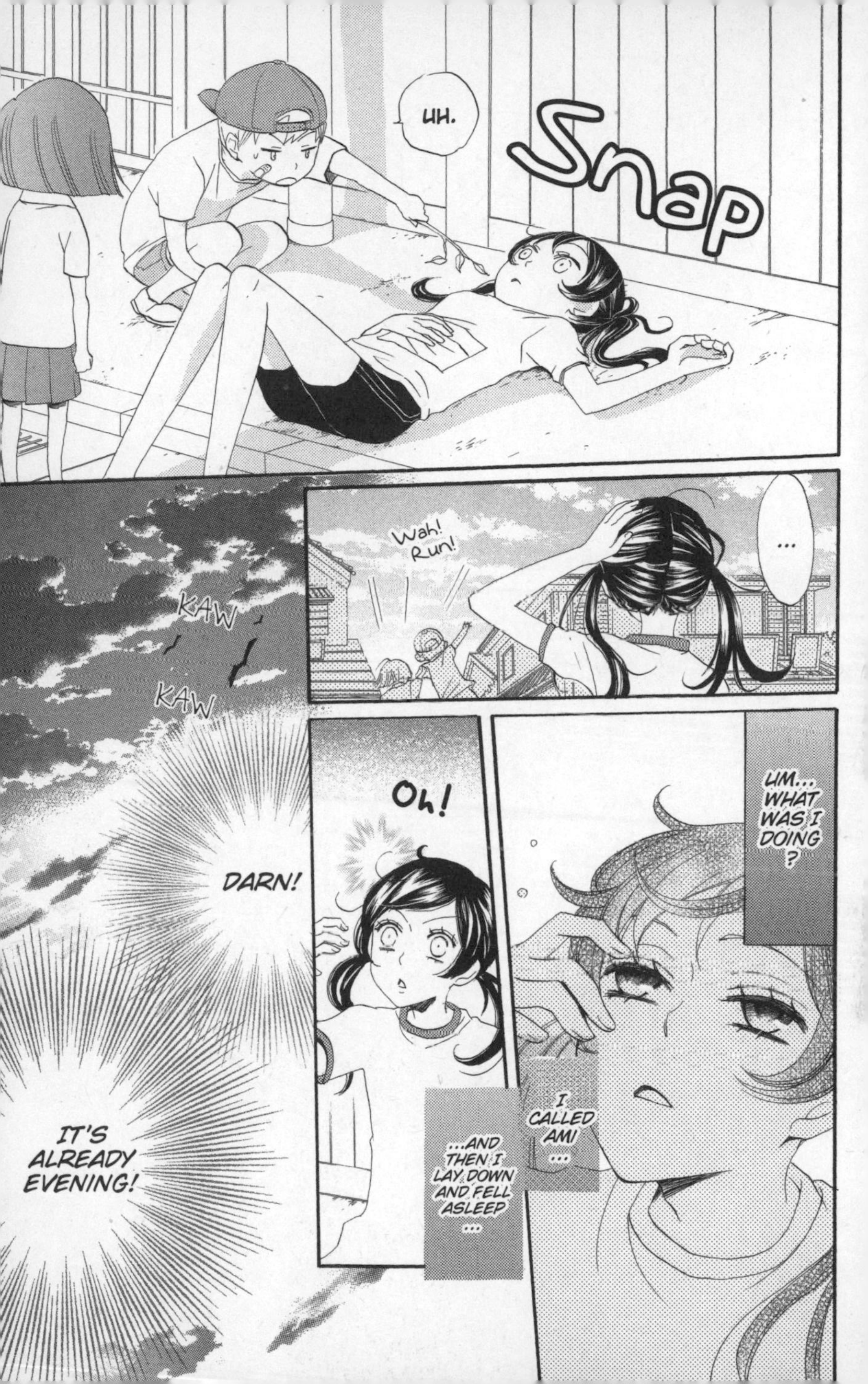
Snap
UH.
...
Wah! Run!
UM... WHAT WAS I DOING?
I CALLED AMI...
...AND THEN I LAY DOWN AND FELL ASLEEP...
Oh!
KAW
KAW
DARN!
IT'S ALREADY EVENING!

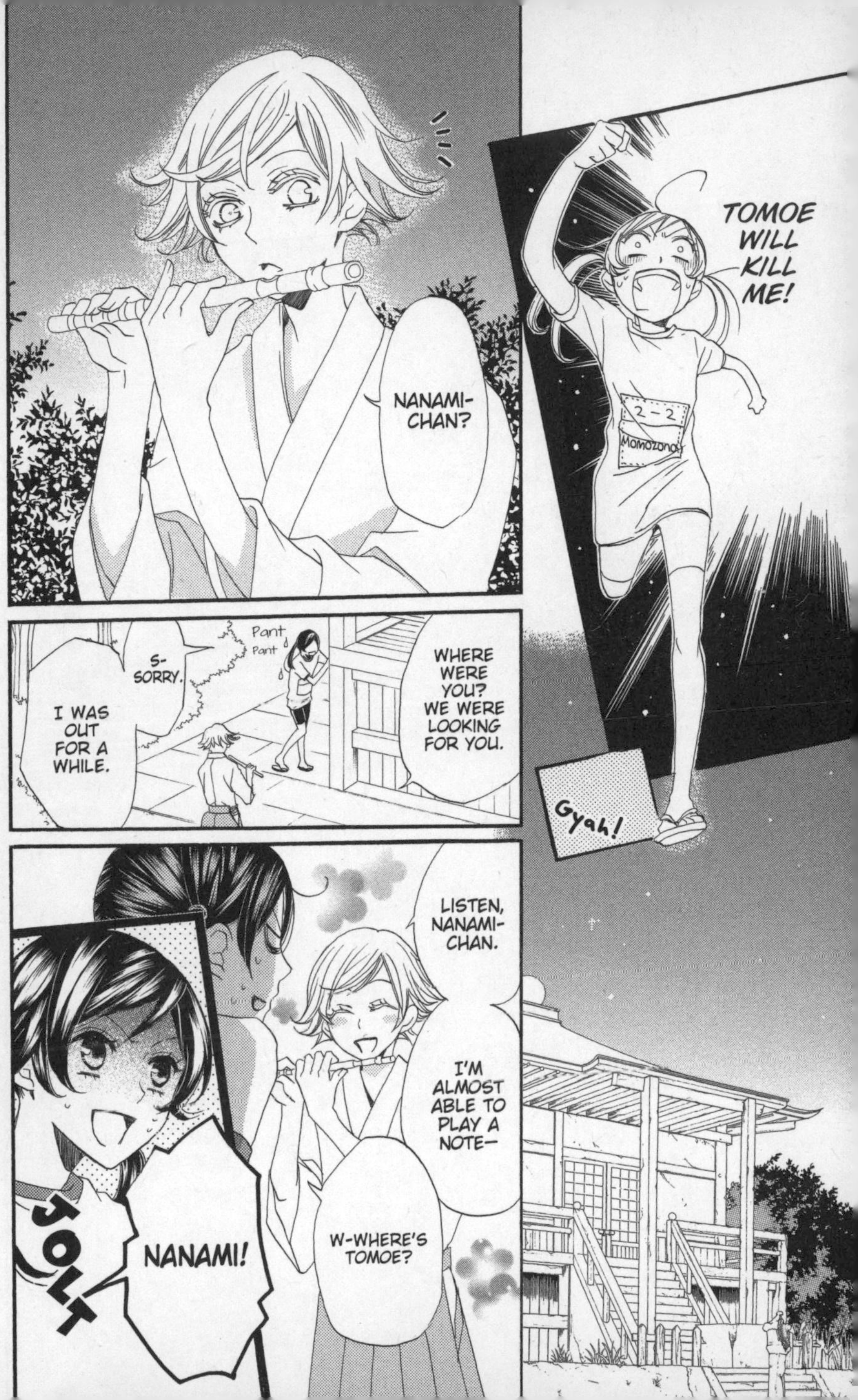
TOMOE WILL KILL ME!
2-2
Momozono
Gyah!
NANAMI-CHAN?
WHERE WERE YOU? WE WERE LOOKING FOR YOU.
Pant
Pant
S-SORRY.
I WAS OUT FOR A WHILE.
LISTEN, NANAMI-CHAN.
I'M ALMOST ABLE TO PLAY A NOTE—
W-WHERE'S TOMOE?
JOLT
NANAMI!

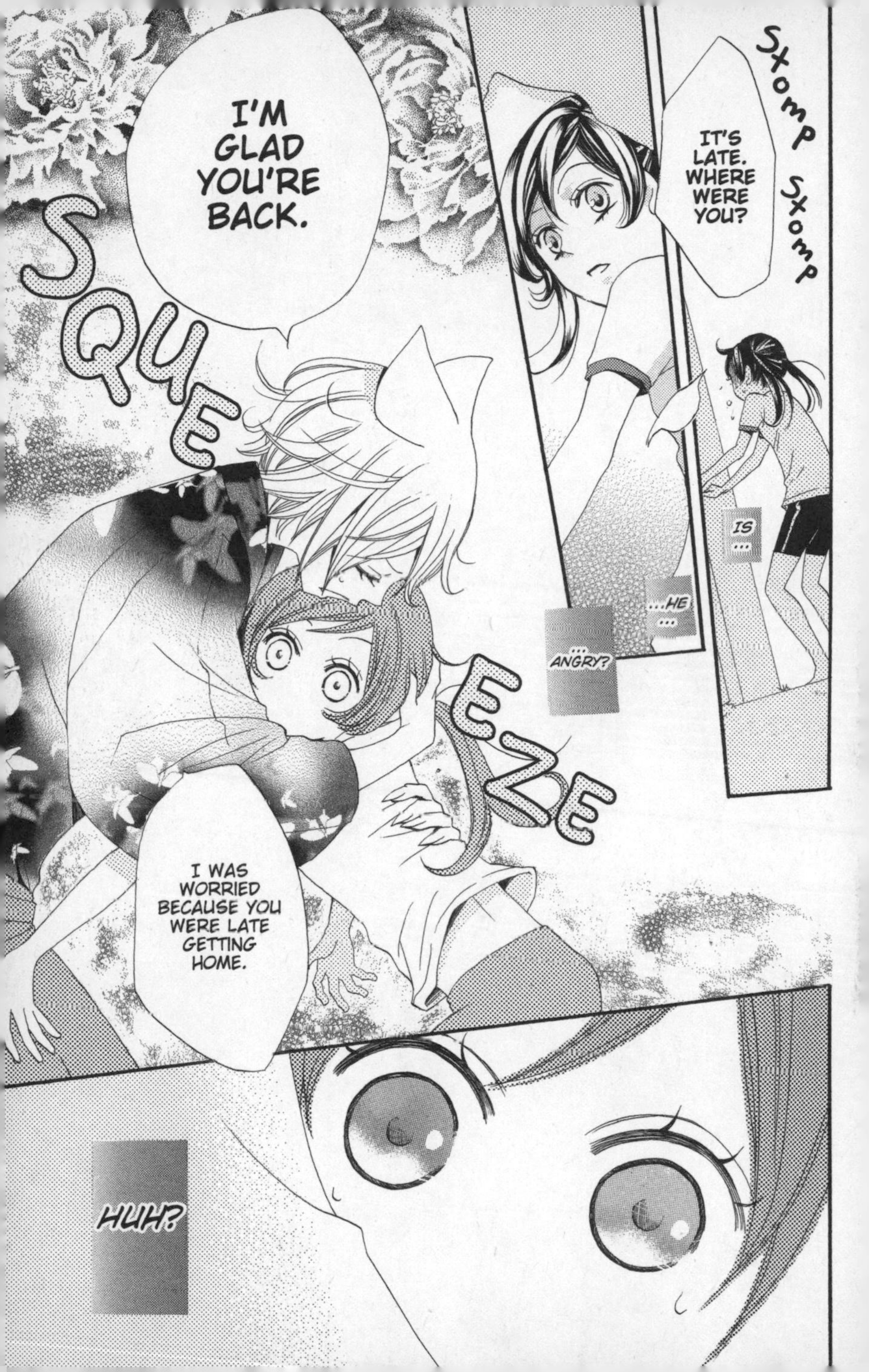
Stomp Stomp
IT'S LATE. WHERE WERE YOU?
IS...
...HE...
...ANGRY?
I'M GLAD YOU'RE BACK.
SQUEEZE
I WAS WORRIED BECAUSE YOU WERE LATE GETTING HOME.
HUH?

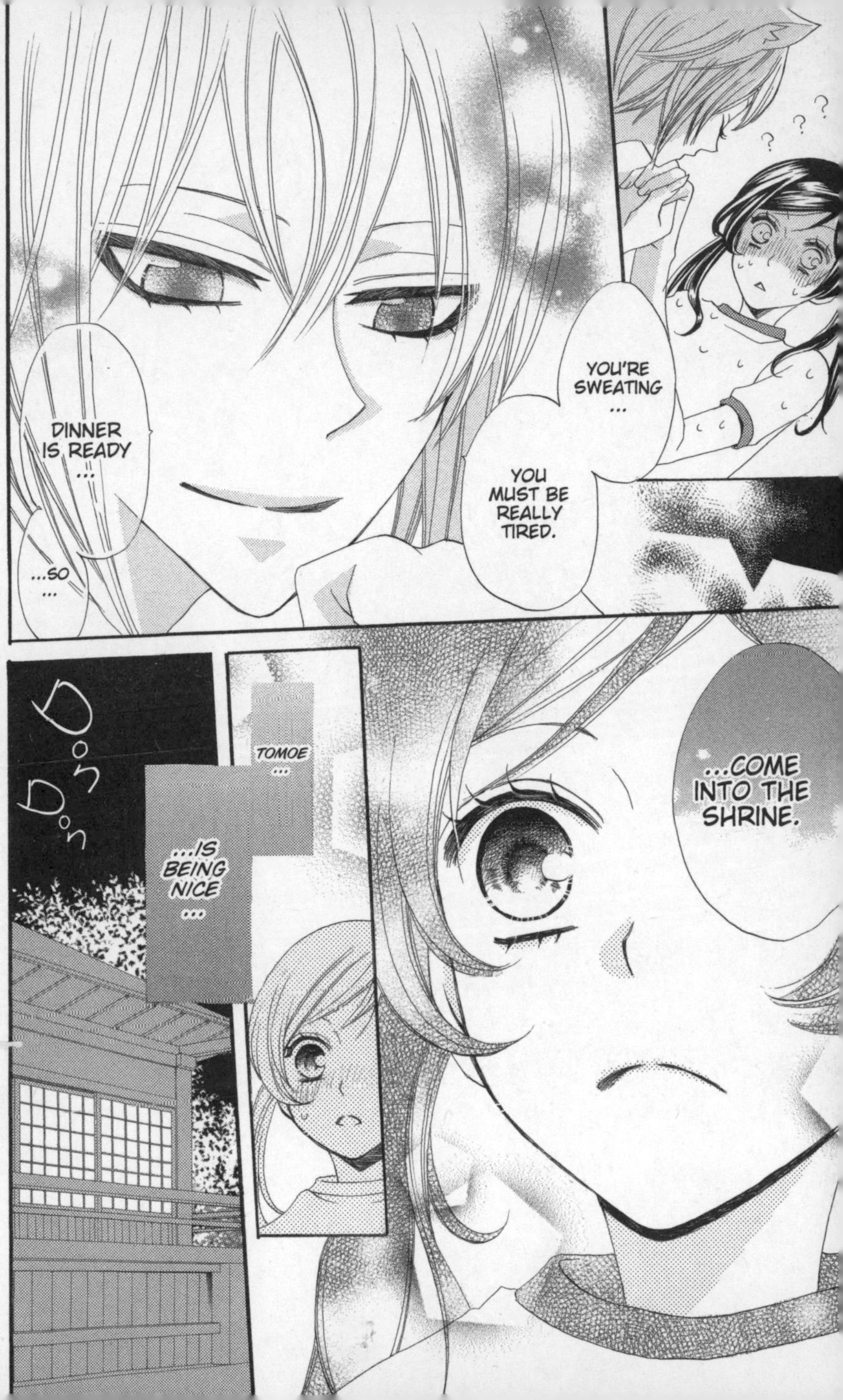
YOU'RE SWEATING ...
YOU MUST BE REALLY TIRED.
DINNER IS READY ...
...SO ...
...COME INTO THE SHRINE.
TOMOE ...
...IS BEING NICE ...

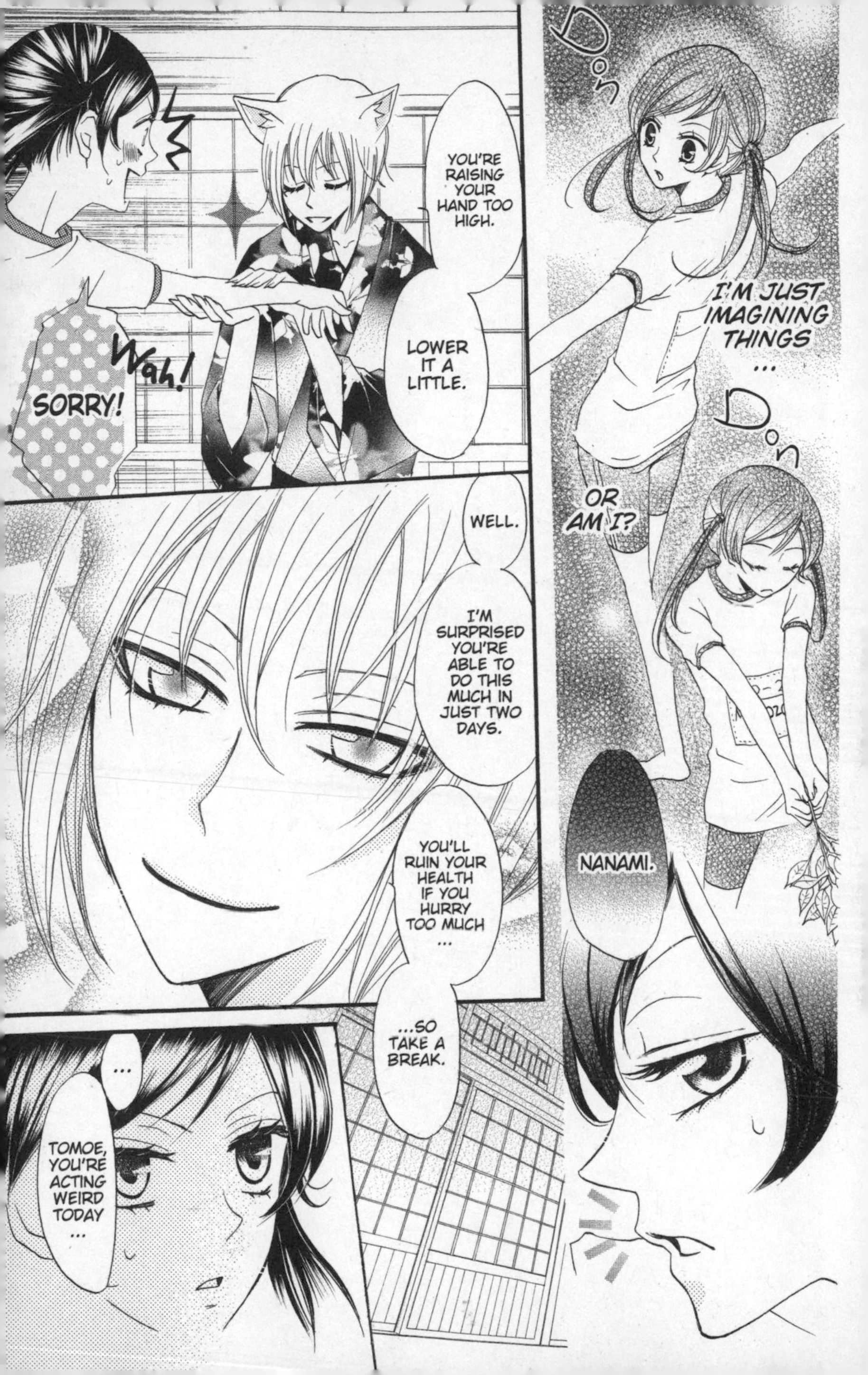
Don
I'M JUST IMAGINING THINGS ...
Don
OR AM I?
YOU'RE RAISING YOUR HAND TOO HIGH.
LOWER IT A LITTLE.
Wah!
SORRY!
WELL.
I'M SURPRISED YOU'RE ABLE TO DO THIS MUCH IN JUST TWO DAYS.
YOU'LL RUIN YOUR HEALTH IF YOU HURRY TOO MUCH ...
...SO TAKE A BREAK.
NANAMI.
...
TOMOE, YOU'RE ACTING WEIRD TODAY ...

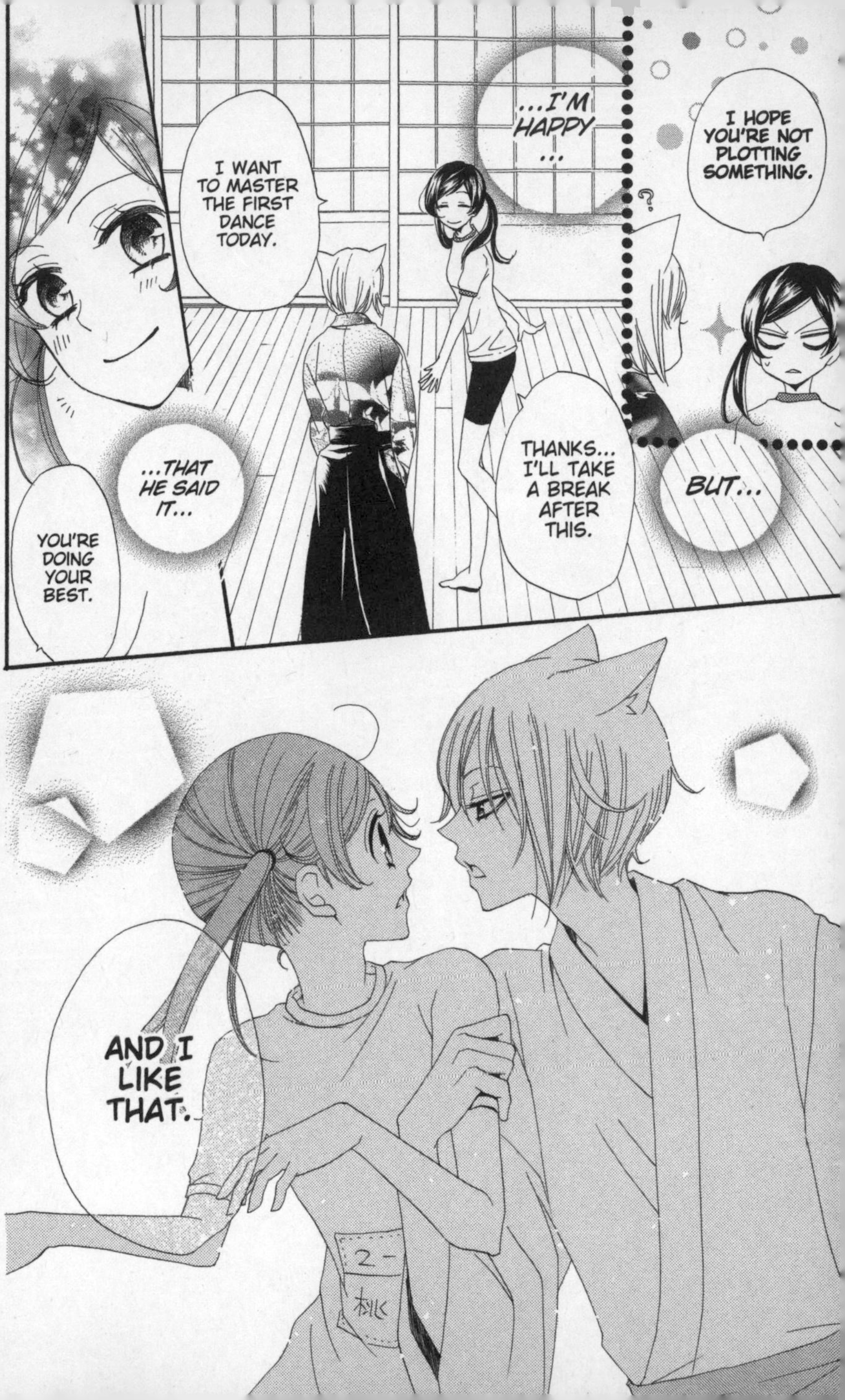
I HOPE YOU'RE NOT PLOTTING SOMETHING.
?
BUT...
...I'M HAPPY...
I WANT TO MASTER THE FIRST DANCE TODAY.
THANKS... I'LL TAKE A BREAK AFTER THIS.
...THAT HE SAID IT...
YOU'RE DOING YOUR BEST.
AND I LIKE THAT.
2-
桃

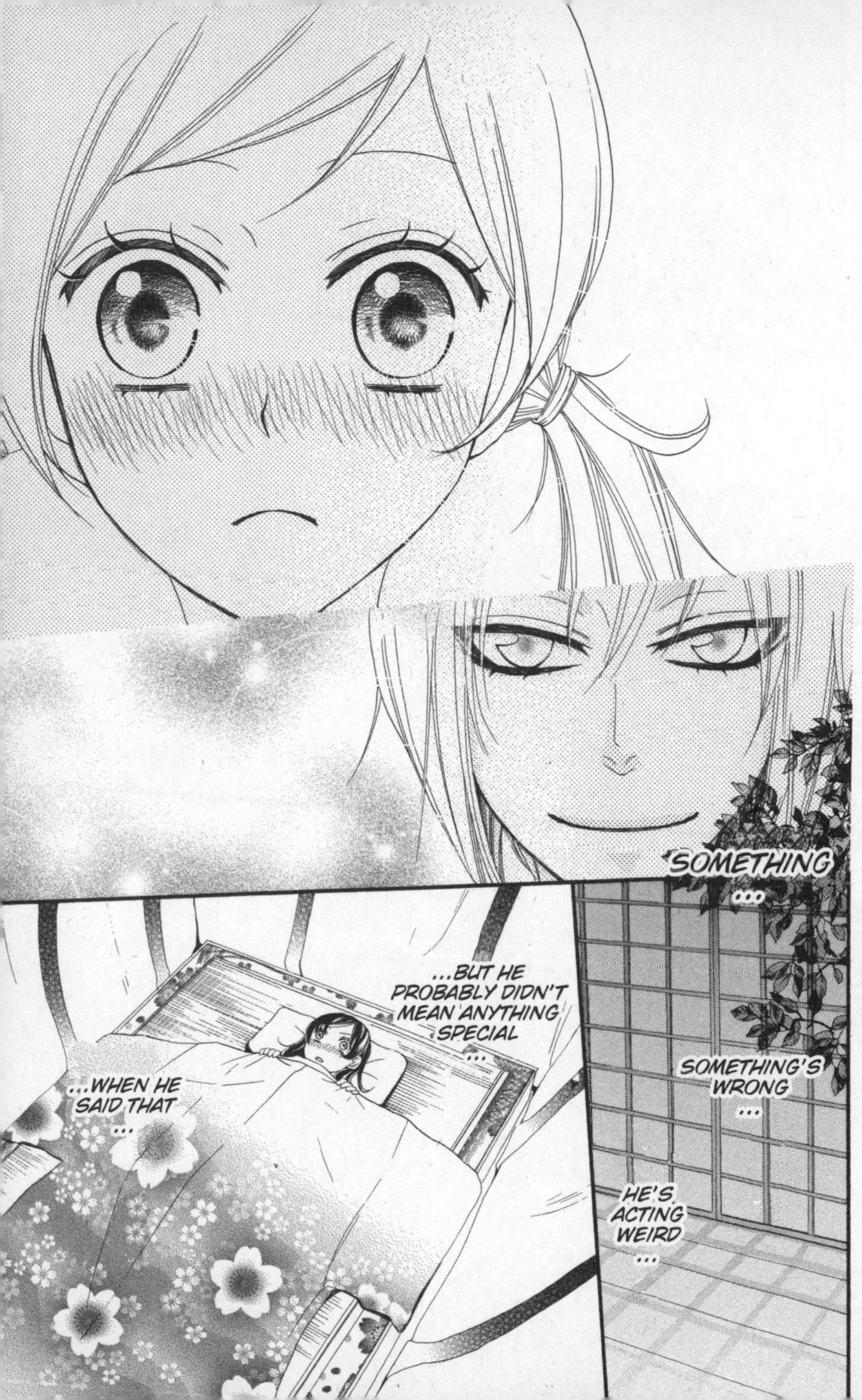
SOMETHING...
SOMETHING'S WRONG...
HE'S ACTING WEIRD...
...BUT HE PROBABLY DIDN'T MEAN ANYTHING SPECIAL...
...WHEN HE SAID THAT...

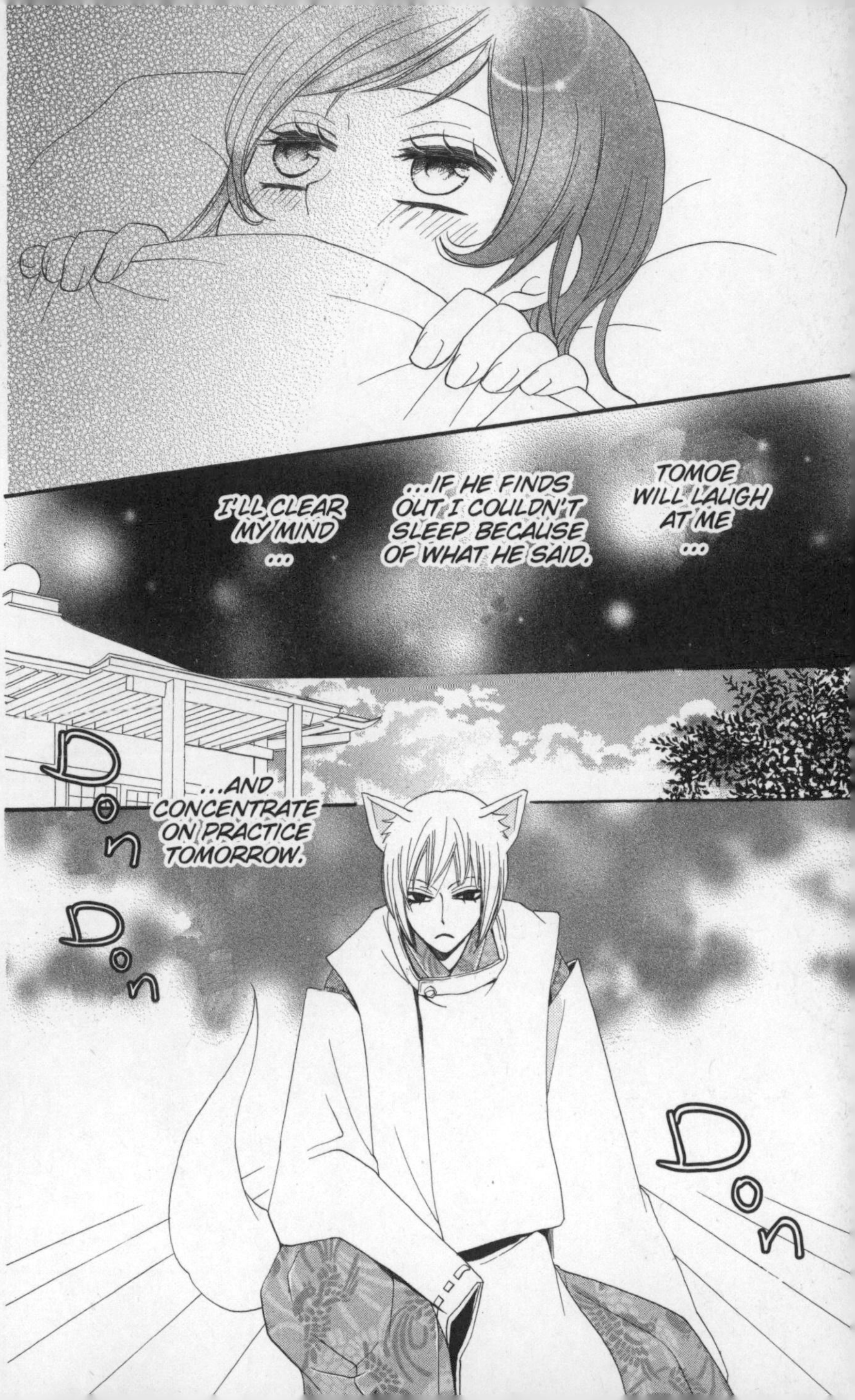
TOMOE WILL LAUGH AT ME ...
...IF HE FINDS OUT I COULDN'T SLEEP BECAUSE OF WHAT HE SAID.
I'LL CLEAR MY MIND ...
...AND CONCENTRATE ON PRACTICE TOMORROW.
Don
Don
Don

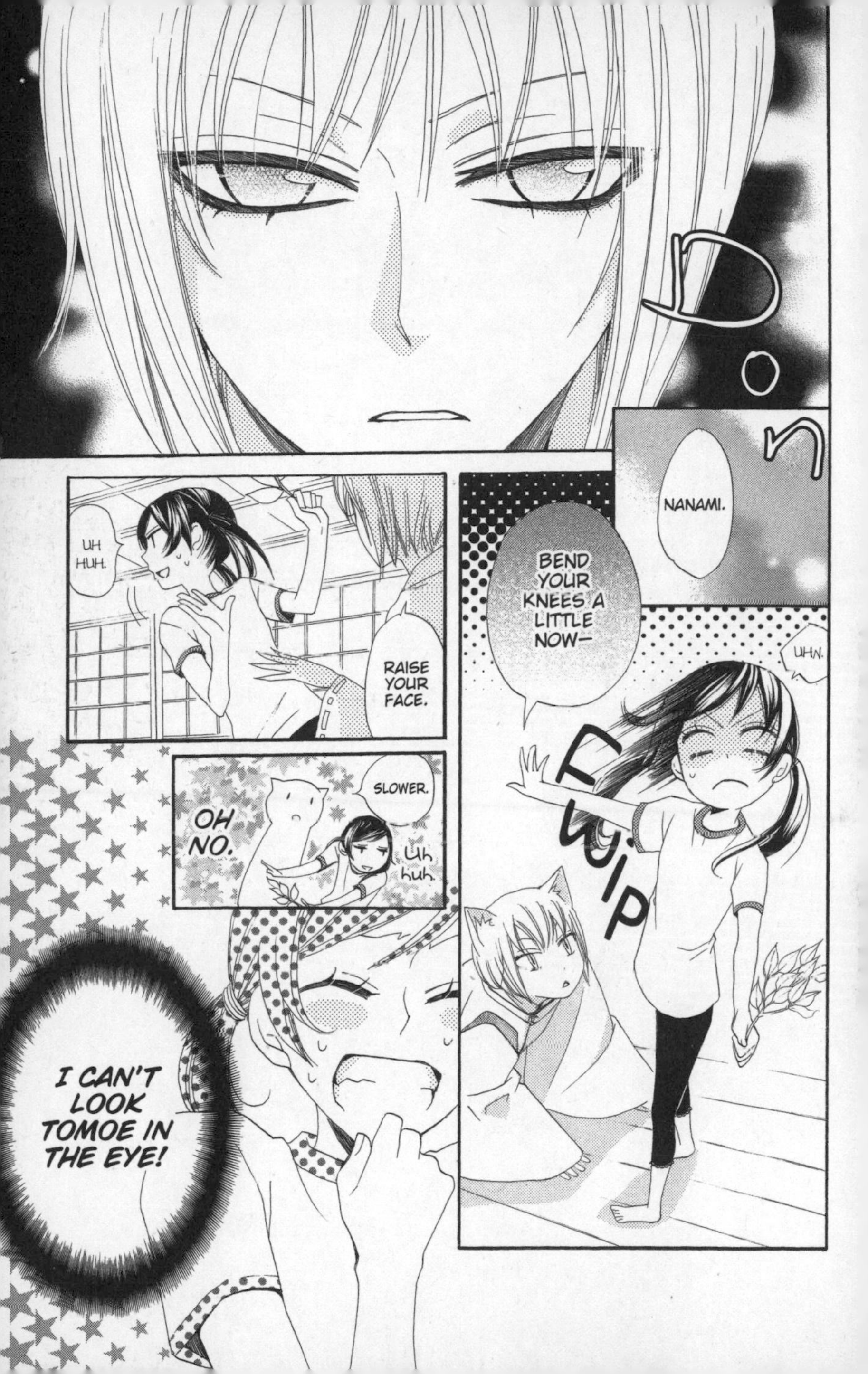
NANAMI.
BEND YOUR KNEES A LITTLE NOW—
UHN.
FWIP
RAISE YOUR FACE.
UH HUH.
SLOWER.
Uh huh.
OH NO.
I CAN'T LOOK TOMOE IN THE EYE!

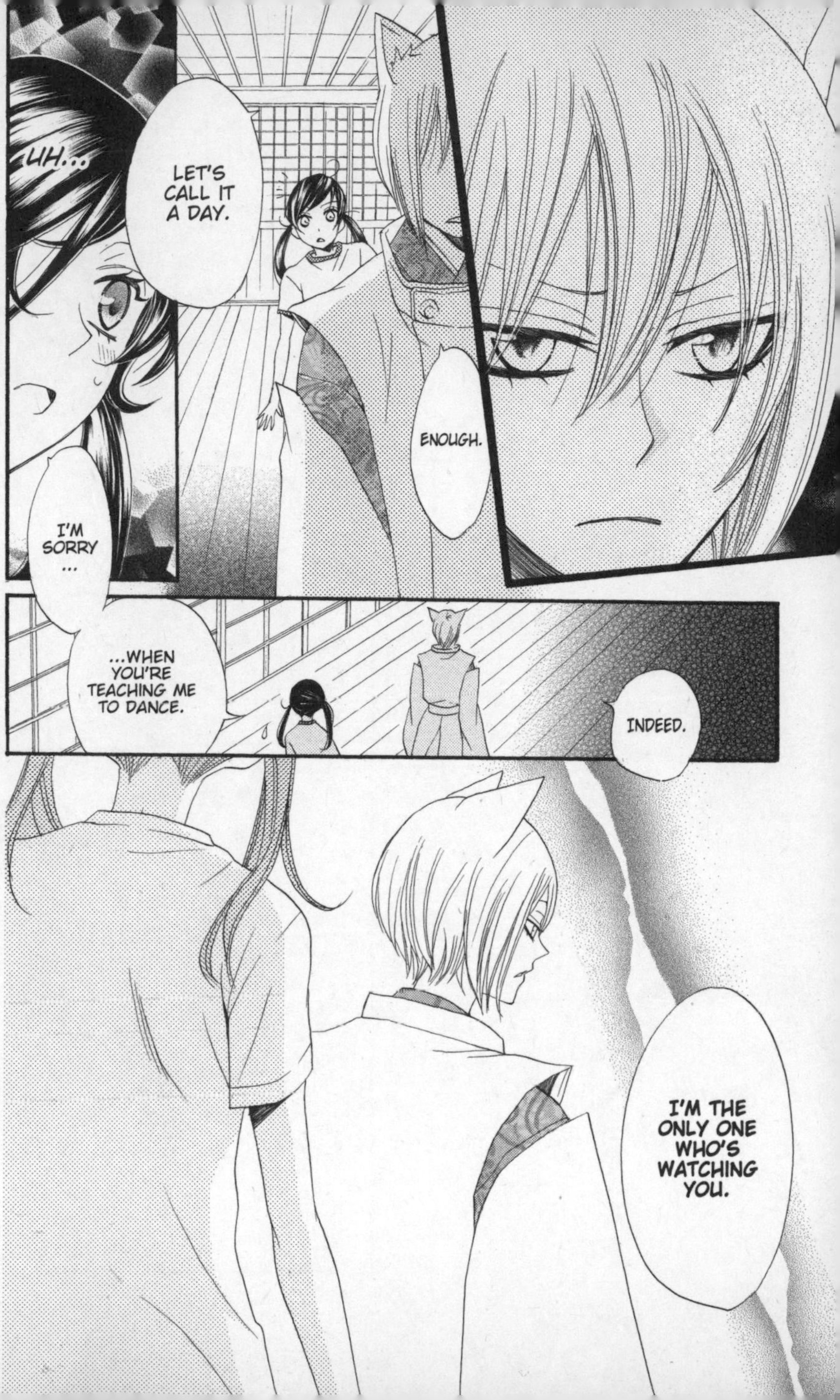
ENOUGH.
LET'S CALL IT A DAY.
UH...
I'M SORRY ...
...WHEN YOU'RE TEACHING ME TO DANCE.
INDEED.
I'M THE ONLY ONE WHO'S WATCHING YOU.

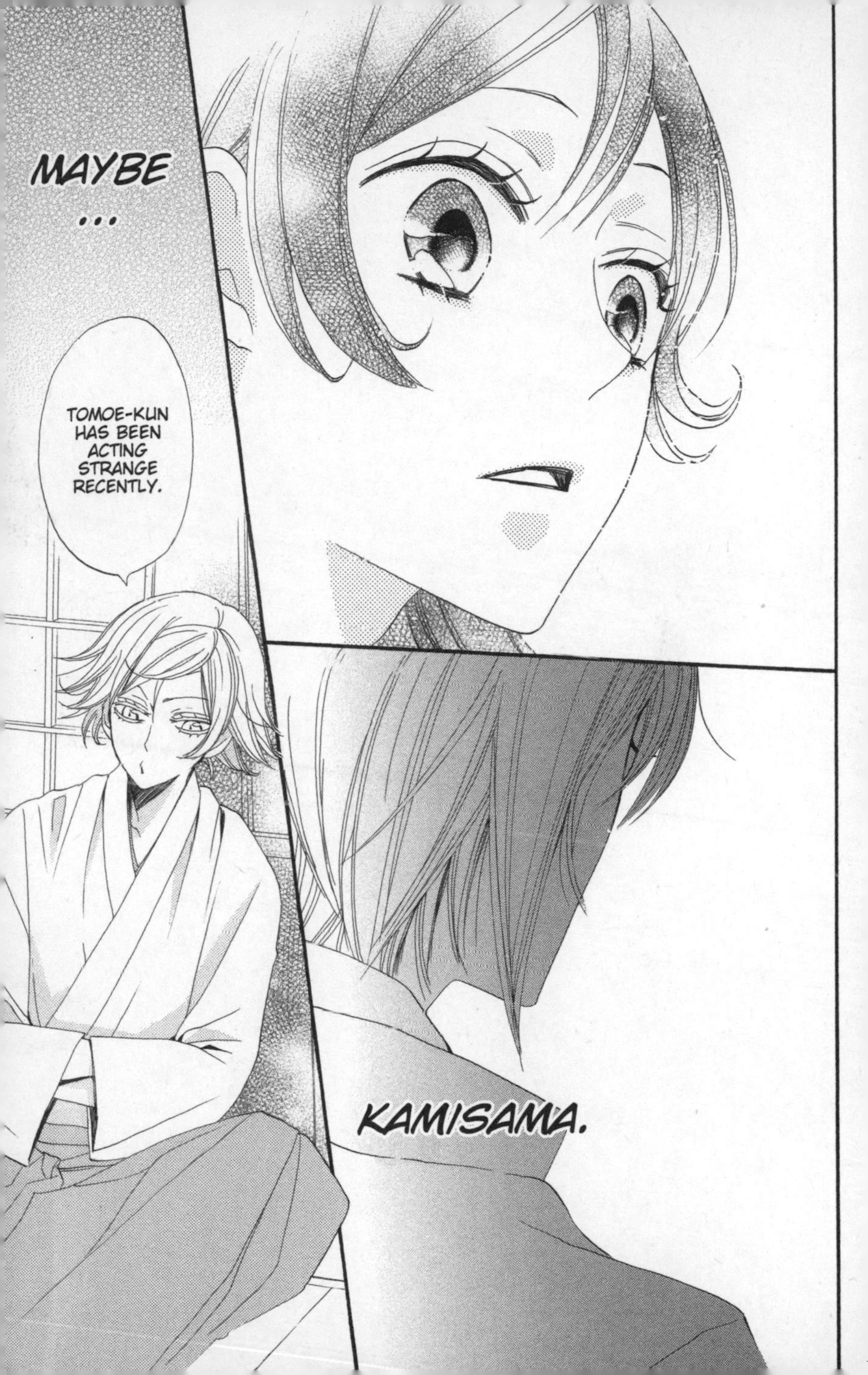
KAMISAMA.
MAYBE ...
TOMOE-KUN HAS BEEN ACTING STRANGE RECENTLY.

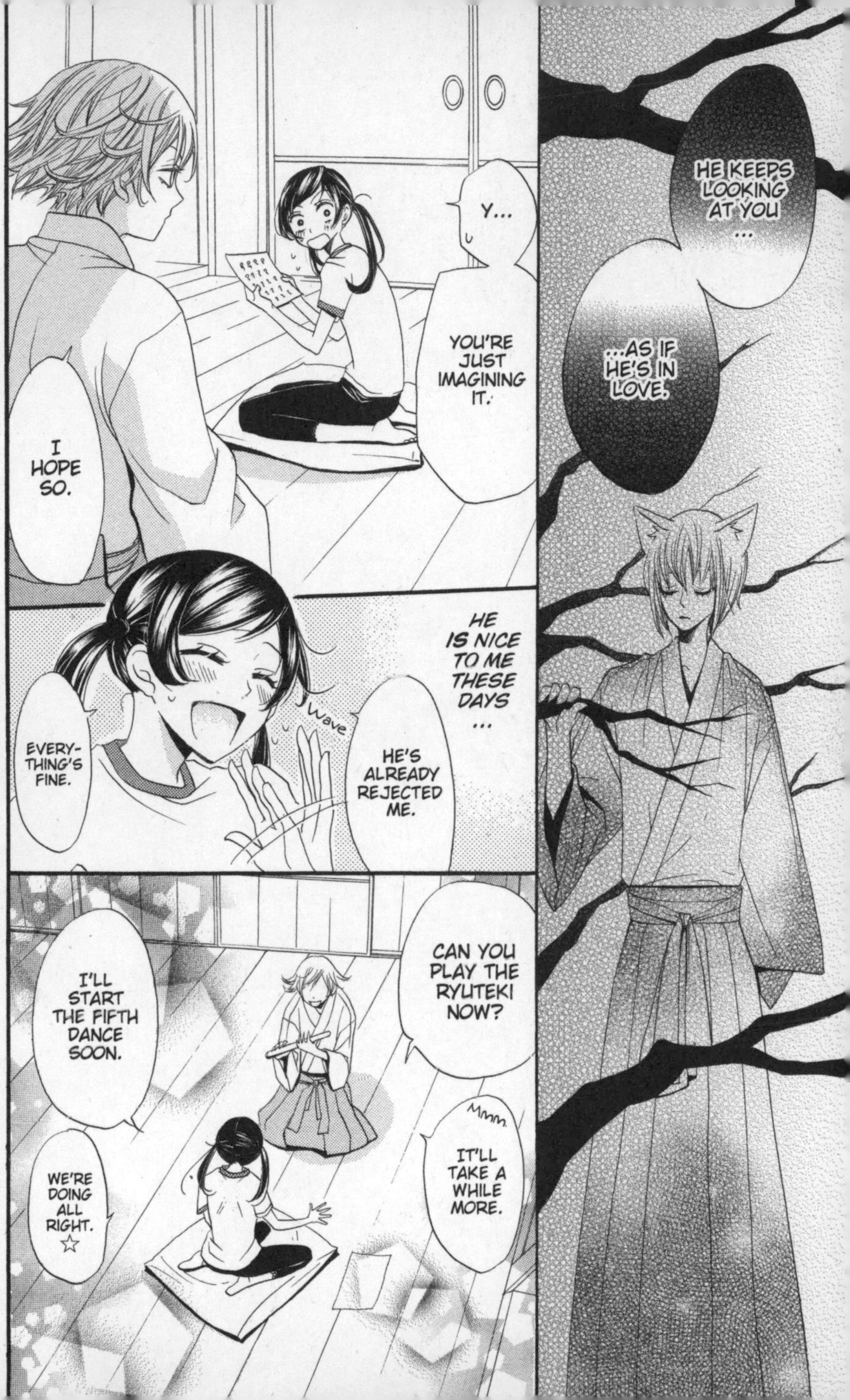
HE KEEPS LOOKING AT YOU ...
...AS IF HE'S IN LOVE.
Y...
YOU'RE JUST IMAGINING IT.
I HOPE SO.
HE IS NICE TO ME THESE DAYS ...
HE'S ALREADY REJECTED ME.
Wave
EVERY-THING'S FINE.
CAN YOU PLAY THE RYUTEKI NOW?
I'LL START THE FIFTH DANCE SOON.
Mmm.
IT'LL TAKE A WHILE MORE.
WE'RE DOING ALL RIGHT. ☆

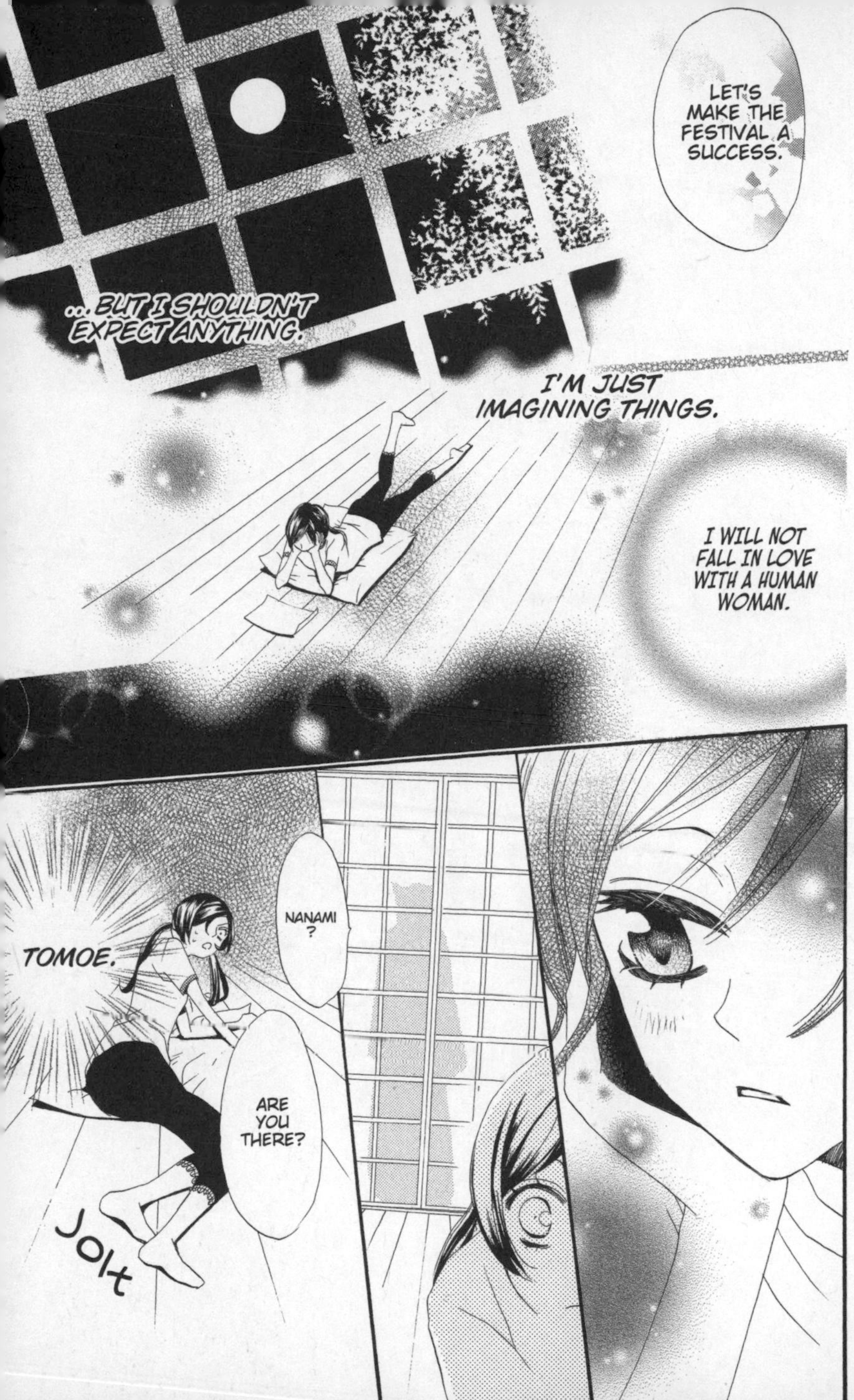
LET'S MAKE THE FESTIVAL A SUCCESS.
...BUT I SHOULDN'T EXPECT ANYTHING.
I'M JUST IMAGINING THINGS.
I WILL NOT FALL IN LOVE WITH A HUMAN WOMAN.
NANAMI?
ARE YOU THERE?
TOMOE.
Jolt

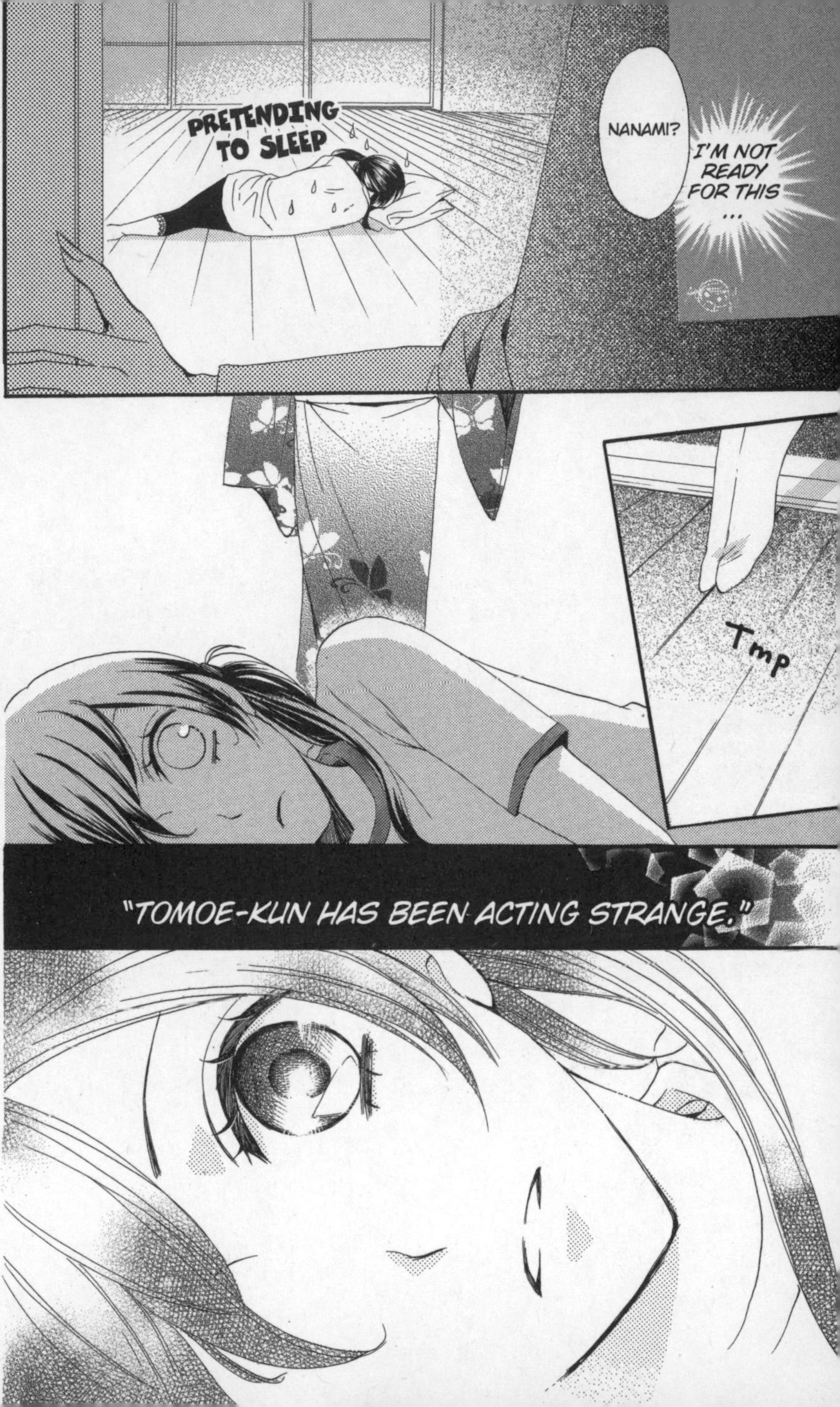
NANAMI?
I'M NOT READY FOR THIS ...
PRETENDING TO SLEEP
Tmp
"TOMOE-KUN HAS BEEN ACTING STRANGE."

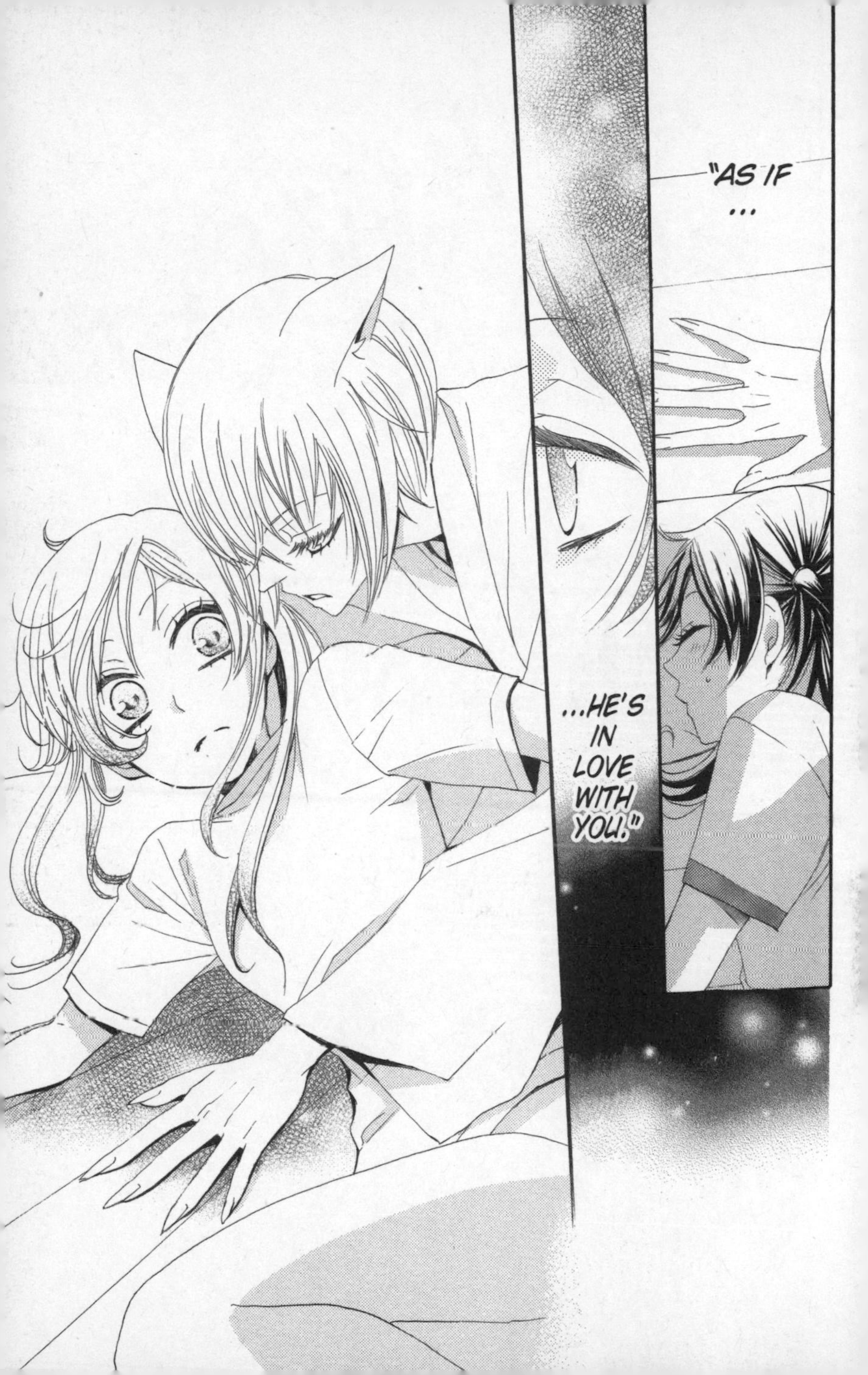
"AS IF ...
...HE'S IN LOVE WITH YOU."

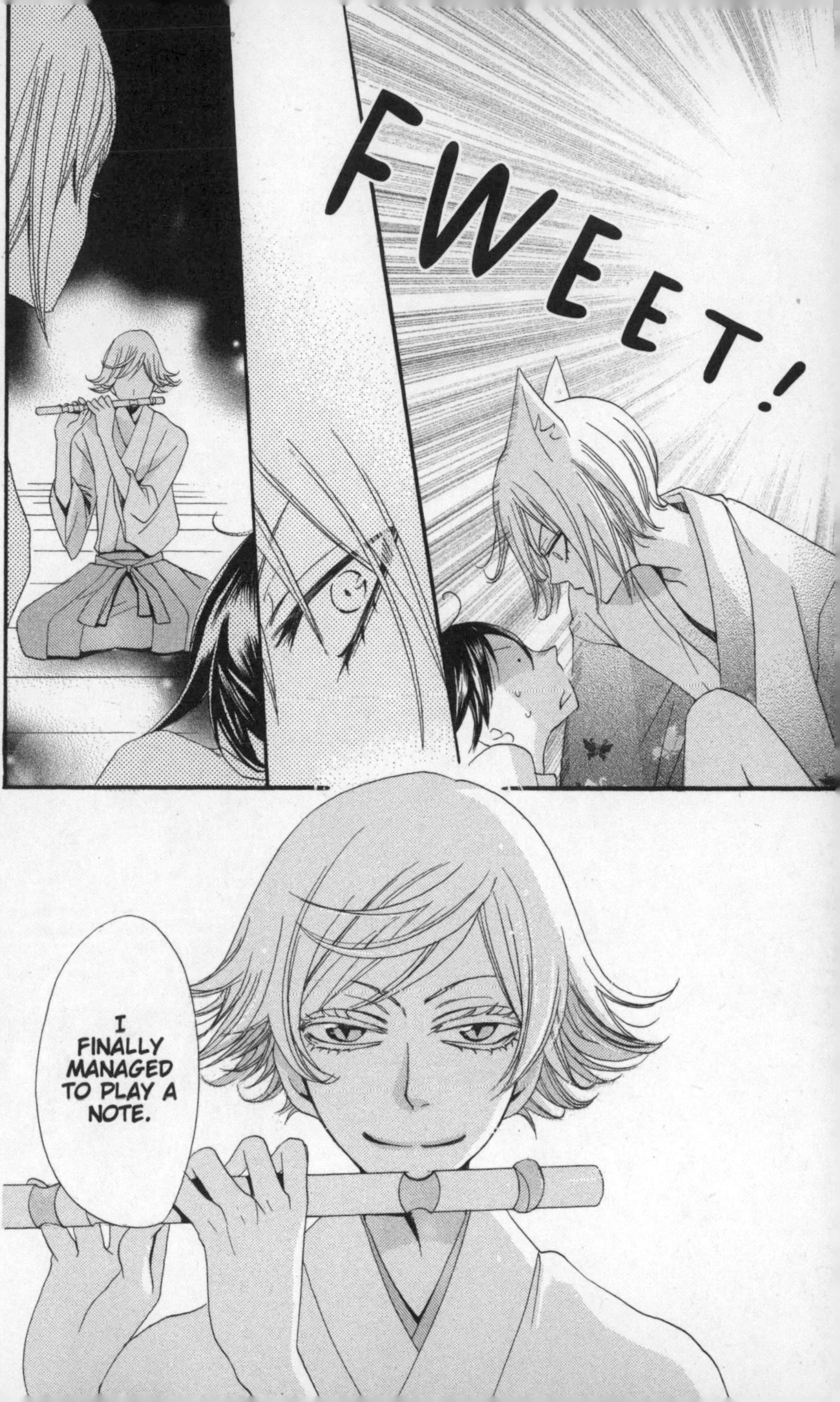
FWEET!
I FINALLY MANAGED TO PLAY A NOTE.

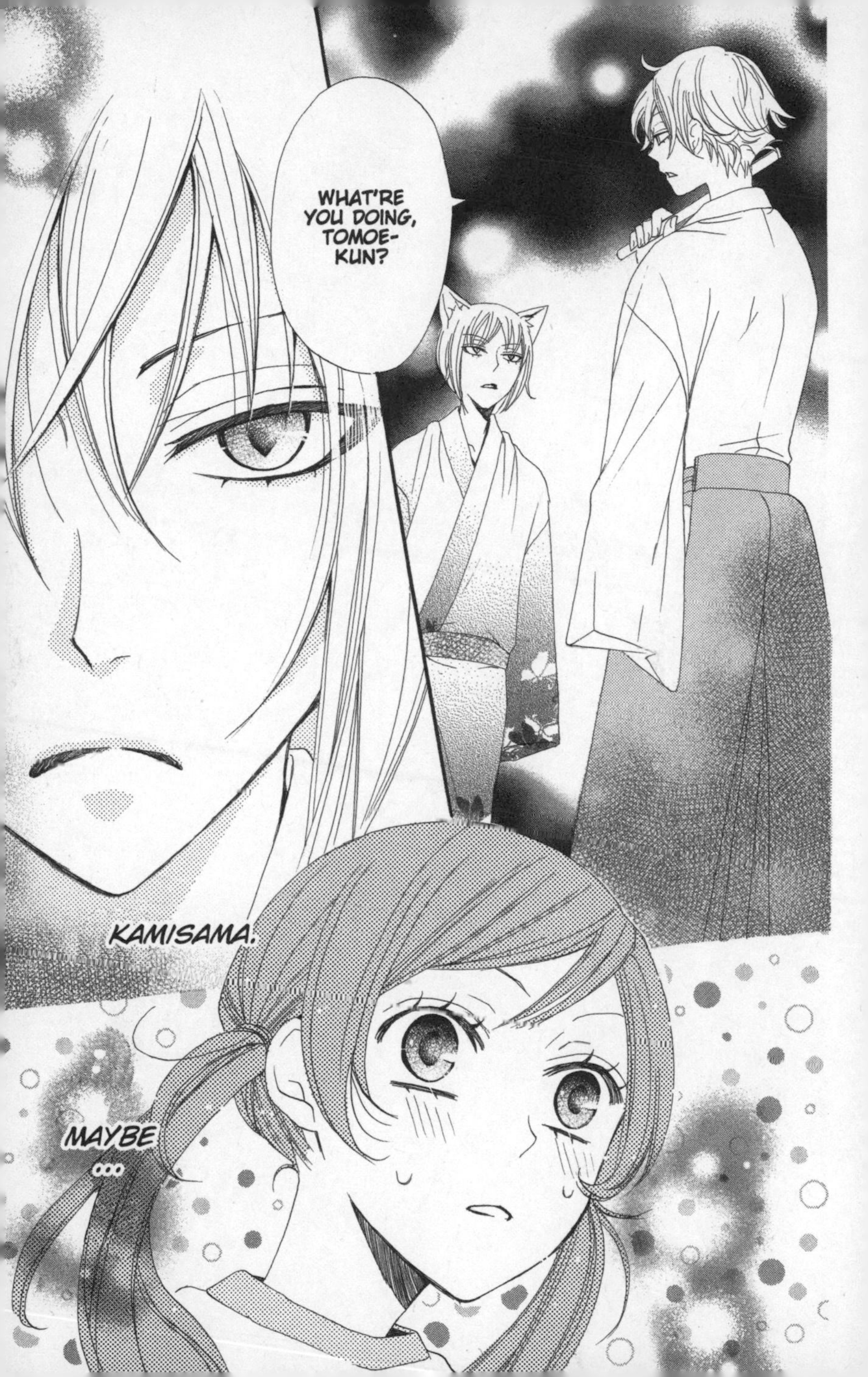
WHAT'RE YOU DOING, TOMOE-KUN?
KAMISAMA.
MAYBE ...

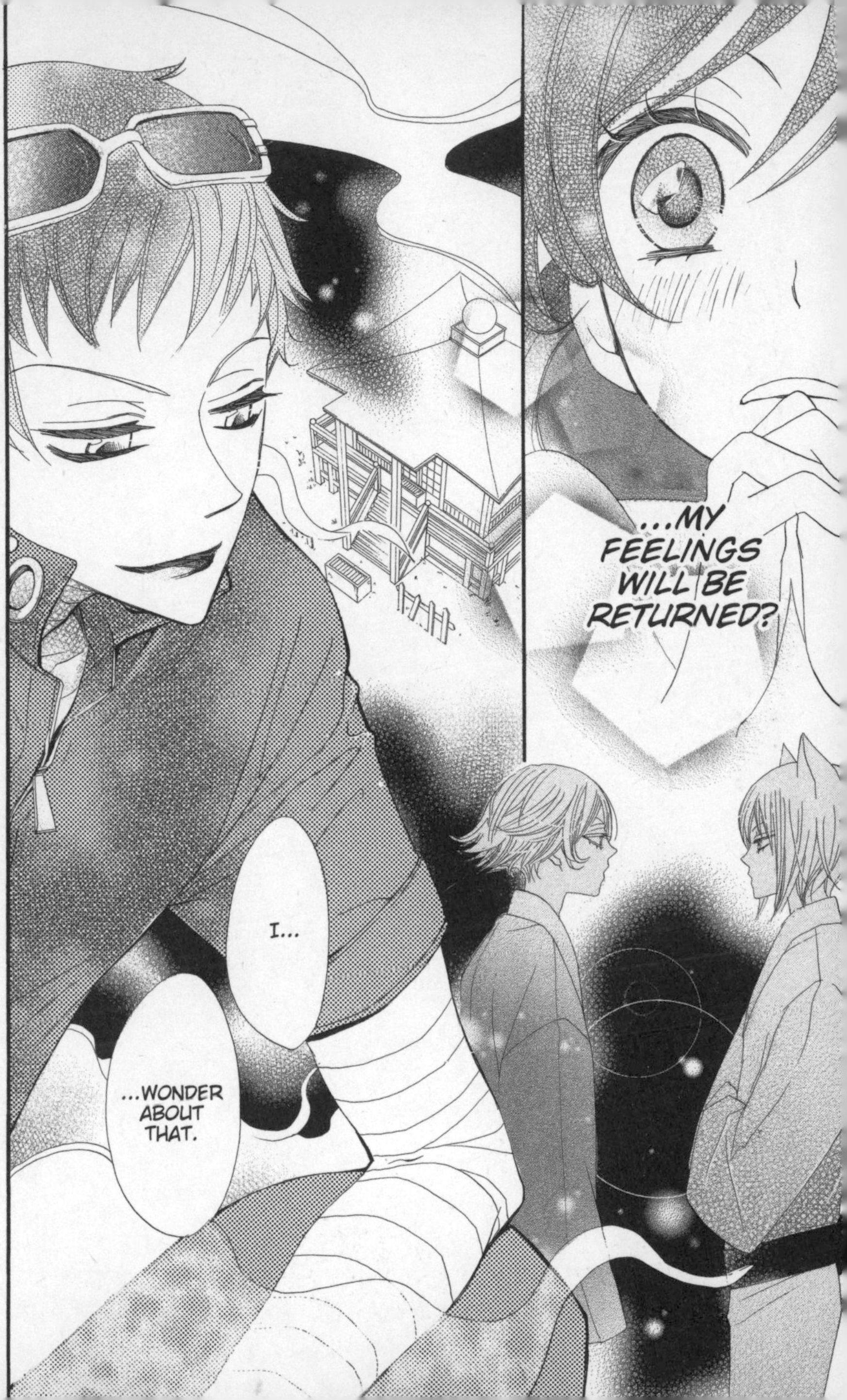
...MY FEELINGS WILL BE RETURNED?
I...
...WONDER ABOUT THAT.

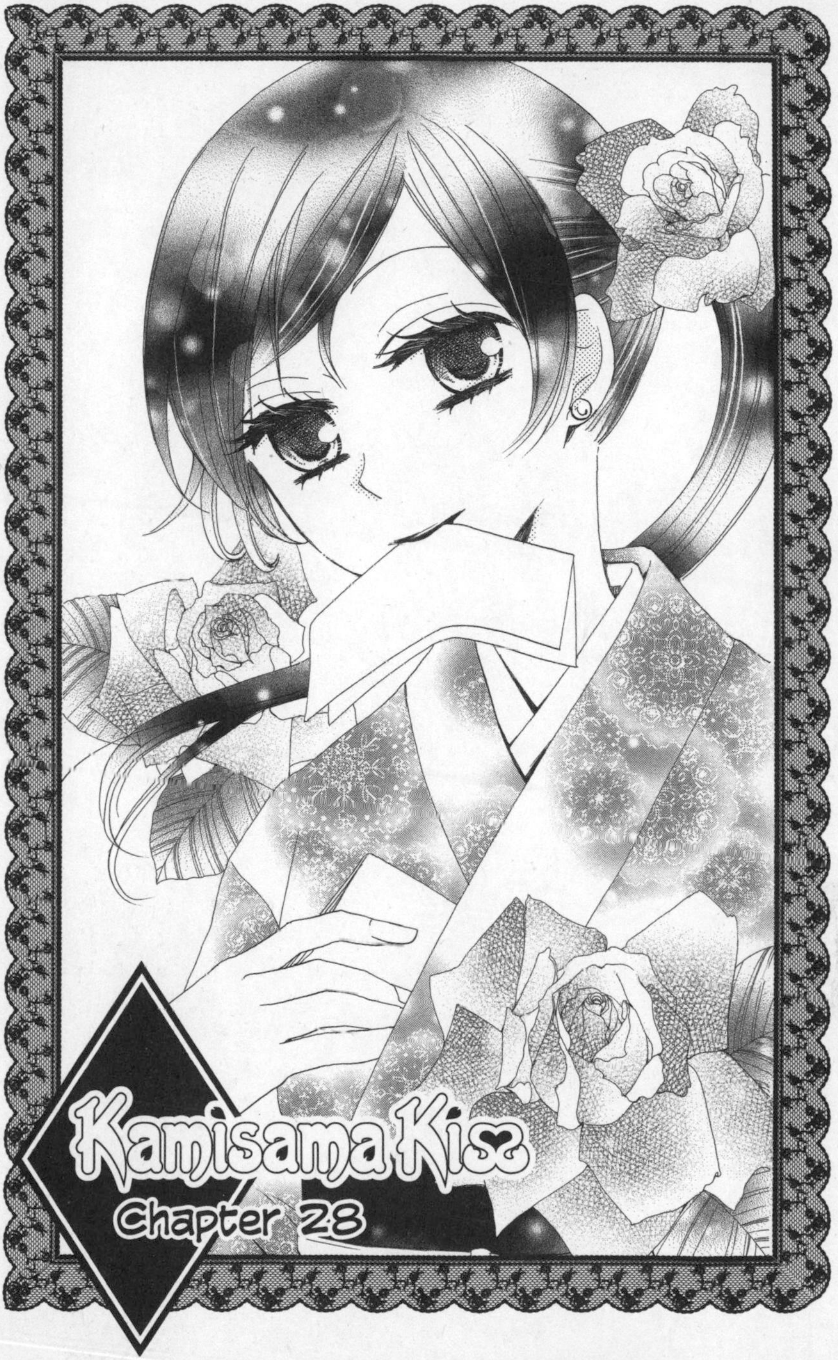
Kamisama Kiss
Chapter 28

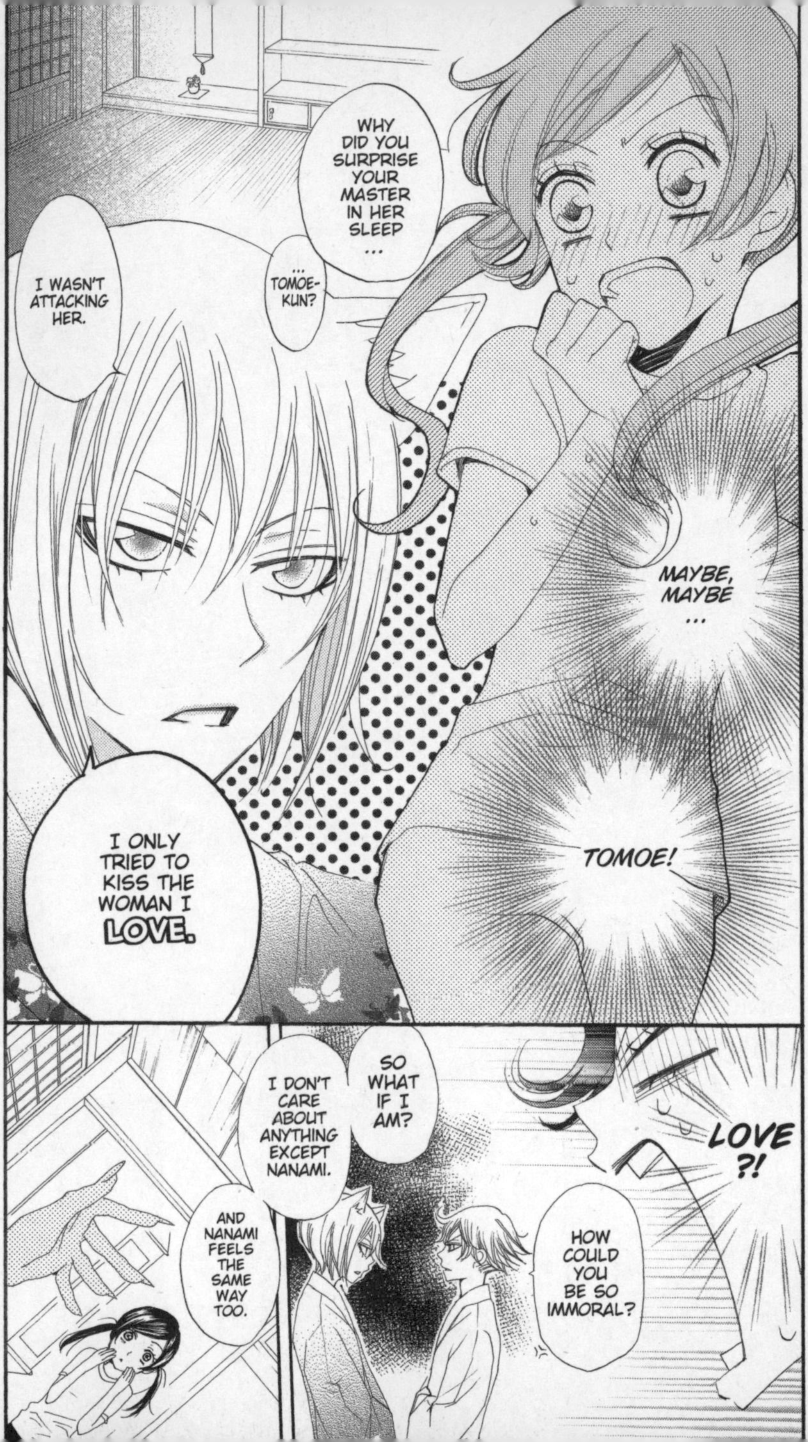
WHY DID YOU SURPRISE YOUR MASTER IN HER SLEEP ...
... TOMOE-KUN?
I WASN'T ATTACKING HER.
MAYBE, MAYBE ...
TOMOE!
I ONLY TRIED TO KISS THE WOMAN I LOVE.
LOVE ?!
HOW COULD YOU BE SO IMMORAL?
SO WHAT IF I AM?
I DON'T CARE ABOUT ANYTHING EXCEPT NANAMI.
AND NANAMI FEELS THE SAME WAY TOO.

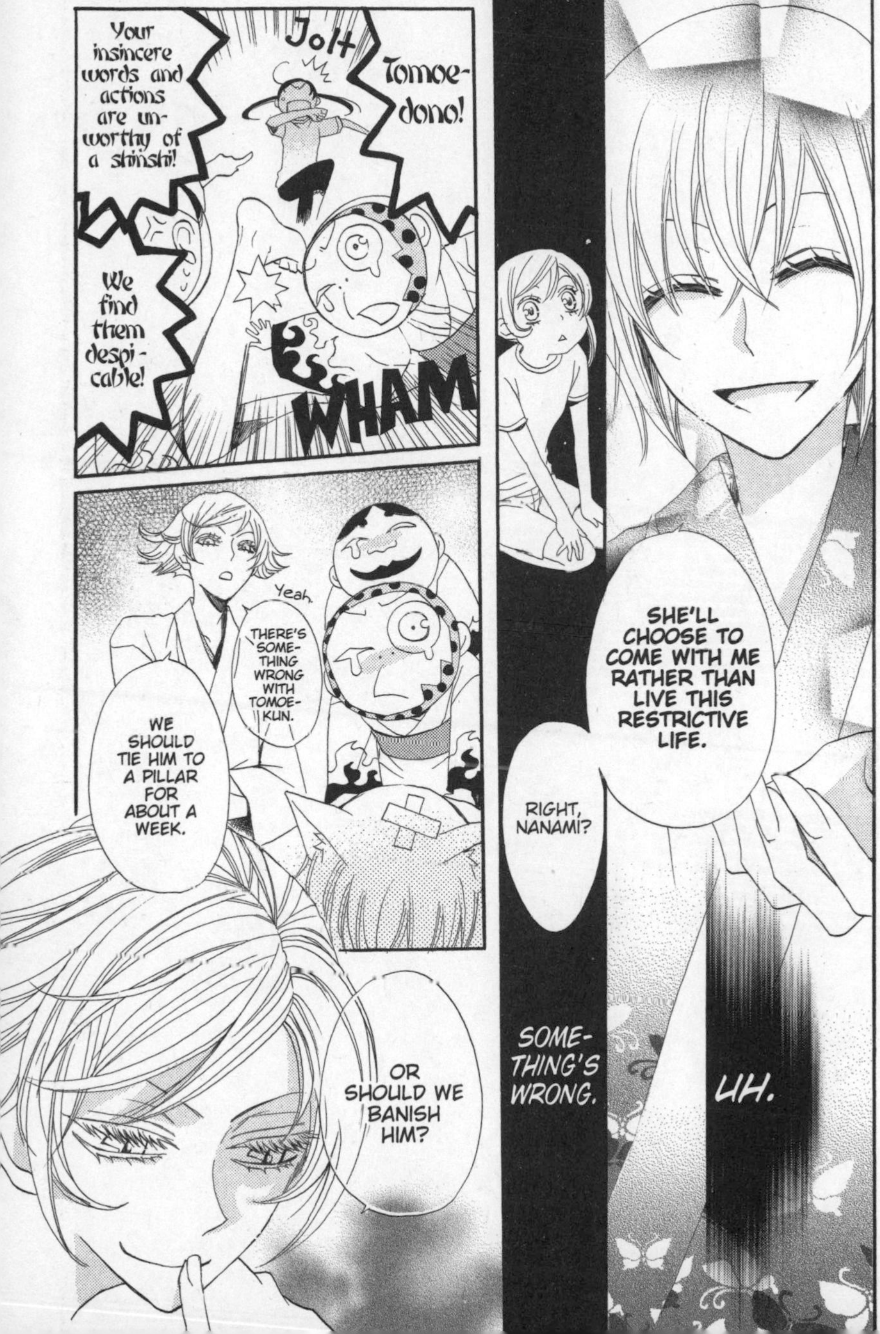
SHE'LL CHOOSE TO COME WITH ME RATHER THAN LIVE THIS RESTRICTIVE LIFE.
RIGHT, NANAMI?
UH.
SOME-THING'S WRONG.
Jolt
Tomoe-dono!
Your insincere words and actions are unworthy of a shinshi!
We find them despicable!
WHAM
Yeah.
THERE'S SOME-THING WRONG WITH TOMOE-KUN.
WE SHOULD TIE HIM TO A PILLAR FOR ABOUT A WEEK.
OR SHOULD WE BANISH HIM?

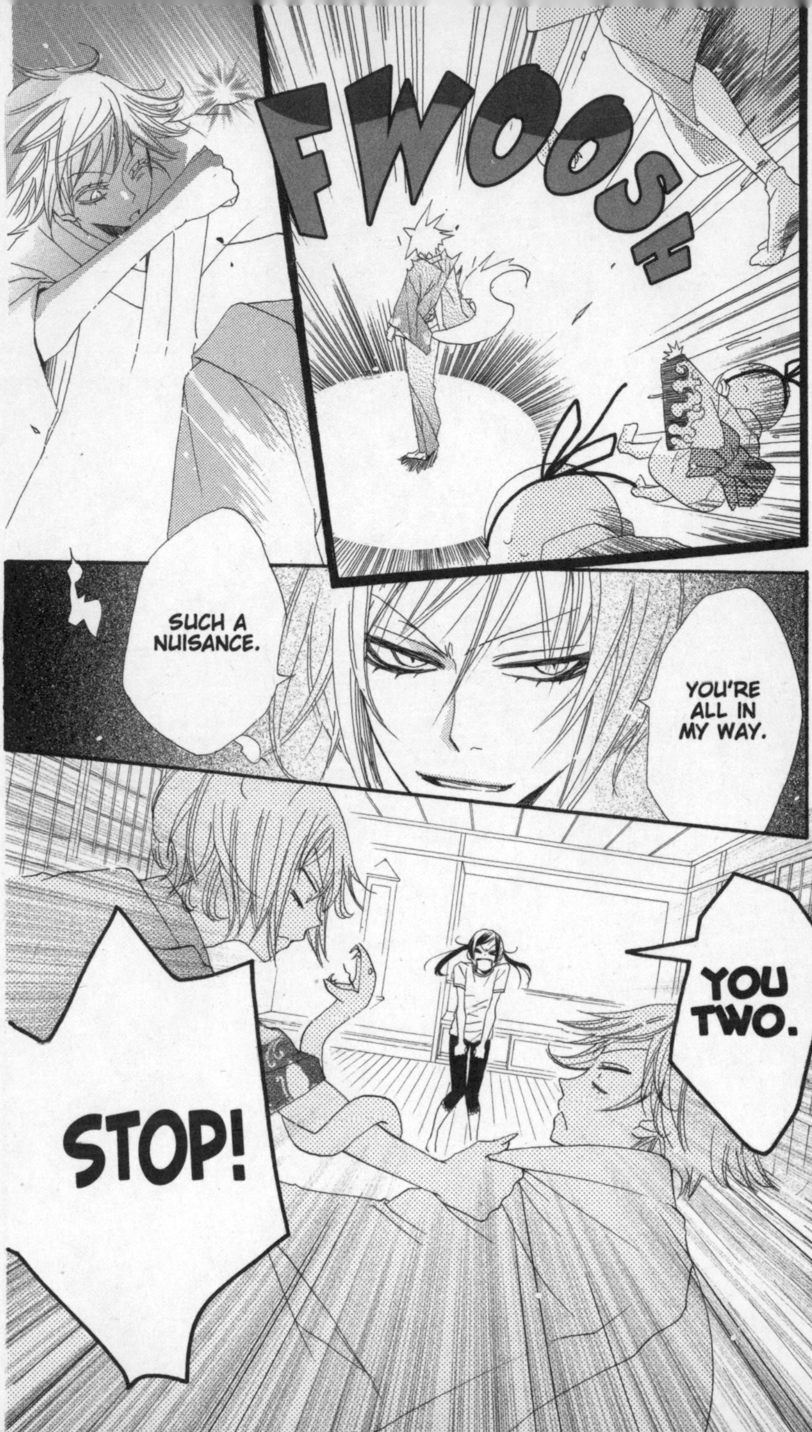
FWOOSH
YOU'RE ALL IN MY WAY.
SUCH A NUISANCE.
YOU TWO.
STOP!

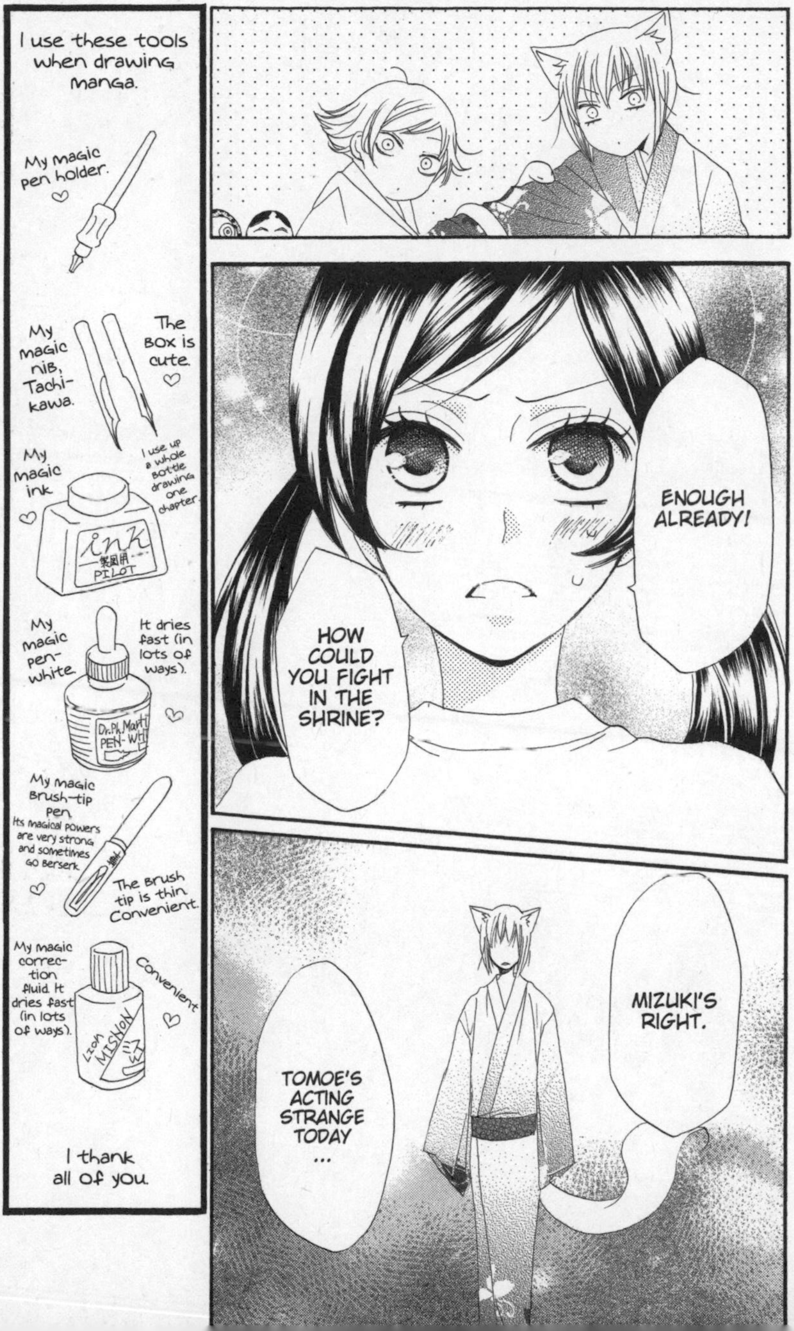
ENOUGH ALREADY!
HOW COULD YOU FIGHT IN THE SHRINE?
MIZUKI'S RIGHT.
TOMOE'S ACTING STRANGE TODAY ...
I use these tools when drawing manga.
My magic pen holder.
My magic nib, Tachi-kawa.
The box is cute.
My magic ink
I use up a whole bottle drawing one chapter.
ink
PILOT
My magic pen-white.
It dries fast (in lots of ways).
My magic brush-tip pen.
Its magical powers are very strong and sometimes go berserk.
The brush tip is thin. Convenient.
My magic correc-tion fluid. It dries fast (in lots of ways).
Convenient
Lion MISHON
I thank all of you.

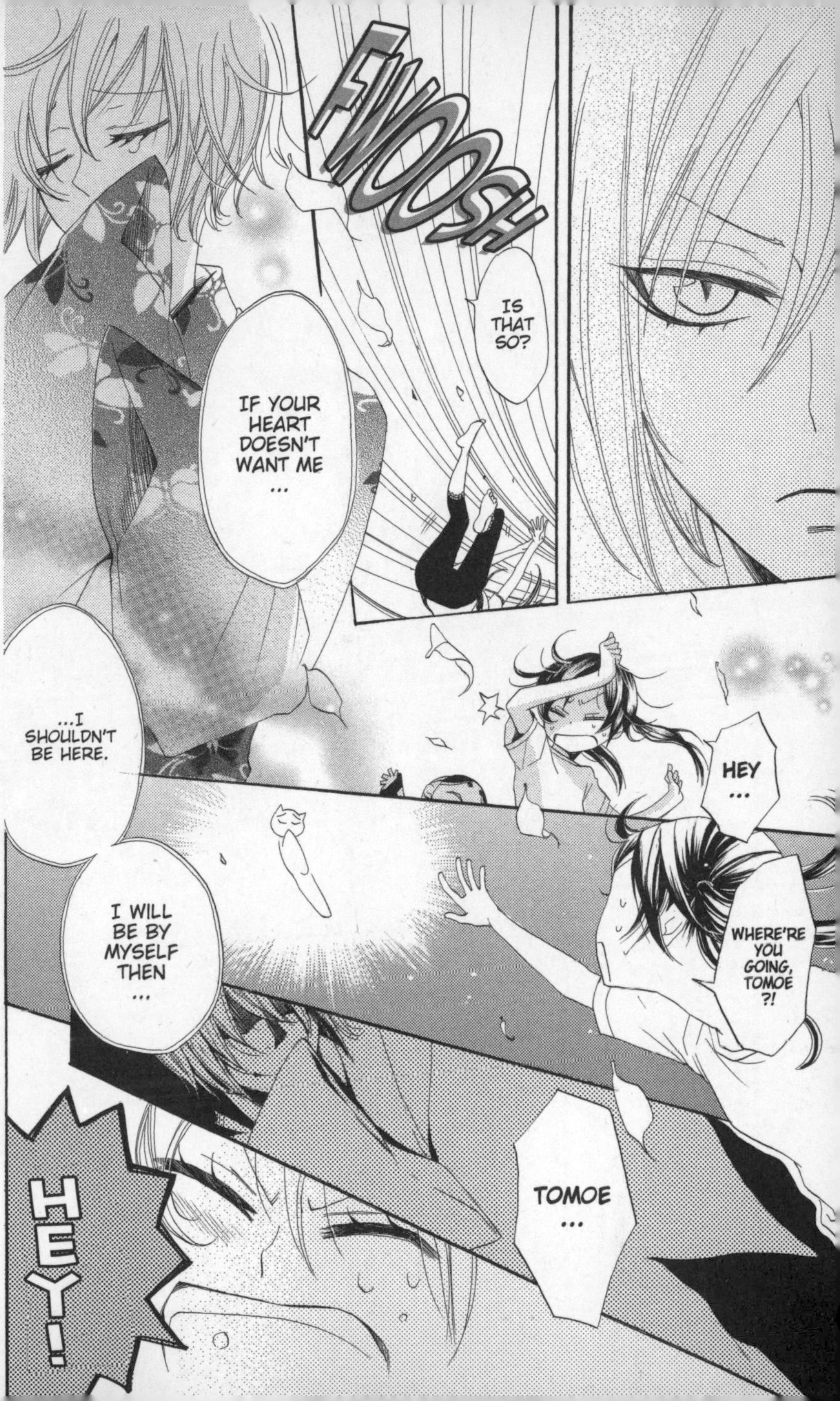
IS THAT SO?
IF YOUR HEART DOESN'T WANT ME ...
...I SHOULDN'T BE HERE.
I WILL BE BY MYSELF THEN ...
FWOOSH
HEY ...
WHERE'RE YOU GOING, TOMOE ?!
TOMOE ...
HEY HEY!

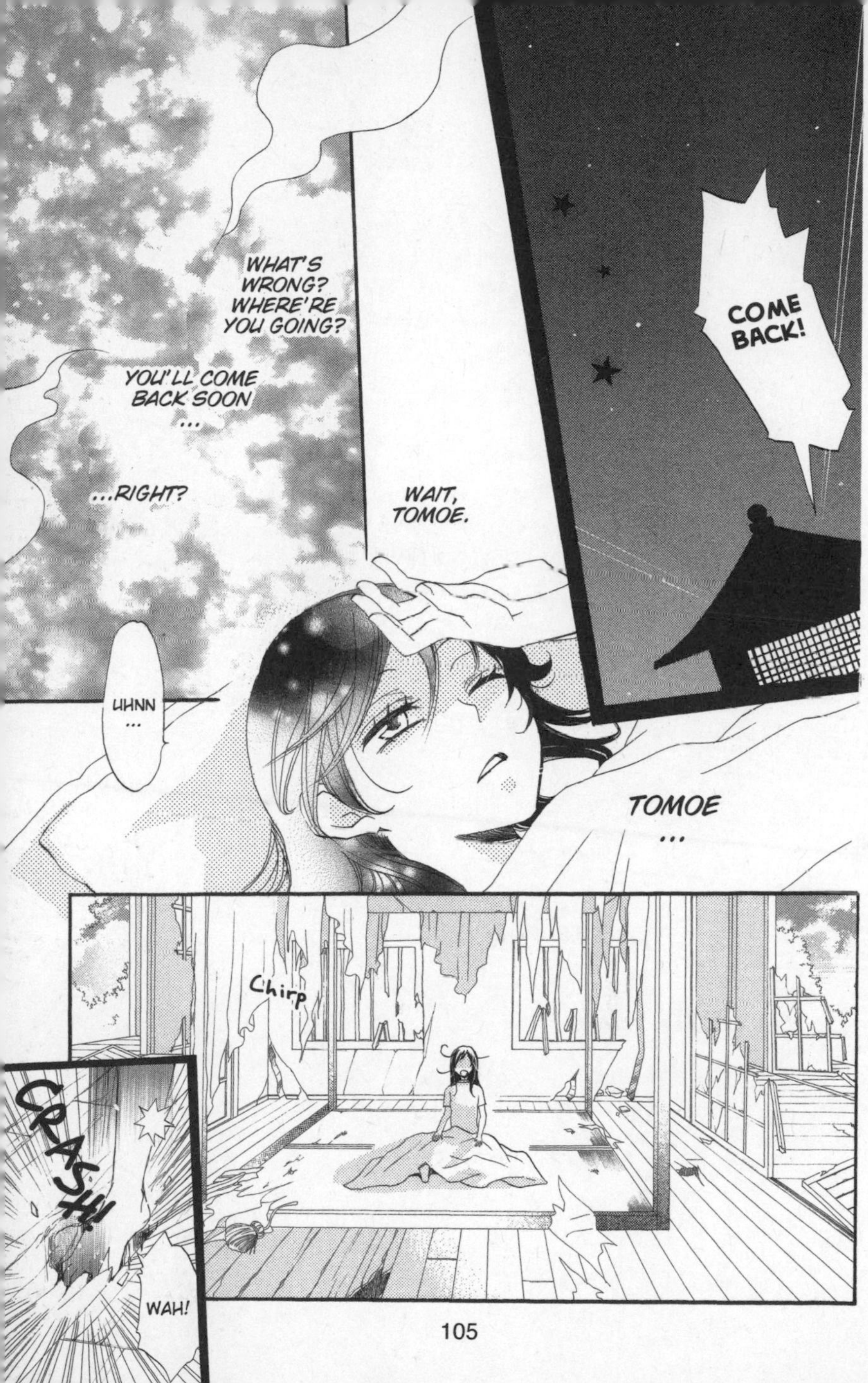
COME BACK!
WAIT, TOMOE.
WHAT'S WRONG? WHERE'RE YOU GOING?
YOU'LL COME BACK SOON ...
...RIGHT?
UHNN ...
TOMOE ...
Chirp
CRASH!
WAH!

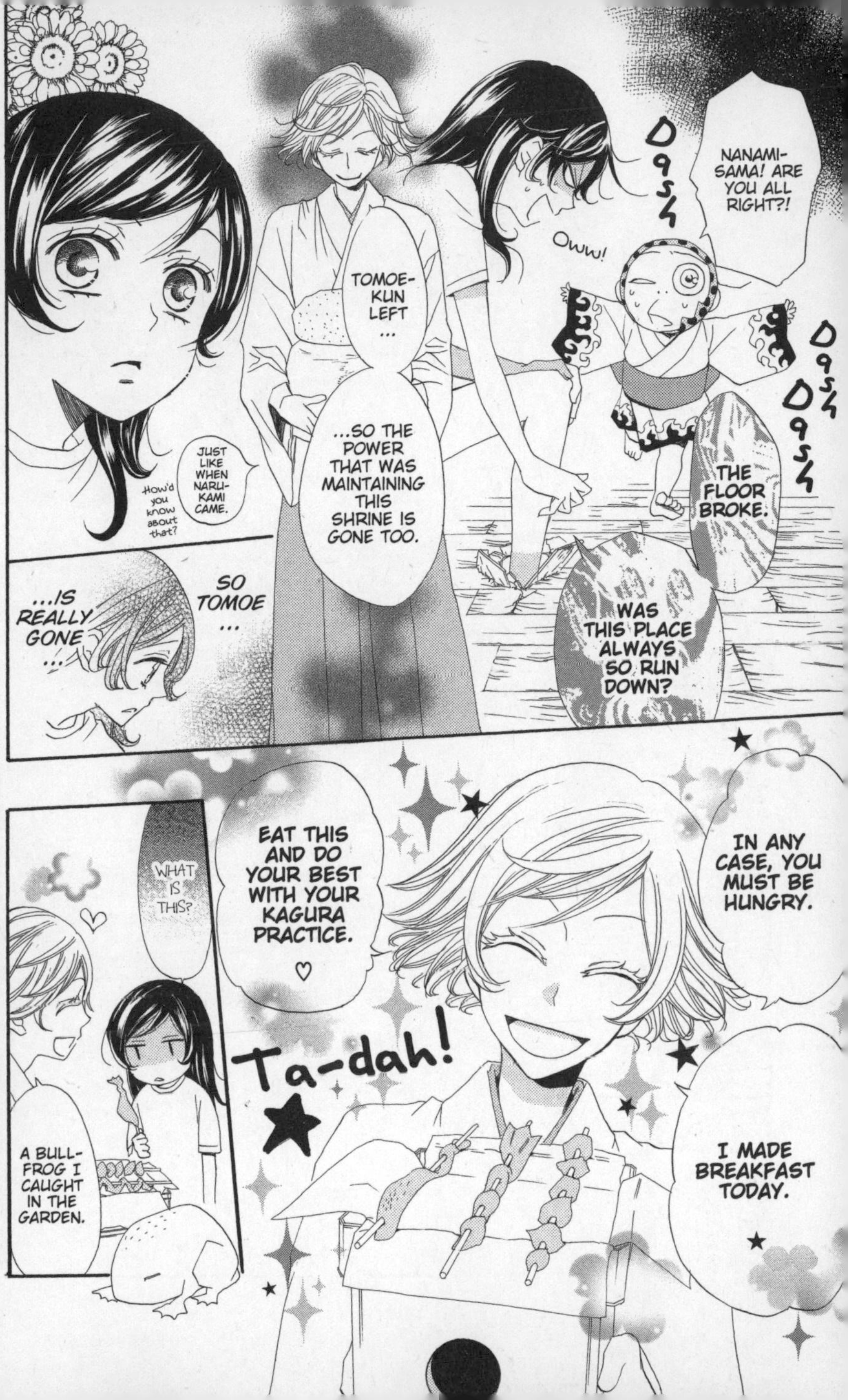
Dash
NANAMI-SAMA! ARE YOU ALL RIGHT?!
Oww!
Dash Dash
THE FLOOR BROKE.
WAS THIS PLACE ALWAYS SO RUN DOWN?
TOMOE-KUN LEFT...
...SO THE POWER THAT WAS MAINTAINING THIS SHRINE IS GONE TOO.
JUST LIKE WHEN NARU-KAMI CAME.
How'd you know about that?
SO TOMOE...
...IS REALLY GONE...
IN ANY CASE, YOU MUST BE HUNGRY.
I MADE BREAKFAST TODAY.
EAT THIS AND DO YOUR BEST WITH YOUR KAGURA PRACTICE. ♡
Ta-dah!
WHAT IS THIS?
A BULL-FROG I CAUGHT IN THE GARDEN.

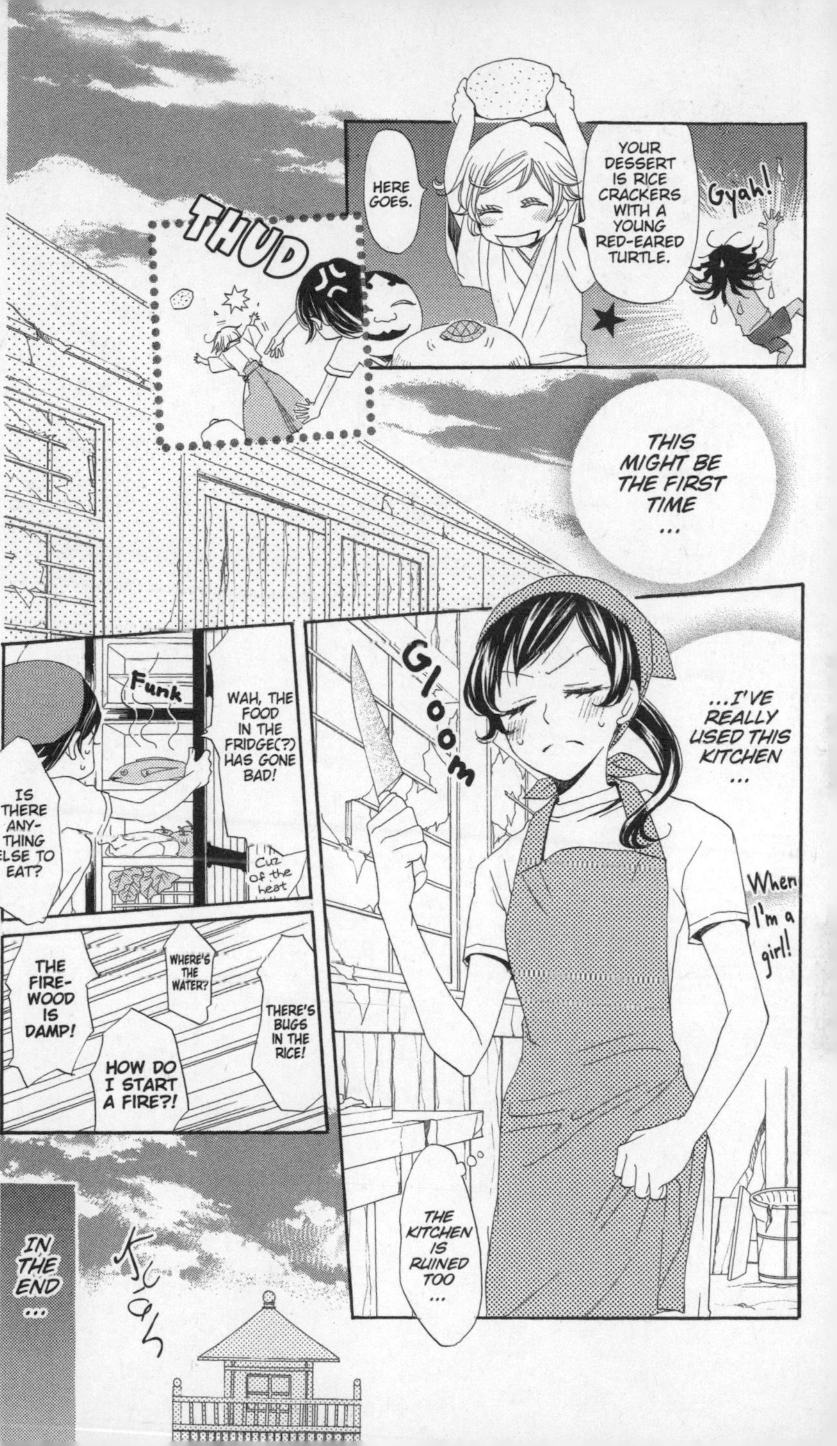
Gyah!
YOUR DESSERT IS RICE CRACKERS WITH A YOUNG RED-EARED TURTLE.
HERE GOES.
THUD
THIS MIGHT BE THE FIRST TIME ...
...I'VE REALLY USED THIS KITCHEN ...
When I'm a girl!
Gloom
THE KITCHEN IS RUINED TOO ...
WAH, THE FOOD IN THE FRIDGE(?) HAS GONE BAD!
Funk
IS THERE ANYTHING ELSE TO EAT?
Cuz of the heat
THERE'S BUGS IN THE RICE!
WHERE'S THE WATER?
THE FIREWOOD IS DAMP!
HOW DO I START A FIRE?!
IN THE END ...

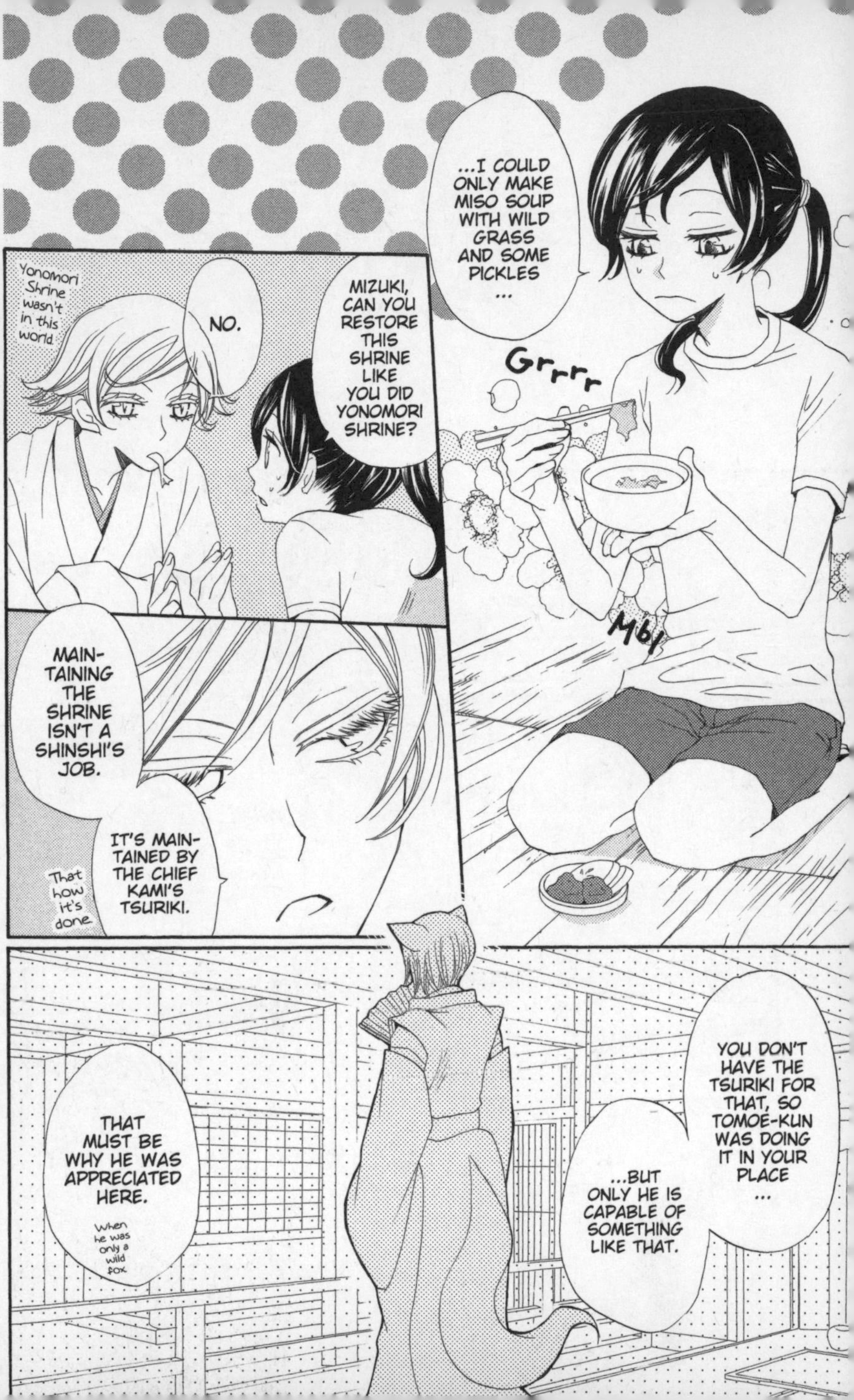
...I COULD ONLY MAKE MISO SOUP WITH WILD GRASS AND SOME PICKLES ...
Grrrr
Mbl
MIZUKI, CAN YOU RESTORE THIS SHRINE LIKE YOU DID YONOMORI SHRINE?
NO.
Yonomori Shrine wasn't in this world.
MAIN-TAINING THE SHRINE ISN'T A SHINSHI'S JOB.
IT'S MAIN-TAINED BY THE CHIEF KAMI'S TSURIKI.
That how it's done.
YOU DON'T HAVE THE TSURIKI FOR THAT, SO TOMOE-KUN WAS DOING IT IN YOUR PLACE ...
...BUT ONLY HE IS CAPABLE OF SOMETHING LIKE THAT.
THAT MUST BE WHY HE WAS APPRECIATED HERE.
When he was only a wild fox.

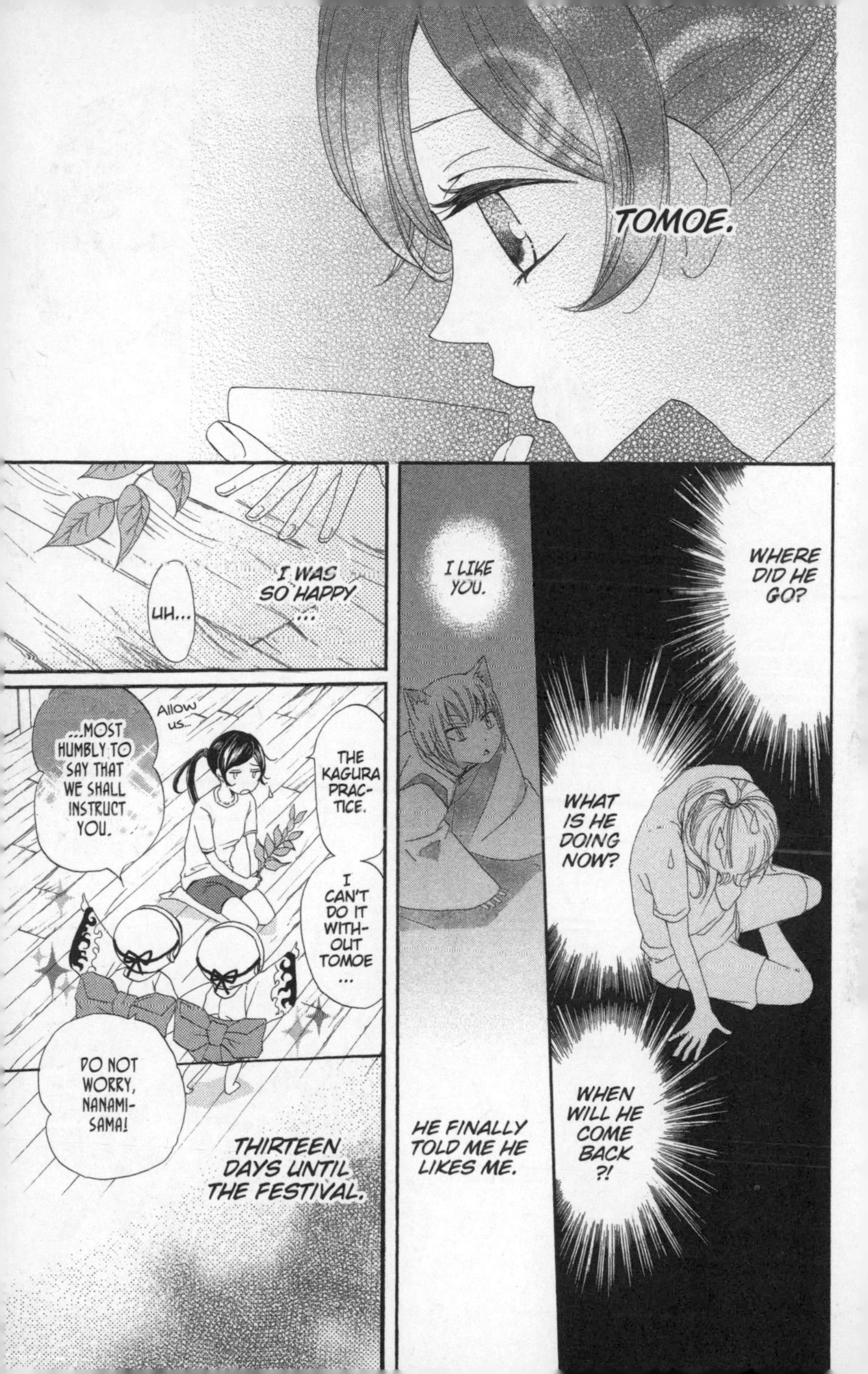
TOMOE.
WHERE DID HE GO?
WHAT IS HE DOING NOW?
WHEN WILL HE COME BACK?!
I LIKE YOU.
HE FINALLY TOLD ME HE LIKES ME.
I WAS SO HAPPY...
UH...
THE KAGURA PRACTICE.
I CAN'T DO IT WITHOUT TOMOE...
Allow us...
...MOST HUMBLY TO SAY THAT WE SHALL INSTRUCT YOU.
DO NOT WORRY, NANAMI-SAMA!
THIRTEEN DAYS UNTIL THE FESTIVAL.

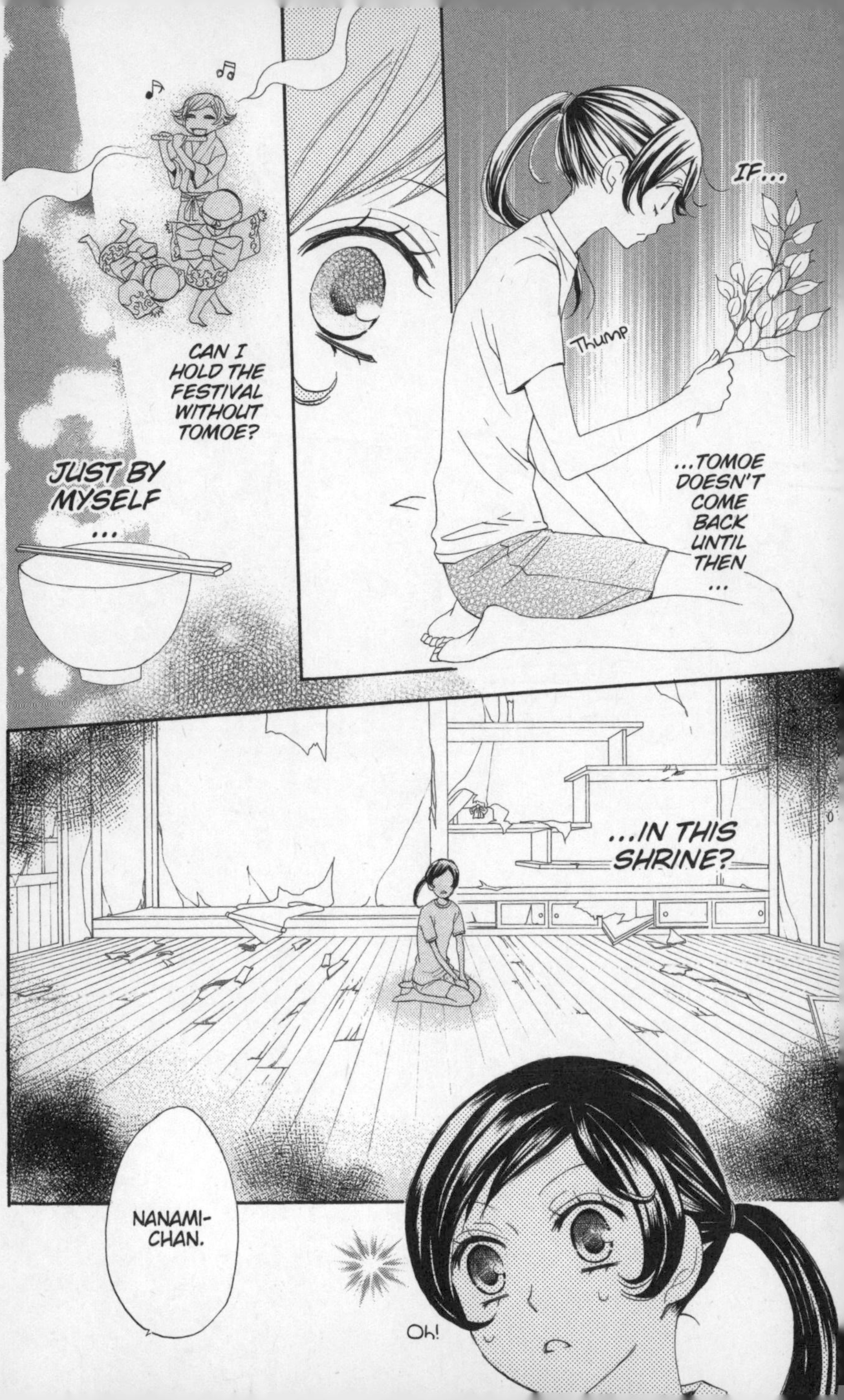
IF...
Thump
...TOMOE DOESN'T COME BACK UNTIL THEN...
CAN I HOLD THE FESTIVAL WITHOUT TOMOE?
JUST BY MYSELF...
...IN THIS SHRINE?
NANAMI-CHAN.
Oh!

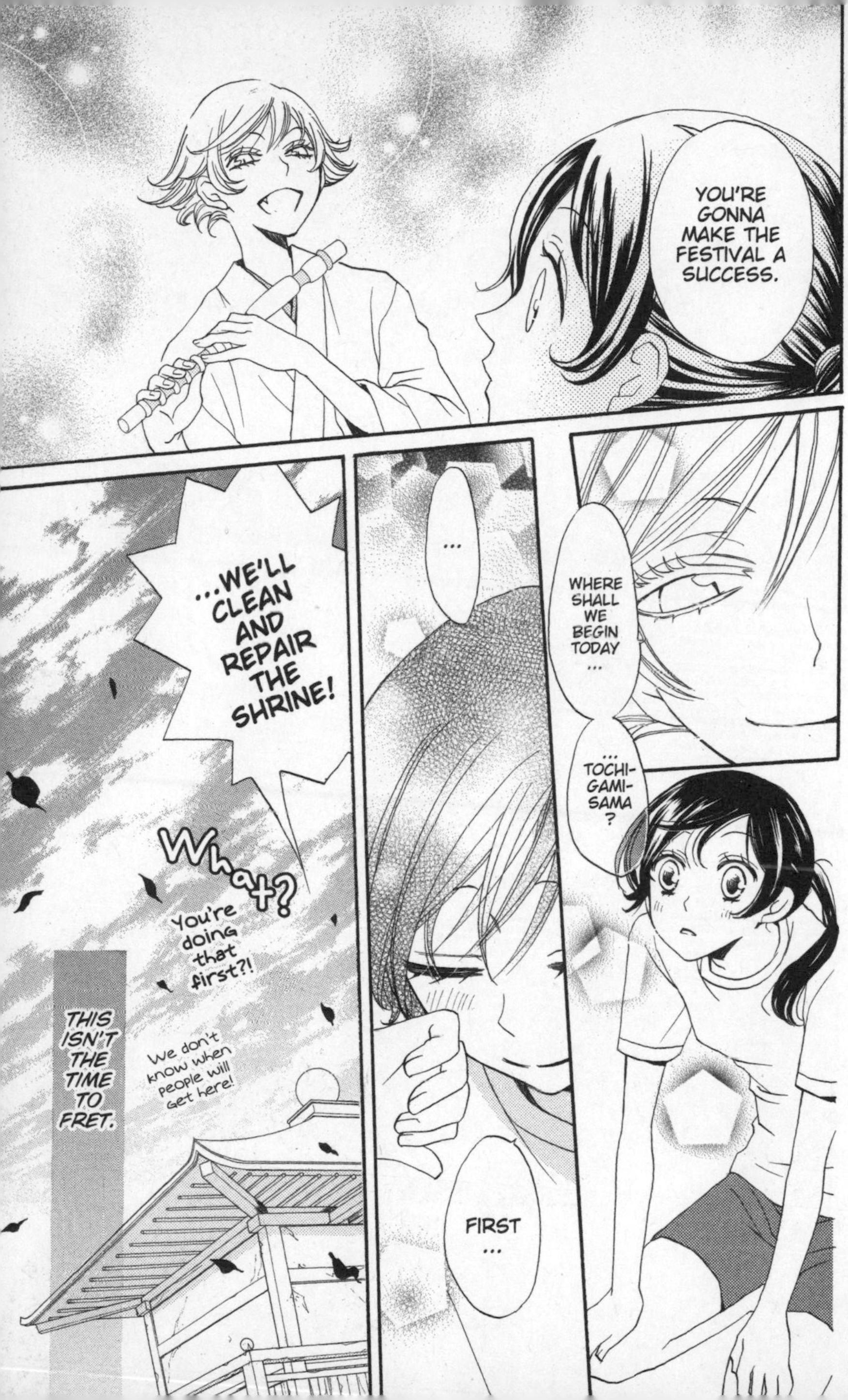
YOU'RE GONNA MAKE THE FESTIVAL A SUCCESS.
WHERE SHALL WE BEGIN TODAY ...
... TOCHI-GAMI-SAMA ?
...
FIRST ...
...WE'LL CLEAN AND REPAIR THE SHRINE!
What?
You're doing that first?!
THIS ISN'T THE TIME TO FRET.
We don't know when people will get here!

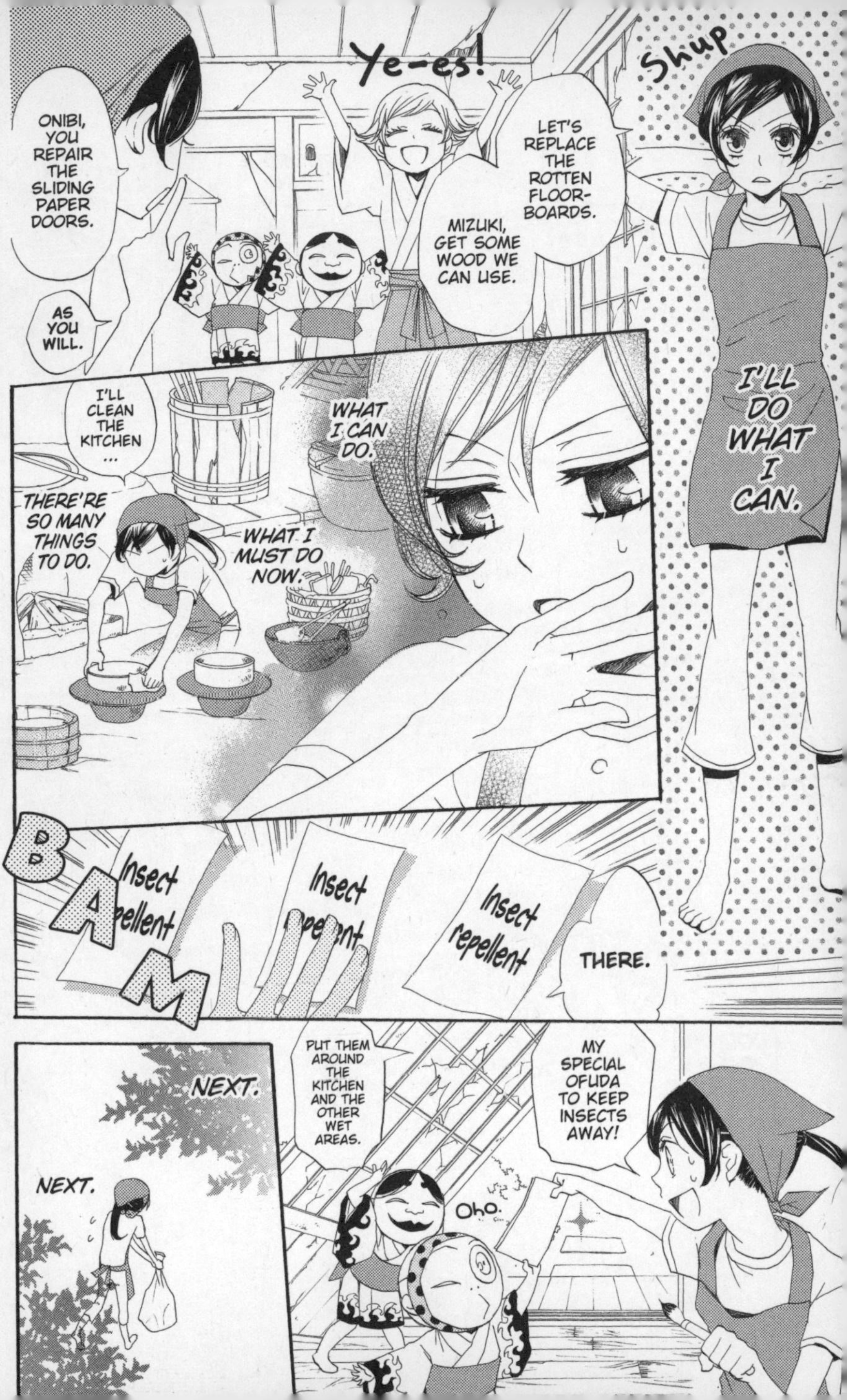
Shup
I'LL DO WHAT I CAN.
LET'S REPLACE THE ROTTEN FLOOR-BOARDS.
MIZUKI, GET SOME WOOD WE CAN USE.
Ye-es!
ONIBI, YOU REPAIR THE SLIDING PAPER DOORS.
AS YOU WILL.
WHAT I CAN DO.
I'LL CLEAN THE KITCHEN ...
WHAT I MUST DO NOW.
THERE'RE SO MANY THINGS TO DO.
THERE.
Insect repellent
Insect repellent
Insect repellent
BAM
MY SPECIAL OFUDA TO KEEP INSECTS AWAY!
PUT THEM AROUND THE KITCHEN AND THE OTHER WET AREAS.
Oho.
NEXT.
NEXT.

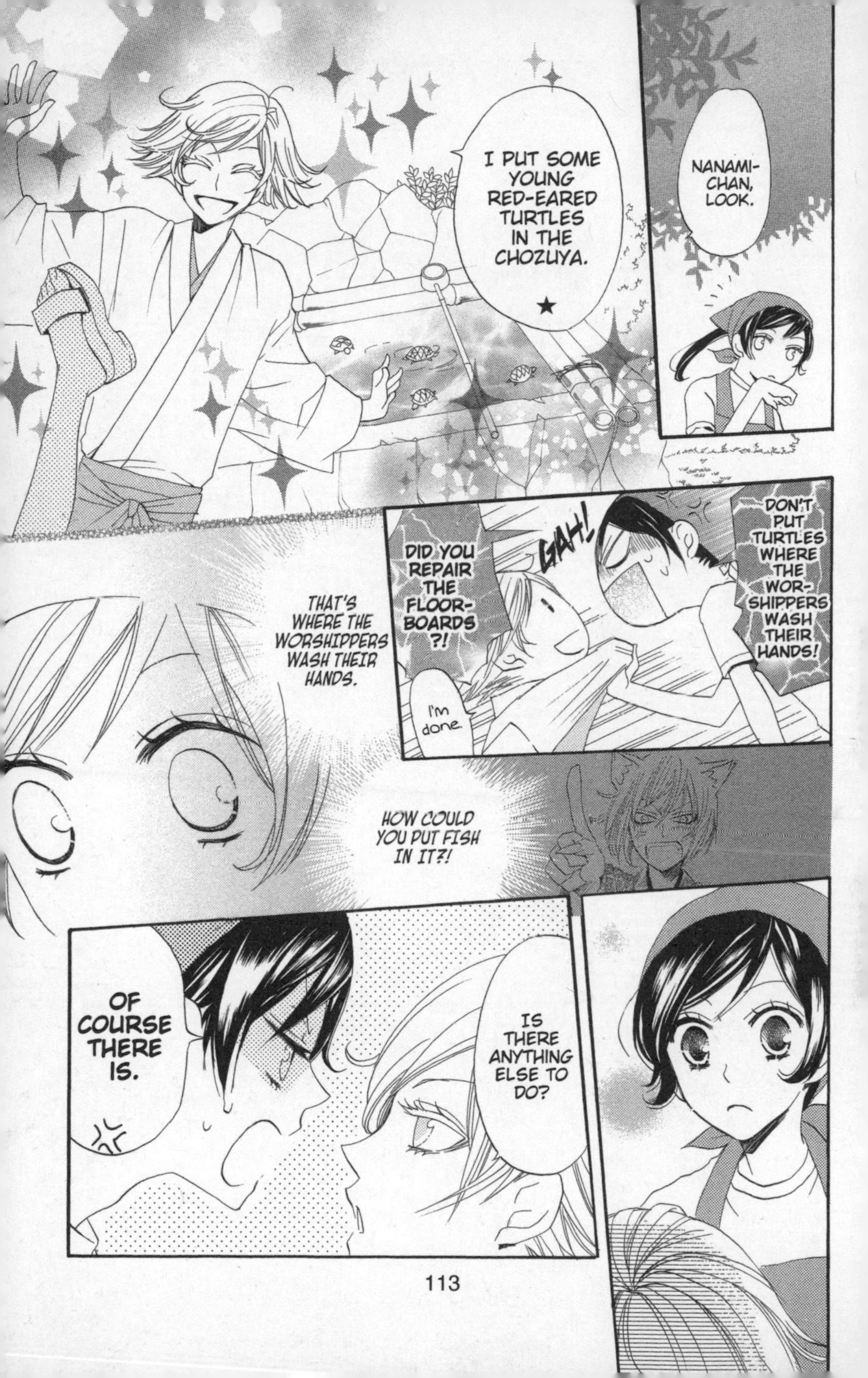
NANAMI-CHAN, LOOK.
I PUT SOME YOUNG RED-EARED TURTLES IN THE CHOZUYA. ★
DON'T PUT TURTLES WHERE THE WOR-SHIPPERS WASH THEIR HANDS!
GAH!
DID YOU REPAIR THE FLOOR-BOARDS?!
I'm done.
THAT'S WHERE THE WORSHIPPERS WASH THEIR HANDS.
HOW COULD YOU PUT FISH IN IT?!
IS THERE ANYTHING ELSE TO DO?
OF COURSE THERE IS.

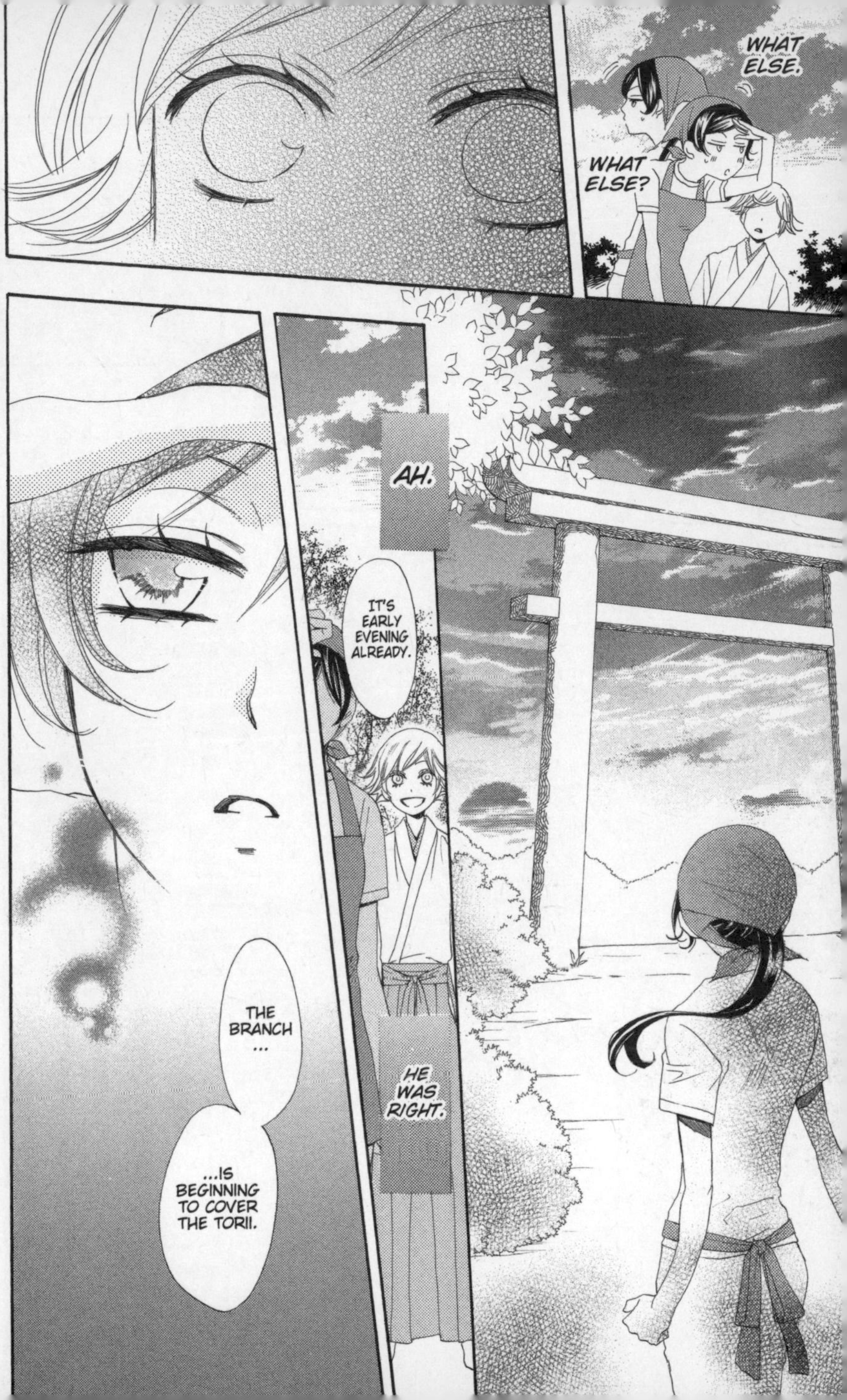
WHAT ELSE.
WHAT ELSE?
AH.
IT'S EARLY EVENING ALREADY.
HE WAS RIGHT.
THE BRANCH...
...IS BEGINNING TO COVER THE TORII.

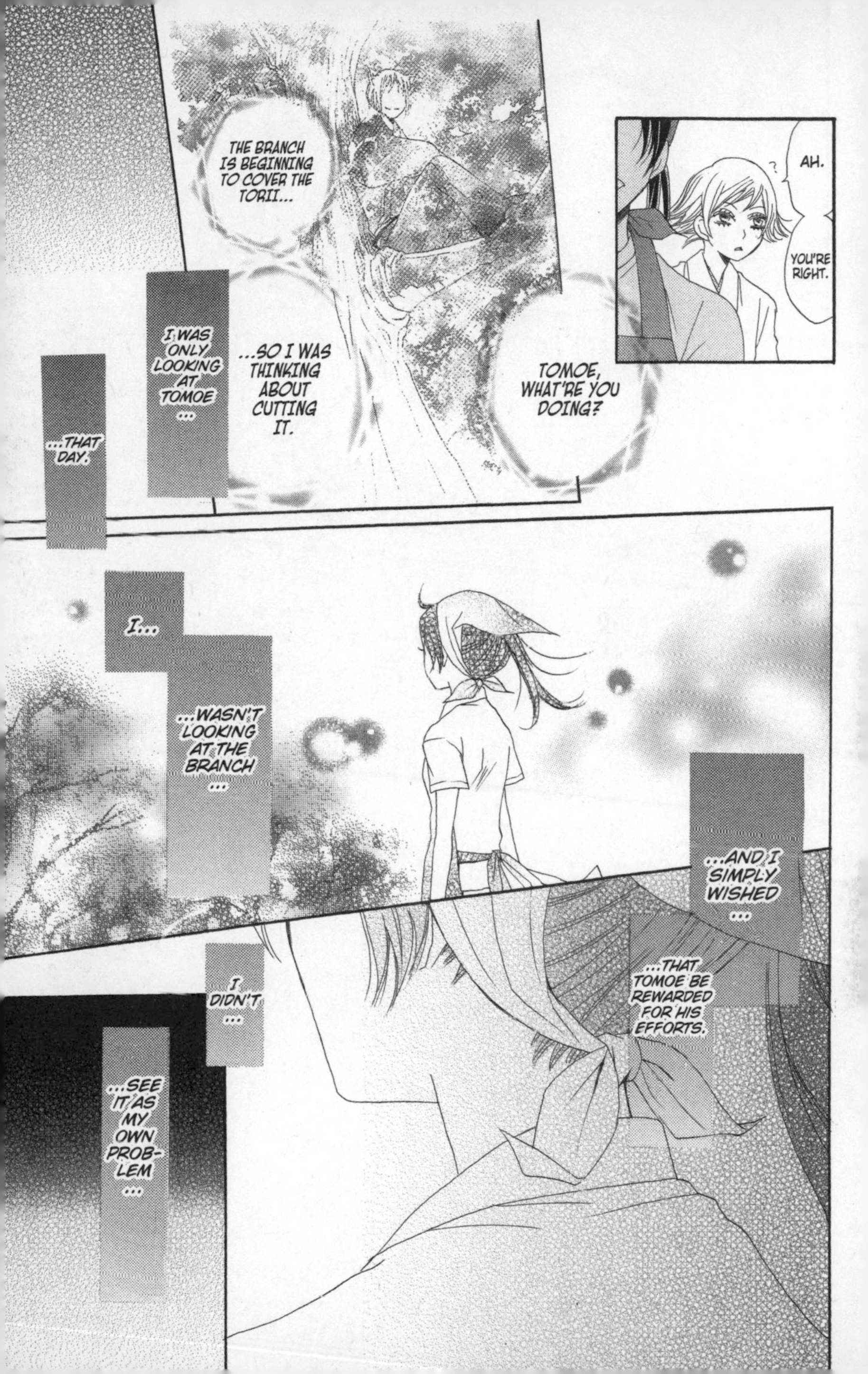
TOMOE, WHAT'RE YOU DOING?
THE BRANCH IS BEGINNING TO COVER THE TORII...
...SO I WAS THINKING ABOUT CUTTING IT.
?
AH.
YOU'RE RIGHT.
I WAS ONLY LOOKING AT TOMOE...
...THAT DAY.
I...
...WASN'T LOOKING AT THE BRANCH...
...AND I SIMPLY WISHED...
...THAT TOMOE BE REWARDED FOR HIS EFFORTS.
I DIDN'T...
...SEE IT AS MY OWN PROB-LEM...

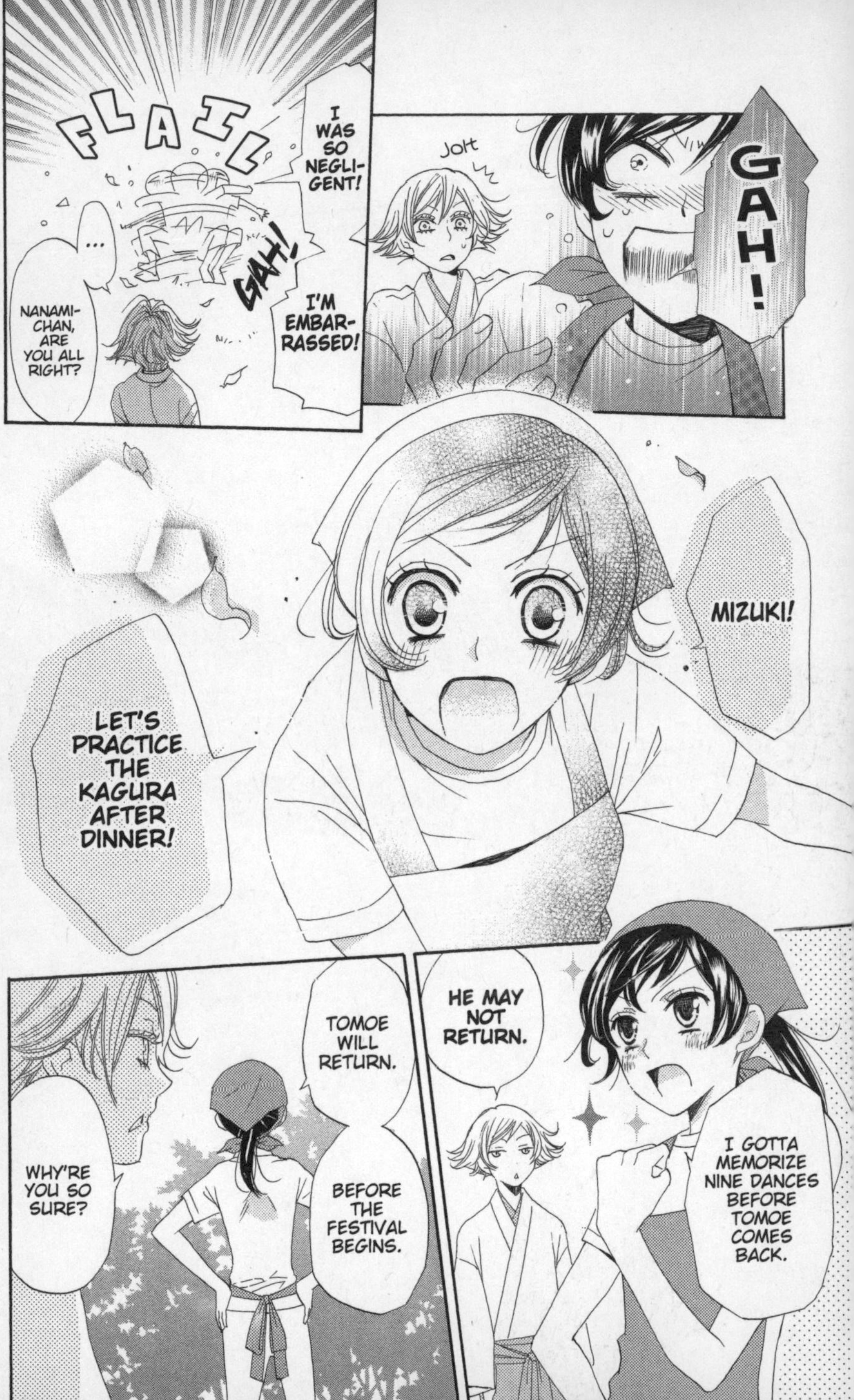
GAH!
Jolt
I WAS SO NEGLIGENT!
FLAIL
GAH!
I'M EMBARRASSED!
...
NANAMI-CHAN, ARE YOU ALL RIGHT?
MIZUKI!
LET'S PRACTICE THE KAGURA AFTER DINNER!
I GOTTA MEMORIZE NINE DANCES BEFORE TOMOE COMES BACK.
HE MAY NOT RETURN.
TOMOE WILL RETURN.
BEFORE THE FESTIVAL BEGINS.
WHY'RE YOU SO SURE?

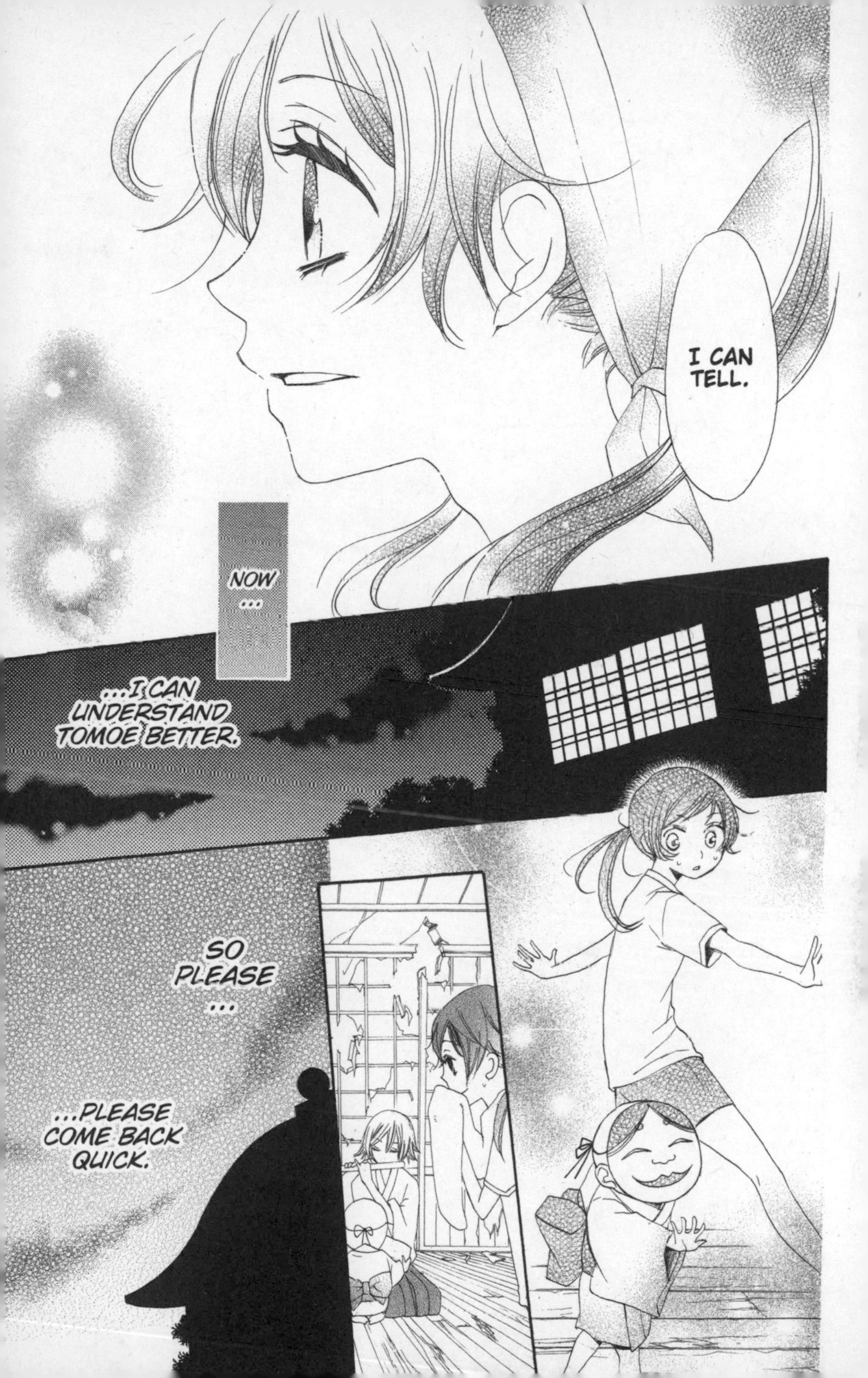
I CAN TELL.
NOW ...
...I CAN UNDERSTAND TOMOE BETTER.
SO PLEASE ...
...PLEASE COME BACK QUICK.

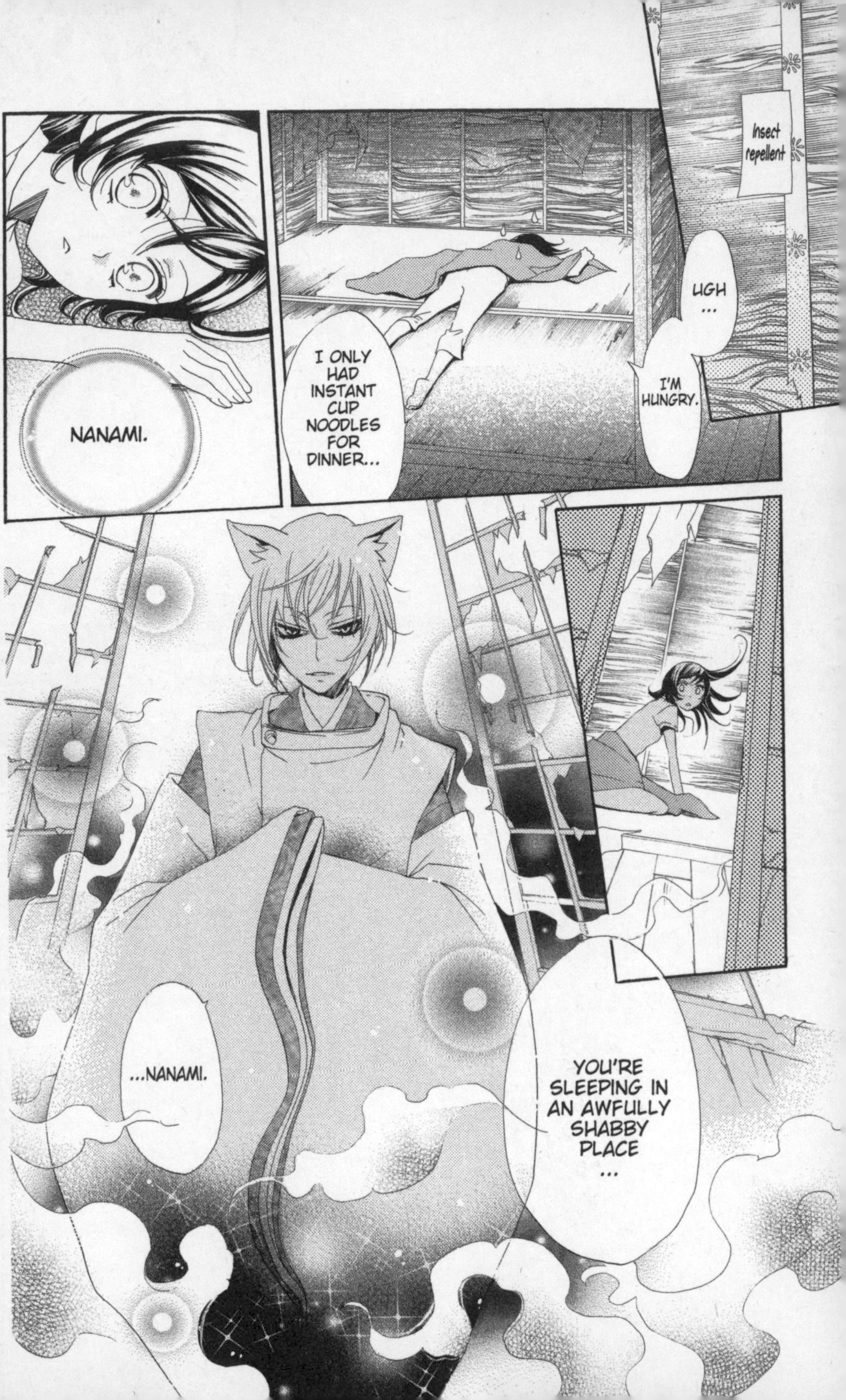
Insect repellent
UGH...
I'M HUNGRY.
I ONLY HAD INSTANT CUP NOODLES FOR DINNER...
NANAMI.
YOU'RE SLEEPING IN AN AWFULLY SHABBY PLACE...
...NANAMI.

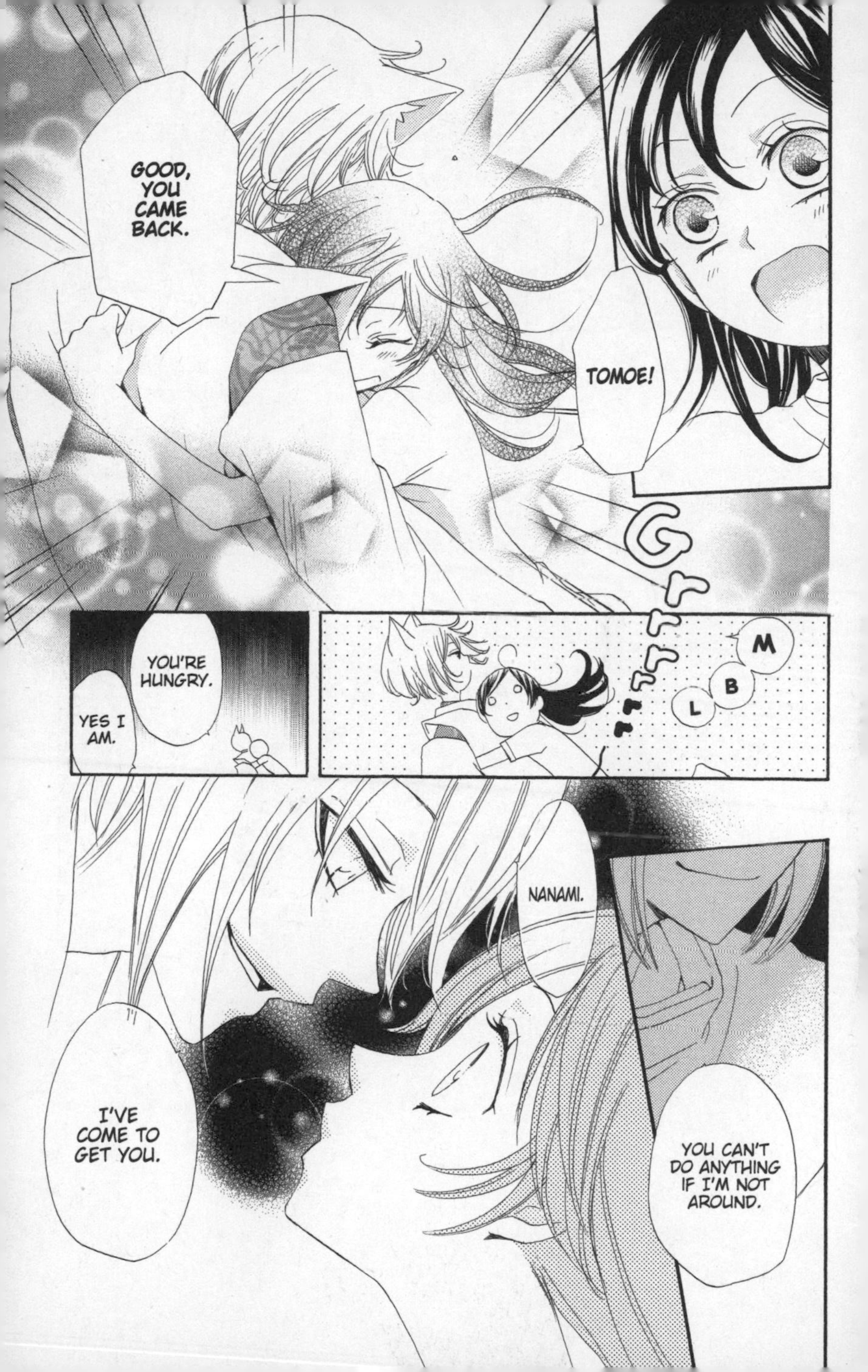
TOMOE!
GOOD, YOU CAME BACK.
Grrrr...
MBL
YOU'RE HUNGRY.
YES I AM.
NANAMI.
YOU CAN'T DO ANYTHING IF I'M NOT AROUND.
I'VE COME TO GET YOU.

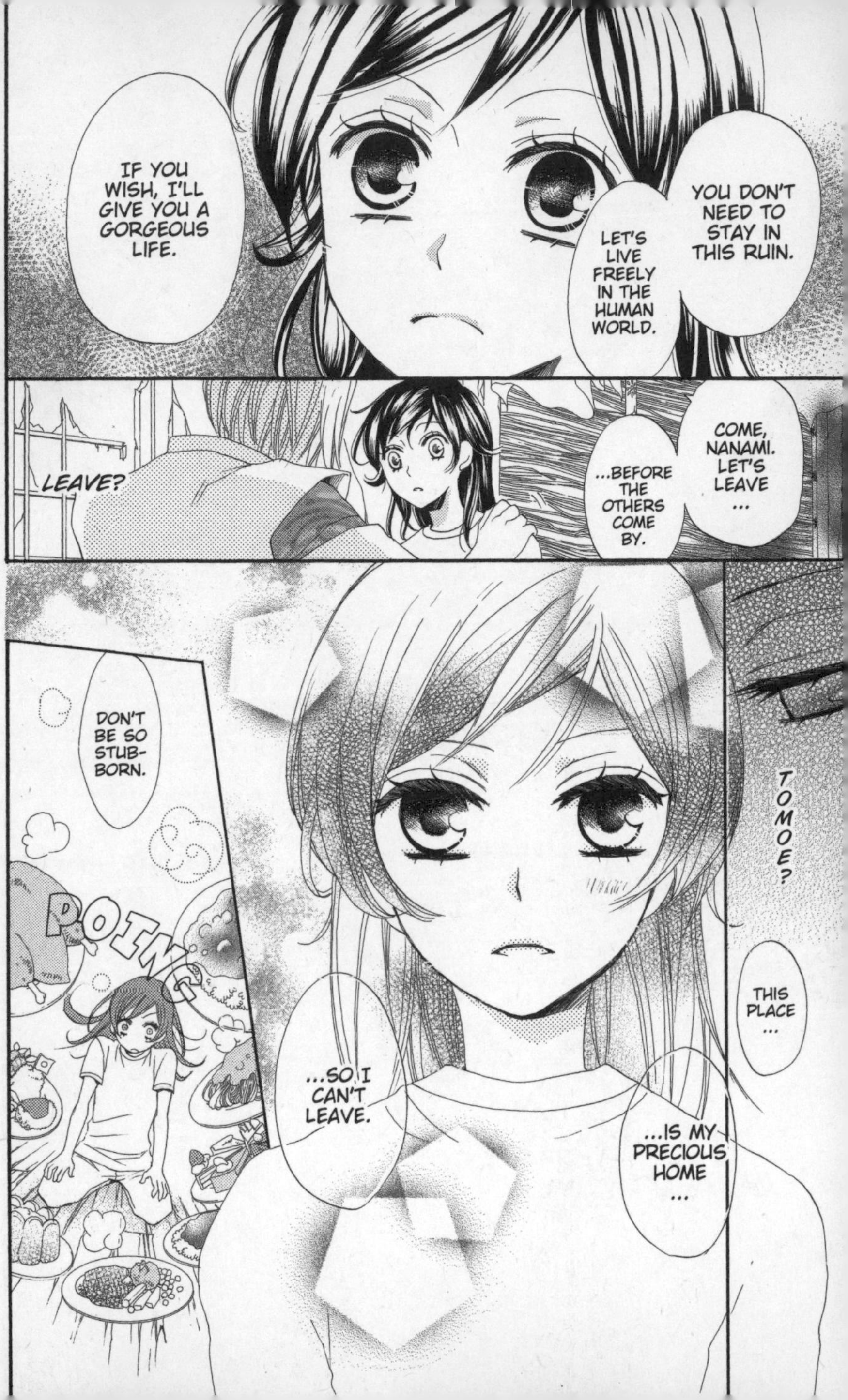
YOU DON'T NEED TO STAY IN THIS RUIN.
LET'S LIVE FREELY IN THE HUMAN WORLD.
IF YOU WISH, I'LL GIVE YOU A GORGEOUS LIFE.
COME, NANAMI. LET'S LEAVE ...
...BEFORE THE OTHERS COME BY.
LEAVE?
TOMOE?
THIS PLACE ...
...IS MY PRECIOUS HOME ...
...SO I CAN'T LEAVE.
DON'T BE SO STUB-BORN.
POING

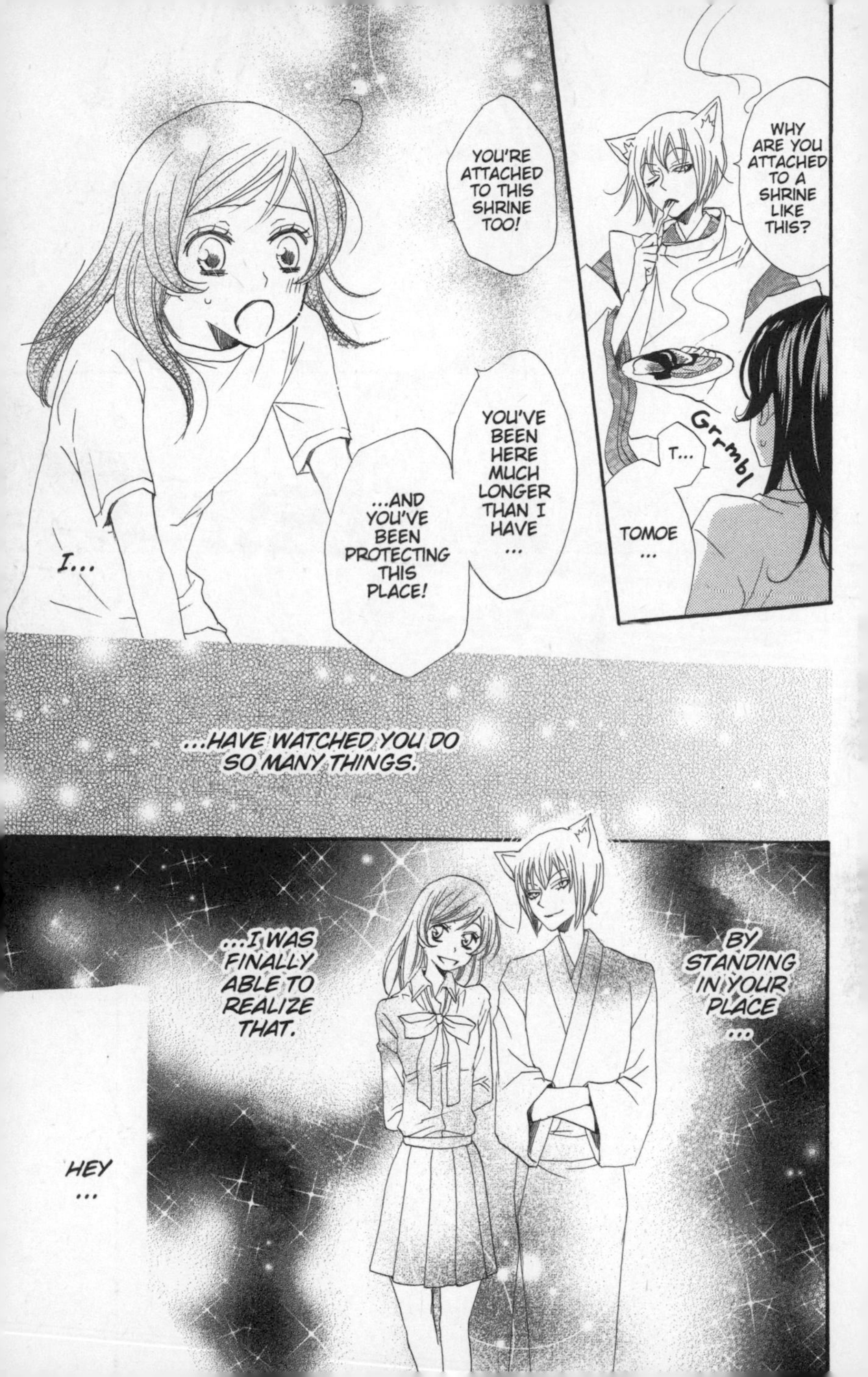
WHY ARE YOU ATTACHED TO A SHRINE LIKE THIS?
Grrmbl
T...
TOMOE ...
YOU'RE ATTACHED TO THIS SHRINE TOO!
YOU'VE BEEN HERE MUCH LONGER THAN I HAVE ...
...AND YOU'VE BEEN PROTECTING THIS PLACE!
I...
...HAVE WATCHED YOU DO SO MANY THINGS.
BY STANDING IN YOUR PLACE ...
...I WAS FINALLY ABLE TO REALIZE THAT.
HEY ...

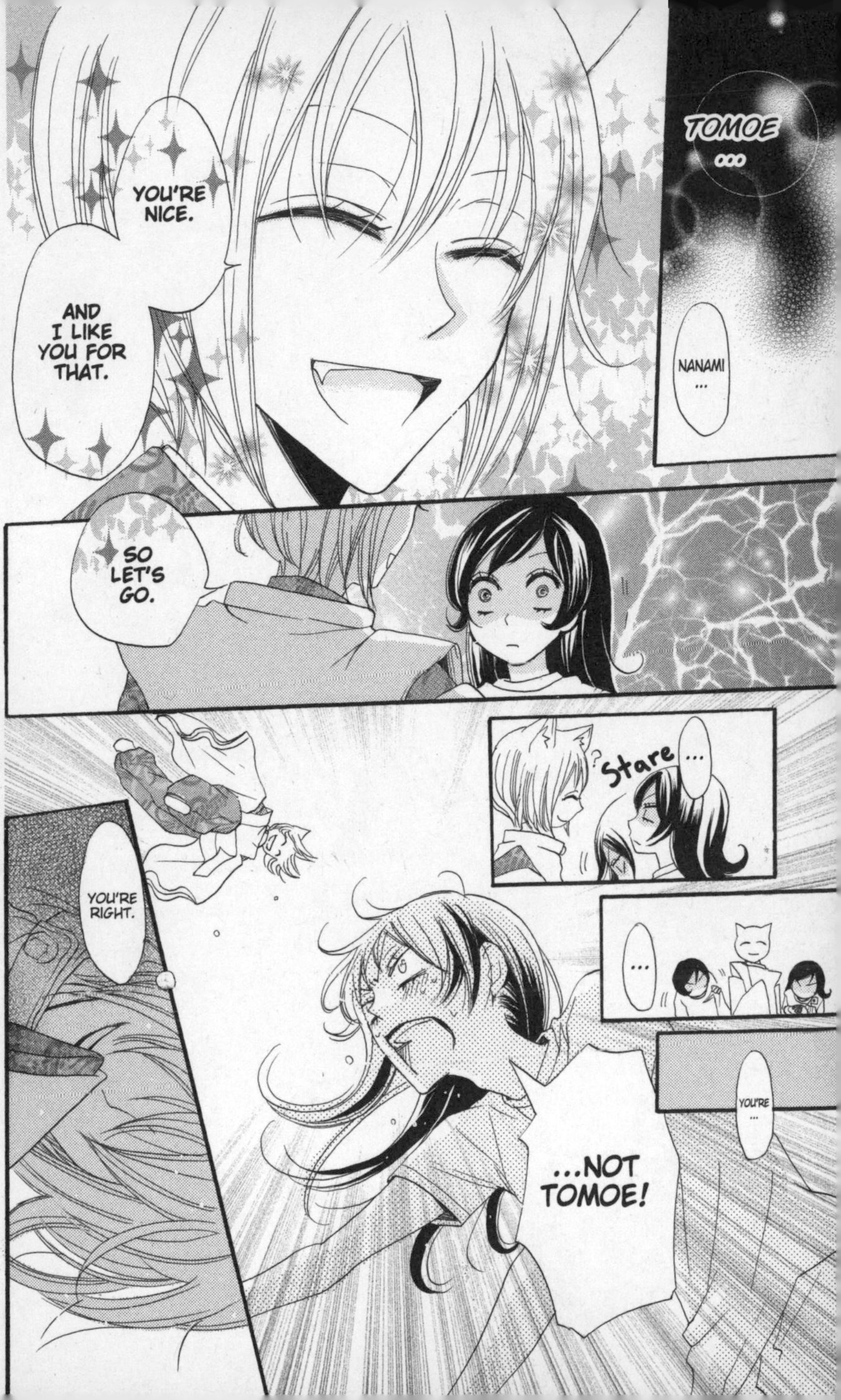
TOMOE ...
NANAMI ...
YOU'RE NICE.
AND I LIKE YOU FOR THAT.
SO LET'S GO.
...
Stare
...
YOU'RE ...
...NOT TOMOE!
YOU'RE RIGHT.

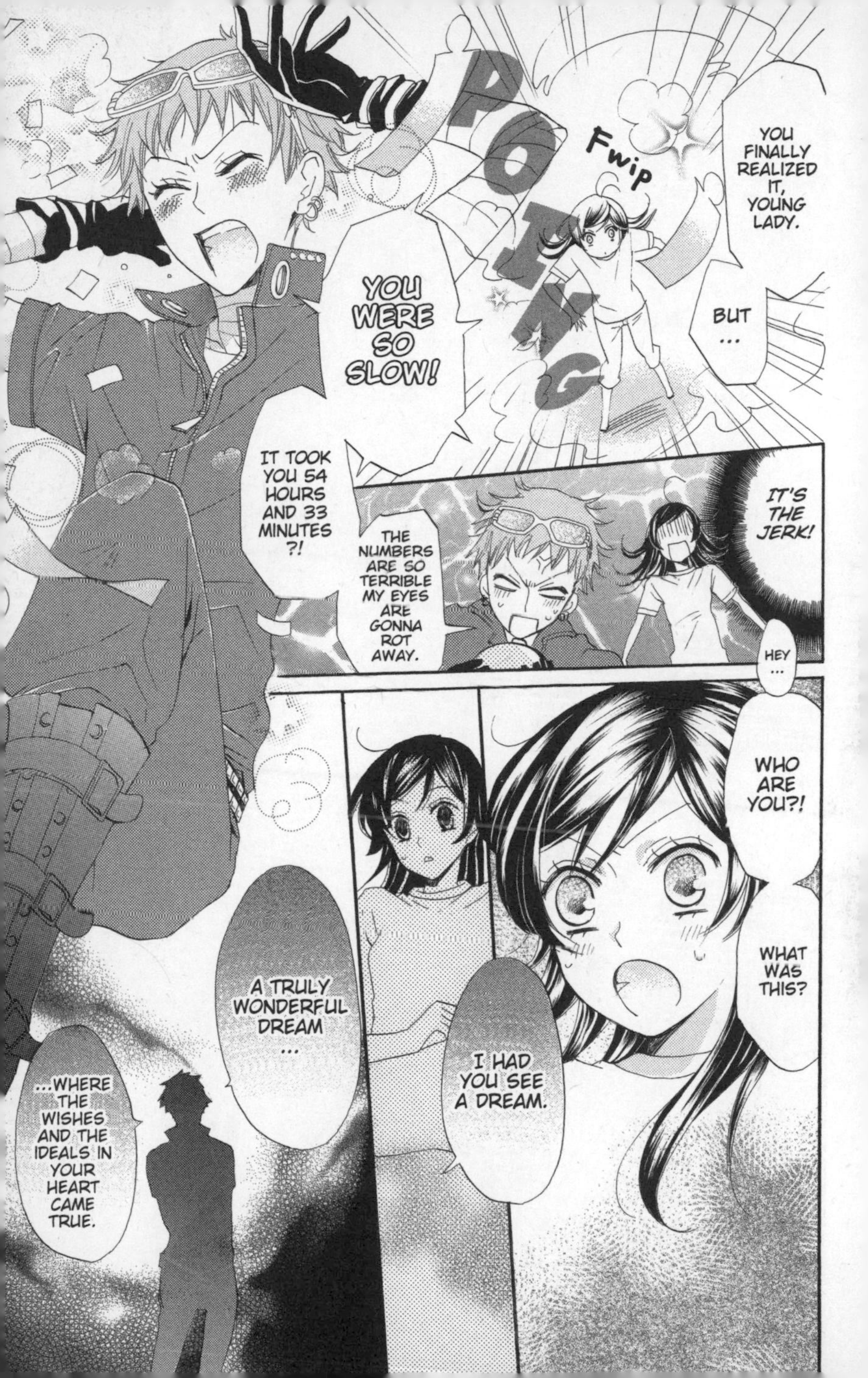

YOU FINALLY REALIZED IT, YOUNG LADY.
Fwip
POING
BUT...
YOU WERE SO SLOW!
IT TOOK YOU 54 HOURS AND 33 MINUTES?!
IT'S THE JERK!
THE NUMBERS ARE SO TERRIBLE MY EYES ARE GONNA ROT AWAY.
HEY...
WHO ARE YOU?!
WHAT WAS THIS?
I HAD YOU SEE A DREAM.
A TRULY WONDERFUL DREAM...
...WHERE THE WISHES AND THE IDEALS IN YOUR HEART CAME TRUE.

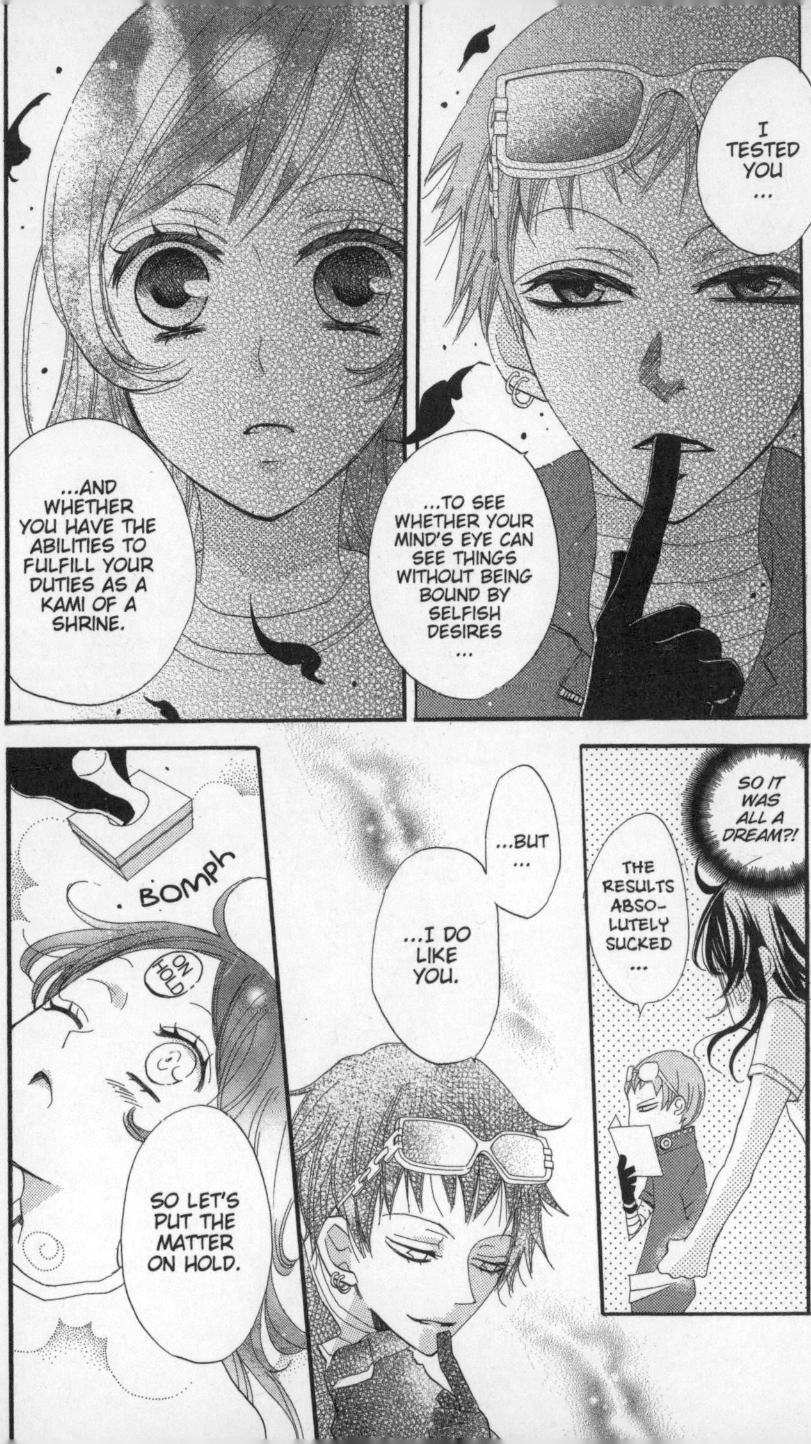
I TESTED YOU ...
...TO SEE WHETHER YOUR MIND'S EYE CAN SEE THINGS WITHOUT BEING BOUND BY SELFISH DESIRES ...
...AND WHETHER YOU HAVE THE ABILITIES TO FULFILL YOUR DUTIES AS A KAMI OF A SHRINE.
SO IT WAS ALL A DREAM?!
THE RESULTS ABSO-LUTELY SUCKED ...
...BUT ...
...I DO LIKE YOU.
SO LET'S PUT THE MATTER ON HOLD.
BOMPH
ON HOLD

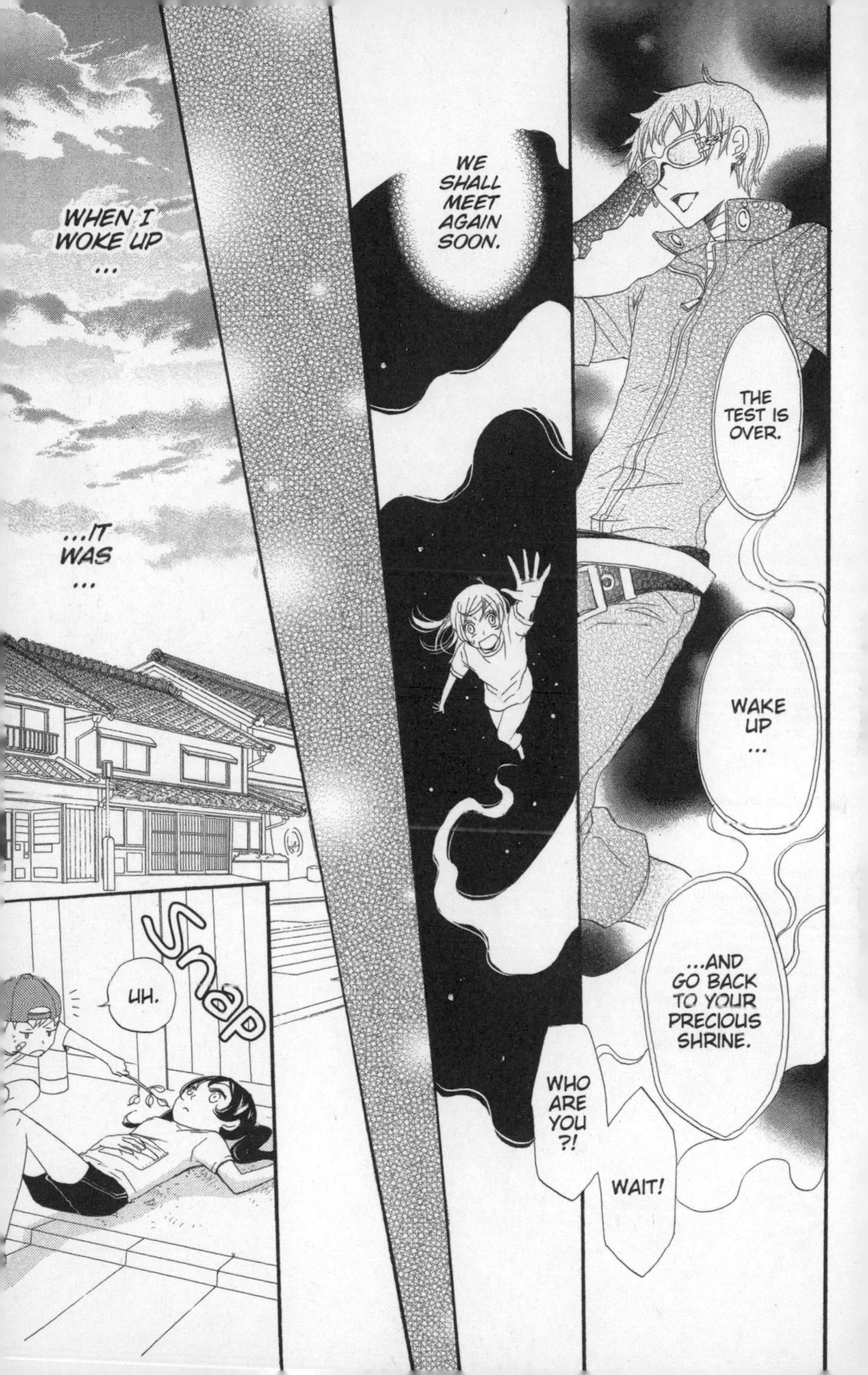
THE TEST IS OVER.
WAKE UP ...
...AND GO BACK TO YOUR PRECIOUS SHRINE.
WHO ARE YOU ?!
WAIT!
WE SHALL MEET AGAIN SOON.
WHEN I WOKE UP ...
...IT WAS ...
Snap
UH.

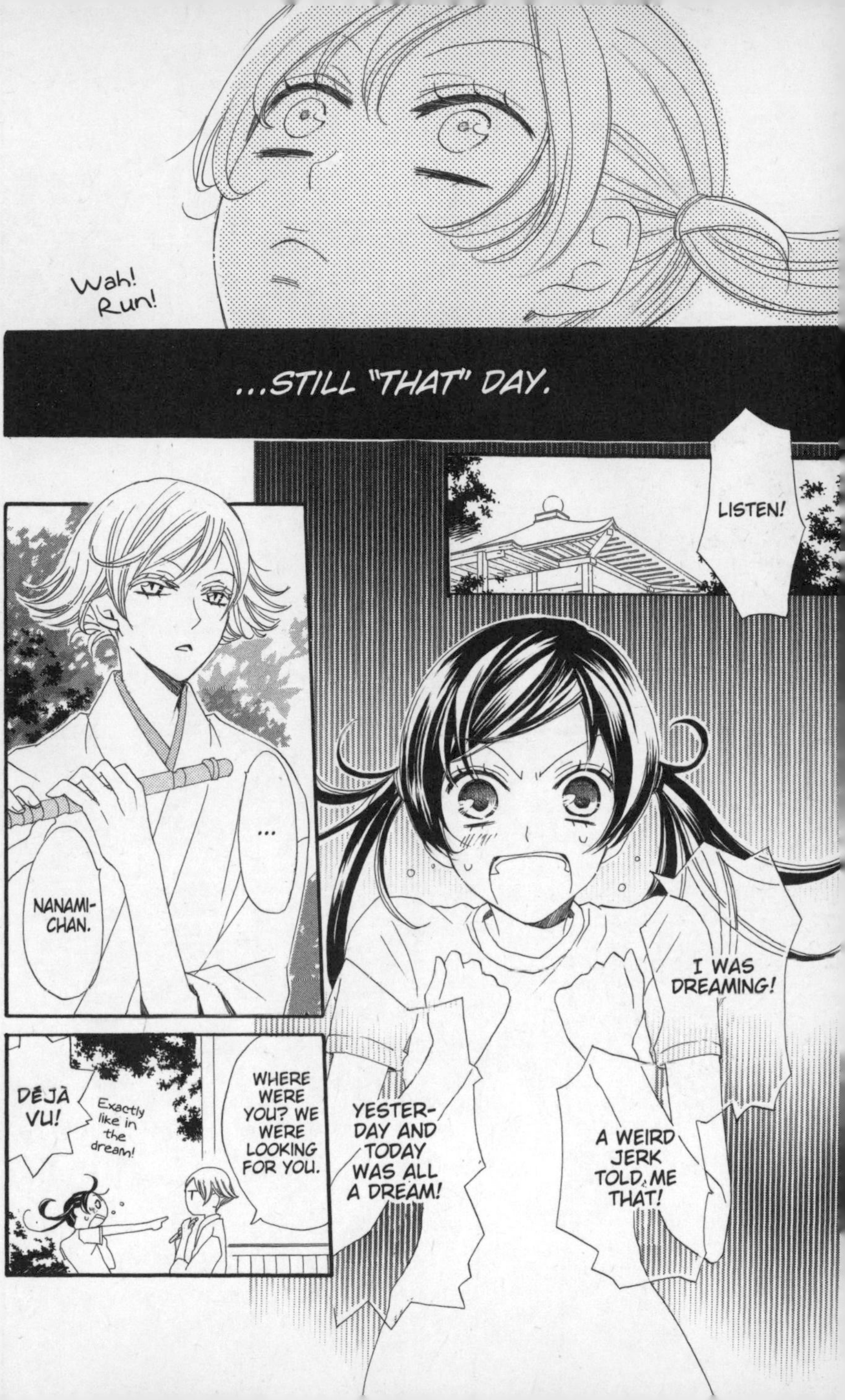
Wah! Run!
...STILL "THAT" DAY.
LISTEN!
I WAS DREAMING!
A WEIRD JERK TOLD ME THAT!
YESTER-DAY AND TODAY WAS ALL A DREAM!
...
NANAMI-CHAN.
WHERE WERE YOU? WE WERE LOOKING FOR YOU.
DÉJÀ VU!
Exactly like in the dream!

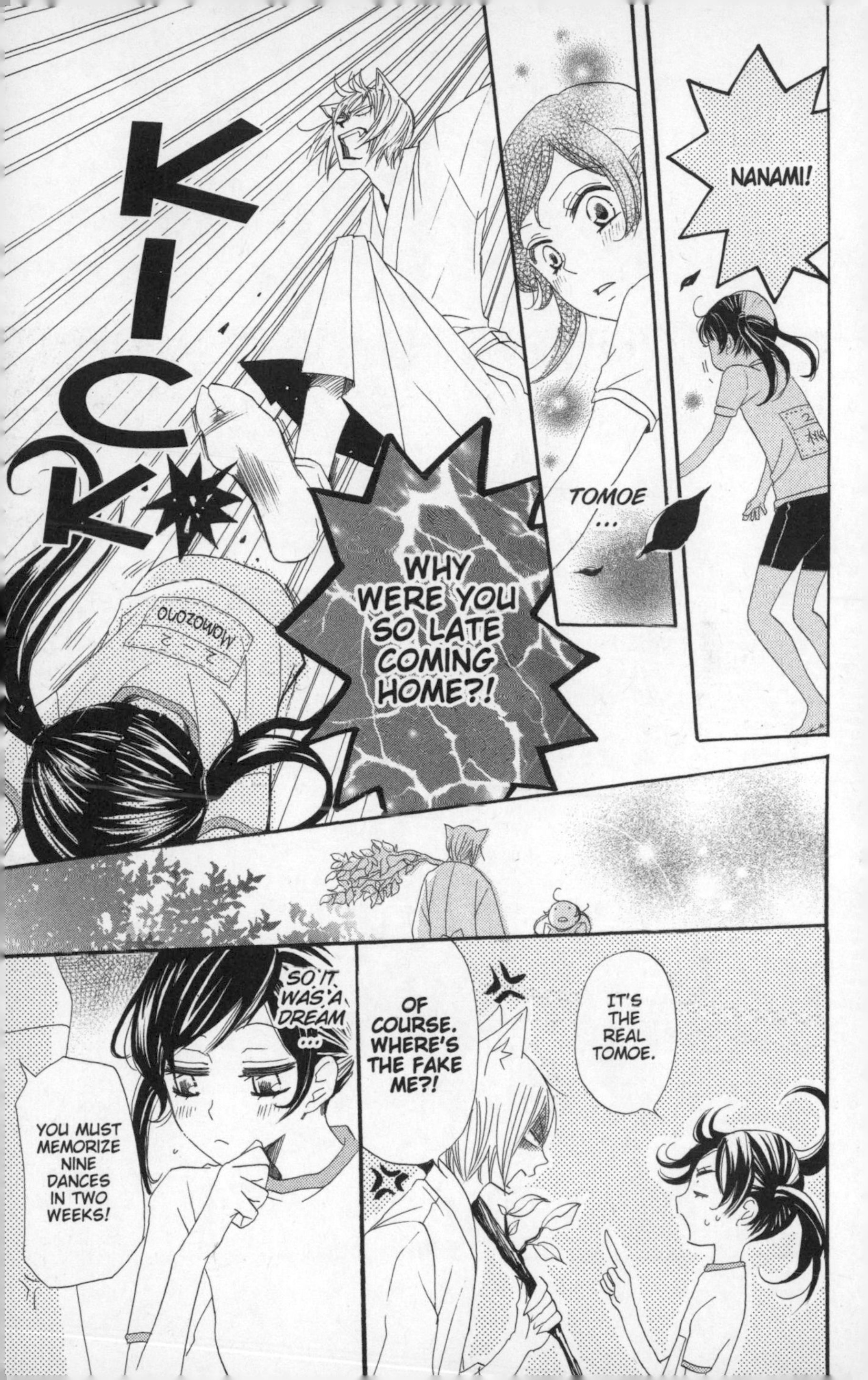
NANAMI!
TOMOE ...
KICK
WHY WERE YOU SO LATE COMING HOME?!
IT'S THE REAL TOMOE.
OF COURSE. WHERE'S THE FAKE ME?!
SO IT WAS A DREAM ...
YOU MUST MEMORIZE NINE DANCES IN TWO WEEKS!

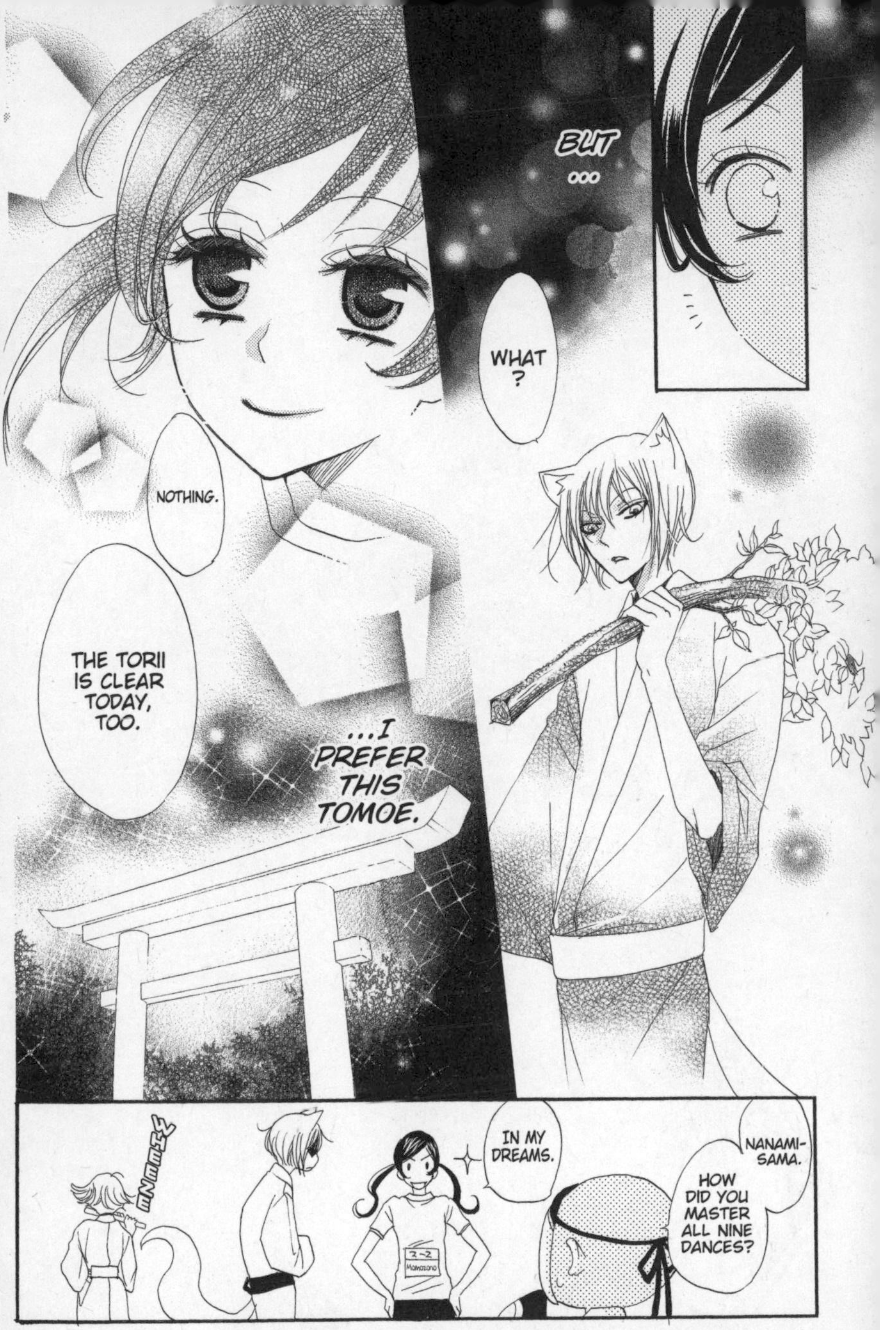
BUT ...
WHAT?
NOTHING.
THE TORII IS CLEAR TODAY, TOO.
...I PREFER THIS TOMOE.
NANAMI-SAMA. HOW DID YOU MASTER ALL NINE DANCES?
IN MY DREAMS.

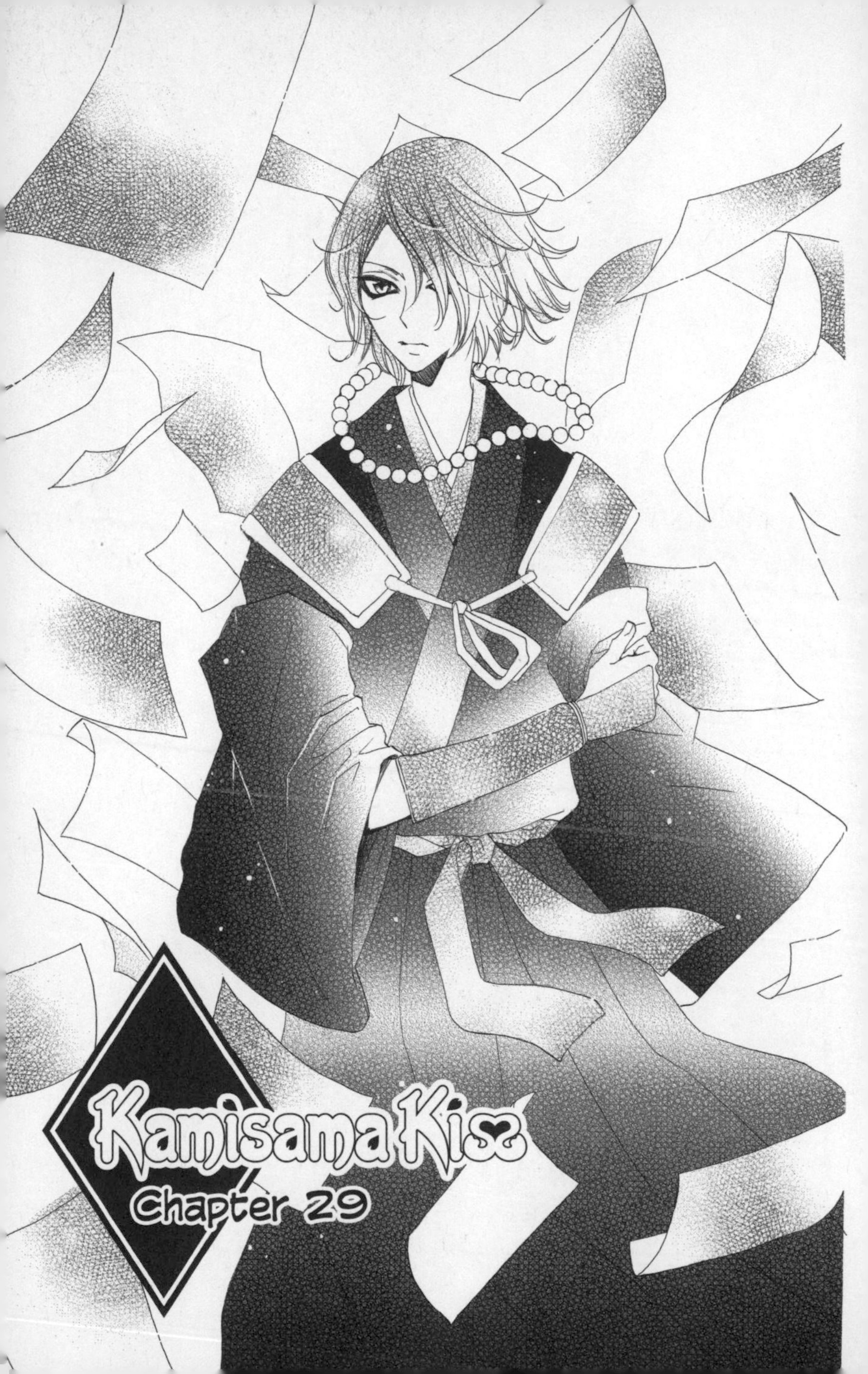
Kamisama Kiss
Chapter 29

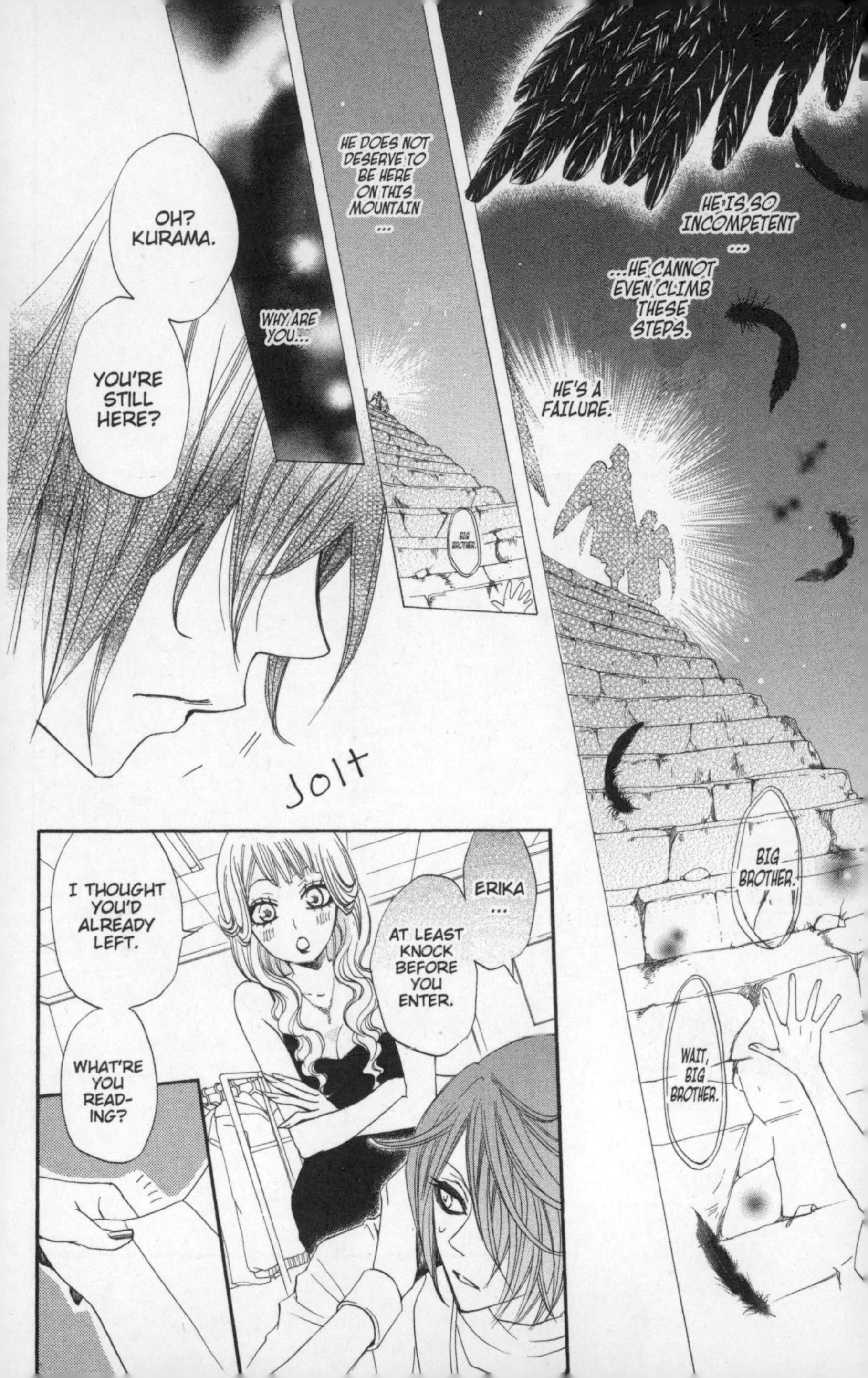
HE IS SO INCOMPETENT...
...HE CANNOT EVEN CLIMB THESE STEPS.
HE'S A FAILURE.
BIG BROTHER.
WAIT, BIG BROTHER.
HE DOES NOT DESERVE TO BE HERE ON THIS MOUNTAIN...
WHY ARE YOU...
BIG BROTHER.
OH? KURAMA.
YOU'RE STILL HERE?
JOLT
ERIKA...
AT LEAST KNOCK BEFORE YOU ENTER.
I THOUGHT YOU'D ALREADY LEFT.
WHAT'RE YOU READING?

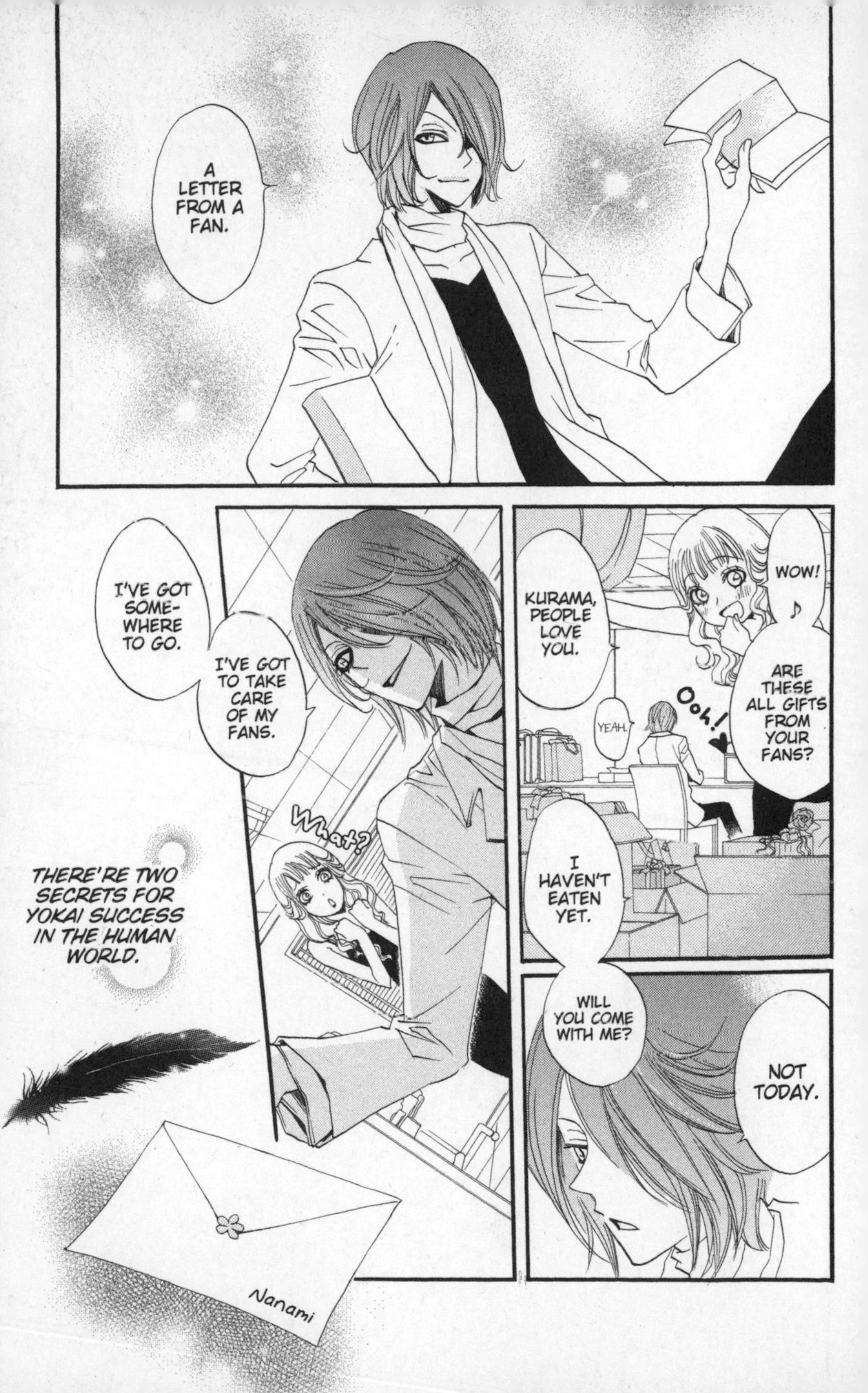
A LETTER FROM A FAN.
WOW!
♪
ARE THESE ALL GIFTS FROM YOUR FANS?
Ooh!
KURAMA, PEOPLE LOVE YOU.
YEAH.
I HAVEN'T EATEN YET.
WILL YOU COME WITH ME?
NOT TODAY.
I'VE GOT TO TAKE CARE OF MY FANS.
I'VE GOT SOME-WHERE TO GO.
What?
THERE'RE TWO SECRETS FOR YOKAI SUCCESS IN THE HUMAN WORLD.
Nanami

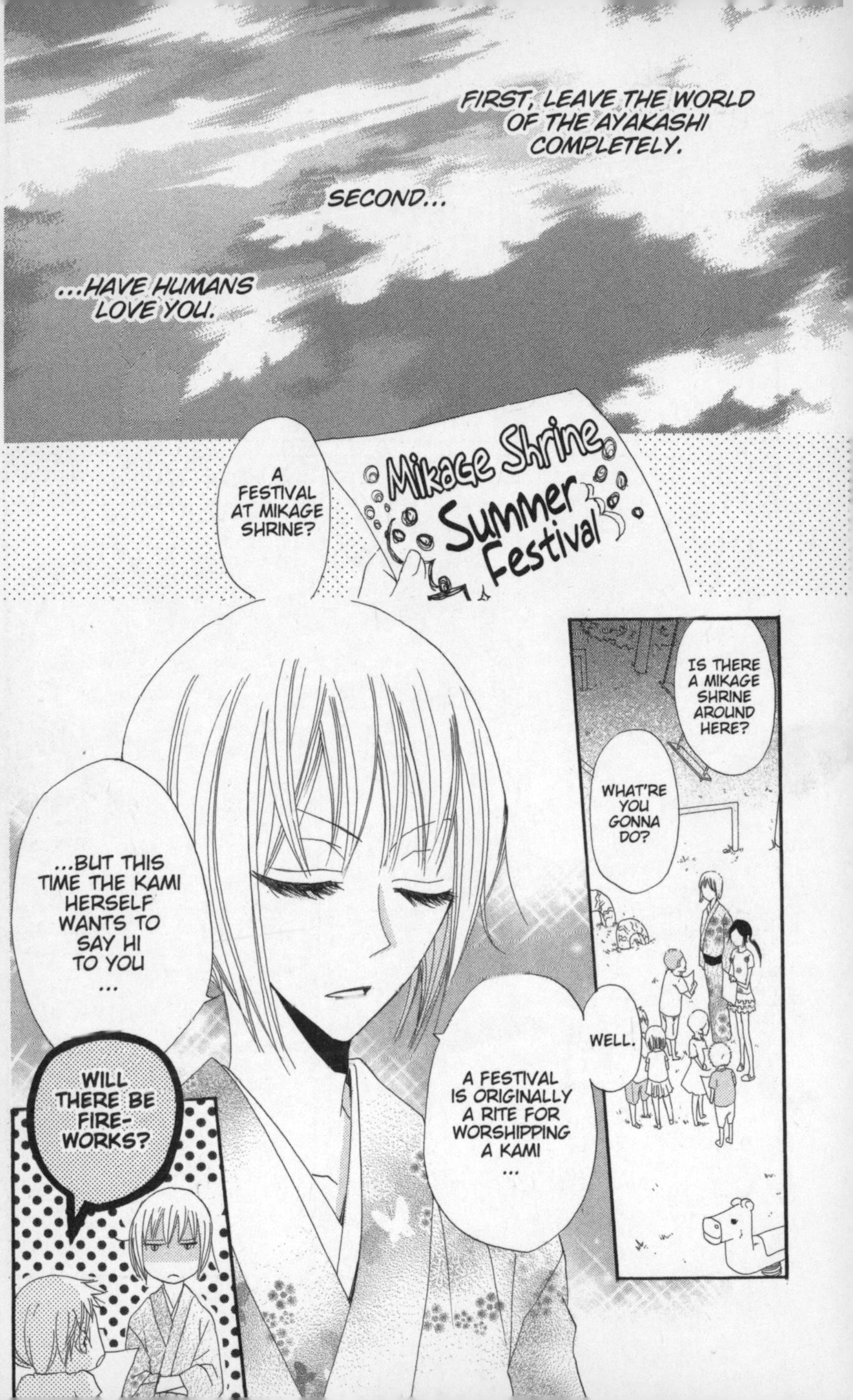
FIRST, LEAVE THE WORLD OF THE AYAKASHI COMPLETELY.
SECOND...
...HAVE HUMANS LOVE YOU.
Mikage Shrine Summer Festival
A FESTIVAL AT MIKAGE SHRINE?
IS THERE A MIKAGE SHRINE AROUND HERE?
WHAT'RE YOU GONNA DO?
WELL.
A FESTIVAL IS ORIGINALLY A RITE FOR WORSHIPPING A KAMI ...
...BUT THIS TIME THE KAMI HERSELF WANTS TO SAY HI TO YOU ...
WILL THERE BE FIRE-WORKS?

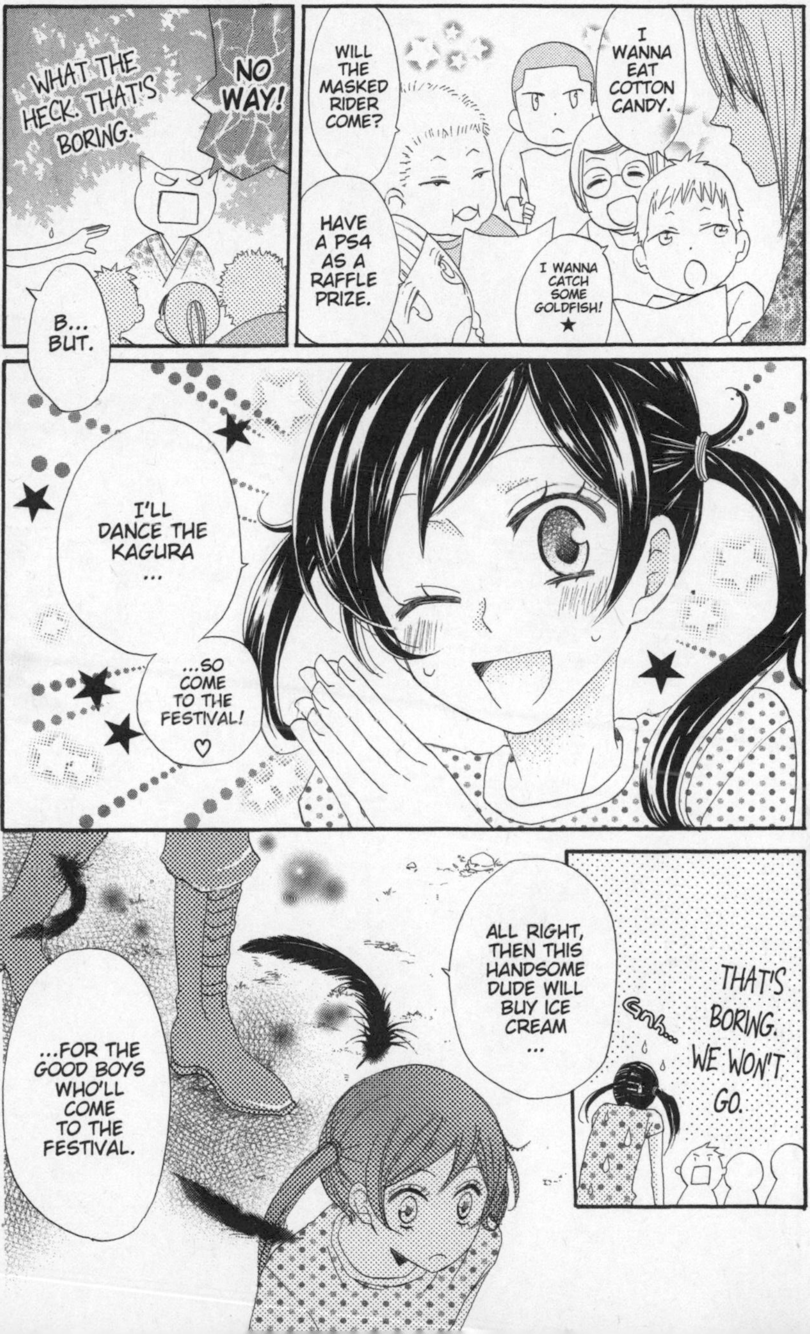
I WANNA EAT COTTON CANDY.
WILL THE MASKED RIDER COME?
I WANNA CATCH SOME GOLDFISH! ★
HAVE A PS4 AS A RAFFLE PRIZE.
NO WAY!
WHAT THE HECK. THAT'S BORING.
B... BUT.
I'LL DANCE THE KAGURA ...
...SO COME TO THE FESTIVAL! ♡
THAT'S BORING. WE WON'T GO.
ALL RIGHT, THEN THIS HANDSOME DUDE WILL BUY ICE CREAM ...
...FOR THE GOOD BOYS WHO'LL COME TO THE FESTIVAL.

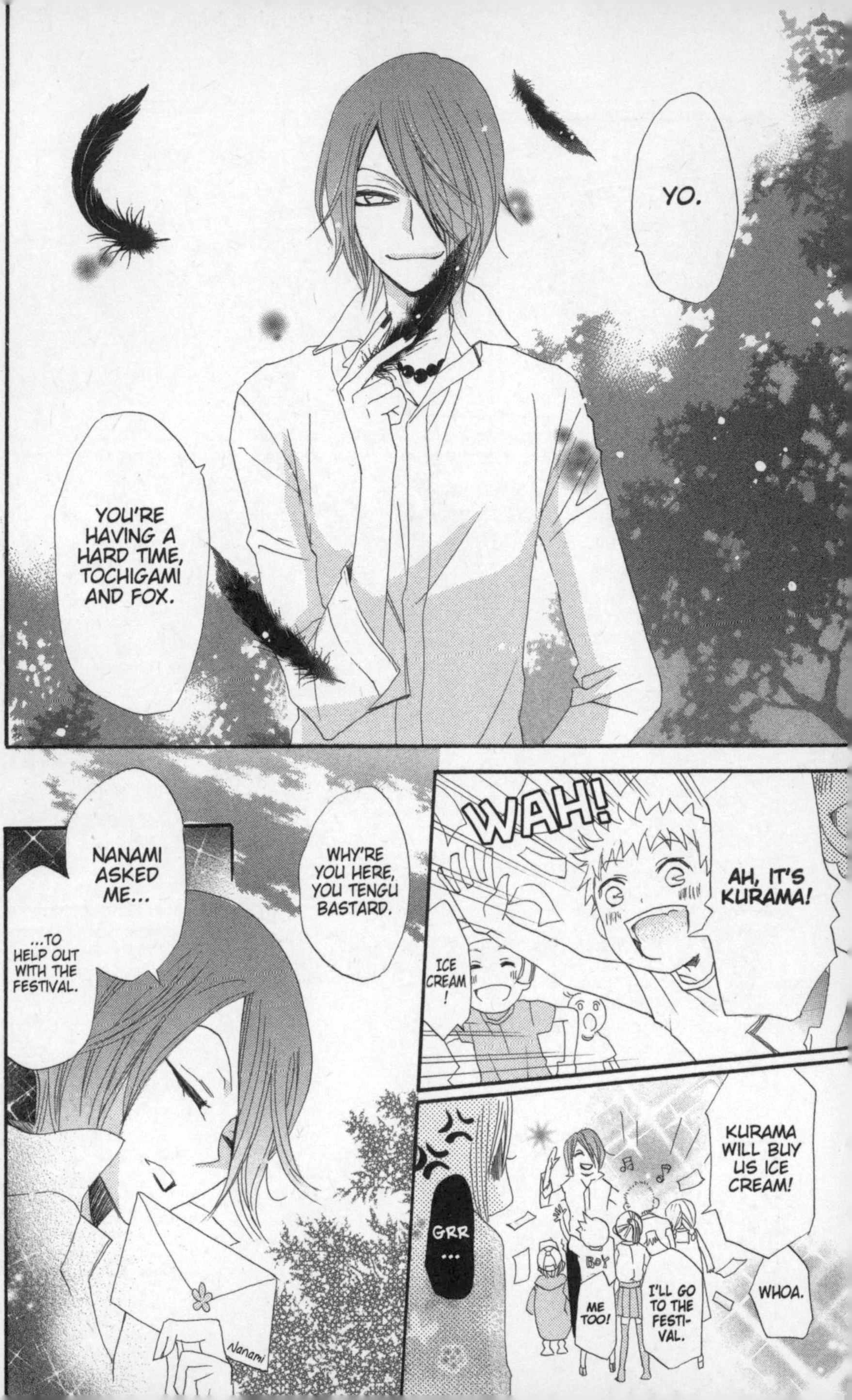
YO.
YOU'RE HAVING A HARD TIME, TOCHIGAMI AND FOX.
WAH!
AH, IT'S KURAMA!
ICE CREAM!
KURAMA WILL BUY US ICE CREAM!
WHOA.
I'LL GO TO THE FESTI-VAL.
ME TOO!
GRR...
WHY'RE YOU HERE, YOU TENGU BASTARD.
NANAMI ASKED ME...
...TO HELP OUT WITH THE FESTIVAL.
Nanami

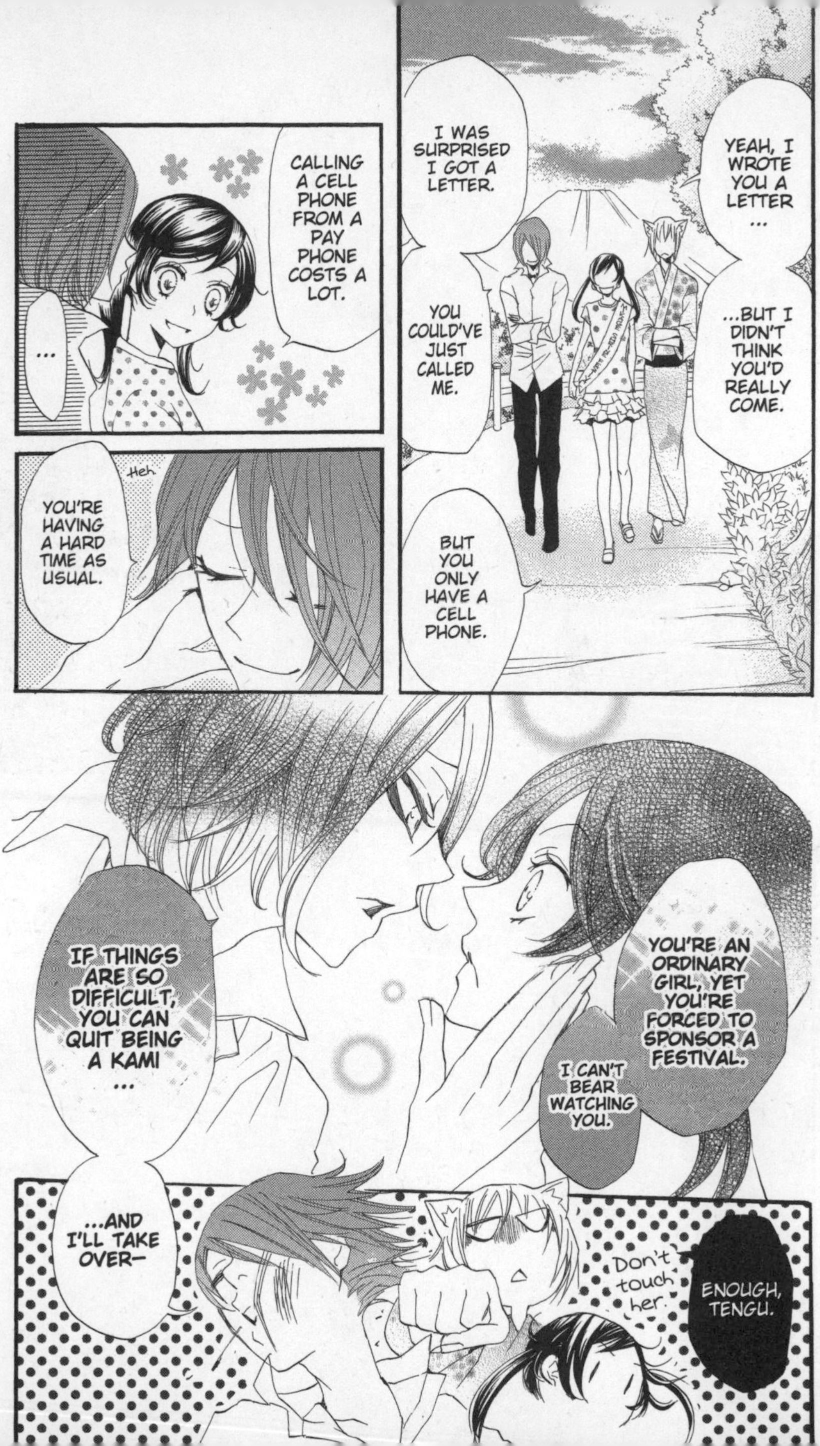
YEAH, I WROTE YOU A LETTER ...
...BUT I DIDN'T THINK YOU'D REALLY COME.
I WAS SURPRISED I GOT A LETTER.
YOU COULD'VE JUST CALLED ME.
BUT YOU ONLY HAVE A CELL PHONE.
CALLING A CELL PHONE FROM A PAY PHONE COSTS A LOT.
...
Heh.
YOU'RE HAVING A HARD TIME AS USUAL.
YOU'RE AN ORDINARY GIRL, YET YOU'RE FORCED TO SPONSOR A FESTIVAL.
I CAN'T BEAR WATCHING YOU.
IF THINGS ARE SO DIFFICULT, YOU CAN QUIT BEING A KAMI ...
...AND I'LL TAKE OVER—
ENOUGH, TENGU.
Don't touch her.

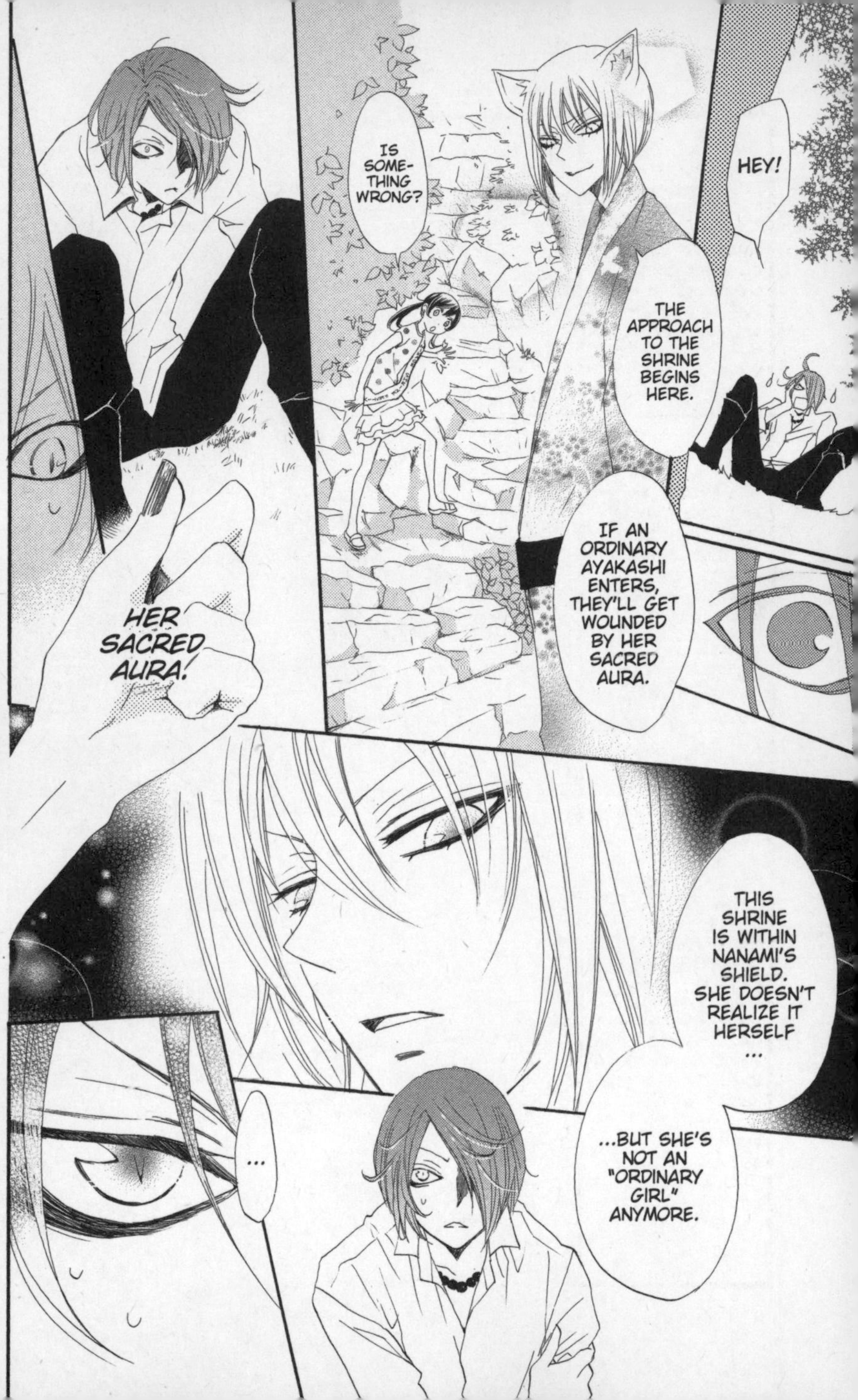
HEY!
IS SOMETHING WRONG?
THE APPROACH TO THE SHRINE BEGINS HERE.
IF AN ORDINARY AYAKASHI ENTERS, THEY'LL GET WOUNDED BY HER SACRED AURA.
HER SACRED AURA!
THIS SHRINE IS WITHIN NANAMI'S SHIELD. SHE DOESN'T REALIZE IT HERSELF...
...
...BUT SHE'S NOT AN "ORDINARY GIRL" ANYMORE.

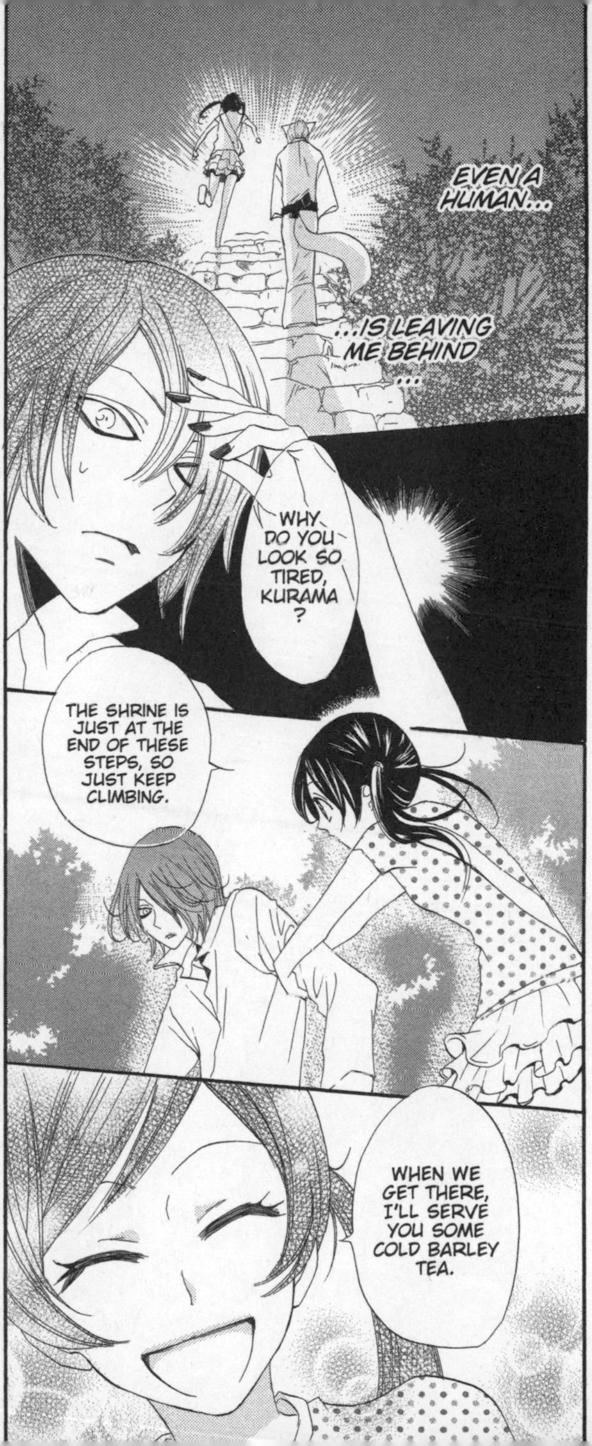
EVEN A HUMAN...
...IS LEAVING ME BEHIND...
WHY DO YOU LOOK SO TIRED, KURAMA?
THE SHRINE IS JUST AT THE END OF THESE STEPS, SO JUST KEEP CLIMBING.
WHEN WE GET THERE, I'LL SERVE YOU SOME COLD BARLEY TEA.

I borrowed a book about the universe.

The book began with the earth, covered dark matter, and was full of photographs taken by NASA and poetic explanations. I found it very interesting.

Even if I'm worried about something, I'm an ant when you think about how big the universe is, so I feel I must be a human who's like dark matter! Thank you for lending me such a wonderful book!

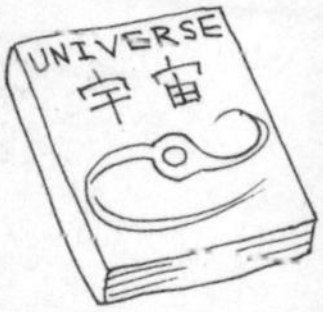
UNIVERSE
宇宙

I'm sorry I haven't returned it yet.

To me, space means Gundam. I've only seen the first series, but I love the way the sense of air and space is portrayed in the movie version! Though there's no air in space!

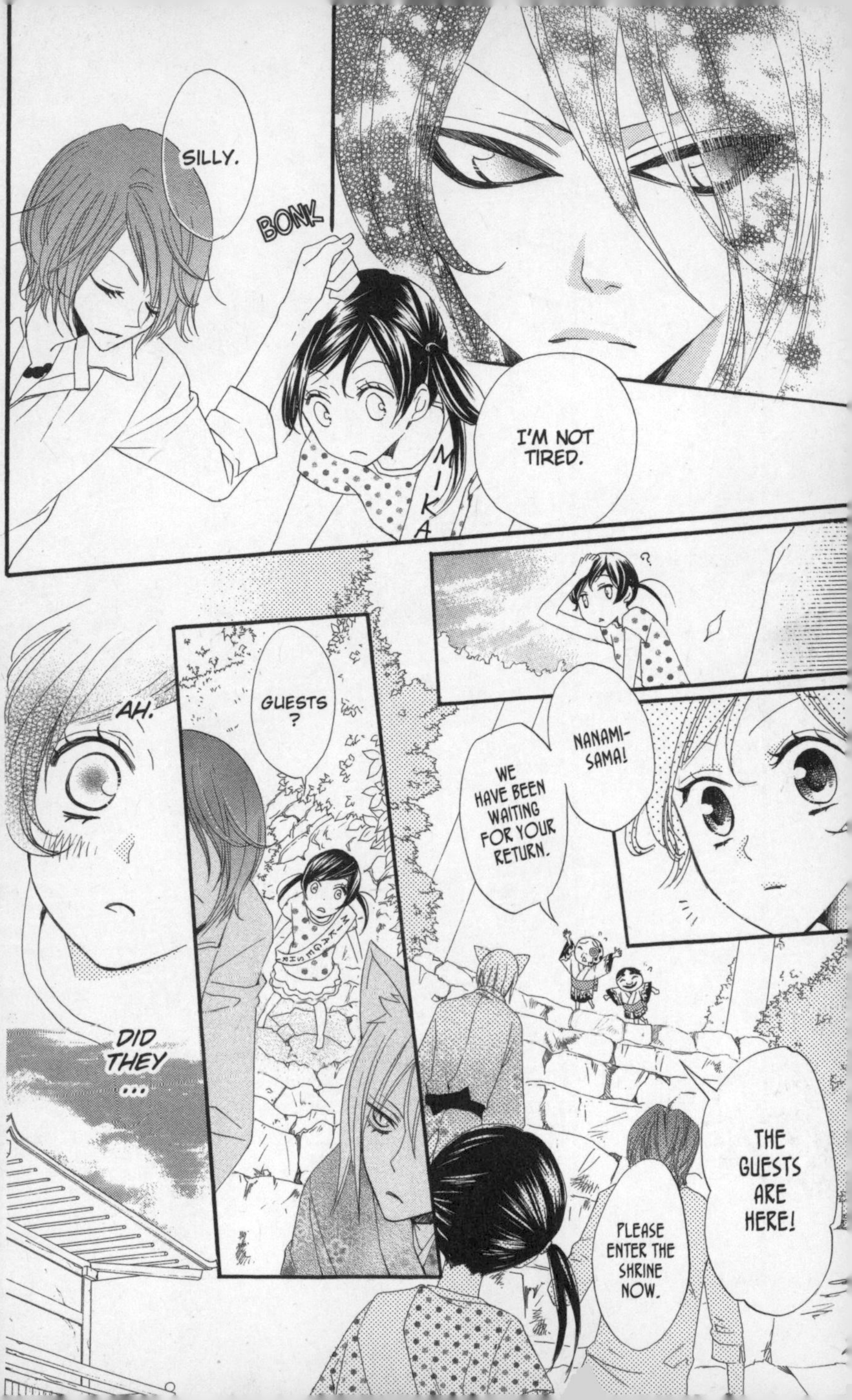
I'M NOT TIRED.
MIKA
SILLY.
BONK
NANAMI-SAMA!
WE HAVE BEEN WAITING FOR YOUR RETURN.
GUESTS?
THE GUESTS ARE HERE!
PLEASE ENTER THE SHRINE NOW.
AH.
DID THEY ...

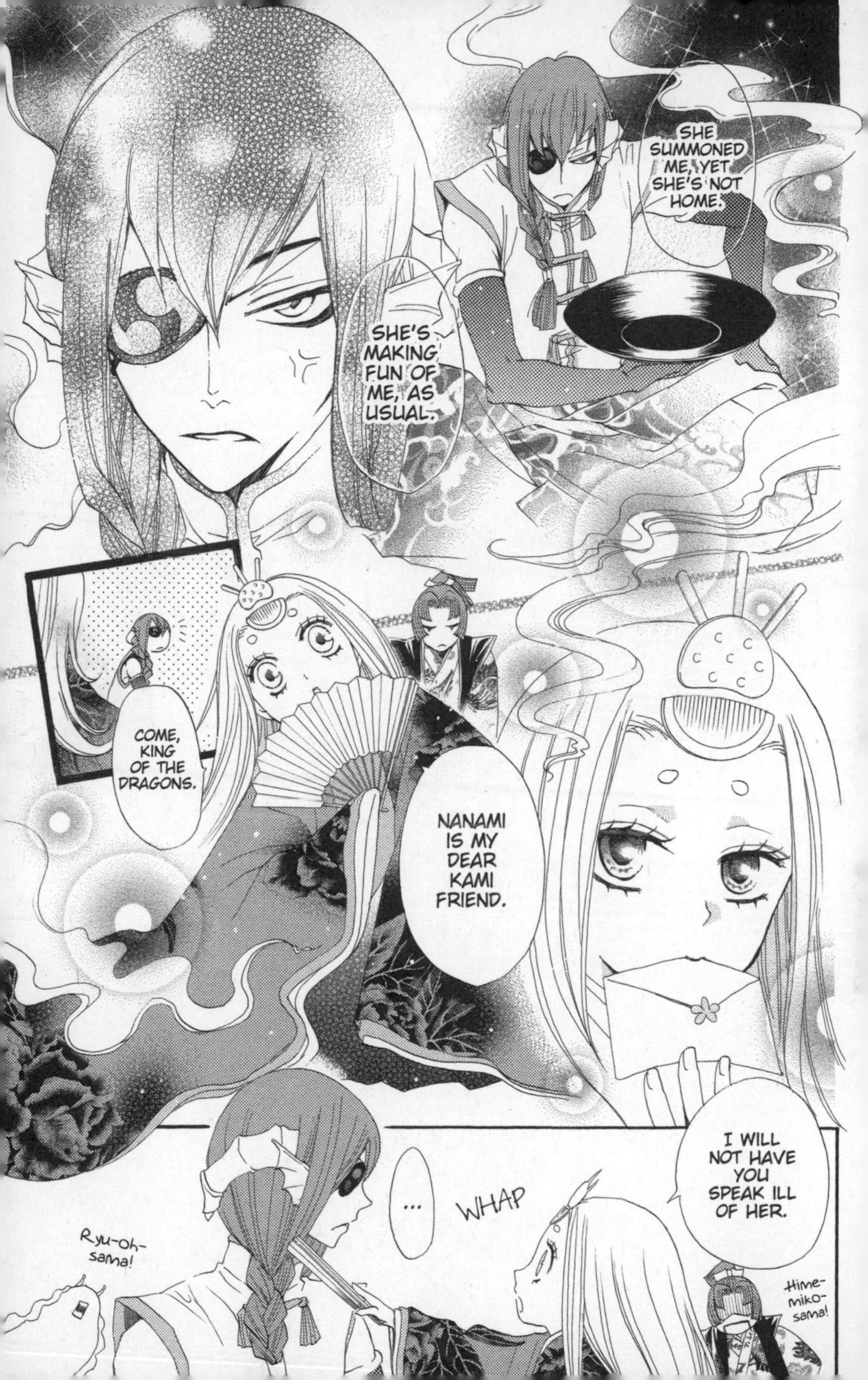
SHE SUMMONED ME, YET SHE'S NOT HOME.
SHE'S MAKING FUN OF ME, AS USUAL.
NANAMI IS MY DEAR KAMI FRIEND.
COME, KING OF THE DRAGONS.
I WILL NOT HAVE YOU SPEAK ILL OF HER.
Hime-miko-sama!
WHAP
...
Ryu-oh-sama!

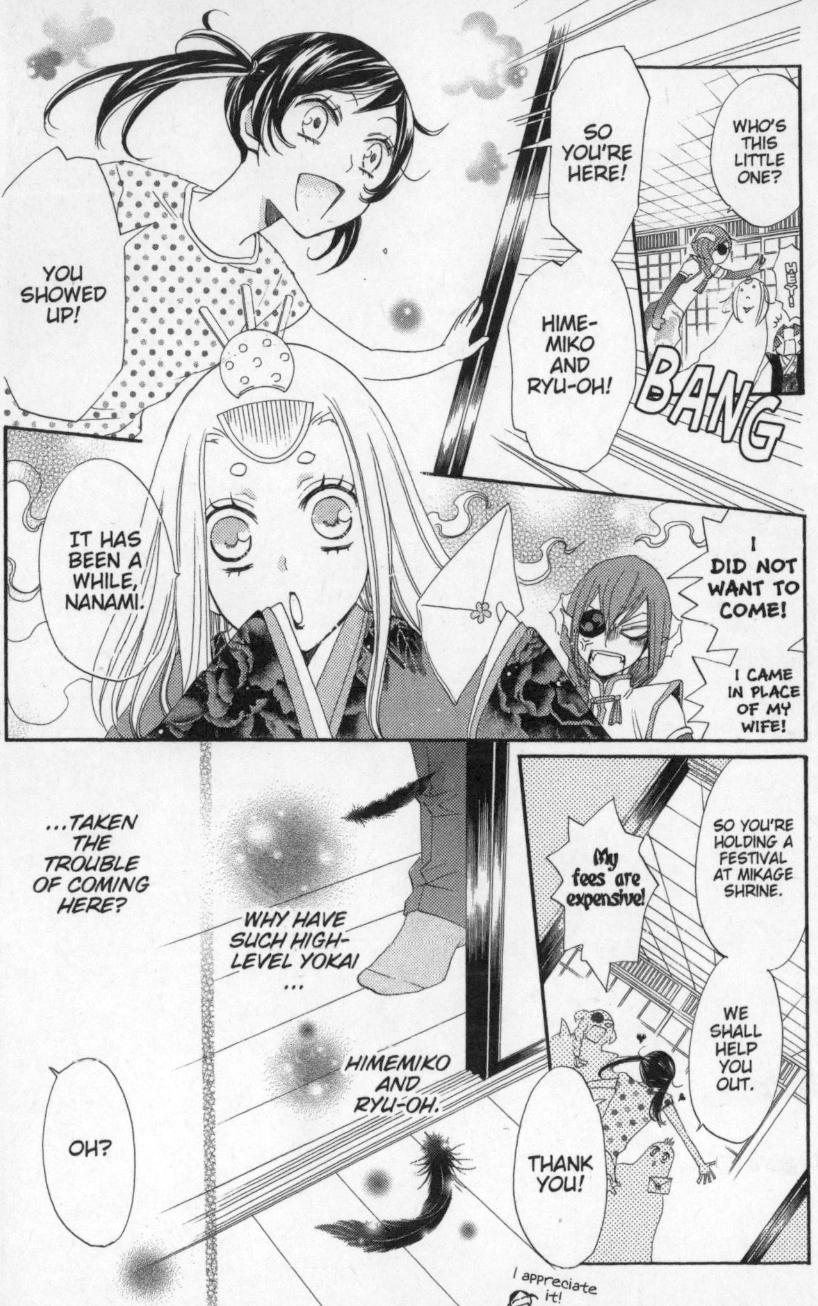
WHO'S THIS LITTLE ONE?
HEY!
BANG
SO YOU'RE HERE!
HIME-MIKO AND RYU-OH!
YOU SHOWED UP!
I DID NOT WANT TO COME!
I CAME IN PLACE OF MY WIFE!
IT HAS BEEN A WHILE, NANAMI.
SO YOU'RE HOLDING A FESTIVAL AT MIKAGE SHRINE.
My fees are expensive!
WE SHALL HELP YOU OUT.
THANK YOU!
I appreciate it!
WHY HAVE SUCH HIGH-LEVEL YOKAI ...
...TAKEN THE TROUBLE OF COMING HERE?
HIMEMIKO AND RYU-OH.
OH?

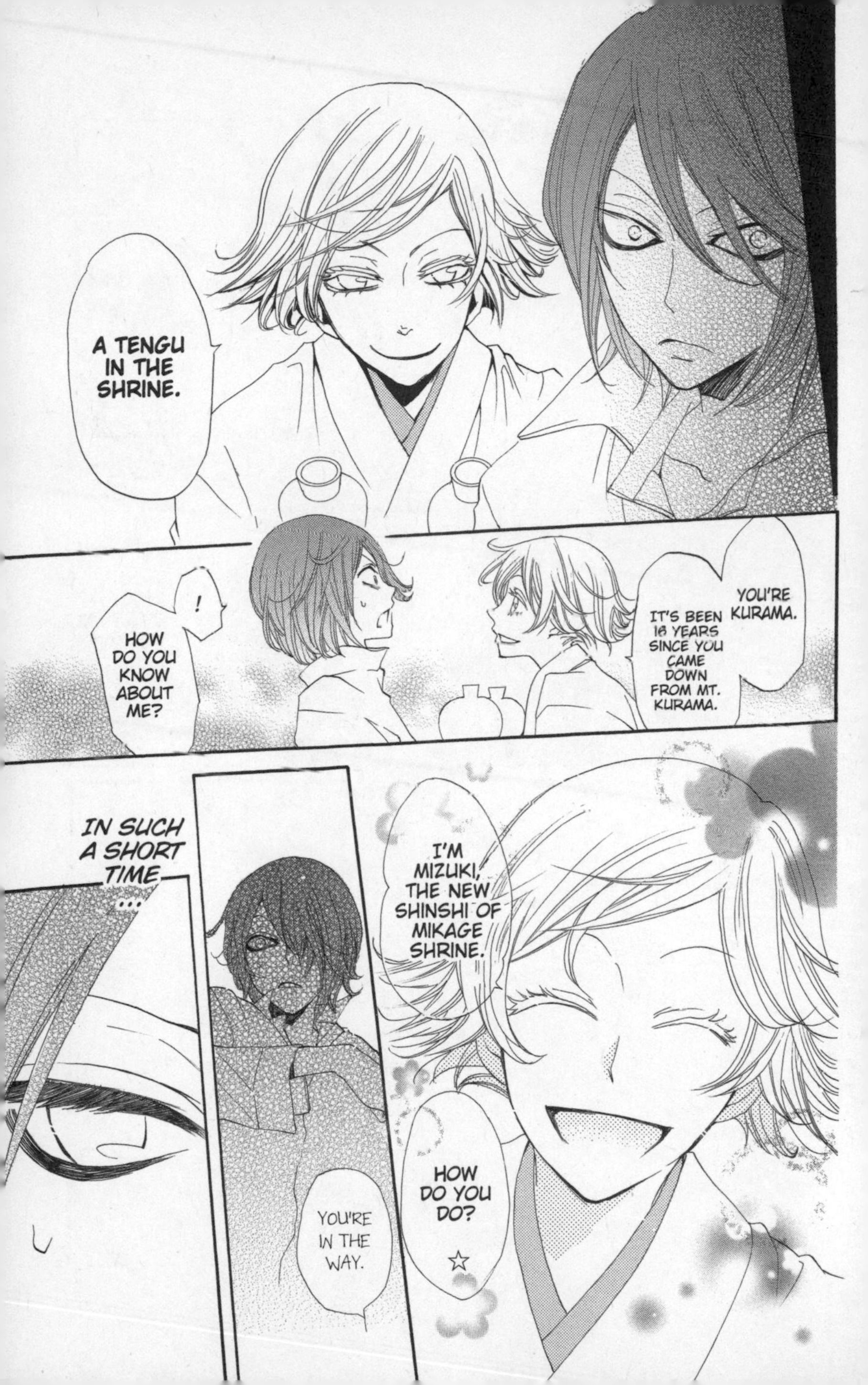
A TENGU IN THE SHRINE.
YOU'RE KURAMA.
IT'S BEEN 16 YEARS SINCE YOU CAME DOWN FROM MT. KURAMA.
!
HOW DO YOU KNOW ABOUT ME?
I'M MIZUKI, THE NEW SHINSHI OF MIKAGE SHRINE.
HOW DO YOU DO? ☆
YOU'RE IN THE WAY.
IN SUCH A SHORT TIME...

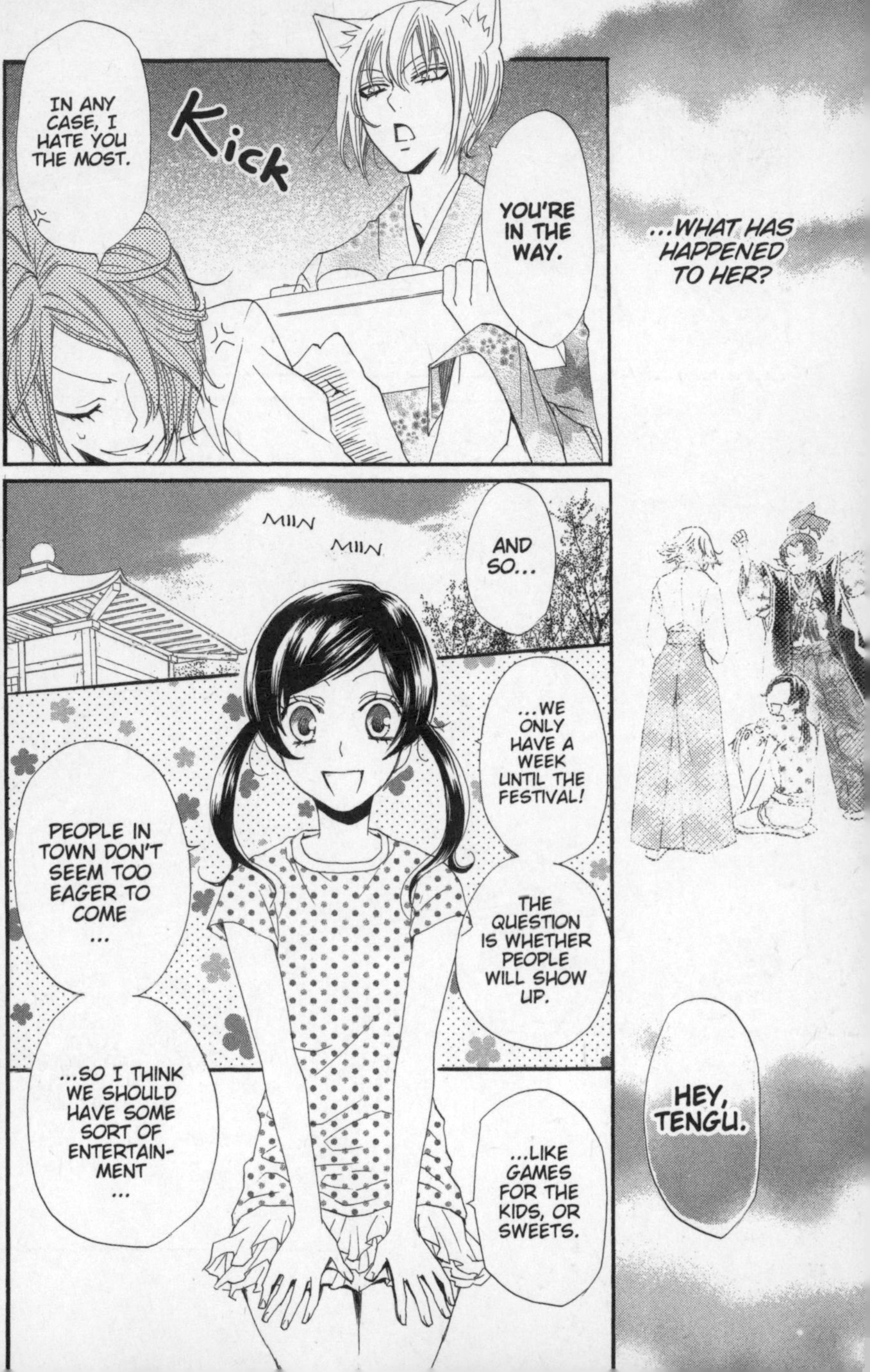
...WHAT HAS HAPPENED TO HER?
HEY, TENGU.
YOU'RE IN THE WAY.
Kick
IN ANY CASE, I HATE YOU THE MOST.
AND SO...
MIIN
MIIN
...WE ONLY HAVE A WEEK UNTIL THE FESTIVAL!
THE QUESTION IS WHETHER PEOPLE WILL SHOW UP.
PEOPLE IN TOWN DON'T SEEM TOO EAGER TO COME ...
...SO I THINK WE SHOULD HAVE SOME SORT OF ENTERTAIN-MENT ...
...LIKE GAMES FOR THE KIDS, OR SWEETS.

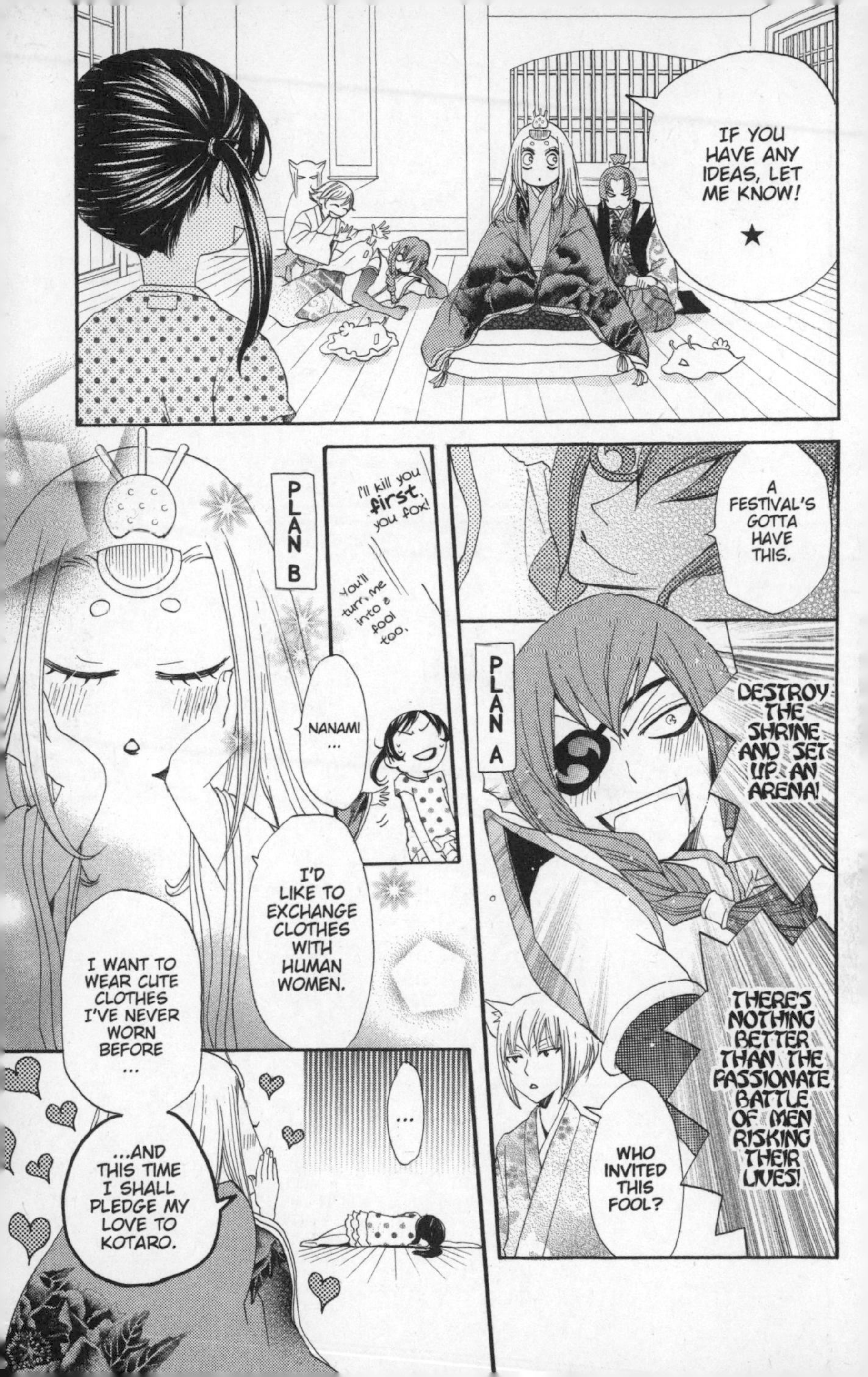
IF YOU HAVE ANY IDEAS, LET ME KNOW! ★
A FESTIVAL'S GOTTA HAVE THIS.
PLAN A
DESTROY THE SHRINE AND SET UP AN ARENA!
THERE'S NOTHING BETTER THAN THE PASSIONATE BATTLE OF MEN RISKING THEIR LIVES!
WHO INVITED THIS FOOL?
I'll kill you first, you fox!
You'll turn me into a fool too.
PLAN B
NANAMI ...
I'D LIKE TO EXCHANGE CLOTHES WITH HUMAN WOMEN.
I WANT TO WEAR CUTE CLOTHES I'VE NEVER WORN BEFORE ...
...AND THIS TIME I SHALL PLEDGE MY LOVE TO KOTARO.
...

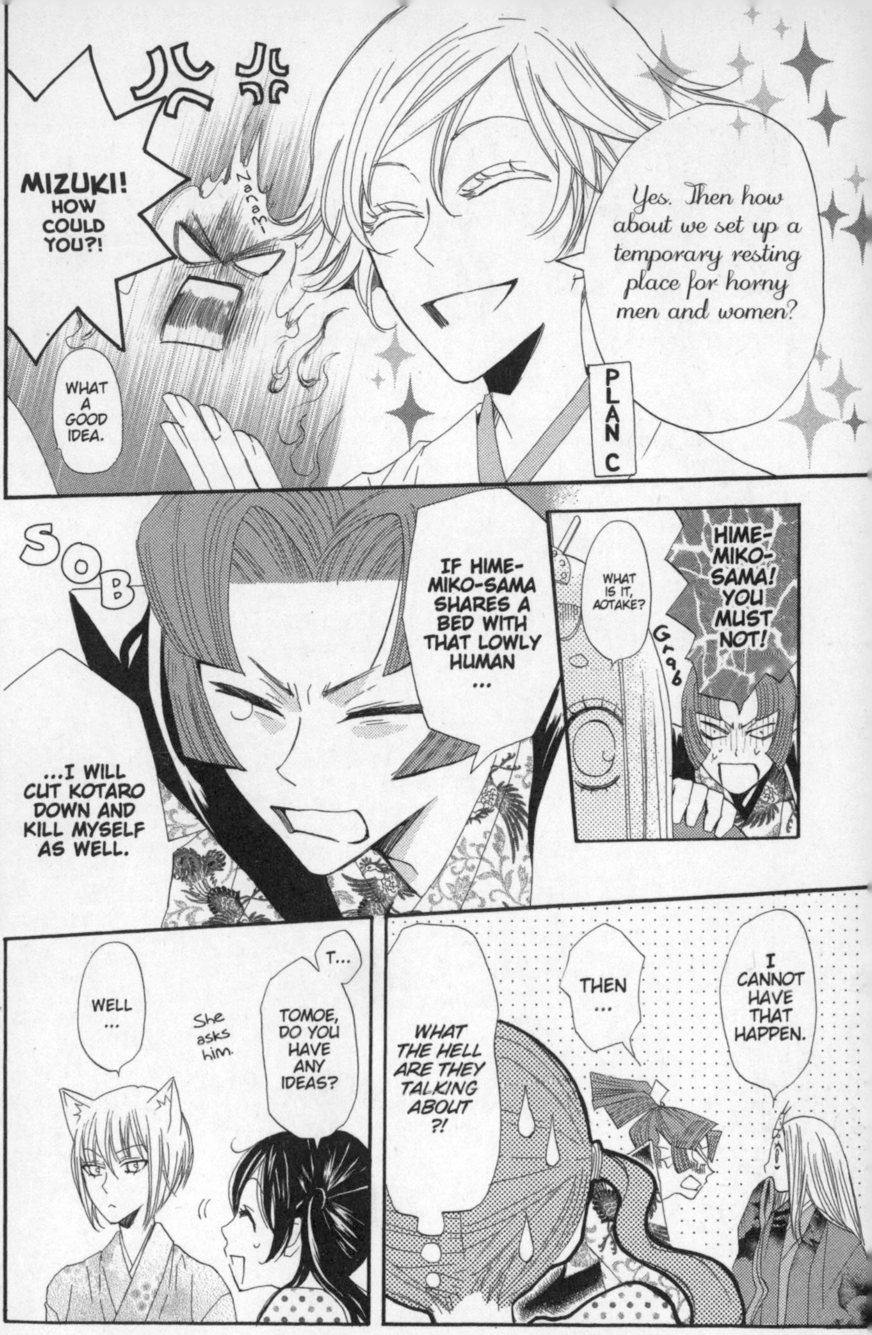
Yes. Then how about we set up a temporary resting place for horny men and women?
PLAN C
Nanami
MIZUKI! HOW COULD YOU?!
WHAT A GOOD IDEA.
HIME-MIKO-SAMA! YOU MUST NOT!
Grab
WHAT IS IT, AOTAKE?
IF HIME-MIKO-SAMA SHARES A BED WITH THAT LOWLY HUMAN ...
SOB
...I WILL CUT KOTARO DOWN AND KILL MYSELF AS WELL.
I CANNOT HAVE THAT HAPPEN.
THEN ...
WHAT THE HELL ARE THEY TALKING ABOUT?!
T...
TOMOE, DO YOU HAVE ANY IDEAS?
She asks him.
WELL ...

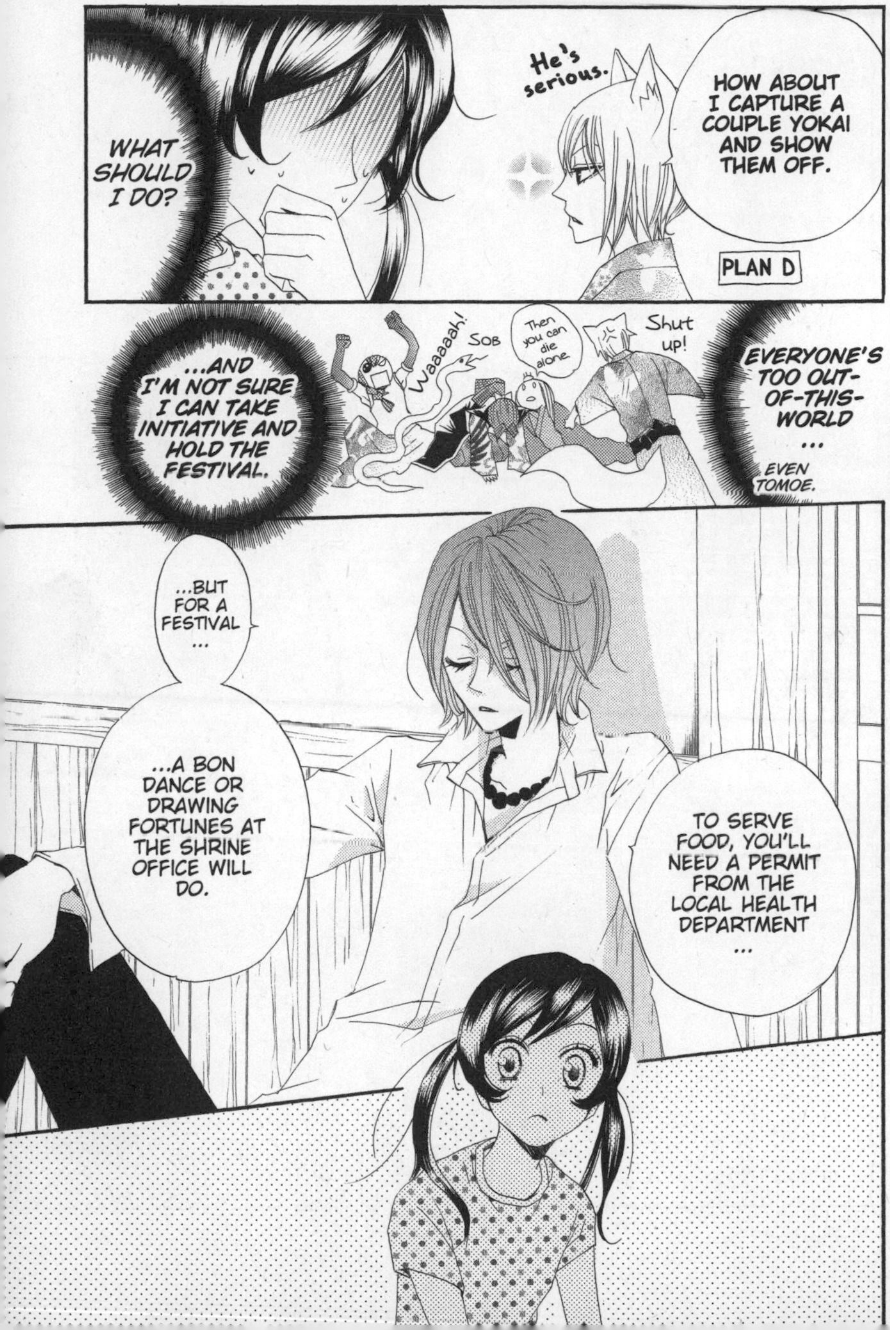
HOW ABOUT I CAPTURE A COUPLE YOKAI AND SHOW THEM OFF.
PLAN D
He's serious.
WHAT SHOULD I DO?
EVERYONE'S TOO OUT-OF-THIS-WORLD...
EVEN TOMOE.
Shut up!
Then you can die alone.
SOB
Waaaaah!
...AND I'M NOT SURE I CAN TAKE INITIATIVE AND HOLD THE FESTIVAL.
TO SERVE FOOD, YOU'LL NEED A PERMIT FROM THE LOCAL HEALTH DEPARTMENT...
...BUT FOR A FESTIVAL...
...A BON DANCE OR DRAWING FORTUNES AT THE SHRINE OFFICE WILL DO.

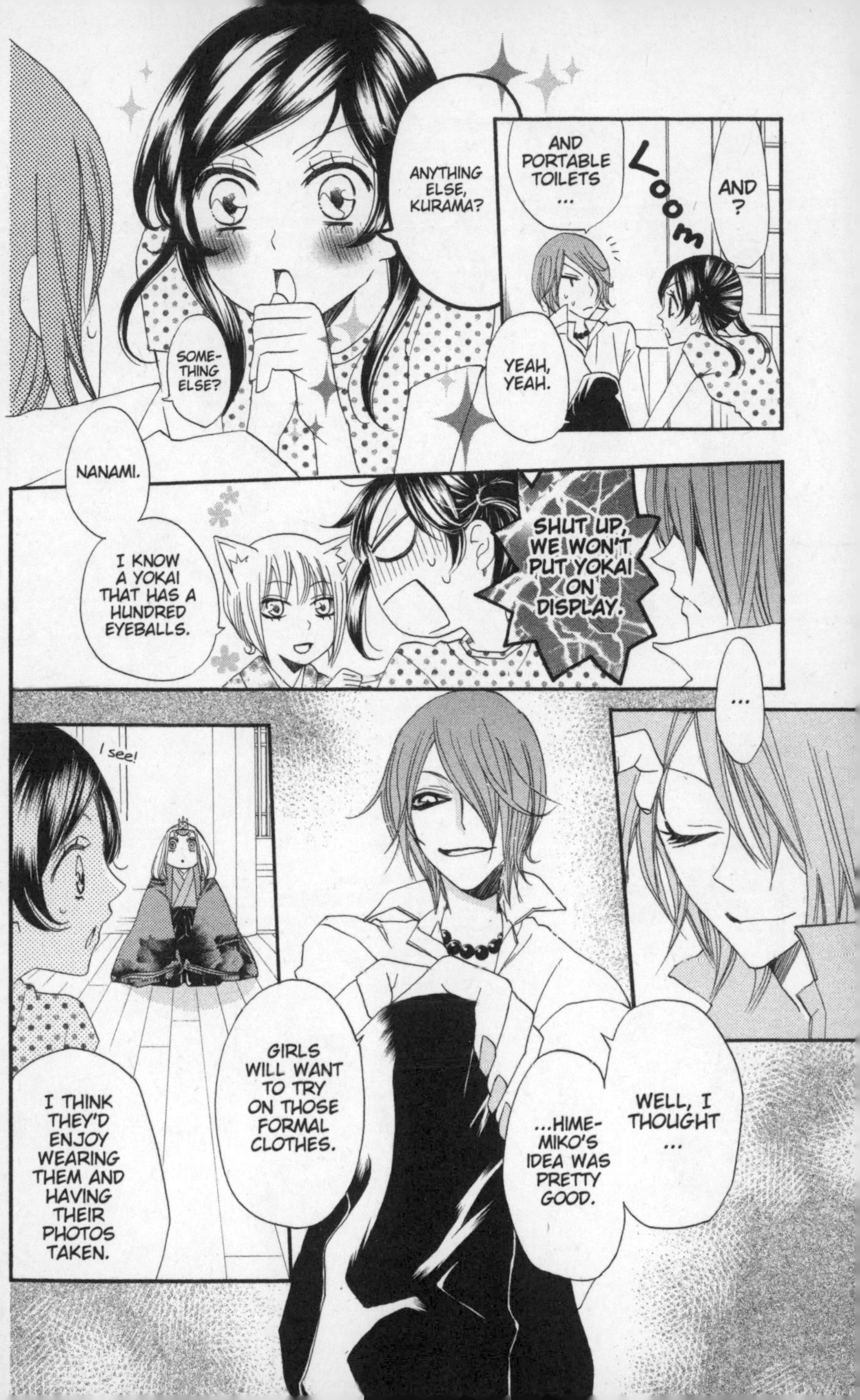
AND ?
AND PORTABLE TOILETS ...
LOOM
YEAH, YEAH.
ANYTHING ELSE, KURAMA?
SOME-THING ELSE?
NANAMI.
I KNOW A YOKAI THAT HAS A HUNDRED EYEBALLS.
SHUT UP, WE WON'T PUT YOKAI ON DISPLAY.
...
WELL, I THOUGHT ...
...HIME-MIKO'S IDEA WAS PRETTY GOOD.
GIRLS WILL WANT TO TRY ON THOSE FORMAL CLOTHES.
I see!
I THINK THEY'D ENJOY WEARING THEM AND HAVING THEIR PHOTOS TAKEN.

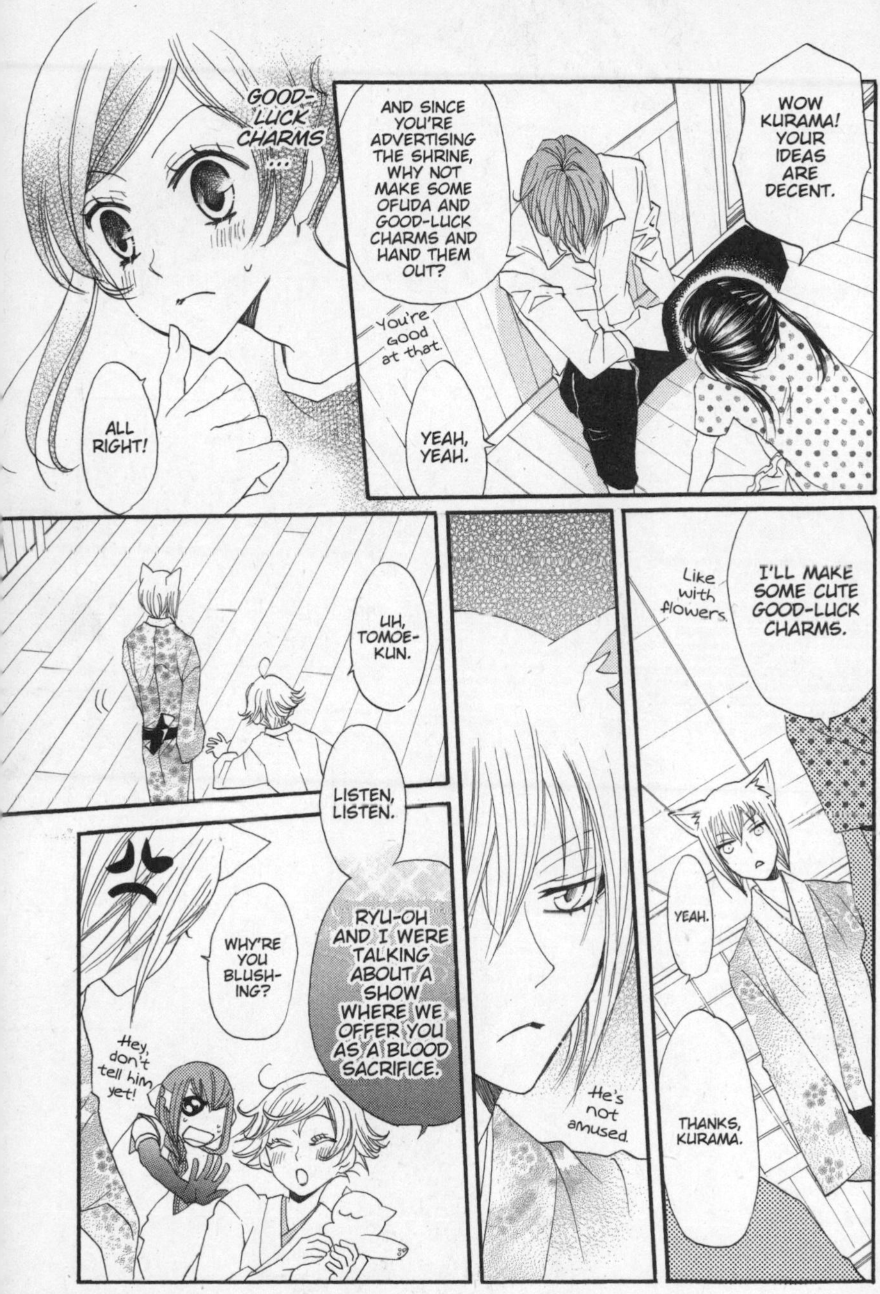
WOW KURAMA! YOUR IDEAS ARE DECENT.
AND SINCE YOU'RE ADVERTISING THE SHRINE, WHY NOT MAKE SOME OFUDA AND GOOD-LUCK CHARMS AND HAND THEM OUT?
You're good at that.
YEAH, YEAH.
GOOD-LUCK CHARMS...
ALL RIGHT!
I'LL MAKE SOME CUTE GOOD-LUCK CHARMS.
Like with flowers.
YEAH.
THANKS, KURAMA.
He's not amused.
UH, TOMOE-KUN.
LISTEN, LISTEN.
RYU-OH AND I WERE TALKING ABOUT A SHOW WHERE WE OFFER YOU AS A BLOOD SACRIFICE.
WHY'RE YOU BLUSHING?
Hey, don't tell him yet!

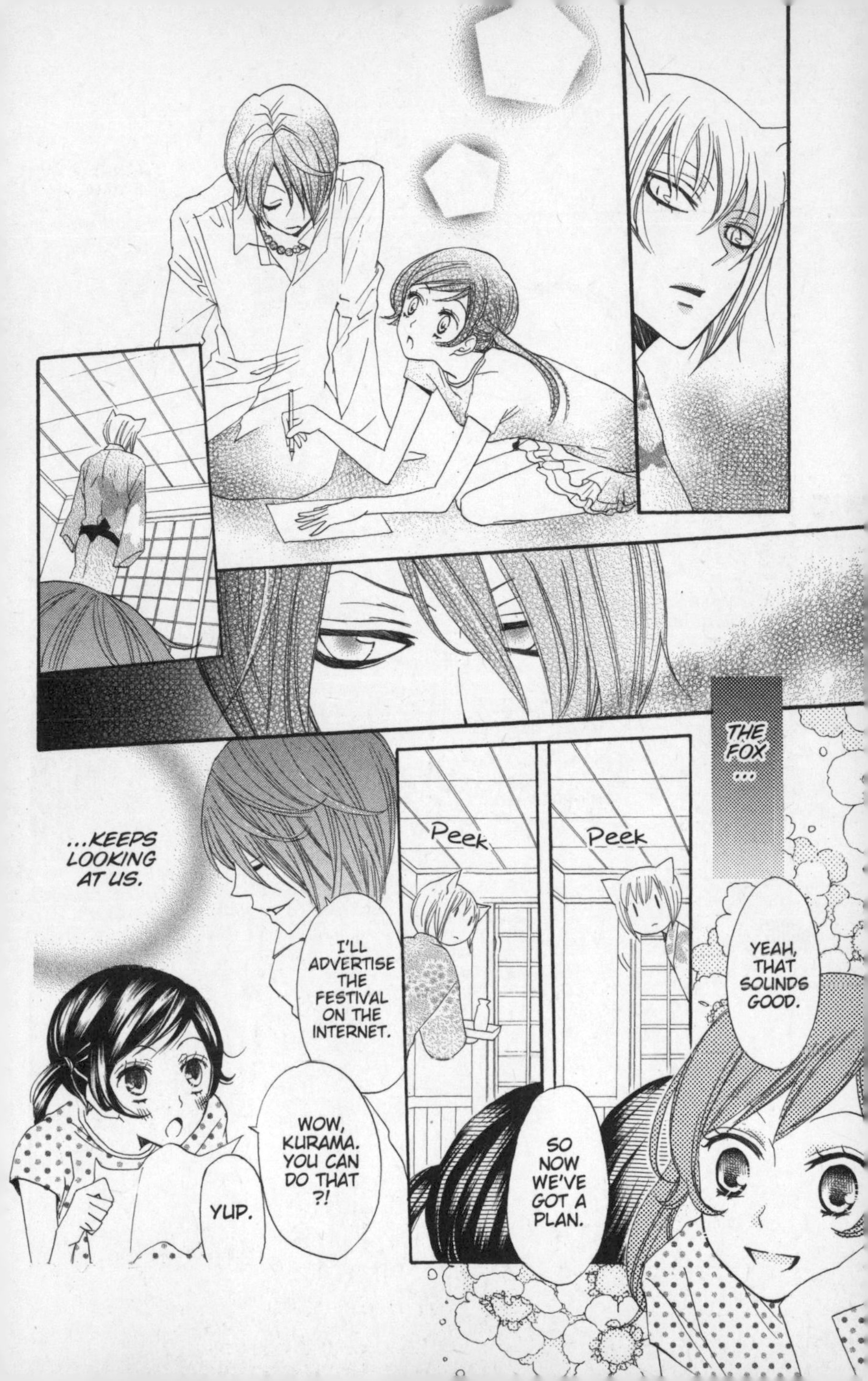
THE FOX ...
...KEEPS LOOKING AT US.
I'LL ADVERTISE THE FESTIVAL ON THE INTERNET.
WOW, KURAMA. YOU CAN DO THAT ?!
YUP.
Peek
Peek
SO NOW WE'VE GOT A PLAN.
YEAH, THAT SOUNDS GOOD.

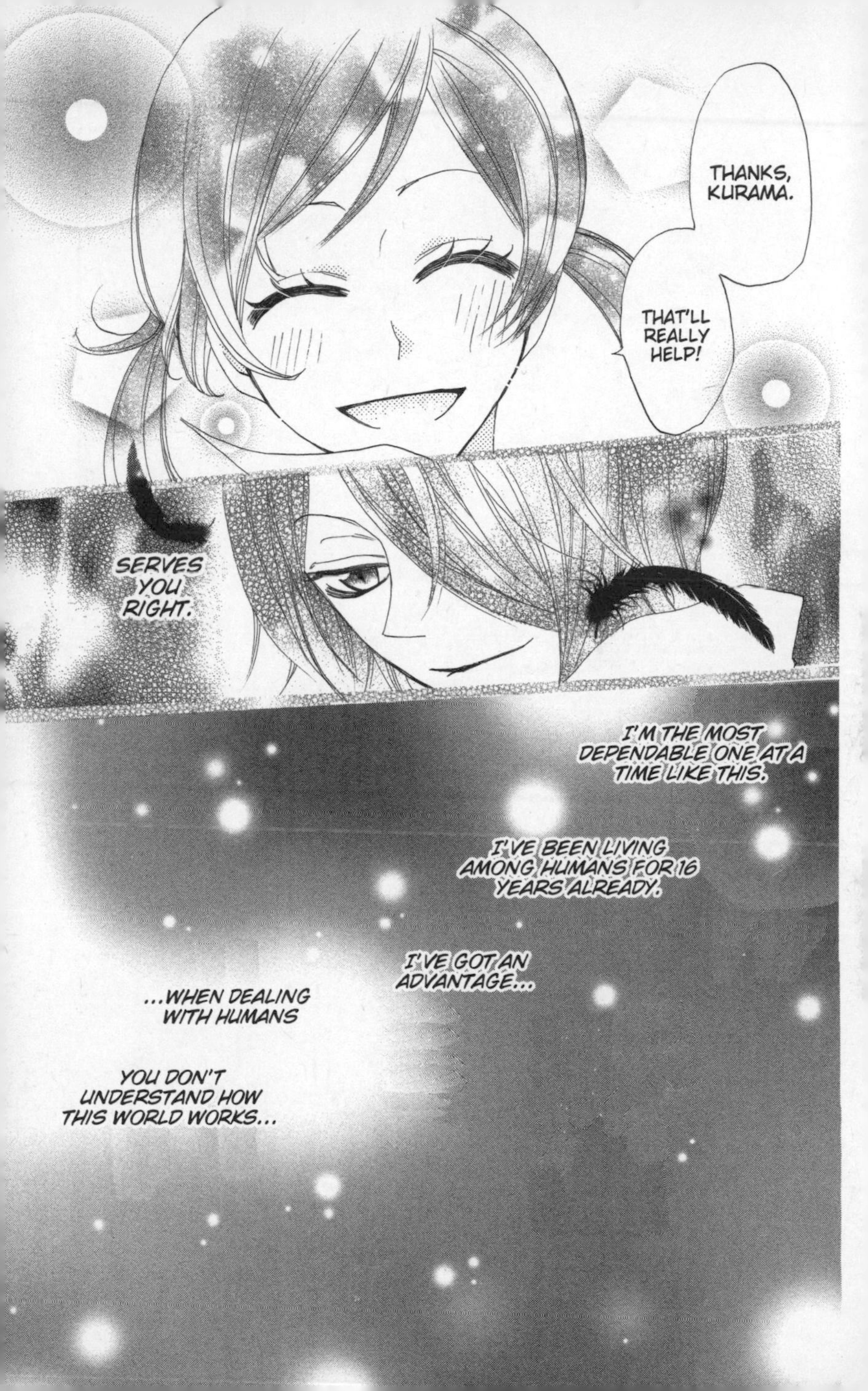
THANKS, KURAMA.
THAT'LL REALLY HELP!
SERVES YOU RIGHT.
I'M THE MOST DEPENDABLE ONE AT A TIME LIKE THIS.
I'VE BEEN LIVING AMONG HUMANS FOR 16 YEARS ALREADY.
I'VE GOT AN ADVANTAGE...
...WHEN DEALING WITH HUMANS
YOU DON'T UNDERSTAND HOW THIS WORLD WORKS...

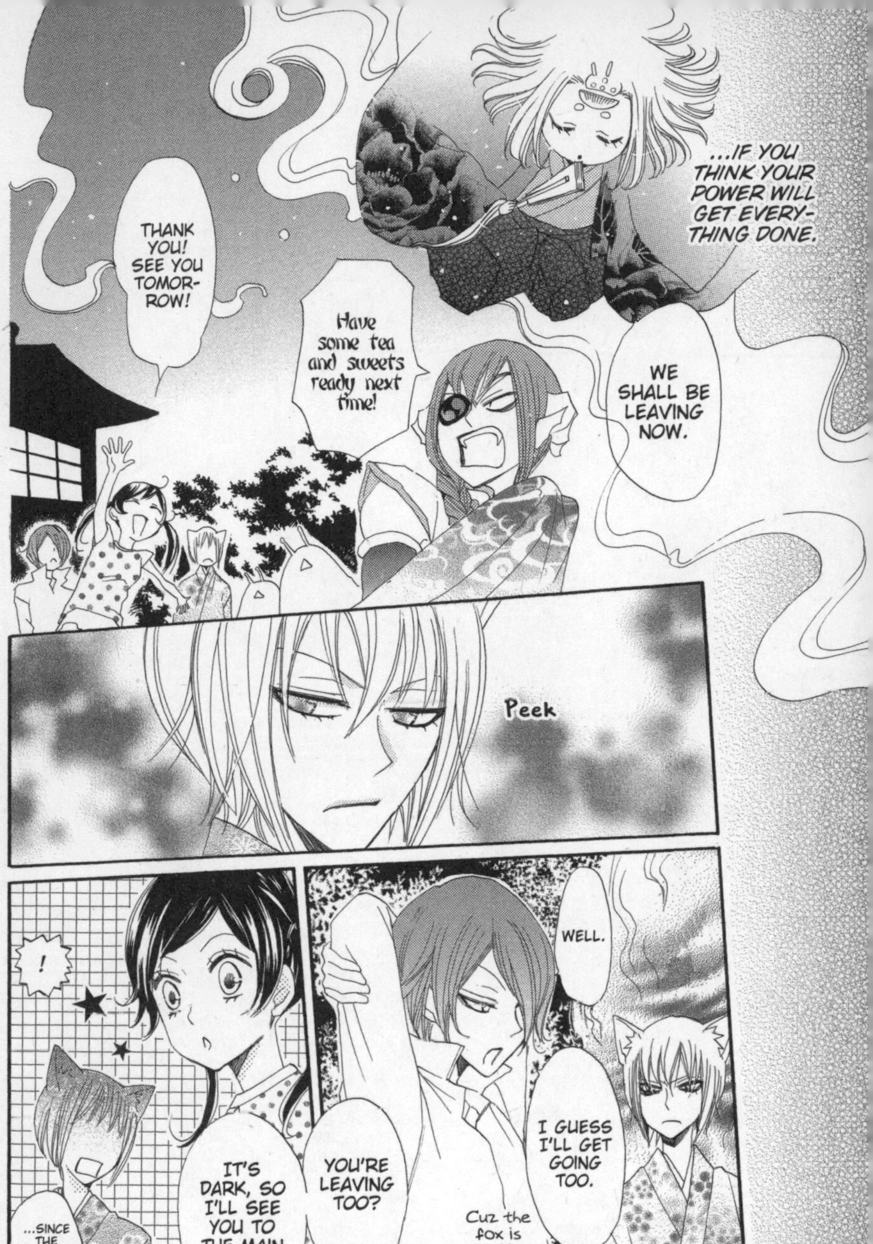
...IF YOU THINK YOUR POWER WILL GET EVERYTHING DONE.
WE SHALL BE LEAVING NOW.
Have some tea and sweets ready next time!
THANK YOU! SEE YOU TOMORROW!
Peek
WELL.
I GUESS I'LL GET GOING TOO.
Cuz the fox is watching.
YOU'RE LEAVING TOO?
IT'S DARK, SO I'LL SEE YOU TO THE MAIN STREET...
...SINCE THE BUSES HAVE STOPPED RUNNING.
!

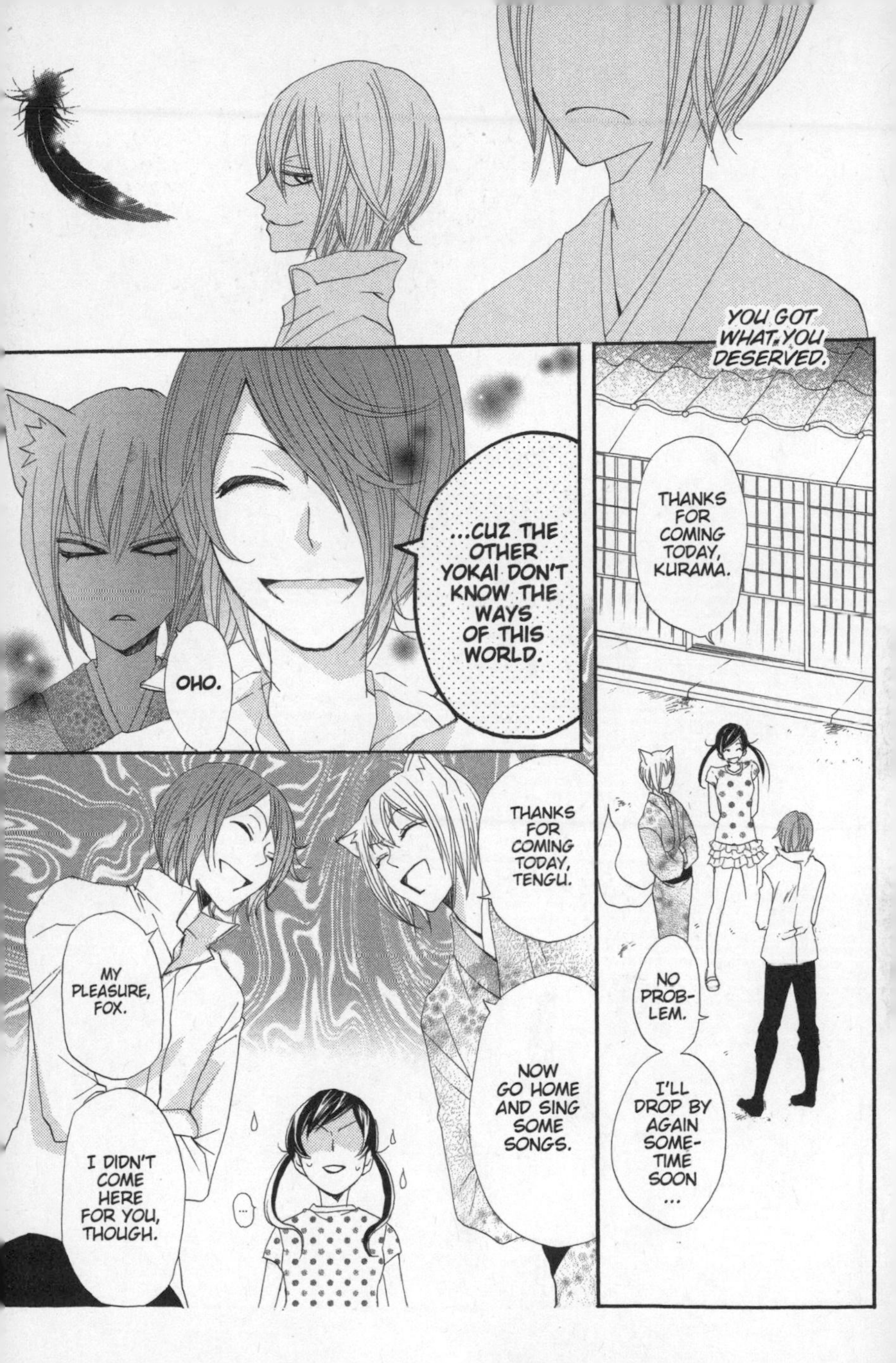
YOU GOT WHAT YOU DESERVED.
THANKS FOR COMING TODAY, KURAMA.
NO PROB-LEM.
I'LL DROP BY AGAIN SOME-TIME SOON...
...CUZ THE OTHER YOKAI DON'T KNOW THE WAYS OF THIS WORLD.
OHO.
THANKS FOR COMING TODAY, TENGU.
MY PLEASURE, FOX.
NOW GO HOME AND SING SOME SONGS.
I DIDN'T COME HERE FOR YOU, THOUGH.
...

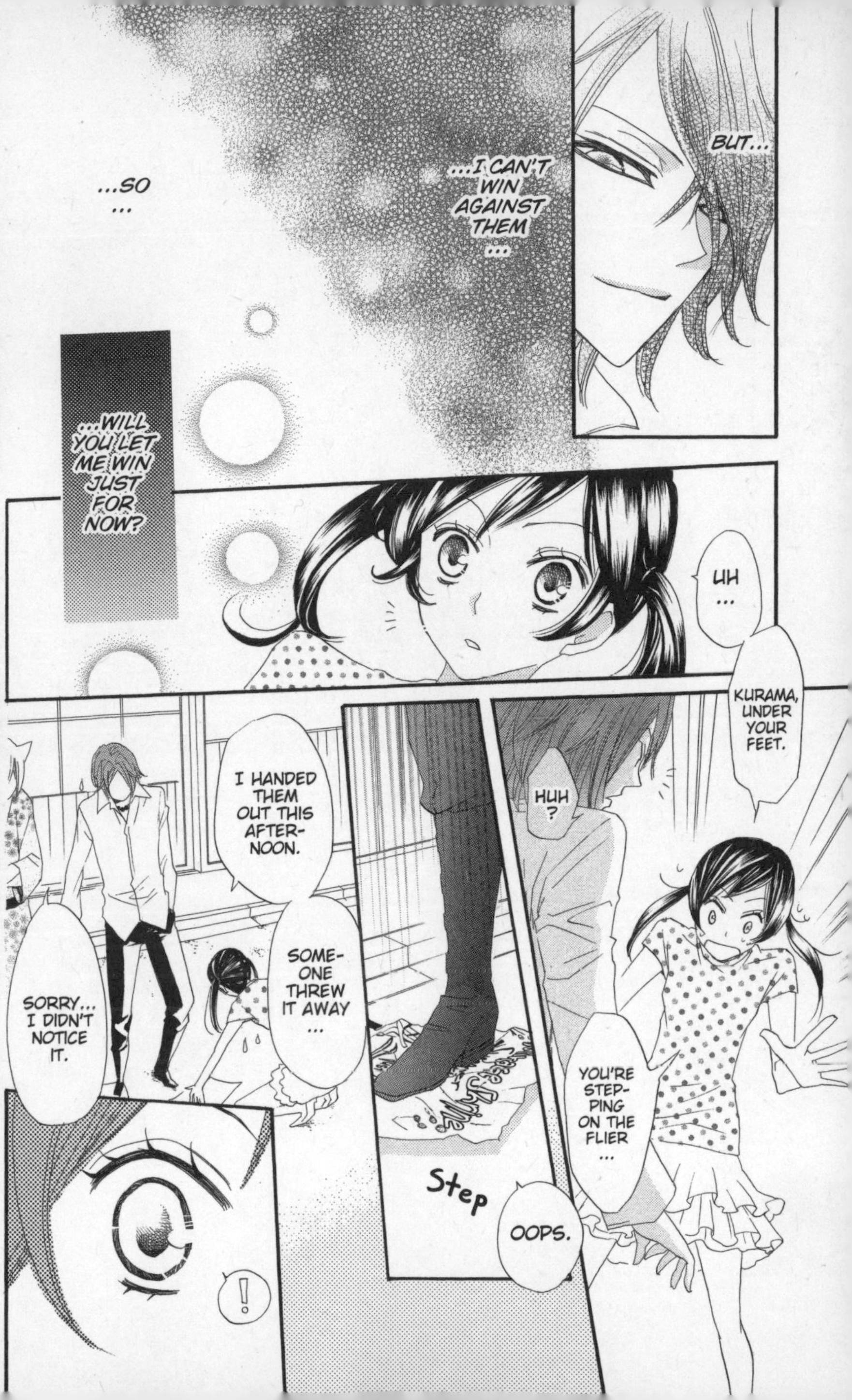
BUT...
...I CAN'T WIN AGAINST THEM...
...SO...
...WILL YOU LET ME WIN JUST FOR NOW?
UH...
KURAMA, UNDER YOUR FEET.
HUH?
YOU'RE STEP-PING ON THE FLIER...
Step
OOPS.
I HANDED THEM OUT THIS AFTER-NOON.
SOME-ONE THREW IT AWAY...
SORRY... I DIDN'T NOTICE IT.
!

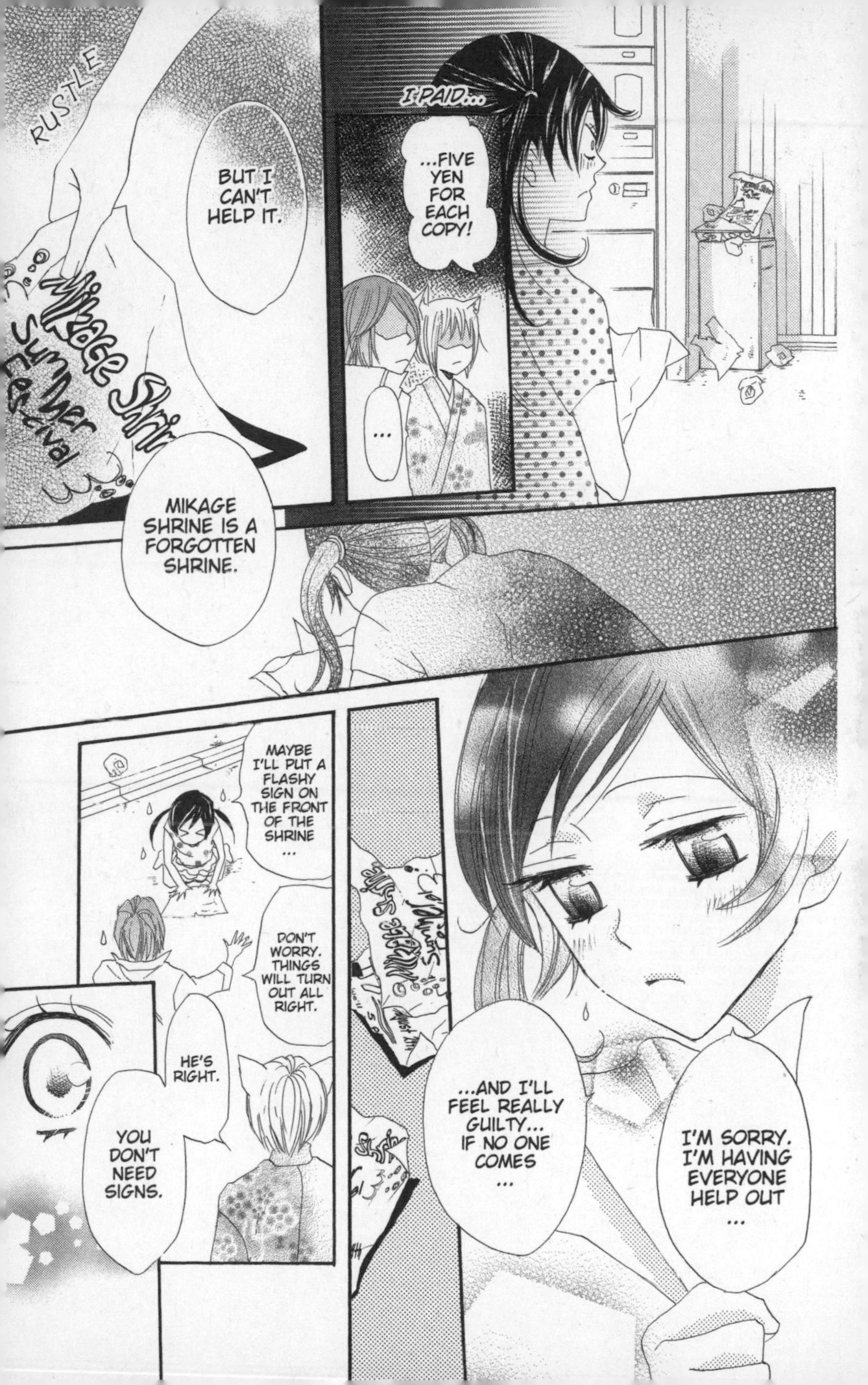
I PAID...
...FIVE YEN FOR EACH COPY!
...
RUSTLE
BUT I CAN'T HELP IT.
MIKAGE SHRINE IS A FORGOTTEN SHRINE.
I'M SORRY. I'M HAVING EVERYONE HELP OUT ...
...AND I'LL FEEL REALLY GUILTY... IF NO ONE COMES ...
MAYBE I'LL PUT A FLASHY SIGN ON THE FRONT OF THE SHRINE ...
DON'T WORRY. THINGS WILL TURN OUT ALL RIGHT.
HE'S RIGHT.
YOU DON'T NEED SIGNS.

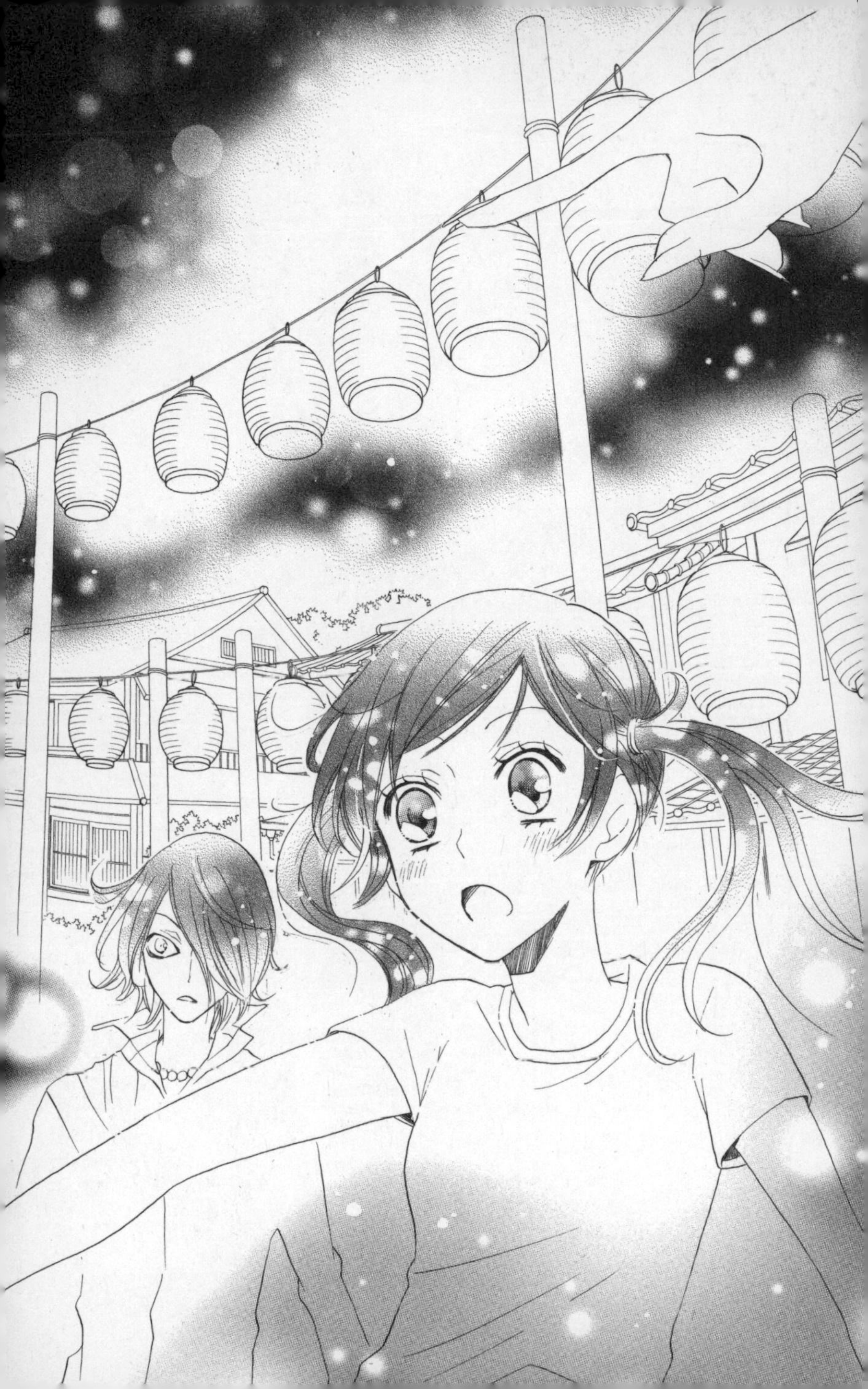

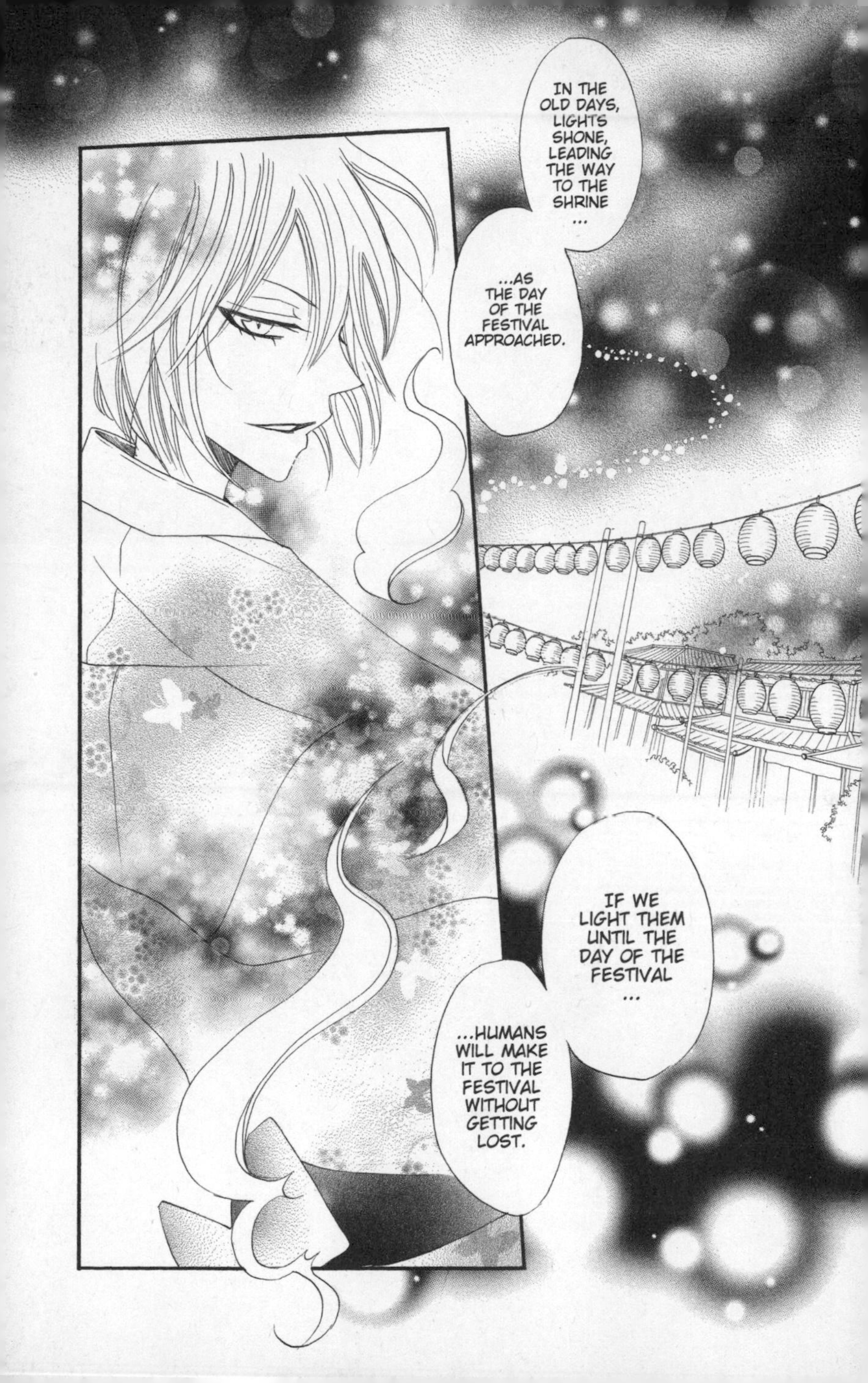
IN THE OLD DAYS, LIGHTS SHONE, LEADING THE WAY TO THE SHRINE...
...AS THE DAY OF THE FESTIVAL APPROACHED.
IF WE LIGHT THEM UNTIL THE DAY OF THE FESTIVAL...
...HUMANS WILL MAKE IT TO THE FESTIVAL WITHOUT GETTING LOST.

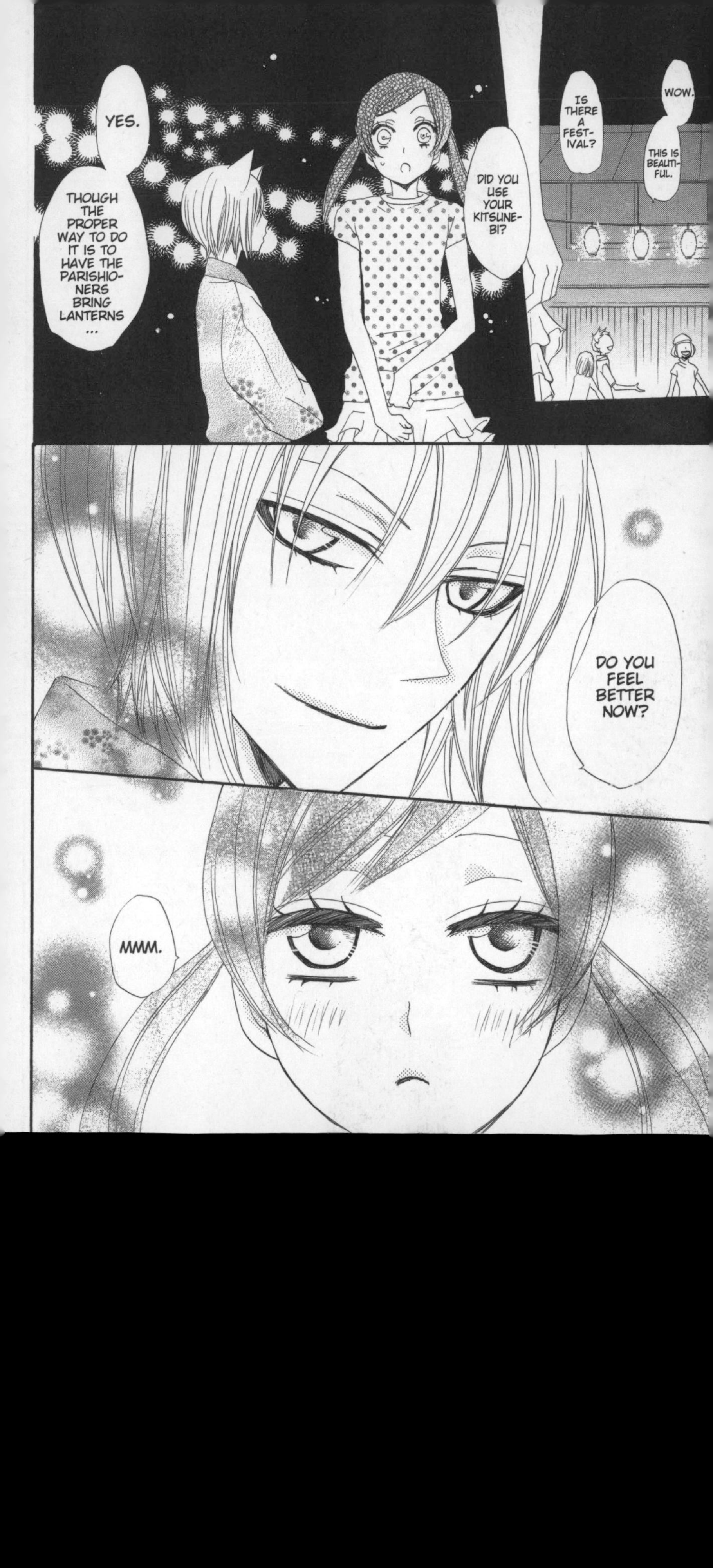
WOW.
THIS IS BEAUTIFUL.
IS THERE A FESTIVAL?
DID YOU USE YOUR KITSUNE-BI?
YES.
THOUGH THE PROPER WAY TO DO IT IS TO HAVE THE PARISHIONERS BRING LANTERNS ...
DO YOU FEEL BETTER NOW?
MMM.

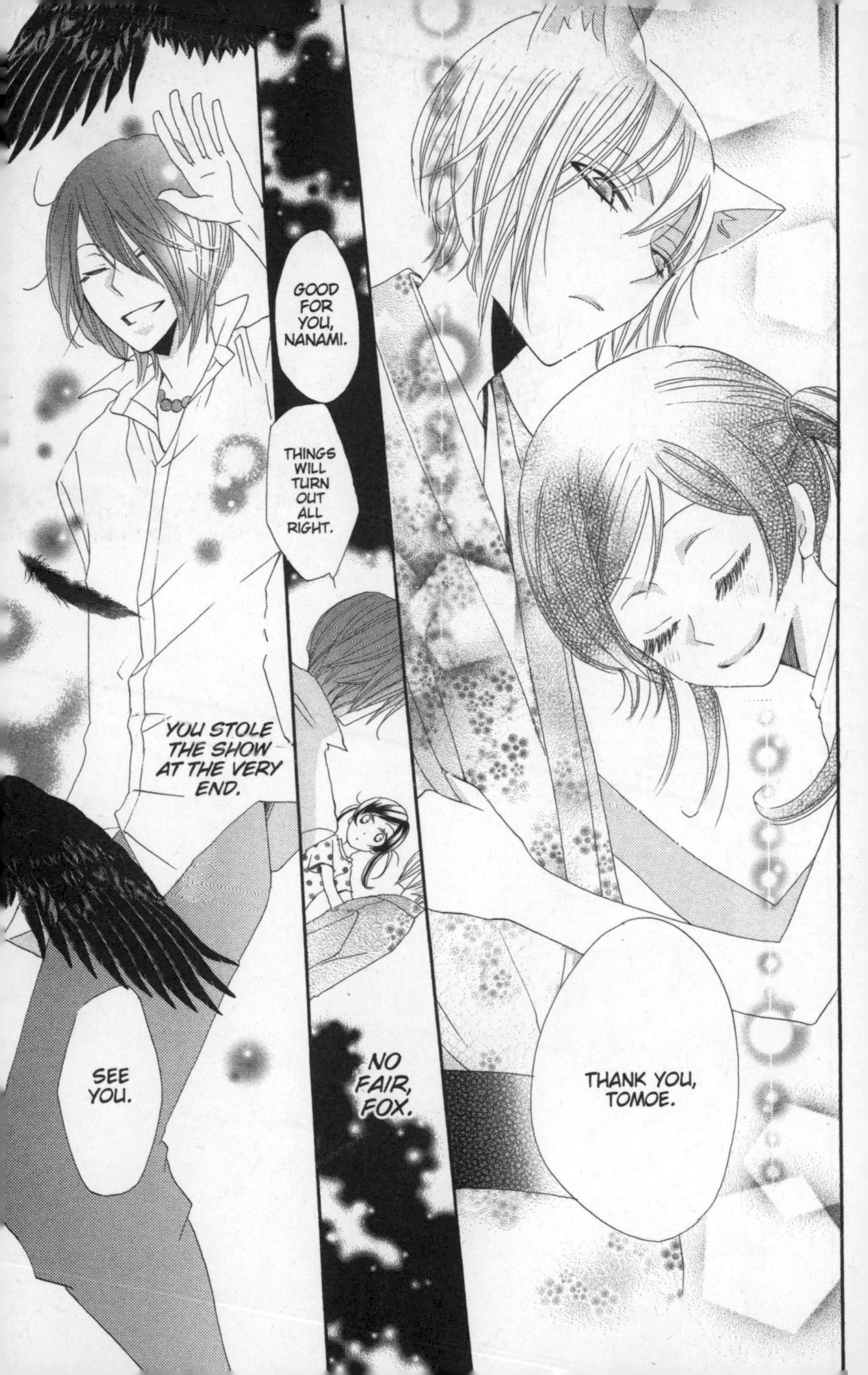
THANK YOU, TOMOE.
GOOD FOR YOU, NANAMI.
THINGS WILL TURN OUT ALL RIGHT.
NO FAIR, FOX.
YOU STOLE THE SHOW AT THE VERY END.
SEE YOU.

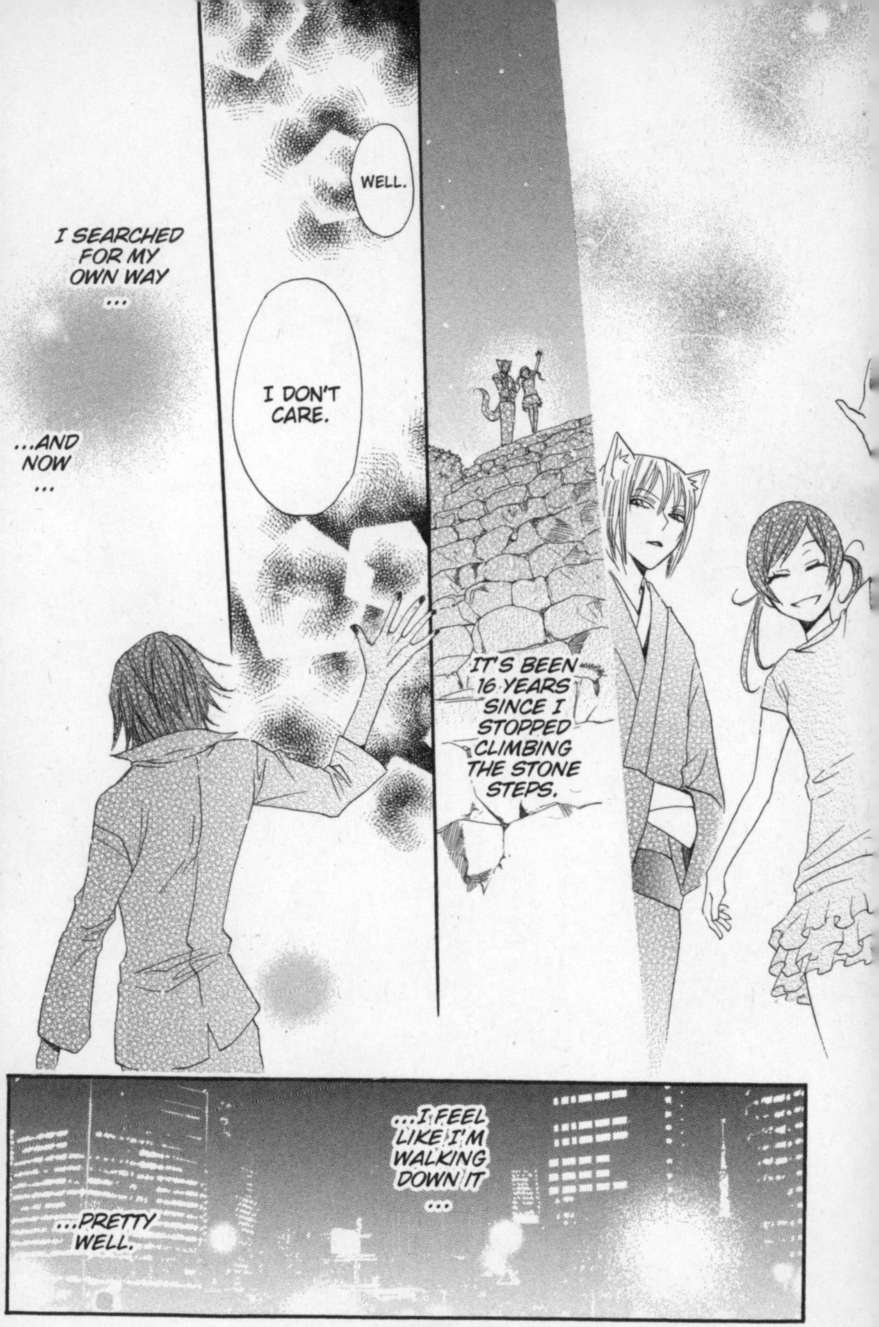
IT'S BEEN 16 YEARS SINCE I STOPPED CLIMBING THE STONE STEPS.
WELL.
I DON'T CARE.
I SEARCHED FOR MY OWN WAY ...
...AND NOW ...
...I FEEL LIKE I'M WALKING DOWN IT ...
...PRETTY WELL.

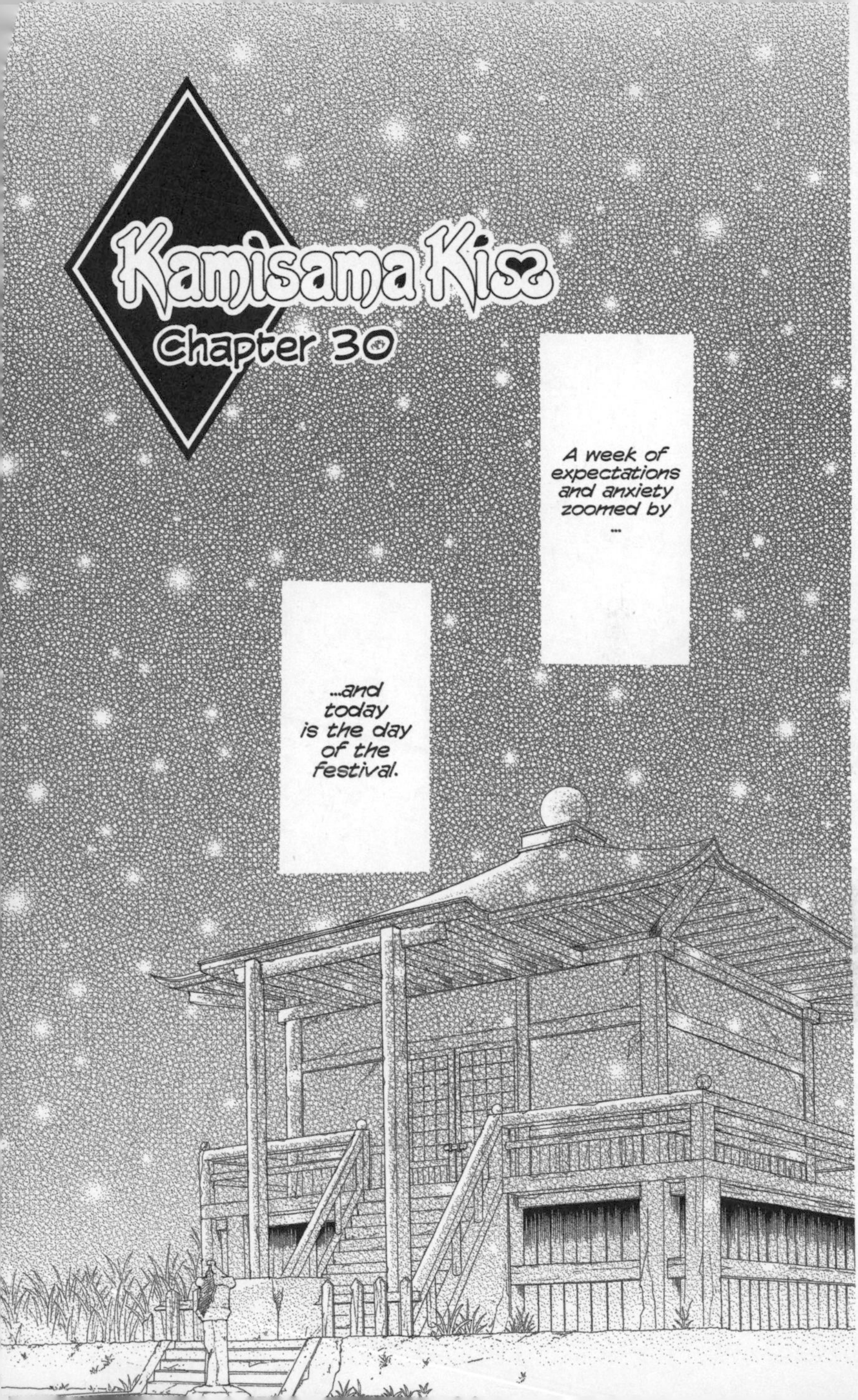
Kamisama Kiss
Chapter 30
A week of expectations and anxiety zoomed by
...
...and today is the day of the festival.

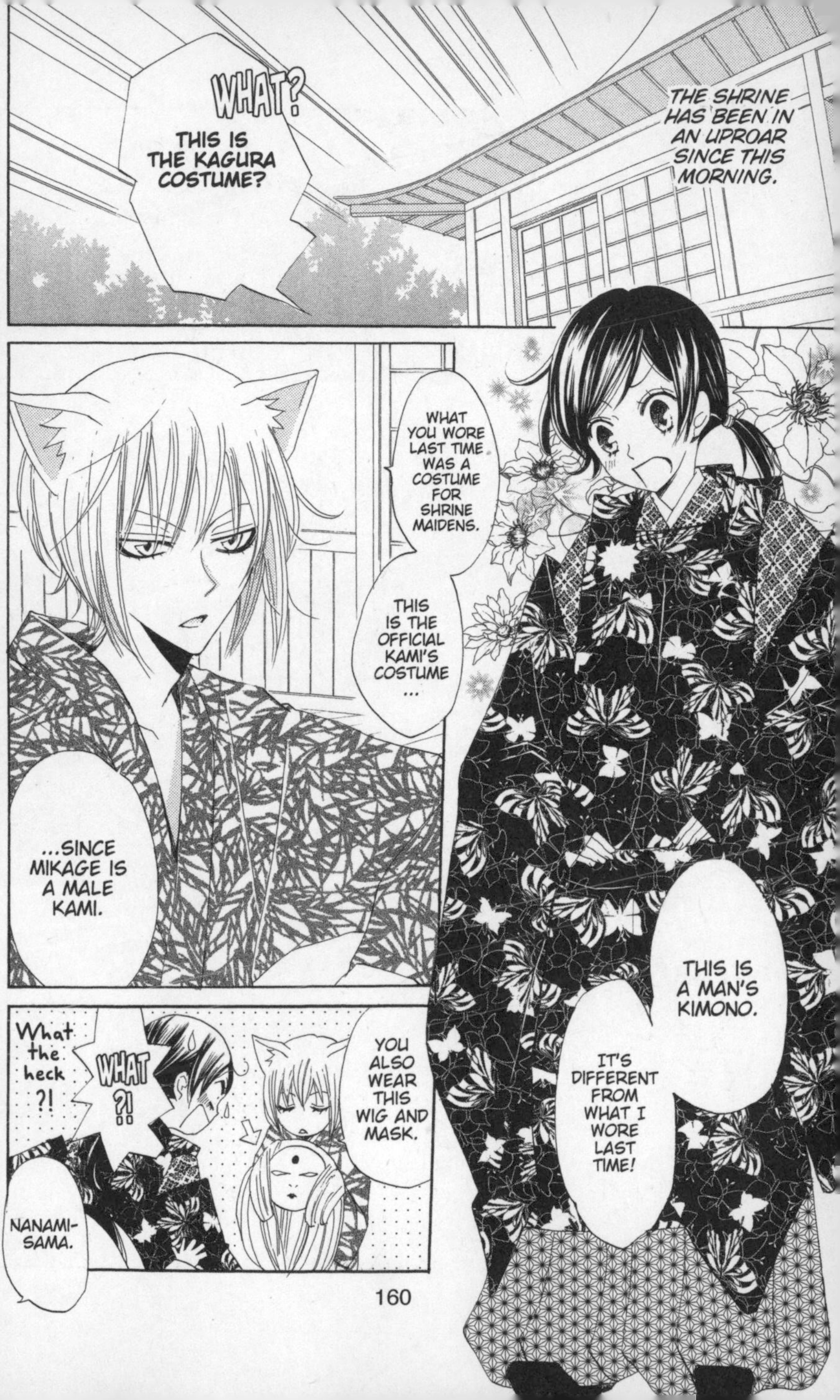
THE SHRINE HAS BEEN IN AN UPROAR SINCE THIS MORNING.
WHAT?
THIS IS THE KAGURA COSTUME?
THIS IS A MAN'S KIMONO.
IT'S DIFFERENT FROM WHAT I WORE LAST TIME!
WHAT YOU WORE LAST TIME WAS A COSTUME FOR SHRINE MAIDENS.
THIS IS THE OFFICIAL KAMI'S COSTUME ...
...SINCE MIKAGE IS A MALE KAMI.
YOU ALSO WEAR THIS WIG AND MASK.
WHAT ?!
What the heck ?!
NANAMI-SAMA.

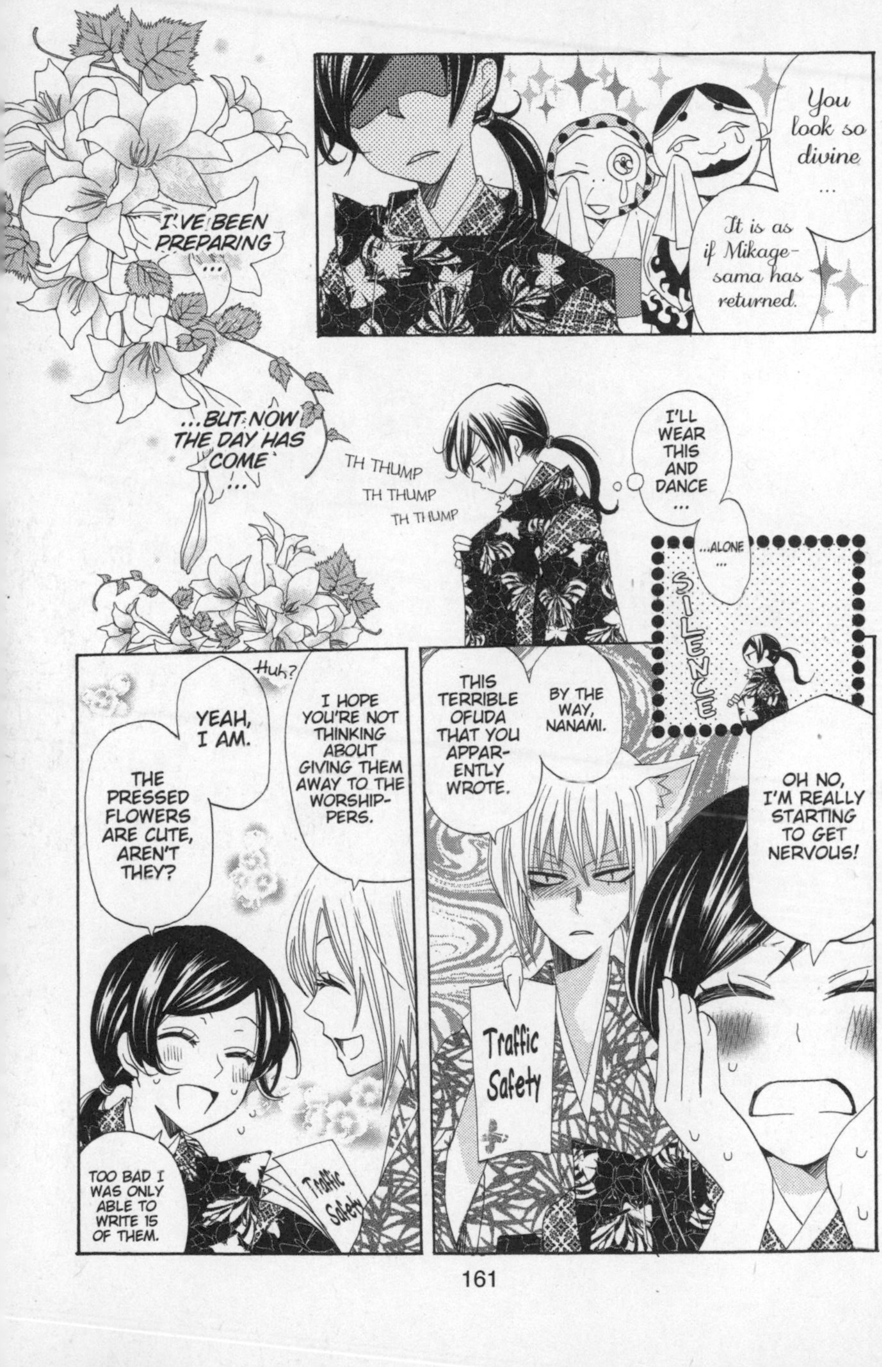
You look so divine ...
It is as if Mikage-sama has returned.
TH THUMP
TH THUMP
TH THUMP
I'LL WEAR THIS AND DANCE ...
...ALONE ...
SILENCE
I'VE BEEN PREPARING ...
...BUT NOW THE DAY HAS COME ...
OH NO, I'M REALLY STARTING TO GET NERVOUS!
BY THE WAY, NANAMI.
THIS TERRIBLE OFUDA THAT YOU APPARENTLY WROTE.
Traffic Safety
I HOPE YOU'RE NOT THINKING ABOUT GIVING THEM AWAY TO THE WORSHIPPERS.
Huh?
YEAH, I AM.
THE PRESSED FLOWERS ARE CUTE, AREN'T THEY?
Traffic Safety
TOO BAD I WAS ONLY ABLE TO WRITE 15 OF THEM.

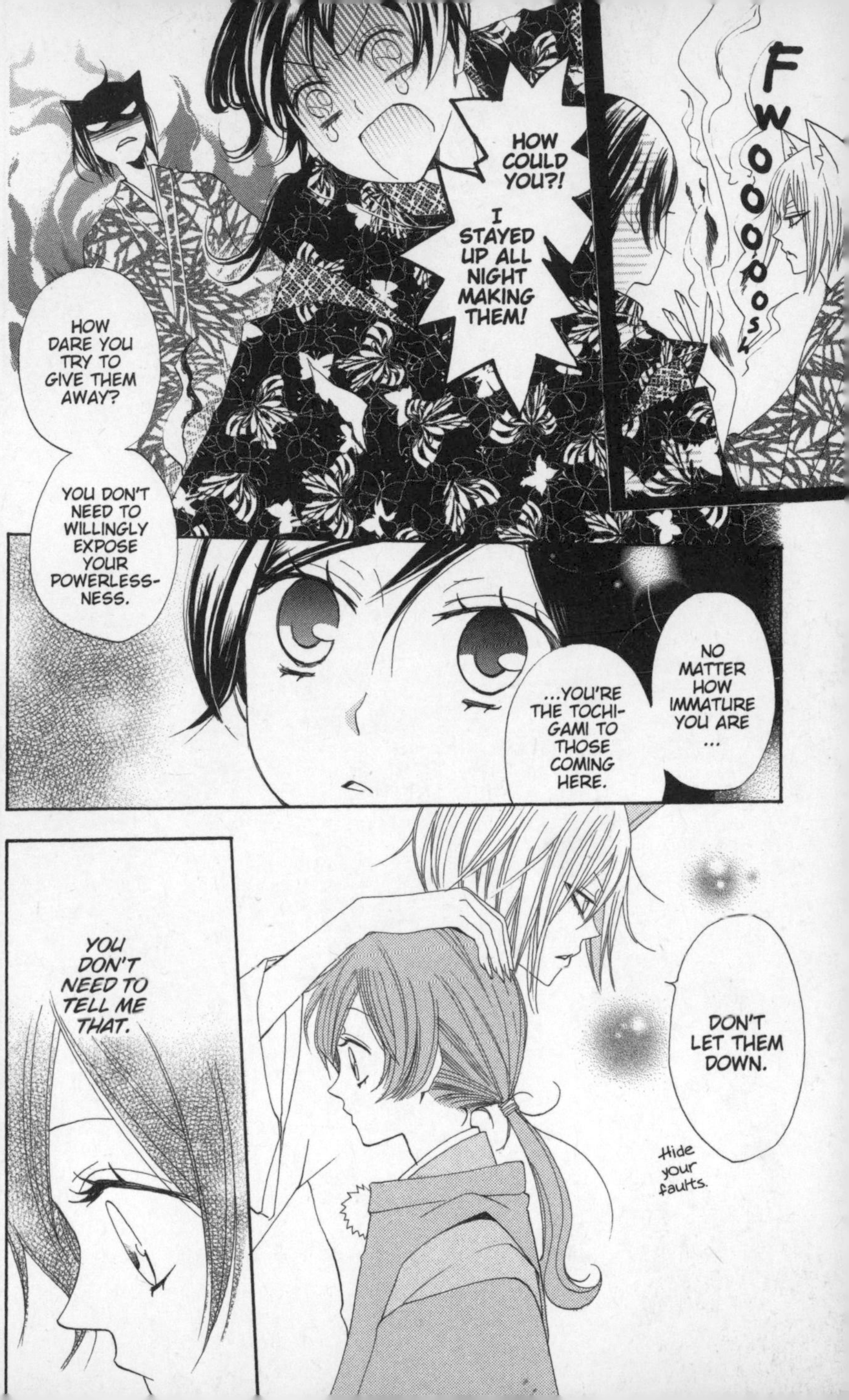
FWOOOOOSH
HOW COULD YOU?!
I STAYED UP ALL NIGHT MAKING THEM!
HOW DARE YOU TRY TO GIVE THEM AWAY?
YOU DON'T NEED TO WILLINGLY EXPOSE YOUR POWERLESS-NESS.
NO MATTER HOW IMMATURE YOU ARE...
...YOU'RE THE TOCHI-GAMI TO THOSE COMING HERE.
DON'T LET THEM DOWN.
Hide your faults.
YOU DON'T NEED TO TELL ME THAT.

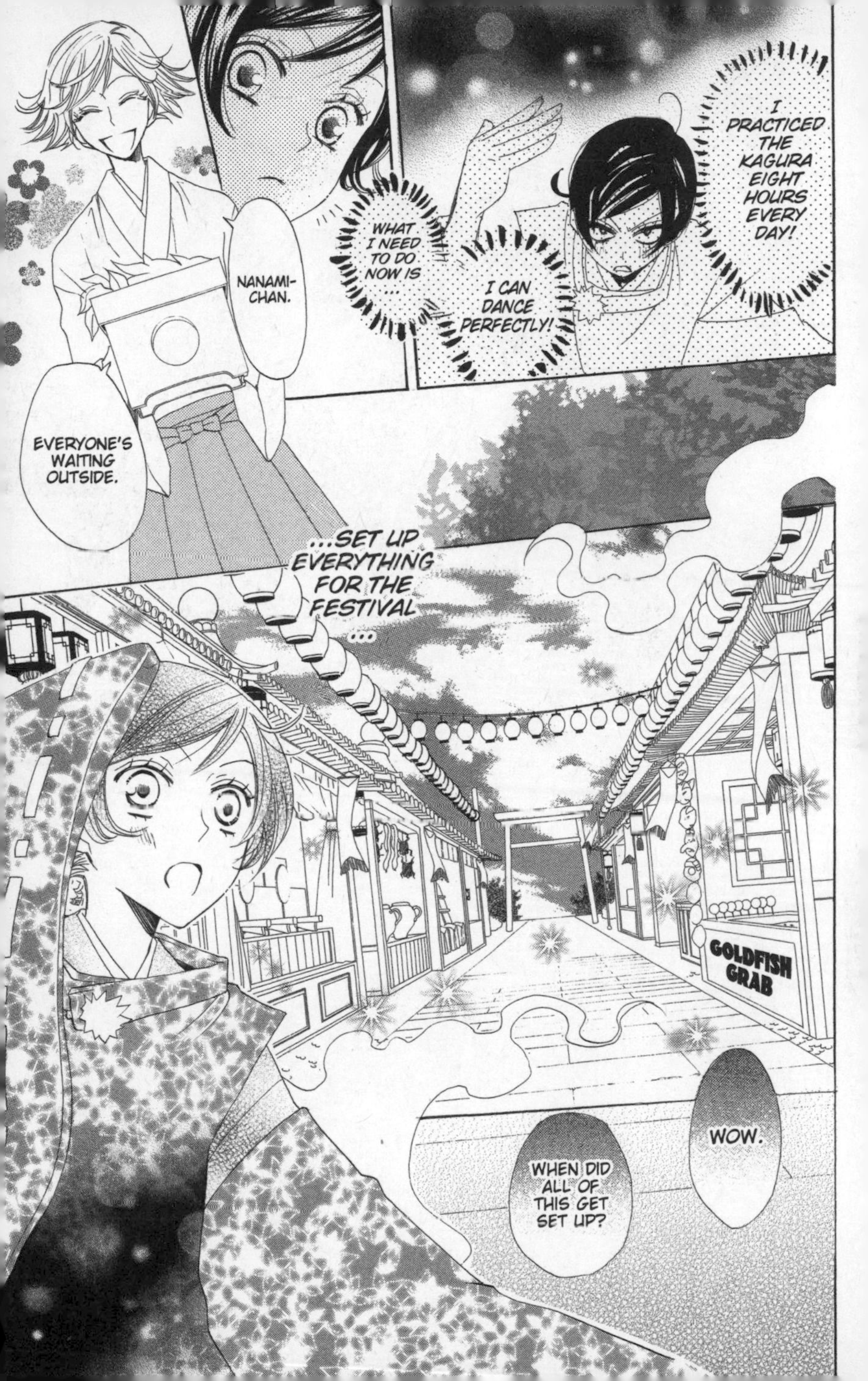
I PRACTICED THE KAGURA EIGHT HOURS EVERY DAY!
I CAN DANCE PERFECTLY!
WHAT I NEED TO DO NOW IS ...
NANAMI-CHAN.
EVERYONE'S WAITING OUTSIDE.
...SET UP EVERYTHING FOR THE FESTIVAL ...
GOLDFISH GRAB
WOW.
WHEN DID ALL OF THIS GET SET UP?

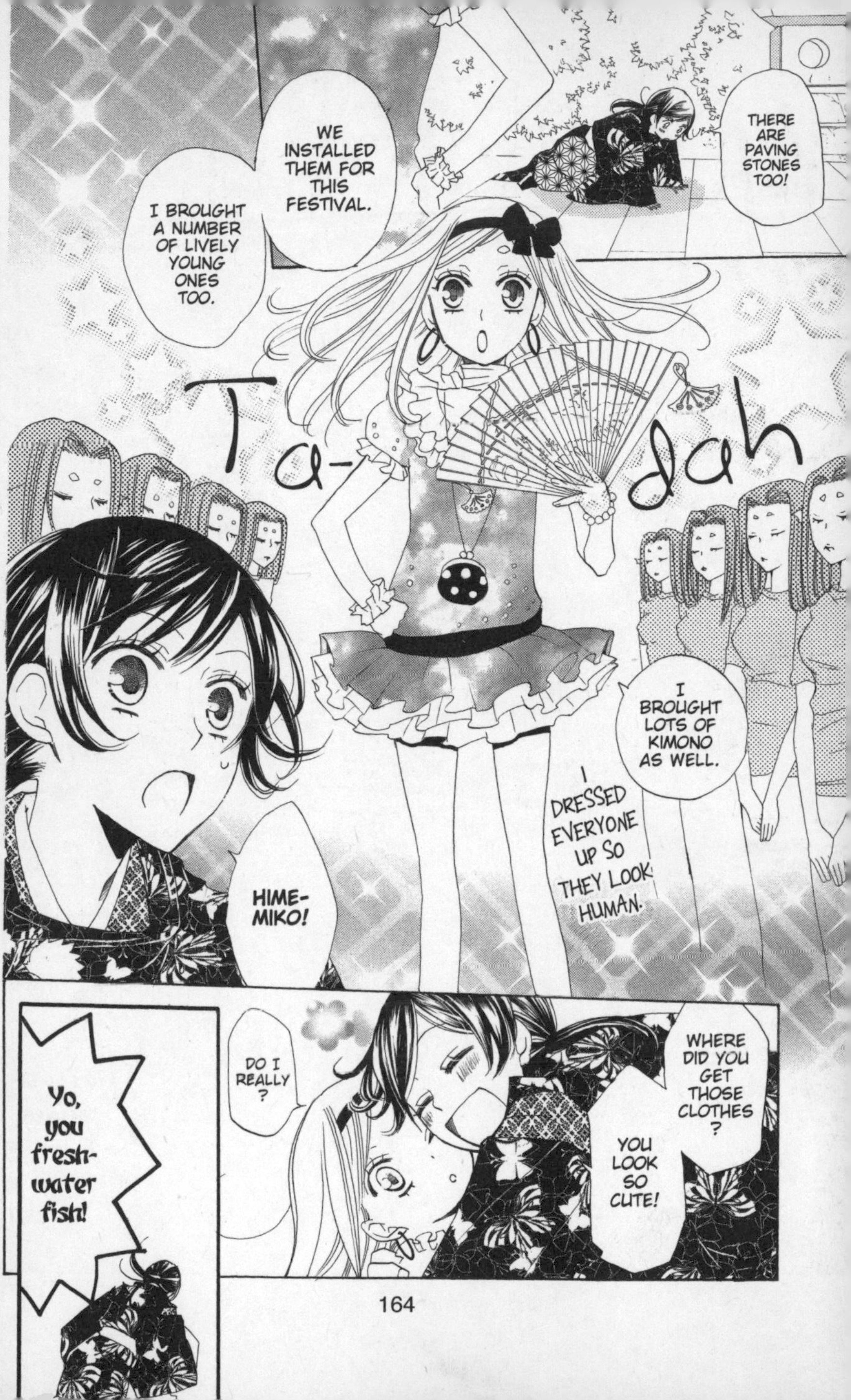
THERE ARE PAVING STONES TOO!
WE INSTALLED THEM FOR THIS FESTIVAL.
I BROUGHT A NUMBER OF LIVELY YOUNG ONES TOO.
Ta-dah
I BROUGHT LOTS OF KIMONO AS WELL.
I DRESSED EVERYONE UP SO THEY LOOK HUMAN.
HIME-MIKO!
WHERE DID YOU GET THOSE CLOTHES?
YOU LOOK SO CUTE!
DO I REALLY?
Yo, you fresh-water fish!

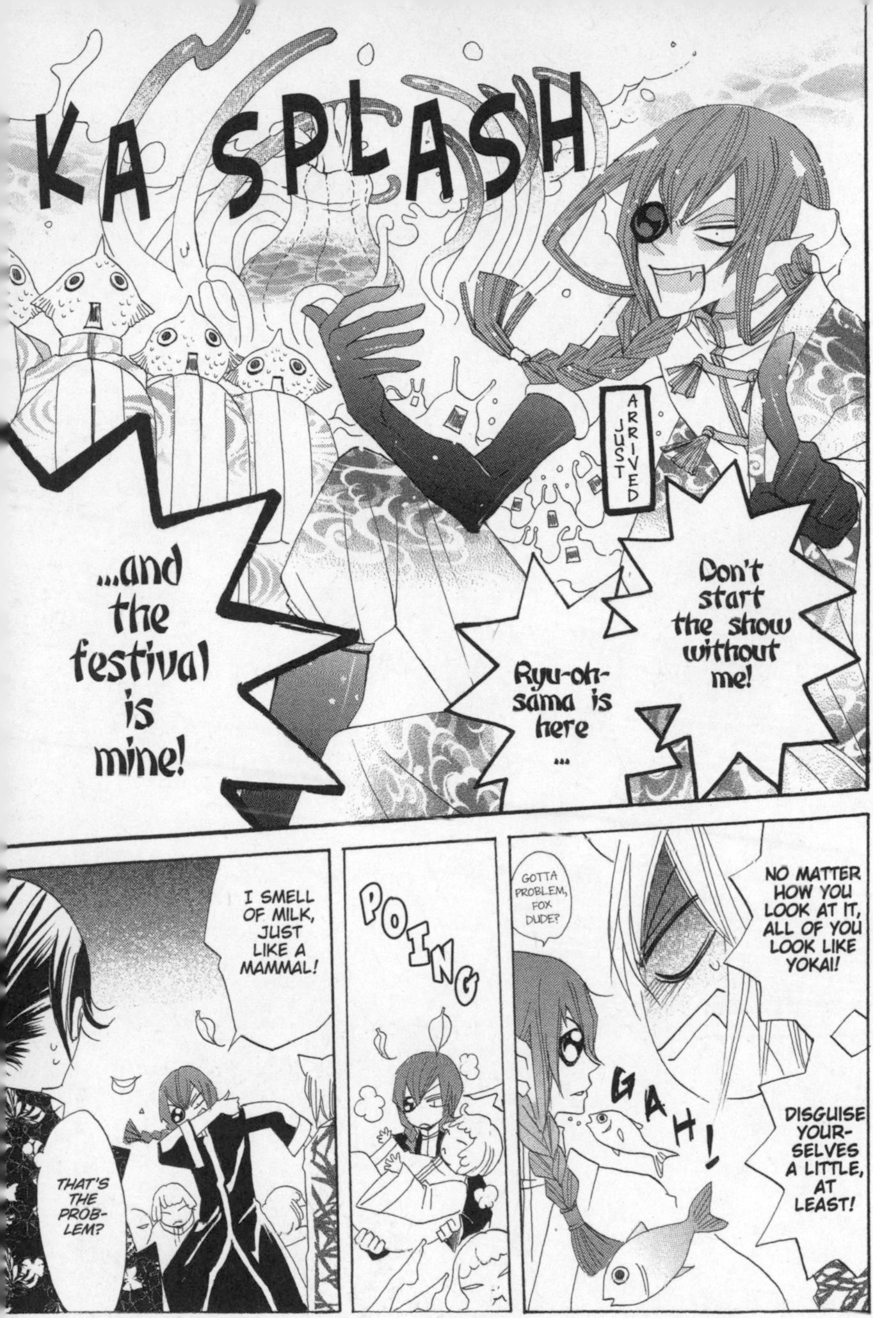
KA SPLASH
JUST ARRIVED
Don't start the show without me!
Ryu-oh-sama is here ...
...and the festival is mine!
NO MATTER HOW YOU LOOK AT IT, ALL OF YOU LOOK LIKE YOKAI!
GOTTA PROBLEM, FOX DUDE?
GAH!
DISGUISE YOURSELVES A LITTLE, AT LEAST!
POING
I SMELL OF MILK, JUST LIKE A MAMMAL!
THAT'S THE PROBLEM?

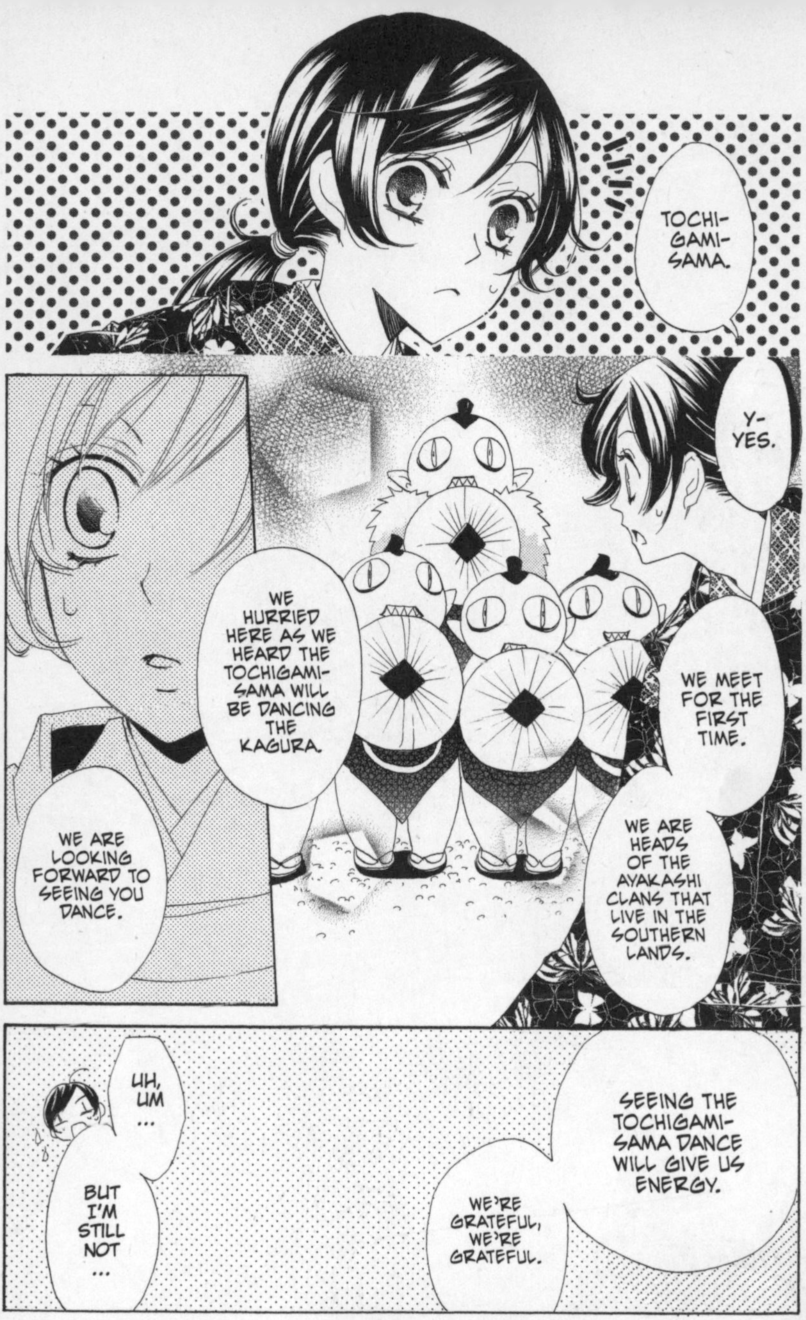
TOCHI-GAMI-SAMA.
Y-YES.
WE MEET FOR THE FIRST TIME.
WE ARE HEADS OF THE AYAKASHI CLANS THAT LIVE IN THE SOUTHERN LANDS.
WE HURRIED HERE AS WE HEARD THE TOCHIGAMI-SAMA WILL BE DANCING THE KAGURA.
WE ARE LOOKING FORWARD TO SEEING YOU DANCE.
SEEING THE TOCHIGAMI-SAMA DANCE WILL GIVE US ENERGY.
WE'RE GRATEFUL, WE'RE GRATEFUL.
UH, UM ...
BUT I'M STILL NOT ...

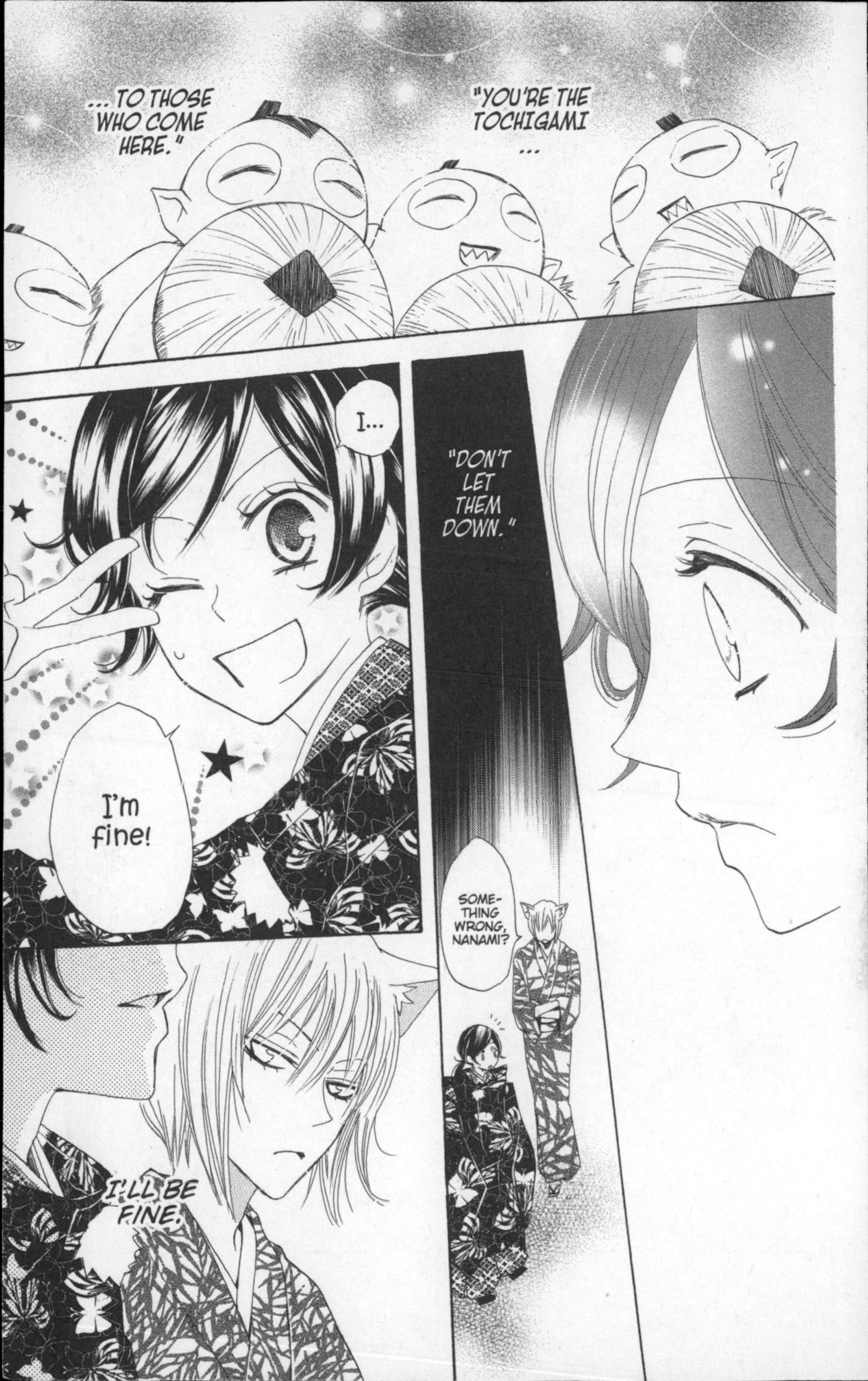
"YOU'RE THE TOCHIGAMI ...
... TO THOSE WHO COME HERE."
"DON'T LET THEM DOWN."
SOME-THING WRONG, NANAMI?
I...
I'm fine!
I'LL BE FINE.

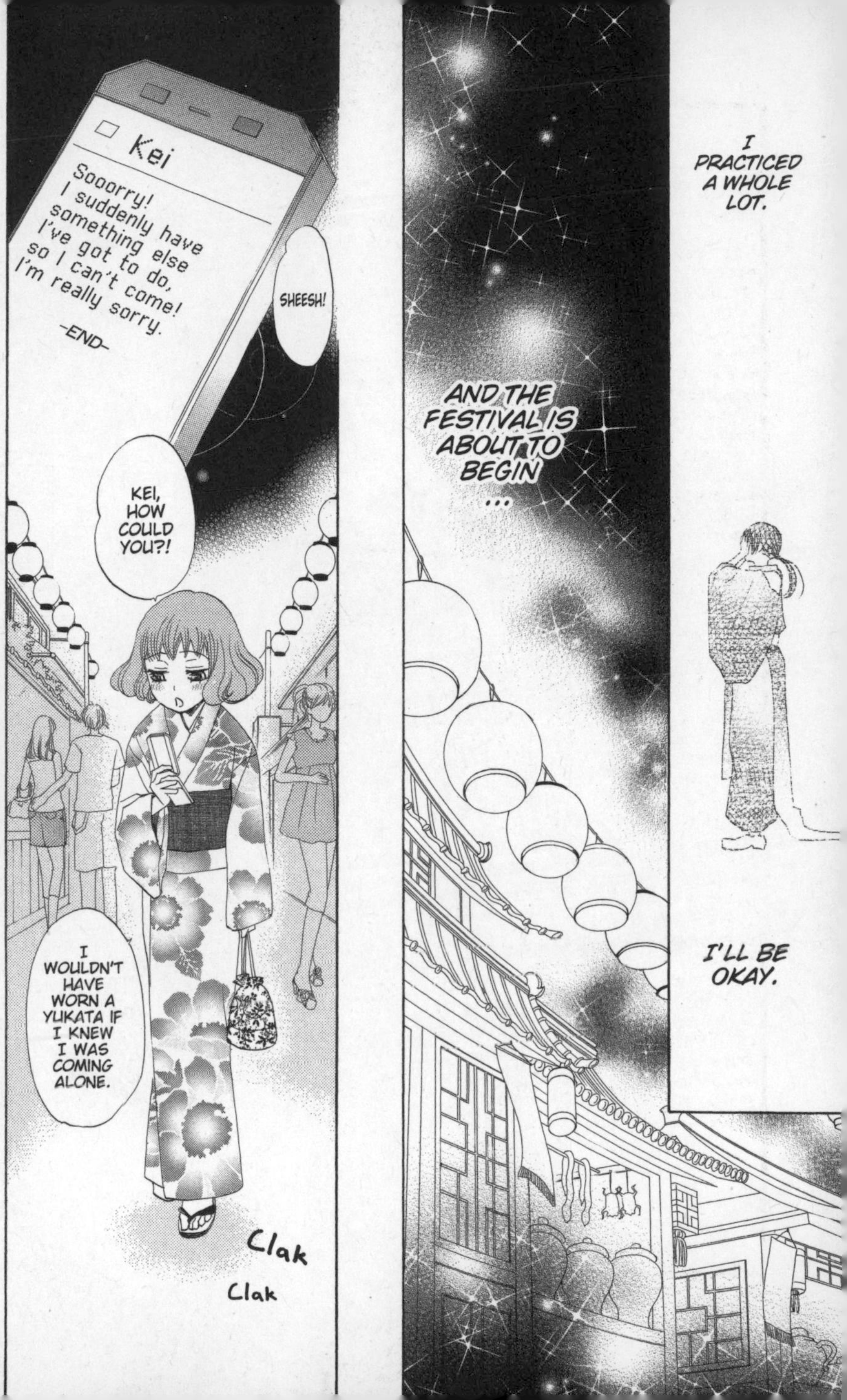
I PRACTICED A WHOLE LOT.
I'LL BE OKAY.
AND THE FESTIVAL IS ABOUT TO BEGIN...
Kei
Sooorry! I suddenly have something else I've got to do, so I can't come! I'm really sorry.
-END-
SHEESH!
KEI, HOW COULD YOU?!
I WOULDN'T HAVE WORN A YUKATA IF I KNEW I WAS COMING ALONE.
Clak
Clak

Thank you for reading this far!

I still have extra pages! What should I write?

Nowadays, I find it difficult drawing manga in complete silence. The engines in my heart have trouble firing up and I want to have some noise while working, so I turn the TV on, then turn down the volume until I can't make out what it's saying. Or I play a foreign movie with subtitles.

My ideal work environment is to draw at a cafe like Starbucks while being surrounded by various sounds, but I can't because I don't want people watching, and also because I'll be worried about the time.

But I've run out of CDs and foreign movies. Hmm, I must think of something else.

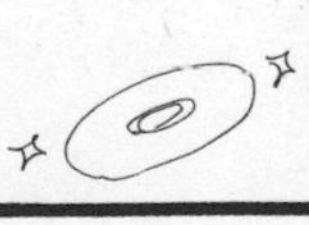

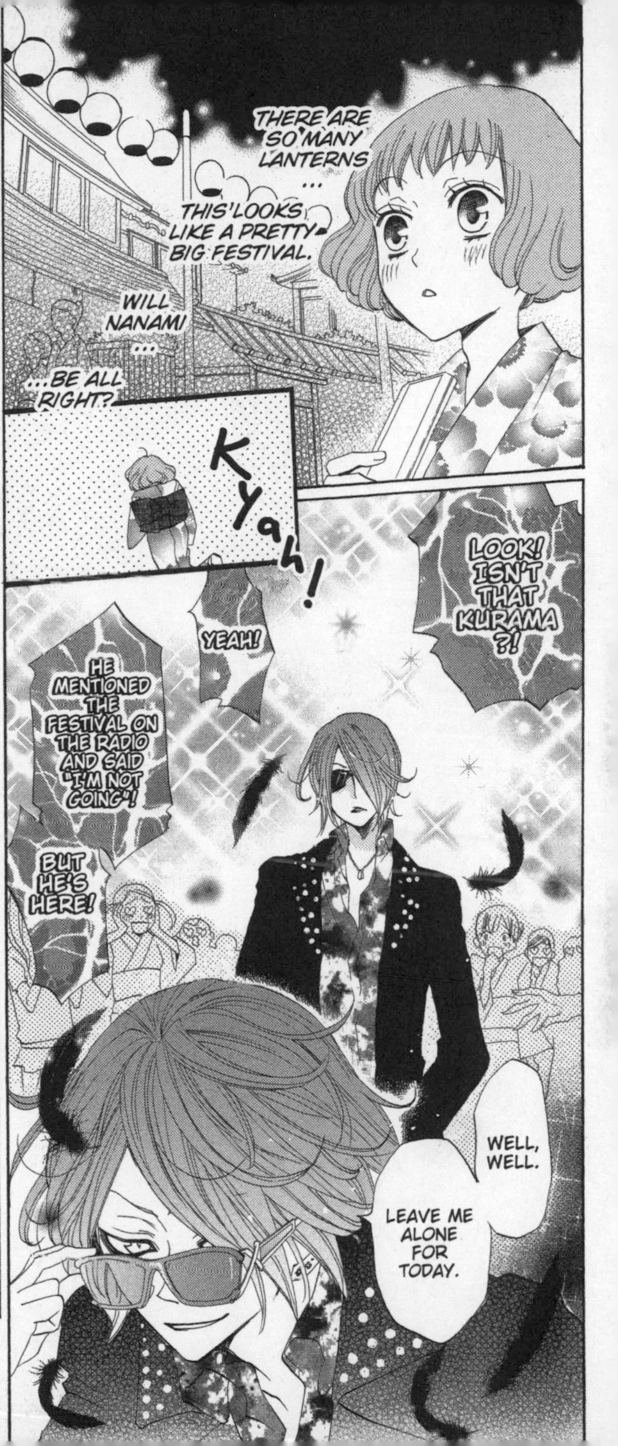
THERE ARE SO MANY LANTERNS...
THIS LOOKS LIKE A PRETTY BIG FESTIVAL.
WILL NANAMI...
...BE ALL RIGHT?
Kyah!
LOOK! ISN'T THAT KURAMA?!
YEAH!
HE MENTIONED THE FESTIVAL ON THE RADIO AND SAID "I'M NOT GOING"!
BUT HE'S HERE!
WELL, WELL.
LEAVE ME ALONE FOR TODAY.

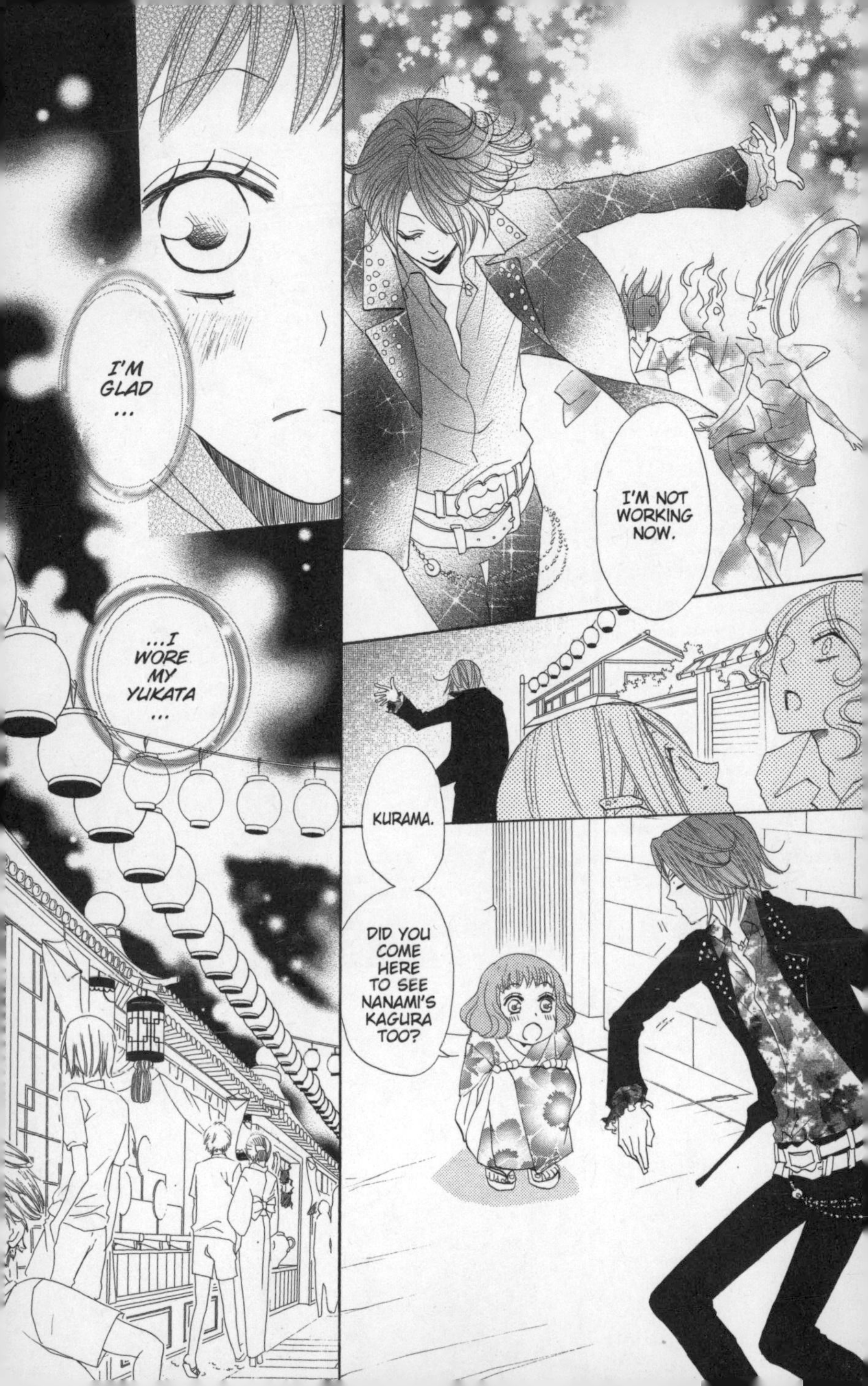
I'M NOT WORKING NOW.
KURAMA.
DID YOU COME HERE TO SEE NANAMI'S KAGURA TOO?
I'M GLAD ...
...I WORE MY YUKATA ...

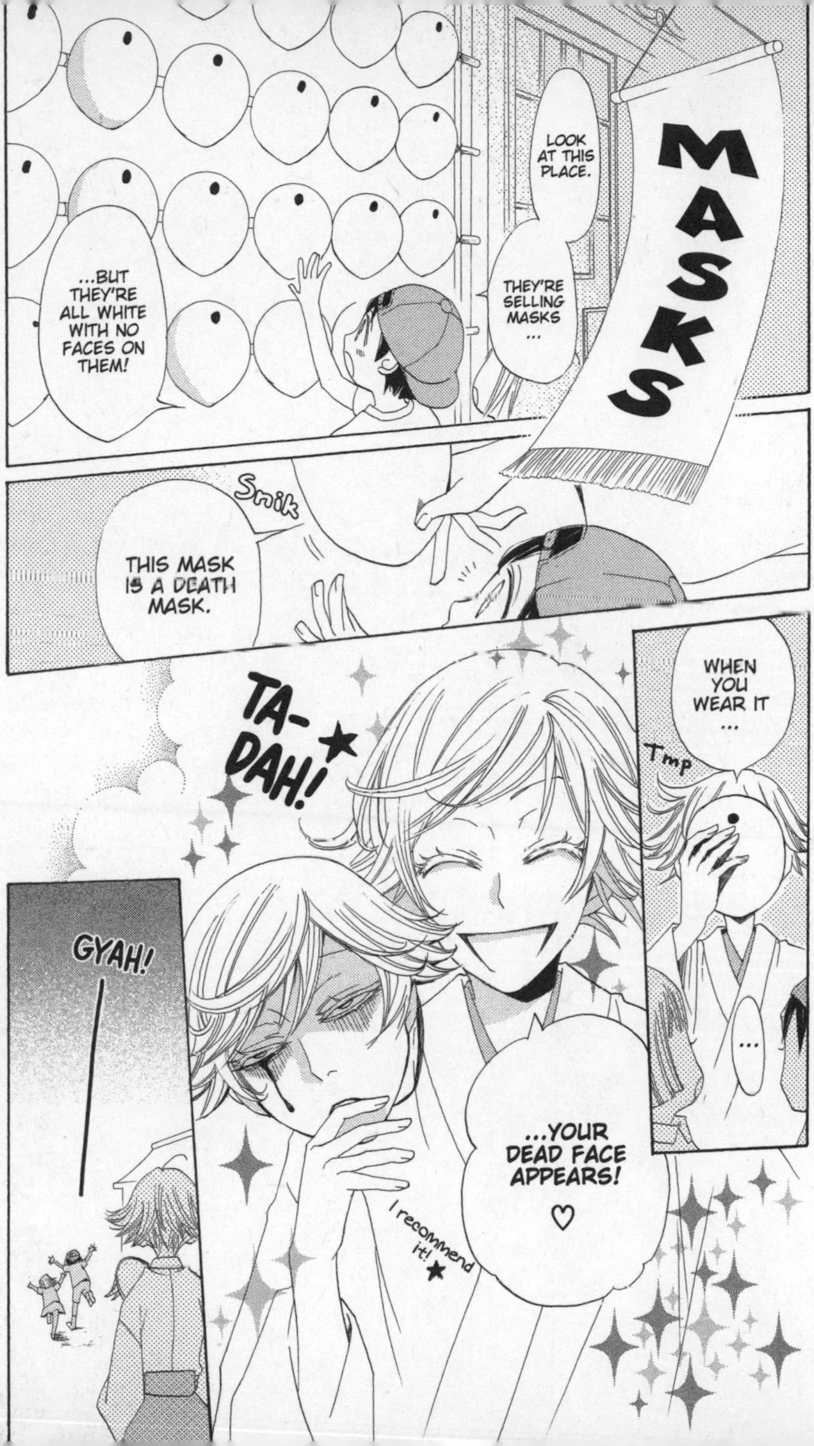
MASKS
LOOK AT THIS PLACE.
THEY'RE SELLING MASKS ...
...BUT THEY'RE ALL WHITE WITH NO FACES ON THEM!
Snik
THIS MASK IS A DEATH MASK.
WHEN YOU WEAR IT ...
Tmp
...
TA-DAH! ★
...YOUR DEAD FACE APPEARS! ♡
I recommend it! ★
GYAH!

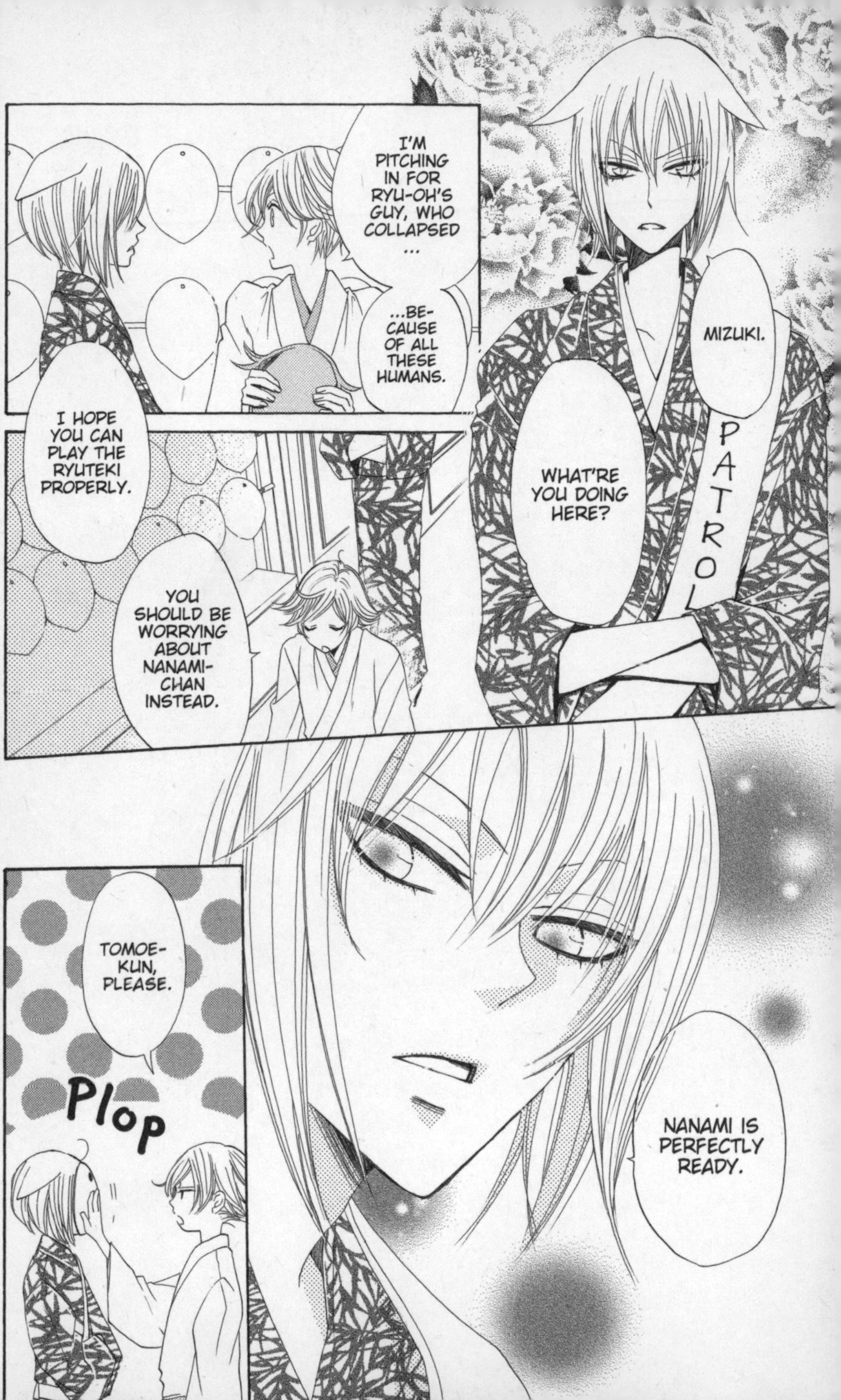
MIZUKI.
WHAT'RE YOU DOING HERE?
PATROL
I'M PITCHING IN FOR RYU-OH'S GUY, WHO COLLAPSED ...
...BECAUSE OF ALL THESE HUMANS.
I HOPE YOU CAN PLAY THE RYUTEKI PROPERLY.
YOU SHOULD BE WORRYING ABOUT NANAMI-CHAN INSTEAD.
NANAMI IS PERFECTLY READY.
TOMOE-KUN, PLEASE.
Plop

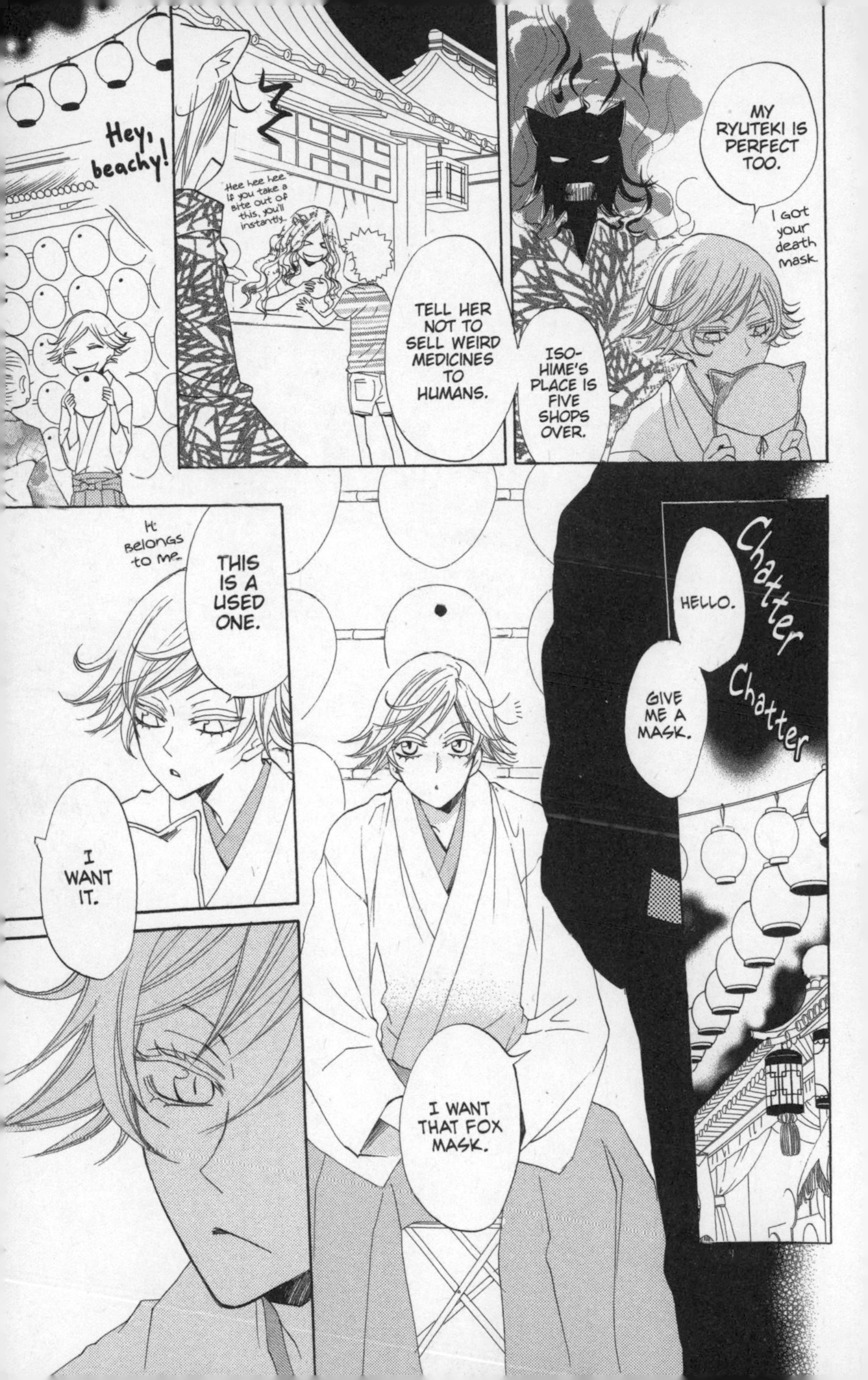

MY RYUTEKI IS PERFECT TOO.
I got your death mask.
ISO-HIME'S PLACE IS FIVE SHOPS OVER.
TELL HER NOT TO SELL WEIRD MEDICINES TO HUMANS.
Hee hee hee If you take a bite out of this, you'll instantly...
Hey, beachy!
Chatter Chatter
HELLO.
GIVE ME A MASK.
I WANT THAT FOX MASK.
THIS IS A USED ONE.
It belongs to me.
I WANT IT.

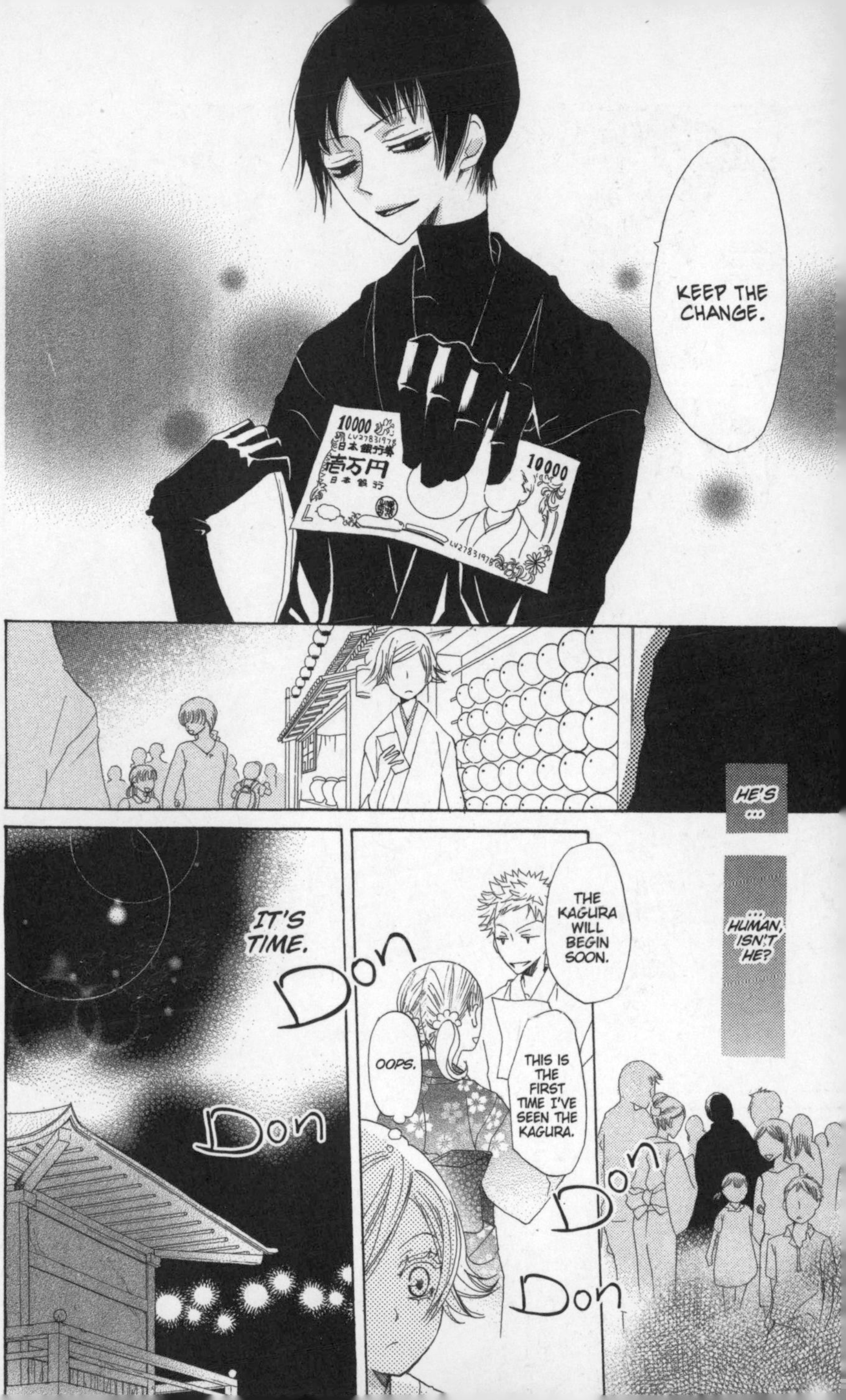
KEEP THE CHANGE.
HE'S...
...HUMAN, ISN'T HE?
THE KAGURA WILL BEGIN SOON.
THIS IS THE FIRST TIME I'VE SEEN THE KAGURA.
OOPS.
Don
Don
Don
IT'S TIME.
Don

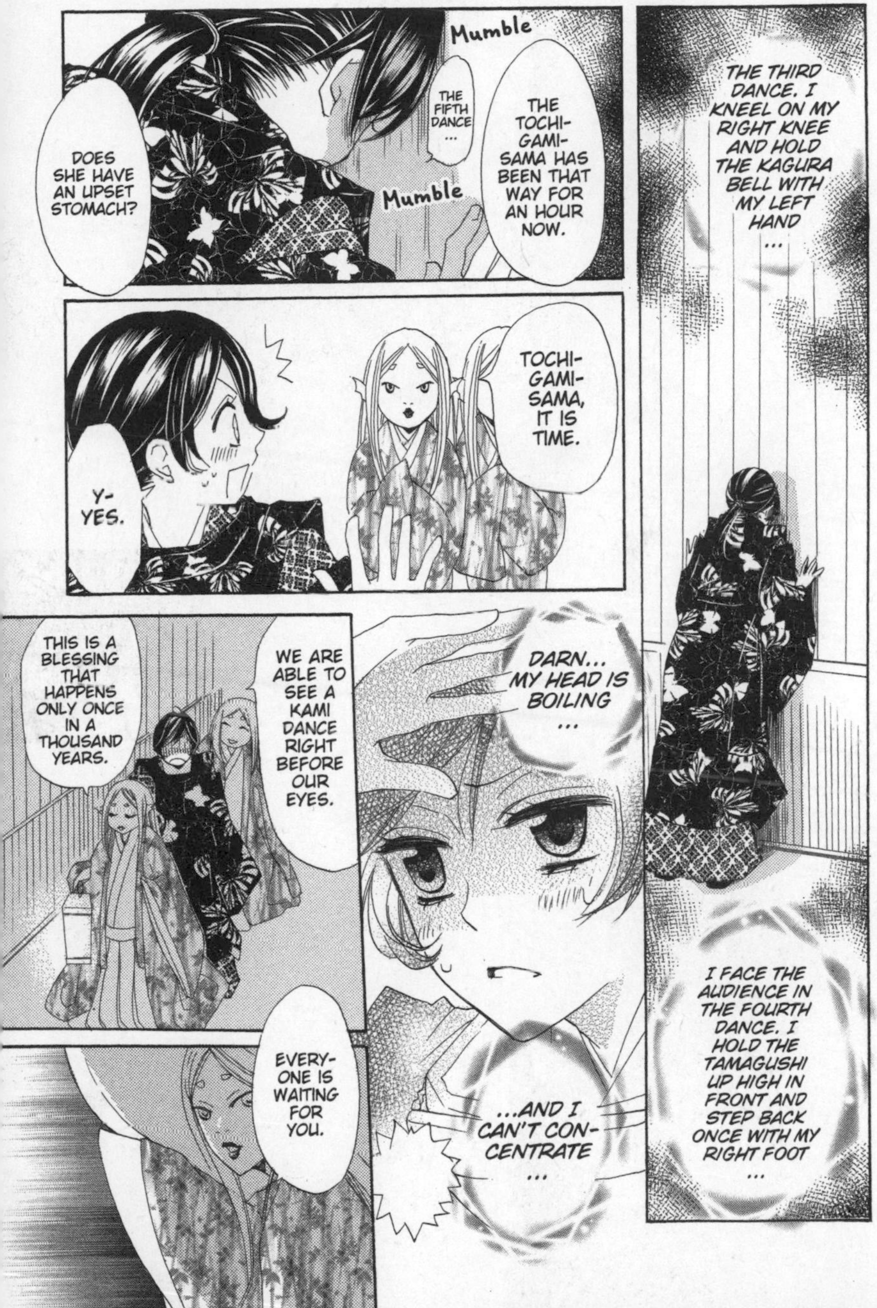
THE THIRD DANCE. I KNEEL ON MY RIGHT KNEE AND HOLD THE KAGURA BELL WITH MY LEFT HAND ...
I FACE THE AUDIENCE IN THE FOURTH DANCE. I HOLD THE TAMAGUSHI UP HIGH IN FRONT AND STEP BACK ONCE WITH MY RIGHT FOOT ...
Mumble
THE TOCHI-GAMI-SAMA HAS BEEN THAT WAY FOR AN HOUR NOW.
THE FIFTH DANCE ...
Mumble
DOES SHE HAVE AN UPSET STOMACH?
TOCHI-GAMI-SAMA, IT IS TIME.
Y-YES.
DARN... MY HEAD IS BOILING ...
WE ARE ABLE TO SEE A KAMI DANCE RIGHT BEFORE OUR EYES.
THIS IS A BLESSING THAT HAPPENS ONLY ONCE IN A THOUSAND YEARS.
...AND I CAN'T CON-CENTRATE ...
EVERY-ONE IS WAITING FOR YOU.

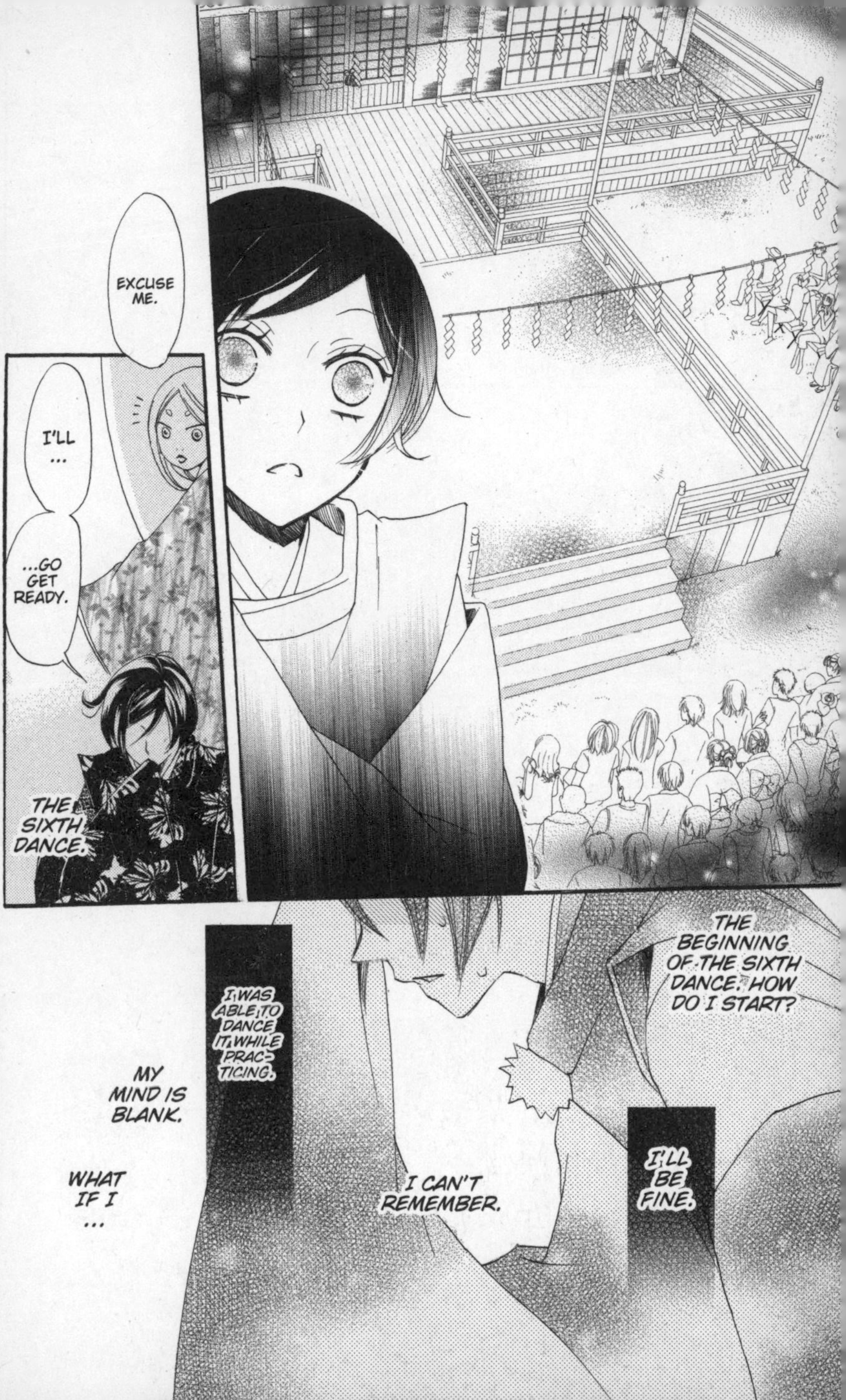
EXCUSE ME.
I'LL ...
...GO GET READY.
THE SIXTH DANCE.
THE BEGINNING OF THE SIXTH DANCE. HOW DO I START?
I'LL BE FINE.
I CAN'T REMEMBER.
I WAS ABLE TO DANCE IT WHILE PRAC-TICING.
MY MIND IS BLANK.
WHAT IF I ...

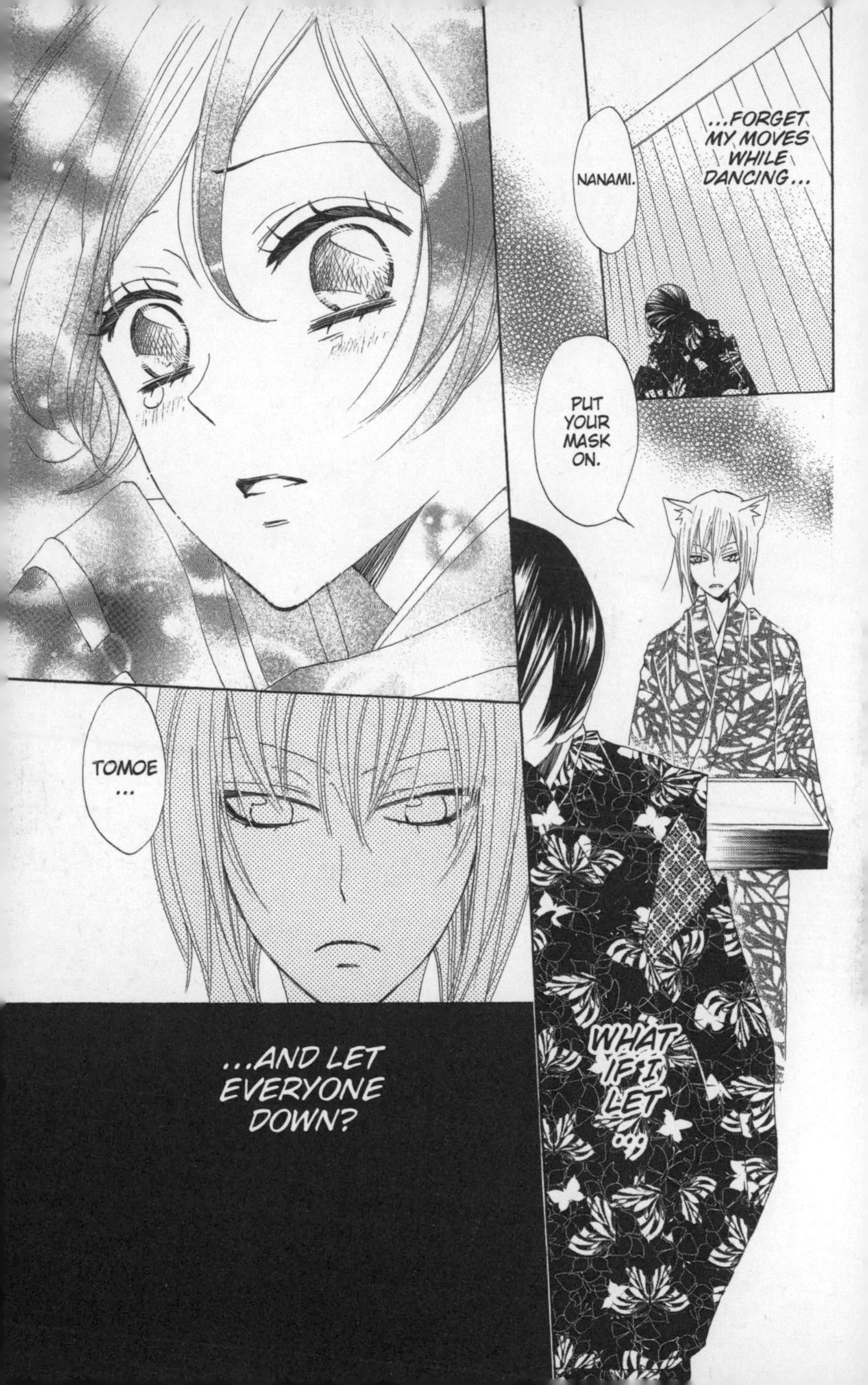
...FORGET MY MOVES WHILE DANCING...
NANAMI.
PUT YOUR MASK ON.
WHAT IF I LET...
TOMOE...
...AND LET EVERYONE DOWN?

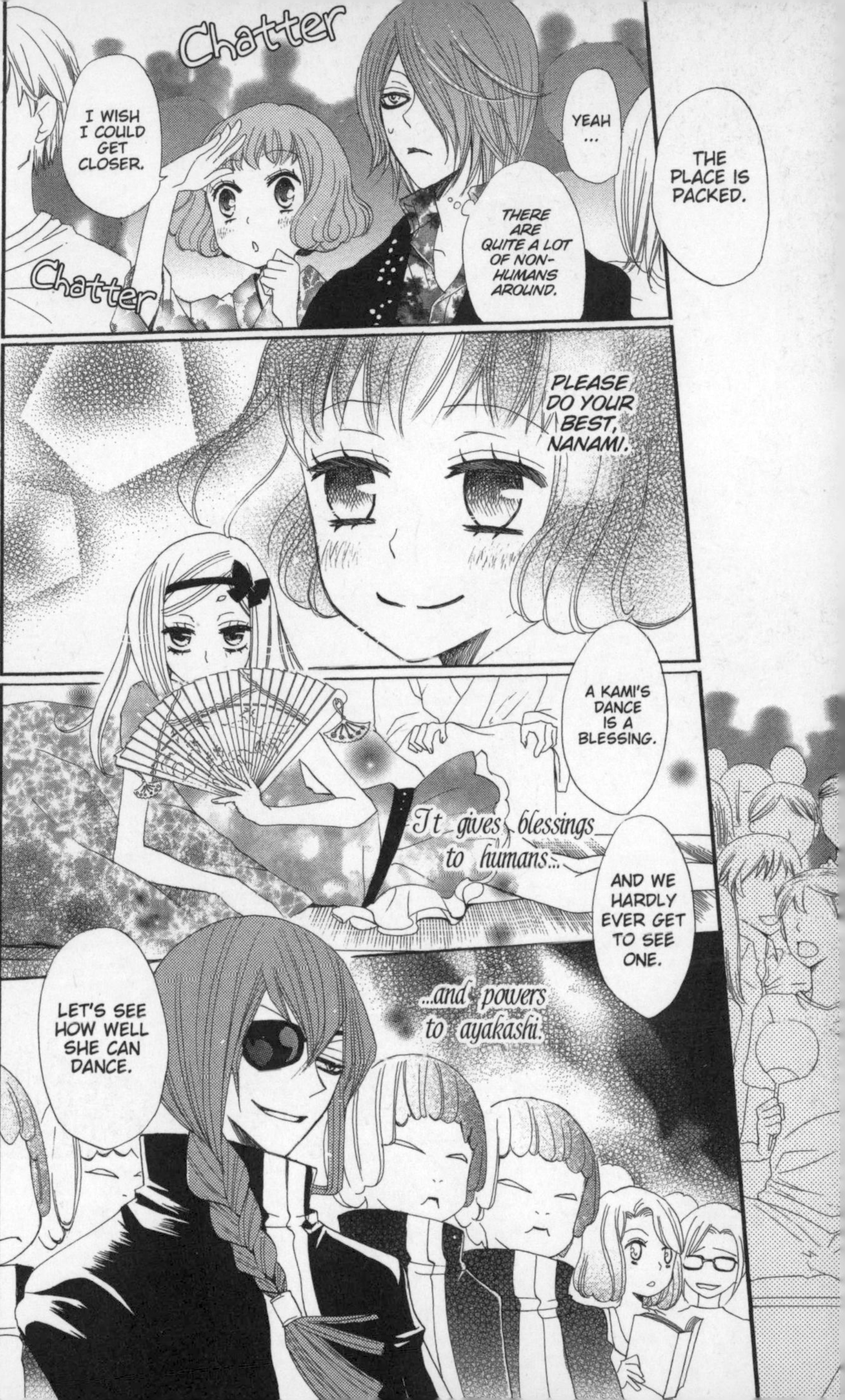
Chatter
THE PLACE IS PACKED.
YEAH...
THERE ARE QUITE A LOT OF NON-HUMANS AROUND.
I WISH I COULD GET CLOSER.
Chatter
PLEASE DO YOUR BEST, NANAMI.
A KAMI'S DANCE IS A BLESSING.
It gives blessings to humans...
AND WE HARDLY EVER GET TO SEE ONE.
...and powers to ayakashi.
LET'S SEE HOW WELL SHE CAN DANCE.

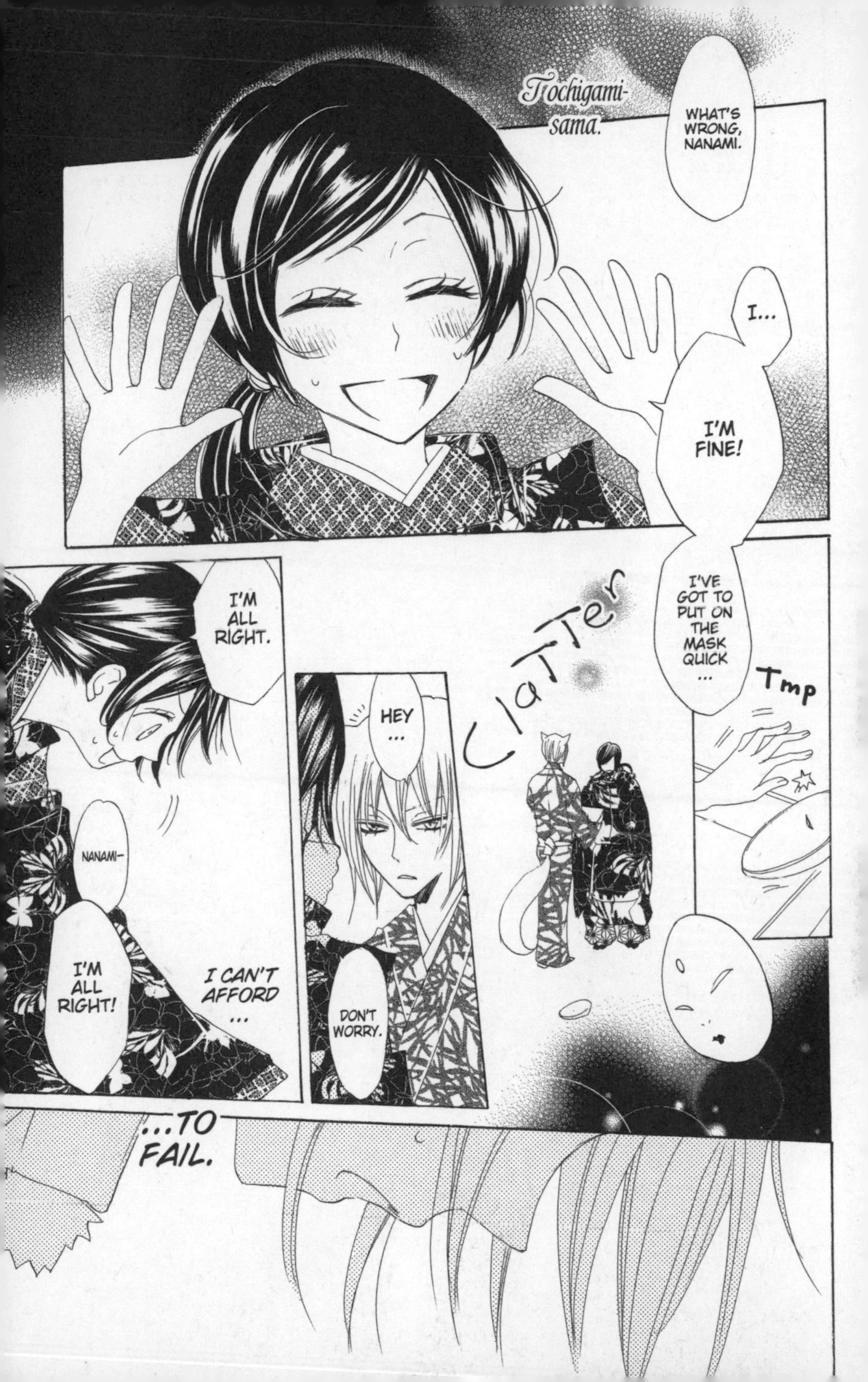
WHAT'S WRONG, NANAMI.
Tochigami-sama.
I...
I'M FINE!
I'VE GOT TO PUT ON THE MASK QUICK ...
Tmp
Clatter
HEY ...
DON'T WORRY.
I'M ALL RIGHT.
NANAMI—
I'M ALL RIGHT!
I CAN'T AFFORD ...
...TO FAIL.

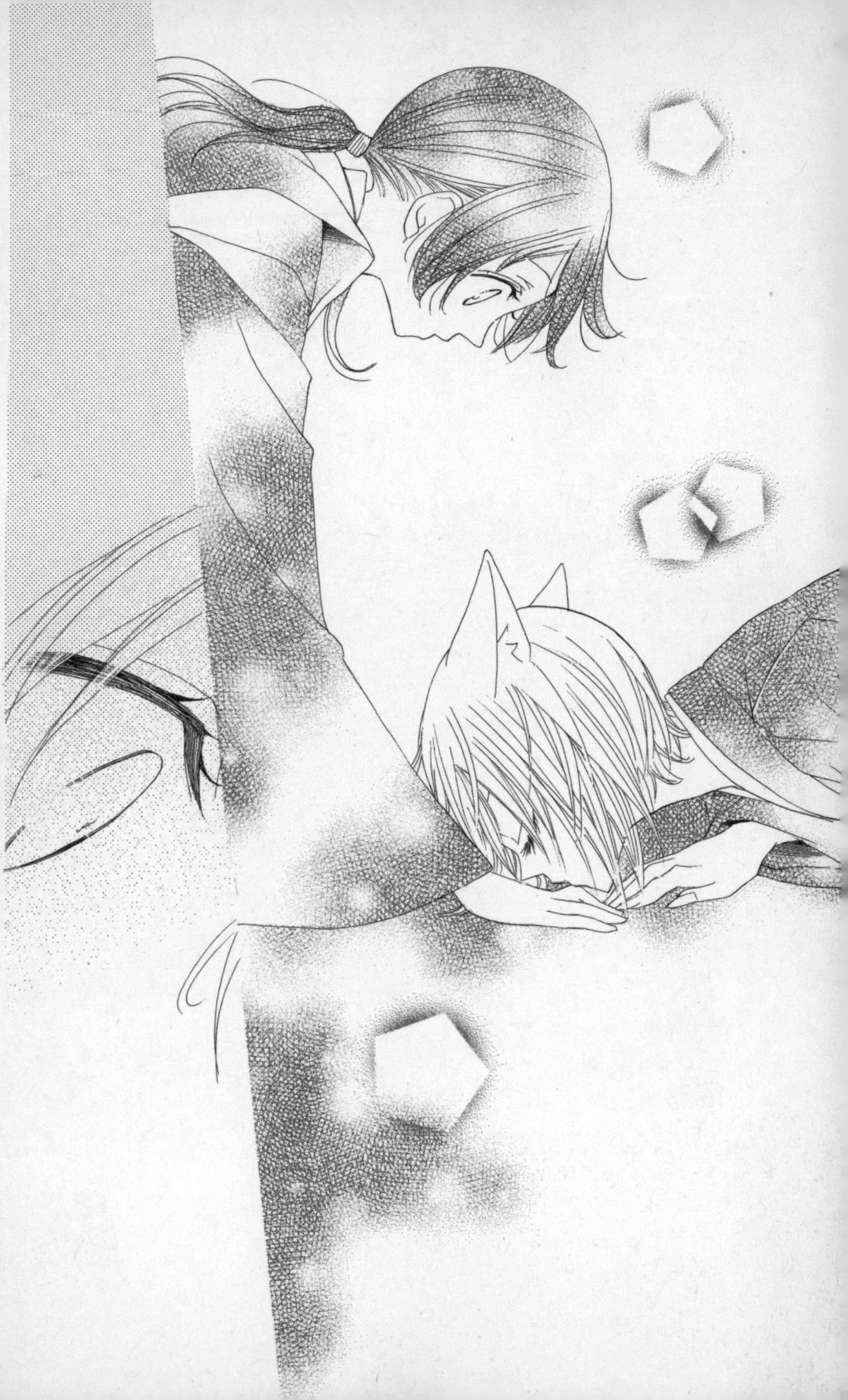

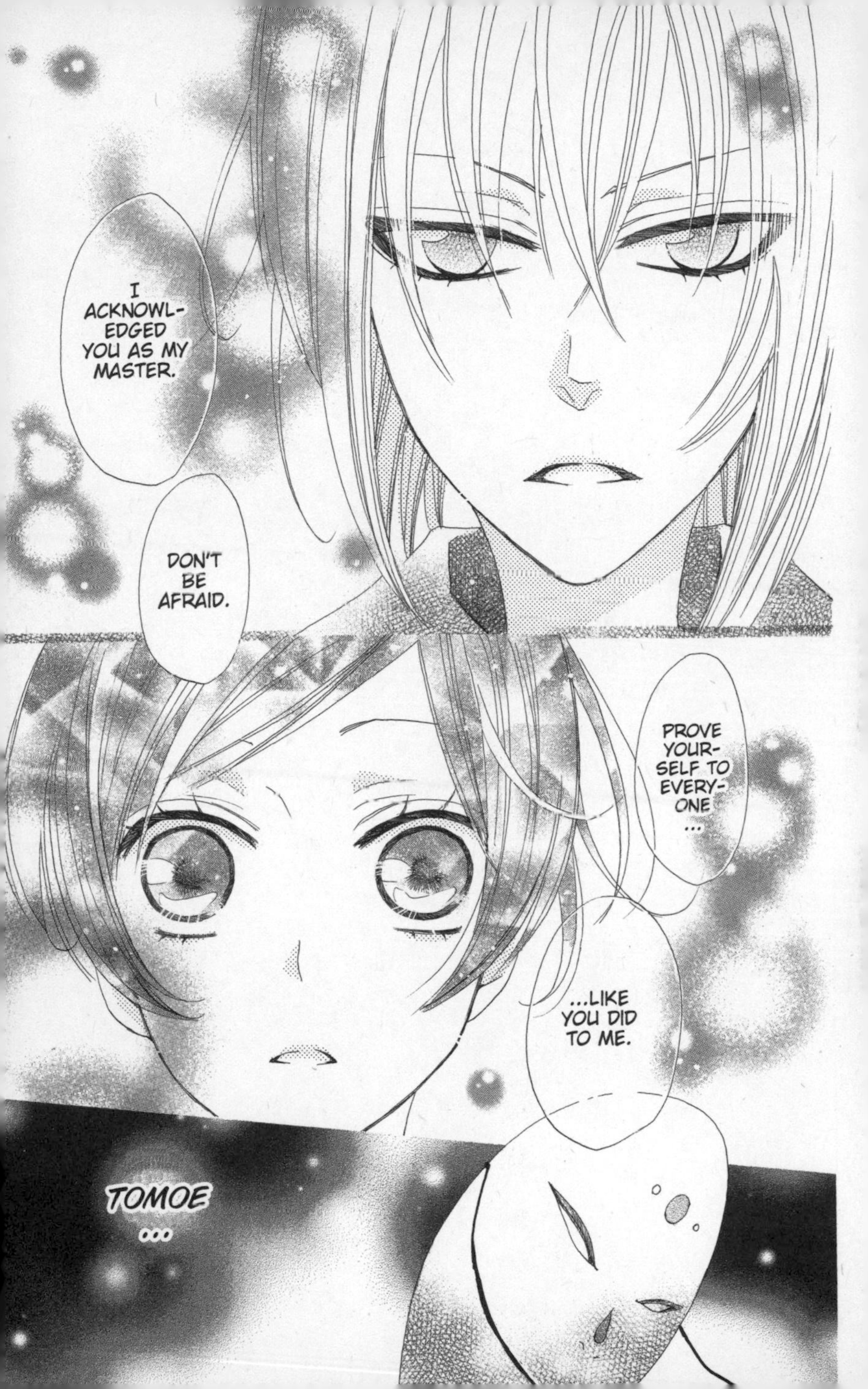
I ACKNOWL-EDGED YOU AS MY MASTER.
DON'T BE AFRAID.
PROVE YOUR-SELF TO EVERY-ONE...
...LIKE YOU DID TO ME.
TOMOE...

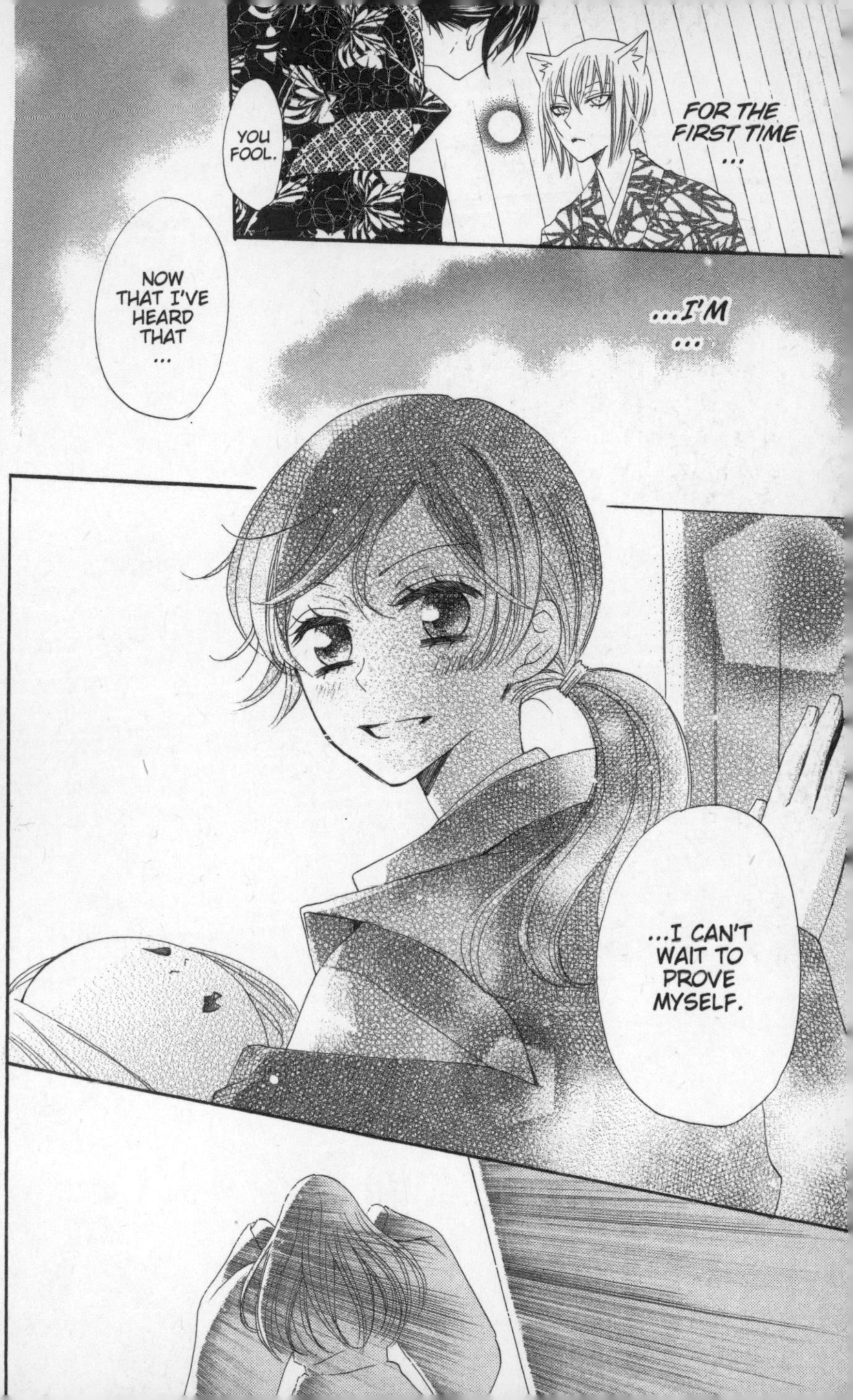
FOR THE FIRST TIME ...
YOU FOOL.
...I'M ...
NOW THAT I'VE HEARD THAT ...
...I CAN'T WAIT TO PROVE MYSELF.

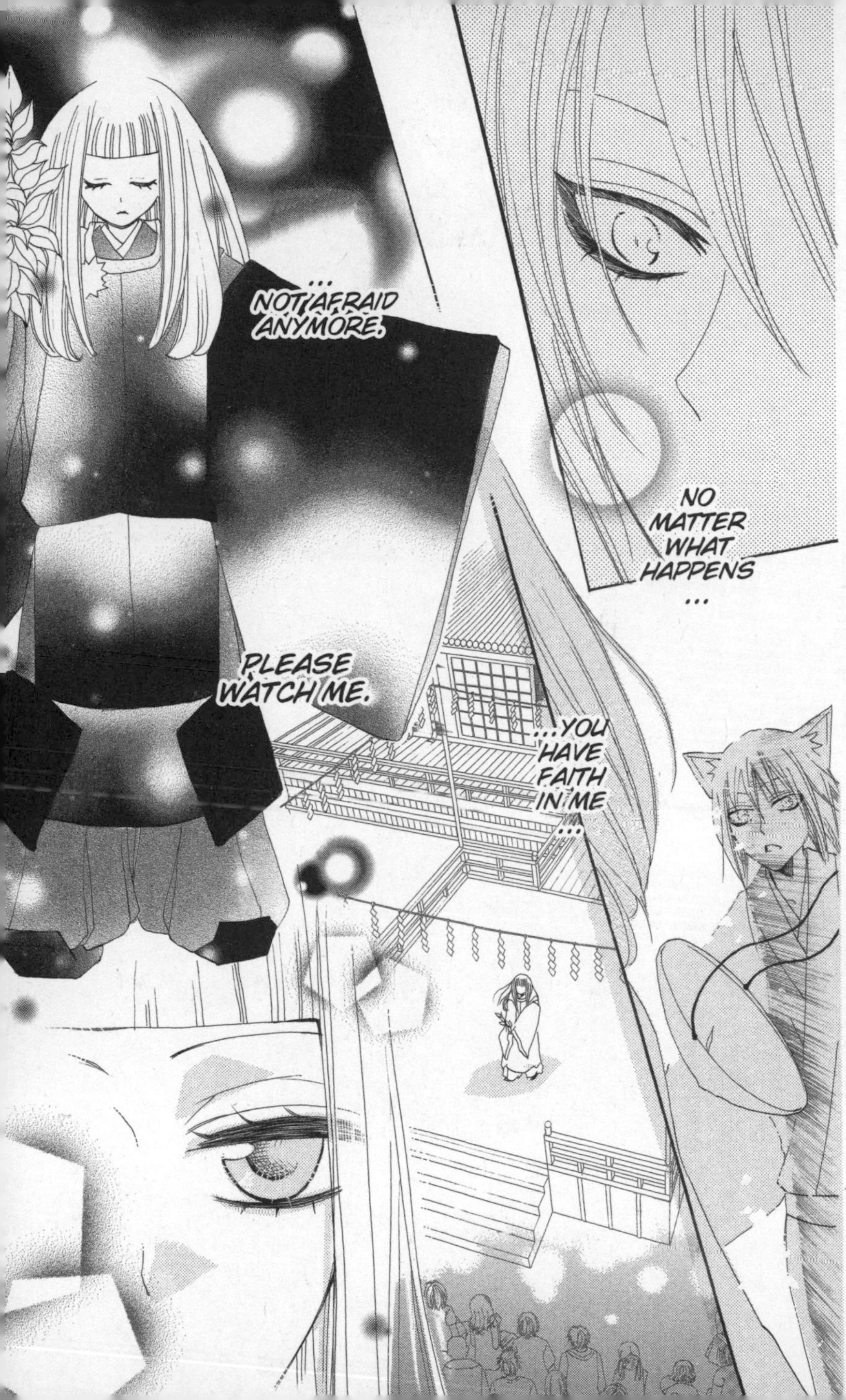
NO MATTER WHAT HAPPENS ...
...YOU HAVE FAITH IN ME ...
... NOT AFRAID ANYMORE.
PLEASE WATCH ME.

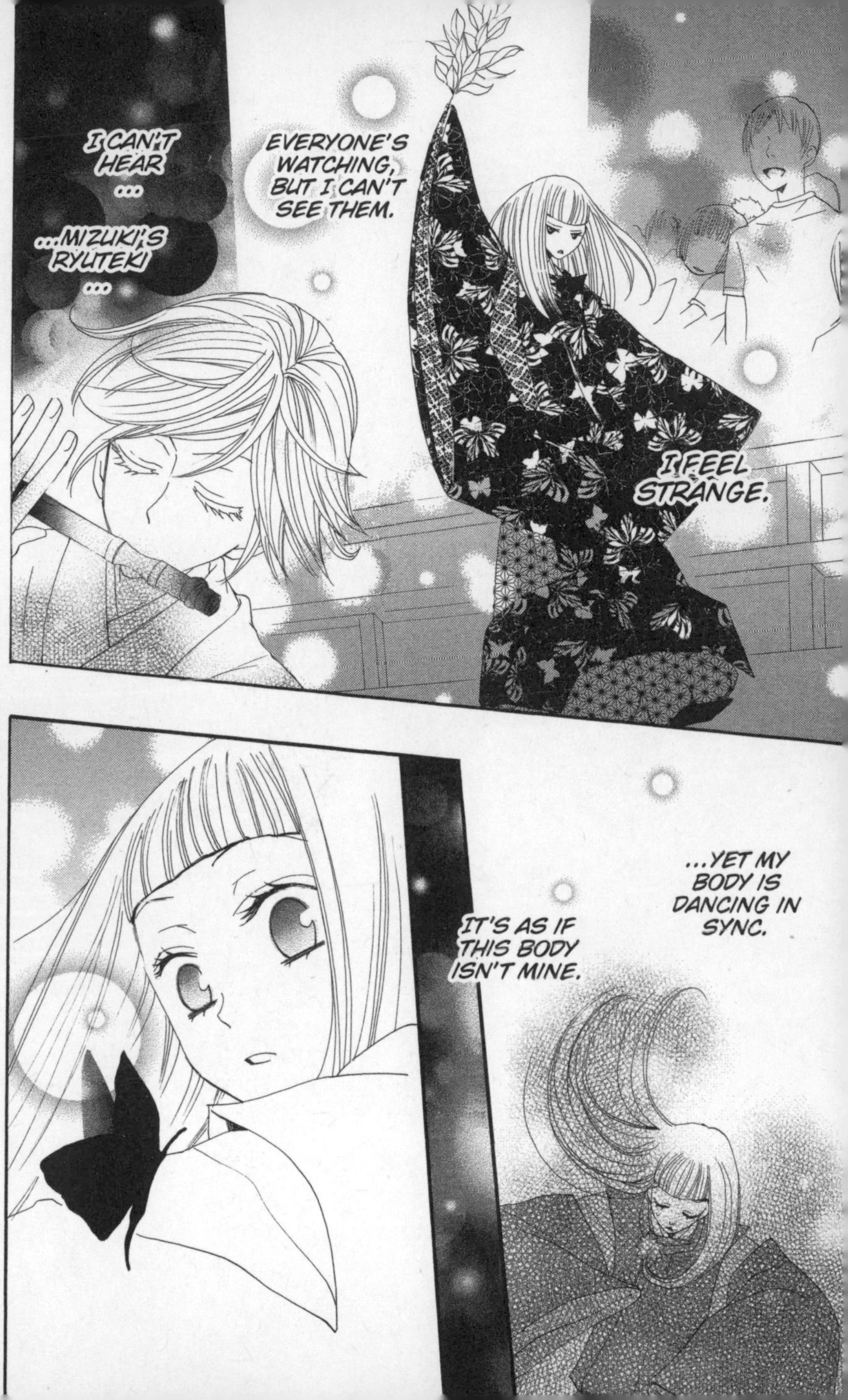
I FEEL STRANGE.
EVERYONE'S WATCHING, BUT I CAN'T SEE THEM.
I CAN'T HEAR...
...MIZUKI'S RYUTEKI...
...YET MY BODY IS DANCING IN SYNC.
IT'S AS IF THIS BODY ISN'T MINE.

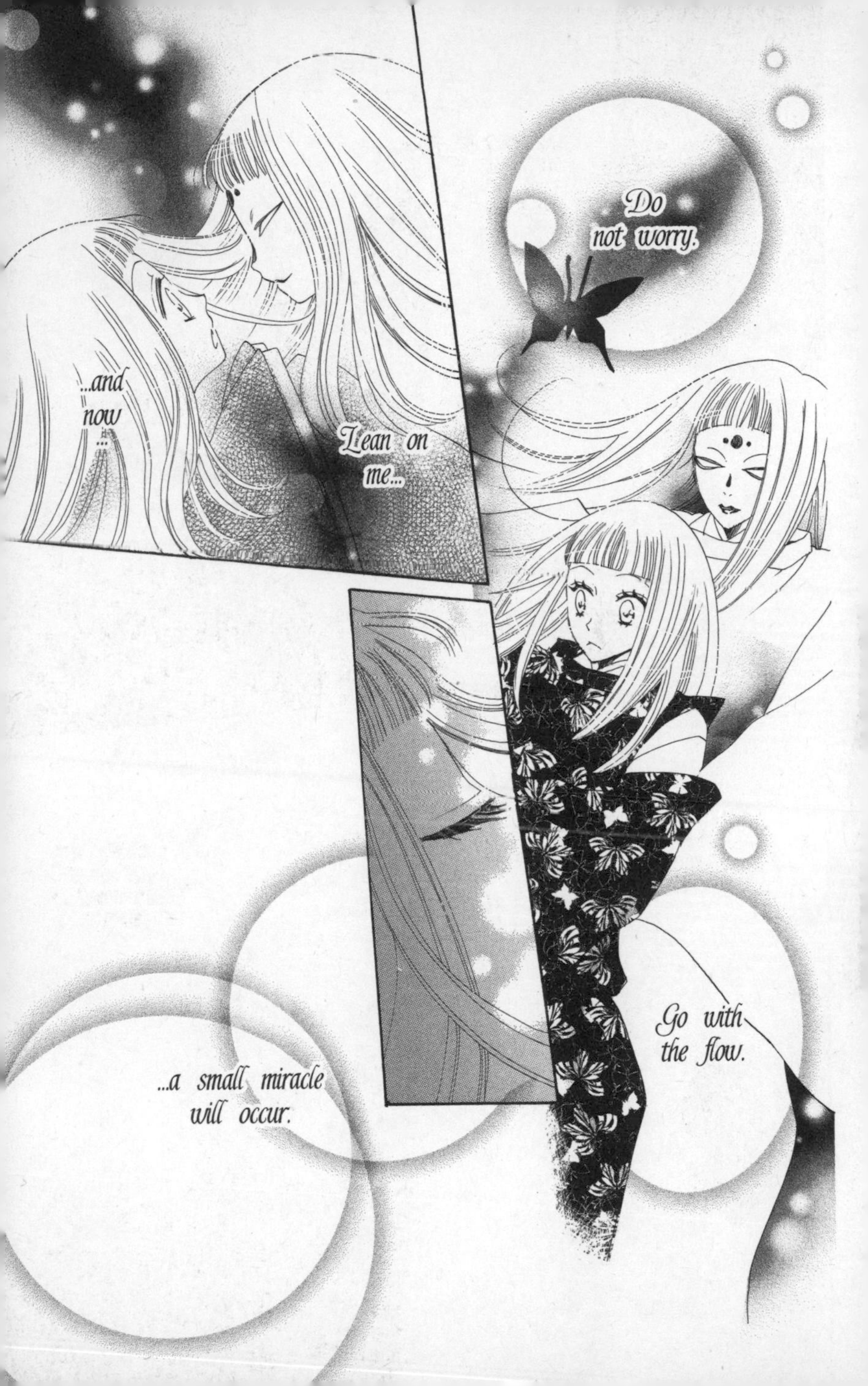

Do not worry.
Lean on me...
...and now...
Go with the flow.
...a small miracle will occur.

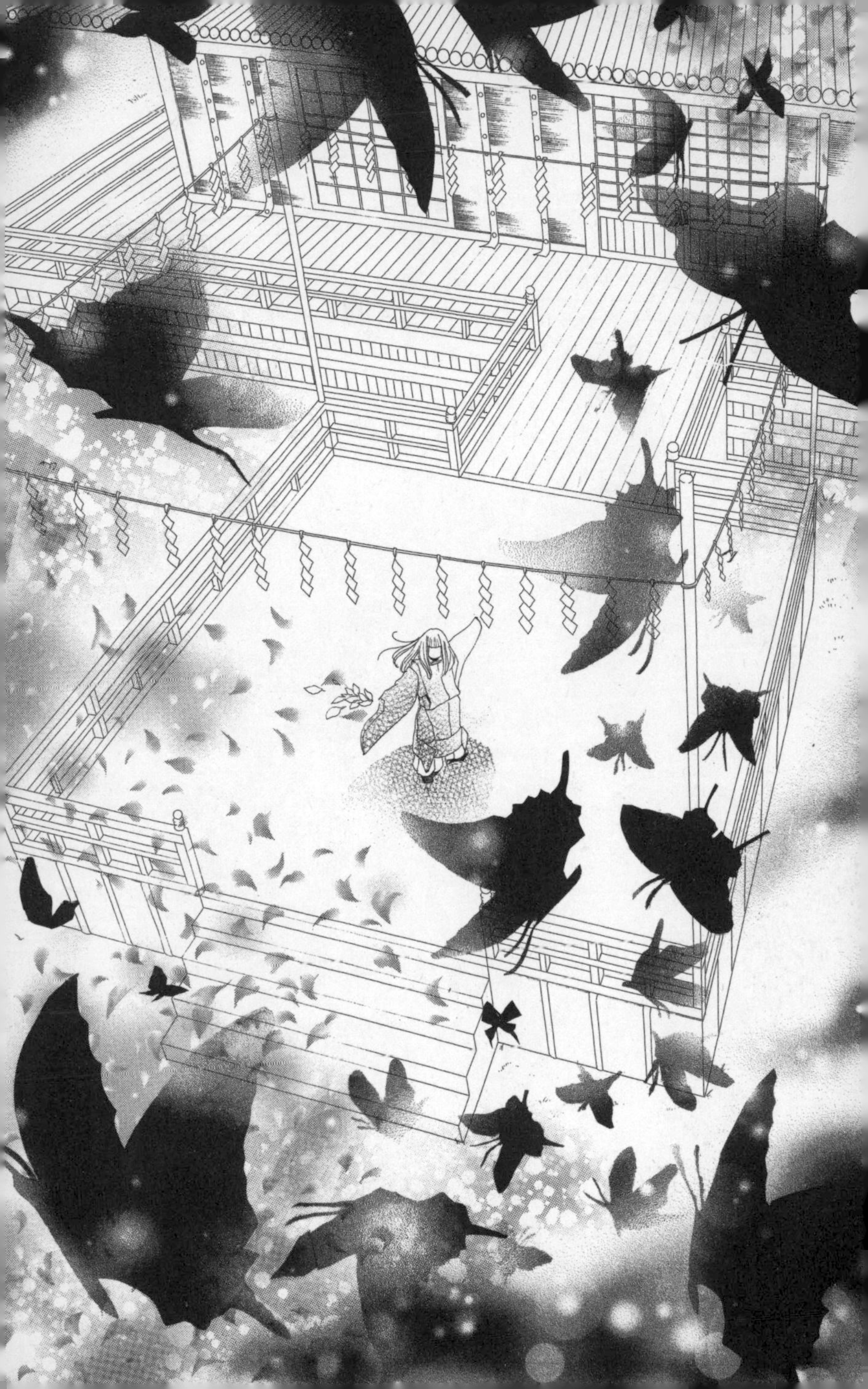

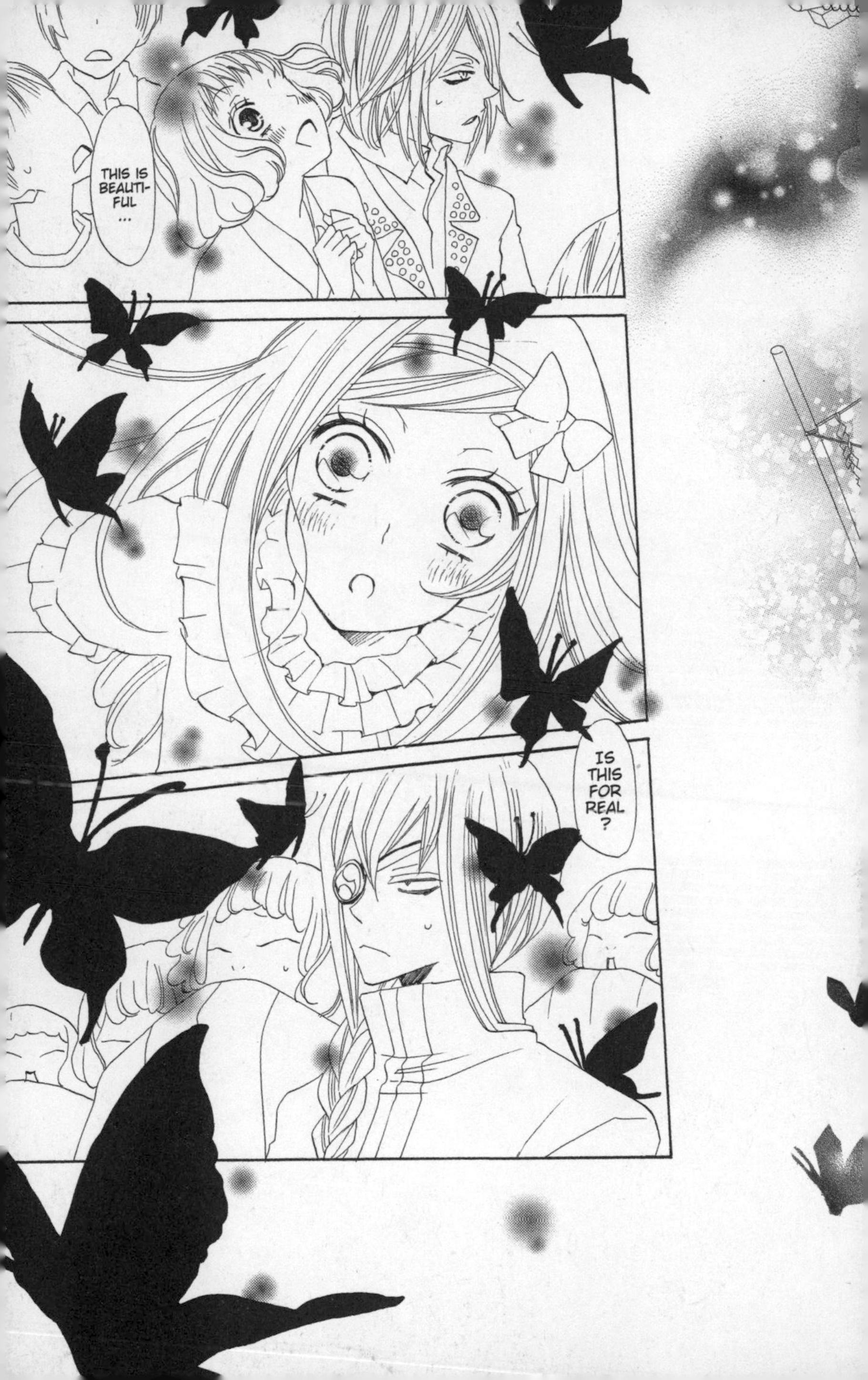
THIS IS BEAUTIFUL...
IS THIS FOR REAL?

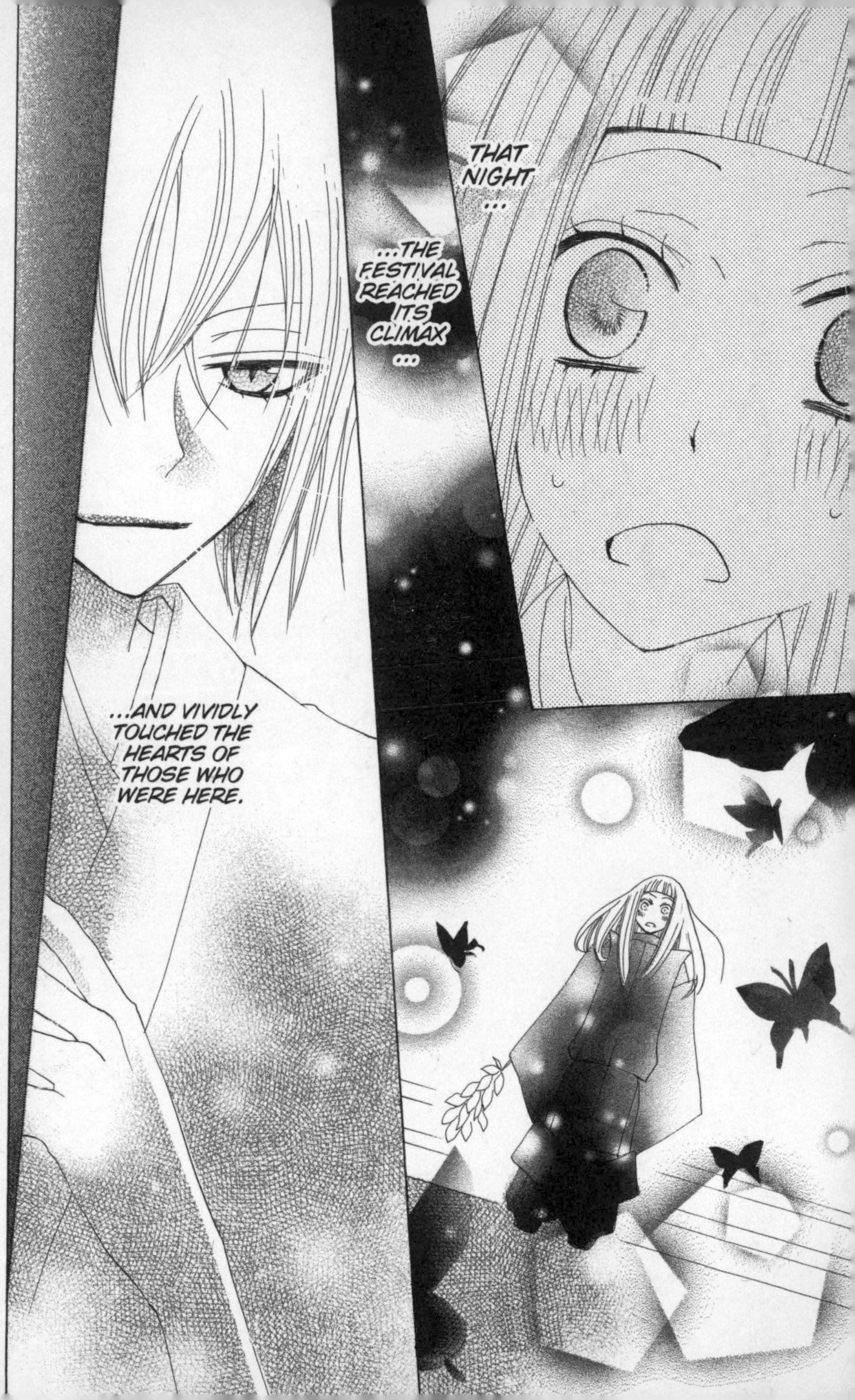
THAT NIGHT ...
...THE FESTIVAL REACHED ITS CLIMAX ...
...AND VIVIDLY TOUCHED THE HEARTS OF THOSE WHO WERE HERE.

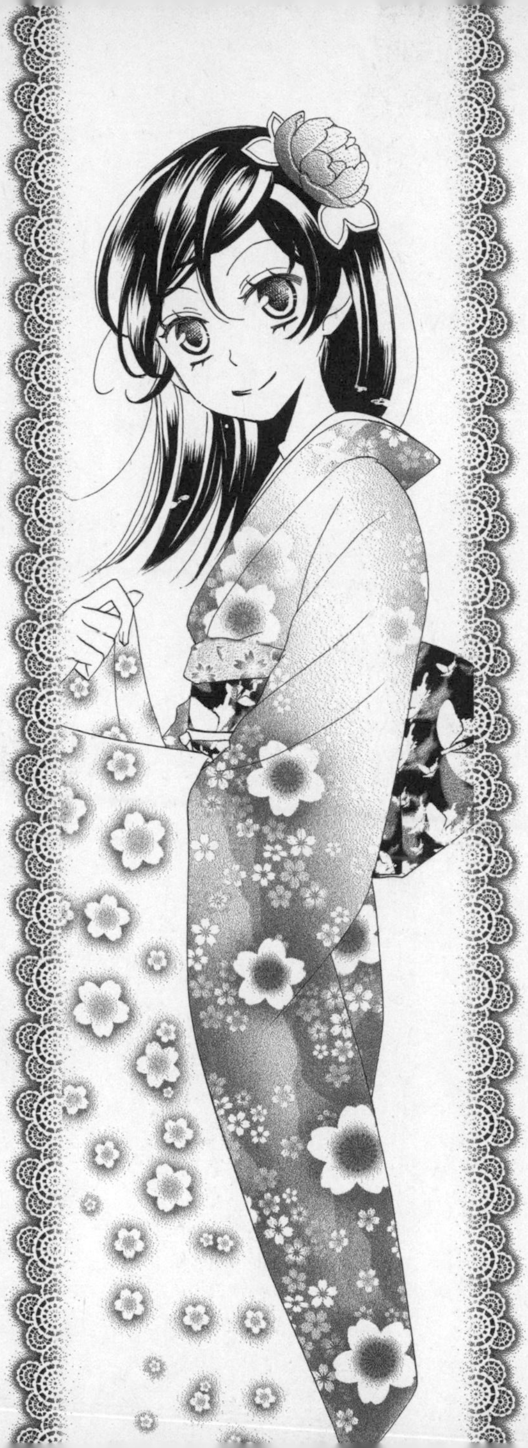

Thank you very much!

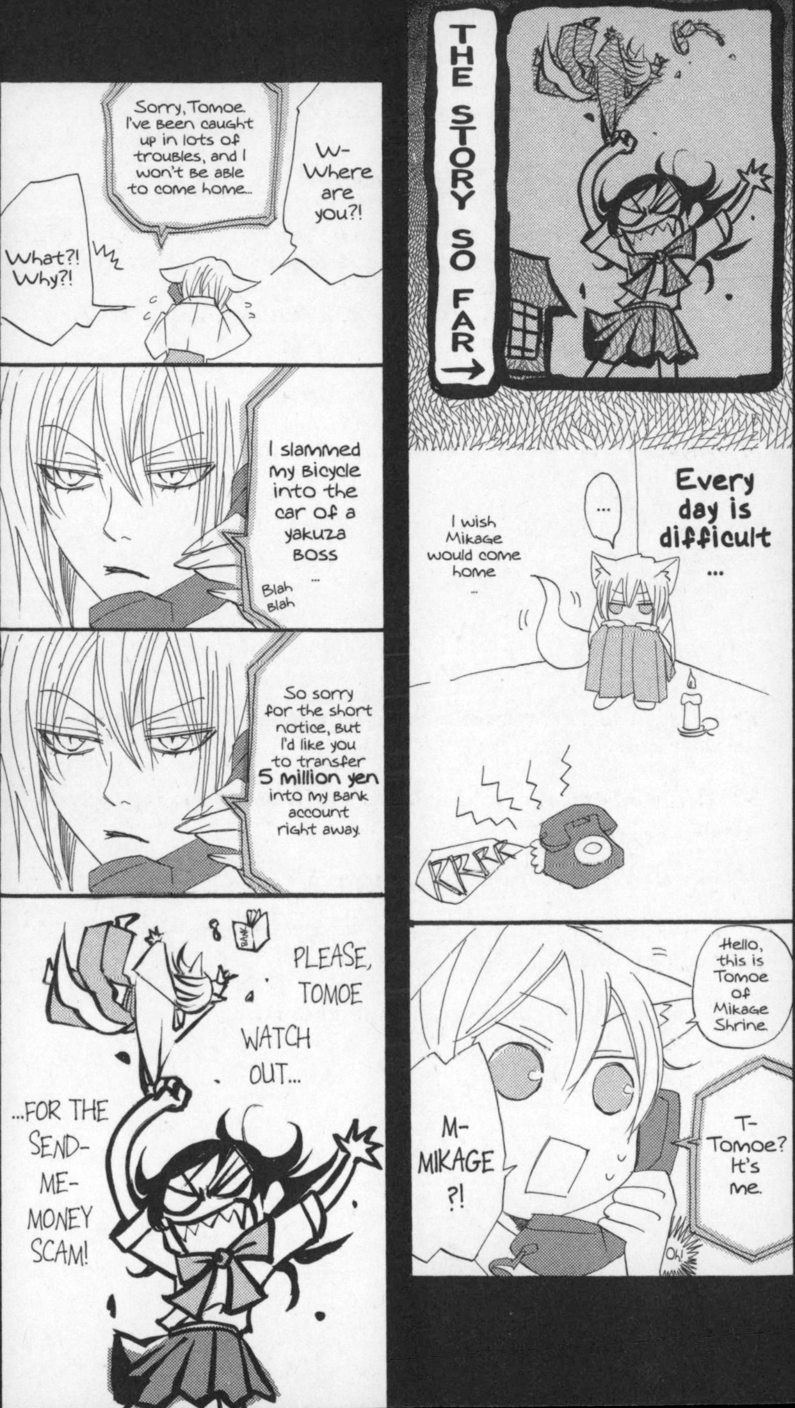
THE STORY SO FAR →
Every day is difficult ...
...
I wish Mikage would come home ...
RRRR
Hello, this is Tomoe of Mikage Shrine.
T-Tomoe? It's me.
Oh!
M-MIKAGE?!
W-Where are you?!
Sorry, Tomoe. I've been caught up in lots of troubles, and I won't be able to come home...
What?! Why?!
I slammed my bicycle into the car of a yakuza boss ...
Blah Blah
So sorry for the short notice, but I'd like you to transfer 5 million yen into my bank account right away.
BANK
PLEASE, TOMOE
WATCH OUT...
...FOR THE SEND-ME-MONEY SCAM!

The Otherworld

Ayakashi is an archaic term for yokai.

Kami are Shinto deities or spirits. The word can be used for a range of creatures, from nature spirits to strong and dangerous gods.

Shinshi are birds, beasts, insects or fish that have a special relationship with a kami.

Tsuriki is a kami's power and becomes stronger the more it is used.

Tengu are a type of yokai. They are sometimes associated with excess pride.

Kitsunebi literally means "foxfire," the flames controlled by fox spirits.

Honorifics

-chan is a diminutive most often used with babies, children or teenage girls.

-dono roughly means "my lord," although not in the aristocratic sense.

-himemiko is a title that means "Imperial princess."

-kun is used by persons of superior rank to their juniors. It can sometimes have a familiar connotation.

-sama is used with people of much higher rank.

Notes

Page 10, panel 1: Yukata
A casual summer kimono made of cotton.

Page 13, author note: Ikaho Onsen, flowers of sulfur
Ikaho Onsen is a famous Japanese hot spring resort in Gunma Prefecture.

Page 13, author note: Flowers of sulfur
"Flowers of sulfur" is another term for powdered sublimed sulfur, which is used medicinally to treat skin conditions and as an anti-parasitic and anti-fungal.

Page 14, panel 2: 300 yen
About $3.66 US.

Page 23, panel 1: Omiki
Ceremonial sake used in Shinto rituals or offered to the kami.

Page 43, panel 2: Torii
The gates that mark the entrance to a Shinto shrine. It literally means "bird perch."

Page 45, author note: Kumade
Kumade are good-luck charm rakes sold at shrines.

Page 45, author note: Tori no Ichi
Tori no Ichi (Rooster Market) are shrine fairs held in November throughout Japan, where luck charms like kumade are sold.

Page 46, panel 5: Omikoshi
Omikoshi are portable Shinto shrines. Kami ride in omikoshi during parades or festivals.

Page 56, panel 1: Chozuya
Also called *temizuya*. The font for water that visitors use to purify their hands or mouths.

Page 59, panel 1: Kagura
Literally "god entertainment." A type of Shinto ceremonial dance.

Page 59, panel 2: Shrine maidens
Miko in Japanese, which literally means "female shaman" but has come to mean "shrine maiden." Modern miko serve as shrine attendants.

Page 72, panel 2: Ryuteki
A type of bamboo flute used in Shinto classical music. It literally means "dragon flute."

Page 75, author note: Cosplay
Short for costume play, or dressing up as a character from manga, comics, anime, movies or video games.

Page 78, panel 4: Jibakurei
Literally "earth-bound spirits." Restless ghosts who can't or won't pass on to the next world.

Page 108, panel 3: Chief kami
Some shrines can house more than one kami.

Page 139, panel 2: Ryu-oh
Literally means "dragon lord."

Page 145, panel 5: Bon dance
Bon dance, or *bon odori*, is the type of dance performed during Obon (the festival to honor the dead).

Page 175, panel 1: Tamagushi
Literallty "jewel skewer." A type of Shinto offering made from branches of the sakai tree decorated with strips of paper, silk or cotton.

Page 190, panel 4: Yakuza
The *yakuza* is the Japanese mafia.

Julietta Suzuki's debut manga *Hoshi ni Naru Hi* (The Day One Becomes a Star) appeared in the 2004 *Hana to Yume Plus*. Her other books include *Akuma to Dolce* (The Devil and Sweets) and *Karakuri Odette*. Born in December in Fukuoka Prefecture, she enjoys having movies play in the background while she works on her manga.

KAMISAMA KISS
VOL. 5
Shojo Beat Edition

STORY AND ART BY
Julietta Suzuki

English Translation & Adaptation / Tomo Kimura
Touch-up Art & Lettering / Joanna Estep
Cover Design / Hidemi Dunn
Interior Design / Yukiko Whitley
Editor / Pancha Diaz

KAMISAMA HAJIMEMASHITA by Julietta Suzuki
© Julietta Suzuki 2010
All rights reserved.
First published in Japan in 2010 by HAKUSENSHA, Inc., Tokyo.
English language translation rights arranged with
HAKUSENSHA, Inc., Tokyo.

The stories, characters and incidents mentioned
in this publication are entirely fictional.

Printed in Canada

Published by VIZ Media, LLC
P.O. Box 77010
San Francisco, CA 94107

10 9 8 7 6 5 4
First printing, October 2011
Fourth printing, January 2015

www.viz.com   www.shojobeat.com

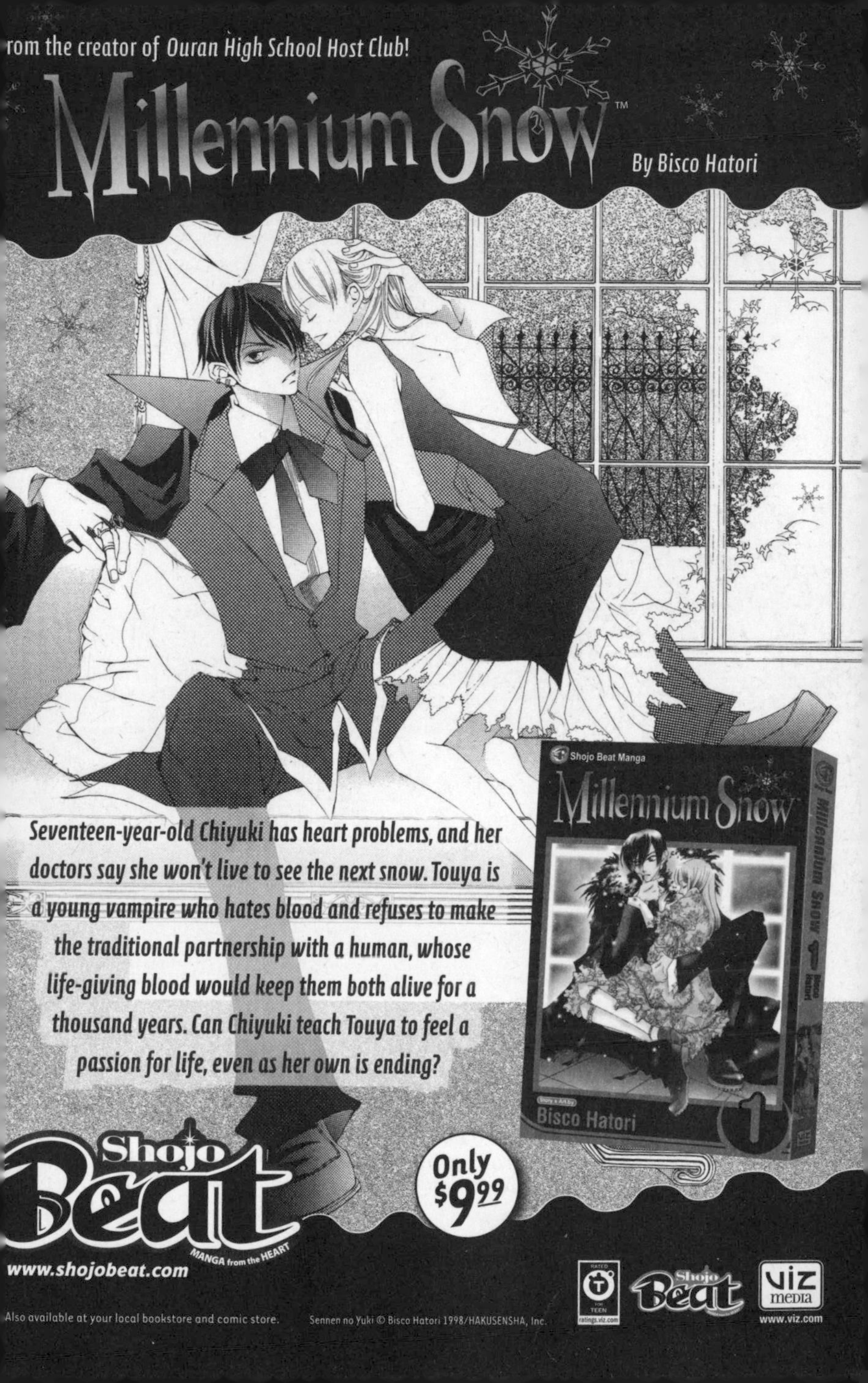
rom the creator of Ouran High School Host Club!
Millennium Snow™
By Bisco Hatori
Seventeen-year-old Chiyuki has heart problems, and her doctors say she won't live to see the next snow. Touya is a young vampire who hates blood and refuses to make the traditional partnership with a human, whose life-giving blood would keep them both alive for a thousand years. Can Chiyuki teach Touya to feel a passion for life, even as her own is ending?
Shojo Beat Manga
Millennium Snow
Bisco Hatori
1
Only $9.99
Shojo Beat
MANGA from the HEART
www.shojobeat.com
RATED T FOR TEEN
ratings.viz.com
VIZ MEDIA
www.viz.com
Also available at your local bookstore and comic store.
Sennen no Yuki © Bisco Hatori 1998/HAKUSENSHA, Inc.

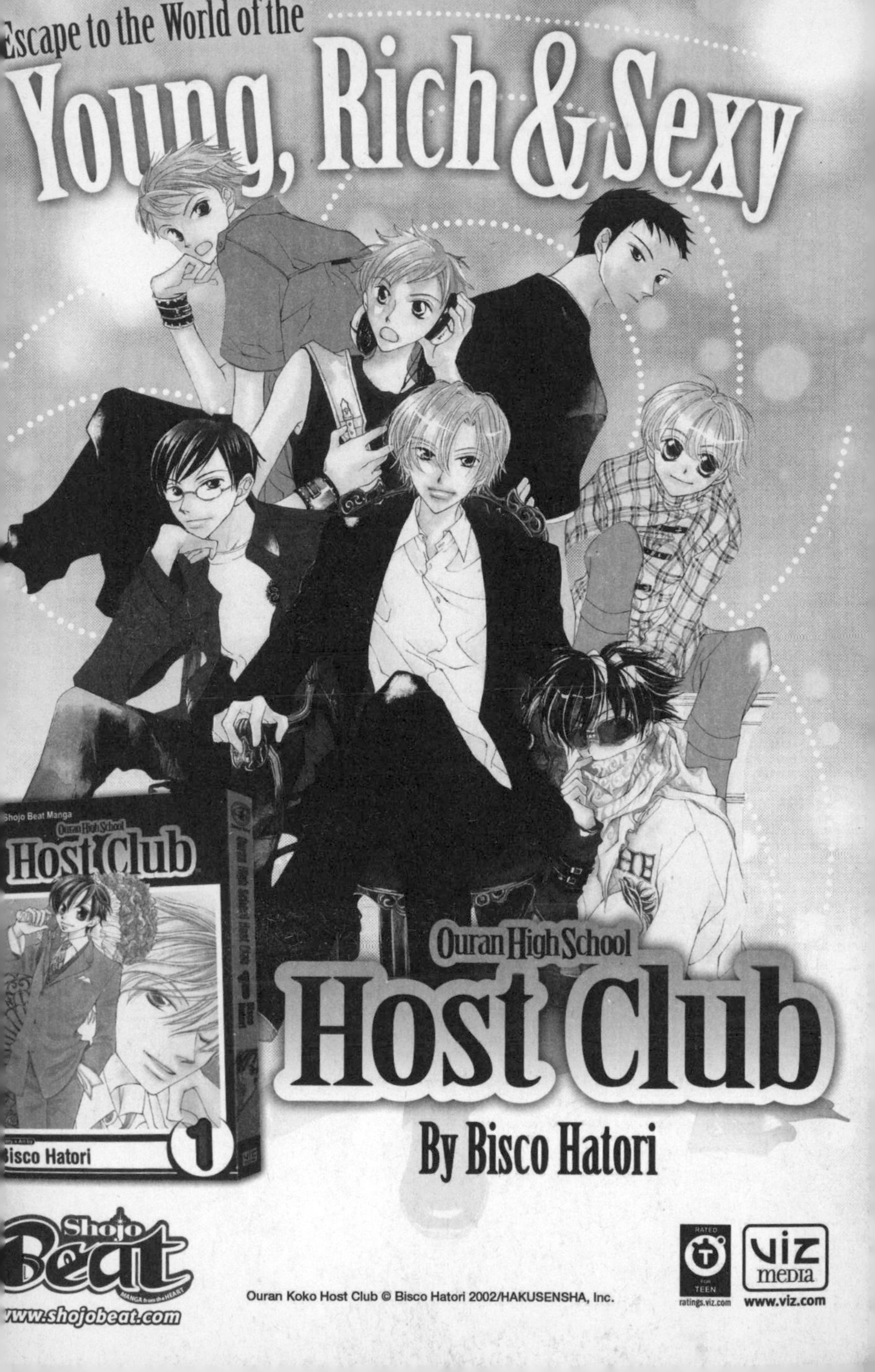
Escape to the World of the
Young, Rich & Sexy
Shojo Beat Manga
Ouran High School
Host Club
Bisco Hatori
1
Ouran High School
Host Club
By Bisco Hatori
Shojo Beat
www.shojobeat.com
Ouran Koko Host Club © Bisco Hatori 2002/HAKUSENSHA, Inc.
RATED T FOR TEEN
ratings.viz.com
VIZ media
www.viz.com

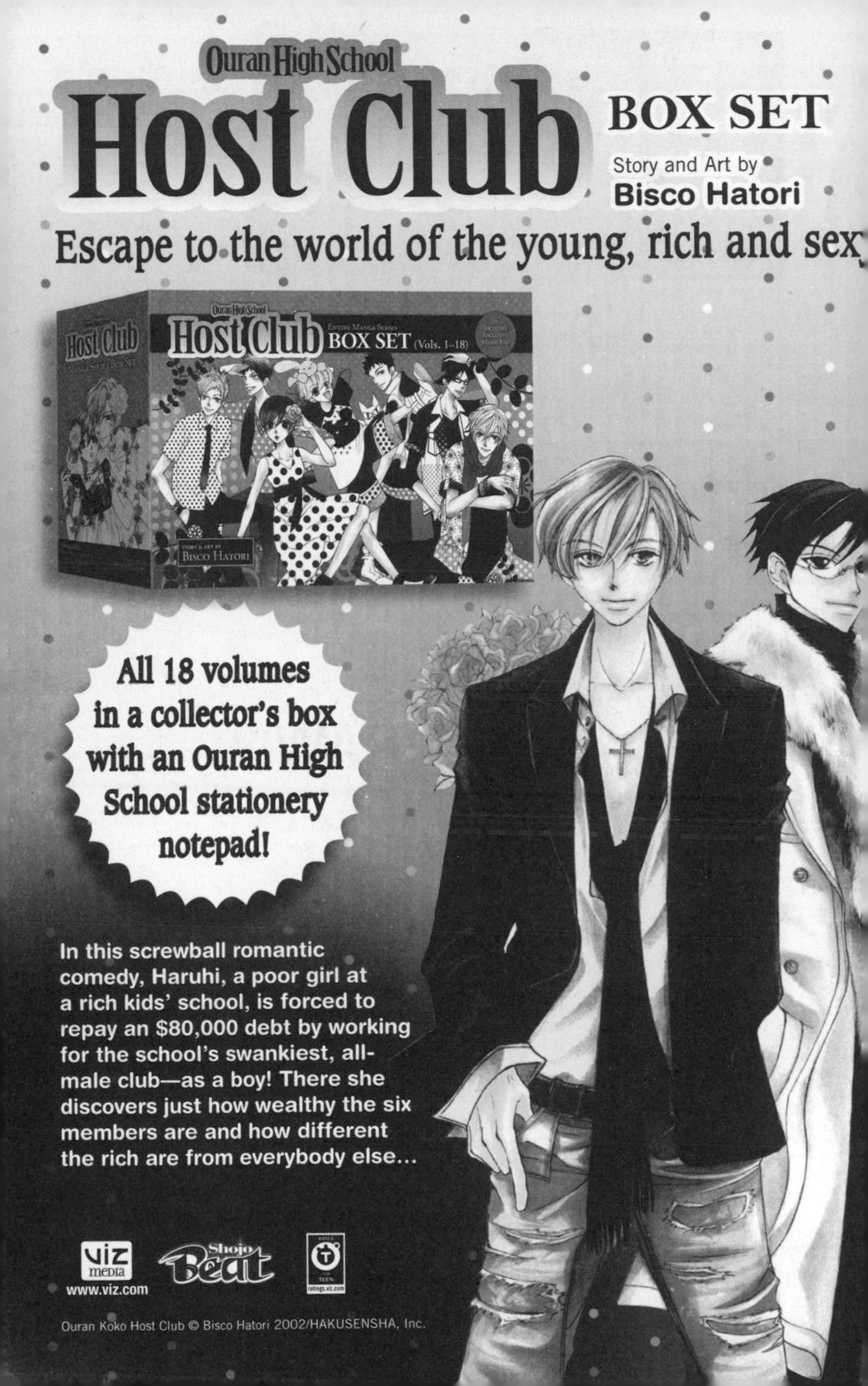

Ouran High School
Host Club
BOX SET
Story and Art by
Bisco Hatori
Escape to the world of the young, rich and sexy
Ouran High School Host Club Box Set (Vols. 1–18)
Bisco Hatori
All 18 volumes in a collector's box with an Ouran High School stationery notepad!
In this screwball romantic comedy, Haruhi, a poor girl at a rich kids' school, is forced to repay an $80,000 debt by working for the school's swankiest, all-male club—as a boy! There she discovers just how wealthy the six members are and how different the rich are from everybody else...
viz media
www.viz.com
Shojo Beat
Rated T for Teen
ratings.viz.com
Ouran Koko Host Club © Bisco Hatori 2002/HAKUSENSHA, Inc.

Th

In keeping with the original Japanese comic format, this book reads from right to left—so action, sound effects, and word balloons are completely reversed. This preserves the orientation of the original artwork—plus, it's fun! Check out the diagram shown here to get the hang of things, and then turn to the other side of the book to get started!

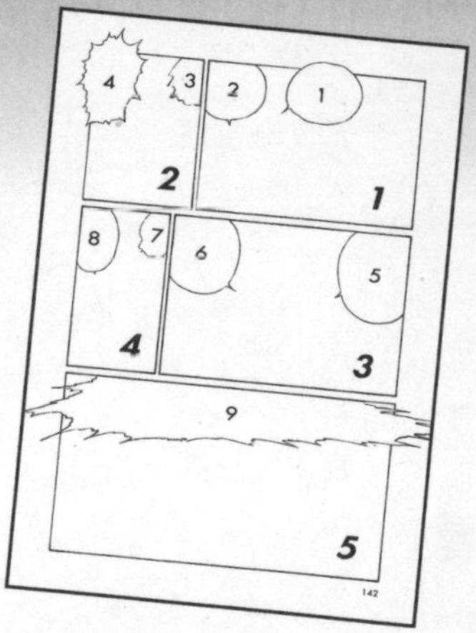
1
2
3
4
1
2
5
6
7
8
3
4
9
5
142

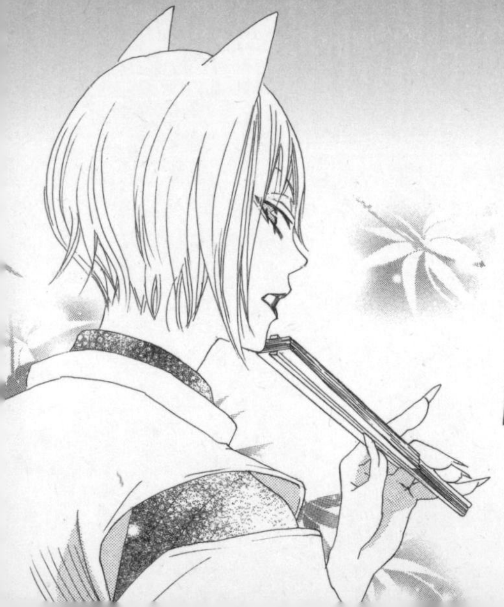